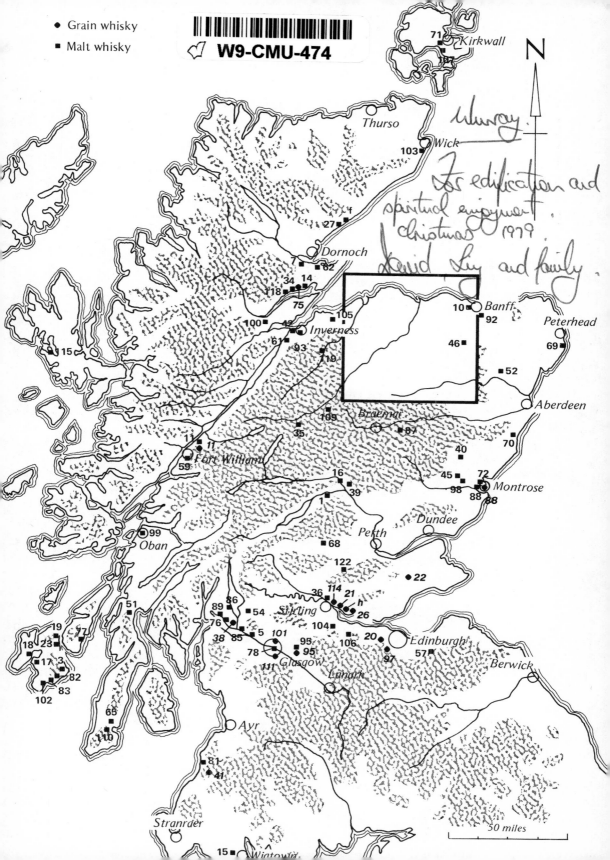

SCOTCH WHISKY
Its Past and Present

DAVID DAICHES

with colour photographs by Alan Daiches

ANDRE DEUTSCH

First published October 1969 by
André Deutsch Limited
105 Great Russell Street London WC1

Second Impression, October 1970
Third revised Impression, June 1978

Set in 'Monotype' Imprint Roman
Printed in Great Britain by Cox & Wyman Ltd
London, Fakenham and Reading

ISBN 0 233 96053 8

Acknowledgements are due to the following for permission to reproduce illustrations in the book:

James Buchanan & Company Limited: pages 95 and 97; Mary Evans
Picture Library: pages 23, 48, 54, 59, 67, 69, 113, 132 and 165; John R.
Freeman & Co. (Photographers) Limited: pages 77, 108 and 118; The
Mansell Collection: pages 30, 34, 51, 61, 72, 75, 111, 130, 142 and 157;
Radio Times Hulton Picture Library: pages 5, 41, 44, 86 and 124;
William Sanderson & Son Limited: pages 27 and 100; The Scottish
Tourist Board: facing page 1 and page 138; John Walker and Sons
Limited: pages 91 and 103.

Contents

Preface

This book does not claim to be a complete and authoritative account of all aspects of Scotch whisky. My concern has been with its social history, its nature, and its present situation. Where matters of taste are concerned, my view is, of course, a personal one, but with respect to matters of fact I have tried to be accurate and objective. I have been helped in this latter endeavour by the kindness and co-operation of people concerned with Scotch whisky at all levels. Firms have sent me their house histories, directors have given up time to talk to me at length, distillery managers have patiently answered my questions and interrupted their work to entertain as well as inform me, brewers, maltmen and stillmen have tolerated with great courtesy my butting in on their routine activities to observe and question. My son has been given every possible facility for taking photographs both in distilleries and in blending and bottling plants. It is true that when I was rash enough to ask one of the great blending firms if they could let me know the proportion of malt and grain whisky in each of the two blends they put out I received a letter informing me that 'it is with regret that I have to tell you that this information is "classified", and that therefore we will not be able to help you with this section of your book'. But on all other matters everybody has been most forthcoming, and my son and I have received nothing but kindness. I have to thank Messrs. Harpers, publishers of *Harpers Wine and Spirit Gazette*, for permission to reproduce their map of the Scotch whisky distilleries.

My expression of gratitude for so much friendly assistance must not, however, obscure the central fact that the opinions expressed in this book are my own. I know that my views on some points are not shared by some of those who have helped me with information, but even when they are shared I must emphasize that nobody but myself is responsible for the views enunciated in various parts of the book. In some respects this is a very personal account of Scotch whisky, for after all the enjoyment of Scotch whisky is a very personal activity. But I have tried to get the facts right.

It is often maintained by those in the Scotch whisky trade that the future of their product depends on the continued expansion of exports. From the point of view of those consumers who most enjoy it, however, it might be said with equal truth that the spread of knowledge and discrimination with respect to it is the best guarantee of its future. Scotch whisky is known throughout the world as a drink of great character and individuality. One purpose of this book is to help increase awareness of that character and individuality so as to preserve and indeed enhance the reputation of Scotch whisky not simply as an alcoholic stimulant but as a civilized drink of great range and subtlety that is best consumed with attention and judgement.

David Daiches

Chapter One

THE ORIGINS AND NATURE
OF SCOTCH WHISKY

A rugged country with a stormy history: Scotland, with its mountains and glens and lochs and streams, captures the visitor with its beauty and its legends, and haunts the exile with insistent memories. The Highlands are the most striking part, with their physical grandeur and their picturesque and sometimes terrible past of clan loyalty and clan warfare. But Scotland has its fertile fields and its great cities as well as its mountain glory, while the Border country, with a scenic display less spectacular but no less appealing than the Highlands, has its own romantic story that finds expression in the great Border Ballads. The popular view of Scotland is understandably somewhat starry-eyed—or perhaps misty-eyed would be the better term: Loch Lomond, the Hebrides, heather-clad hills, and St. Andrews, the silver city by the sea where the royal and ancient game of golf first became an institution. But Scotland has another side too: it was in Glasgow and on Clydeside that the Industrial Revolution began, and that corner of the country is still one of the great industrial areas of the world. And Edinburgh, the capital, with its Castle and its ring of hills, its narrow and history-soaked Old Town and its spacious and elegant New Town, one of the half-dozen most beautiful cities in the world; Aberdeen, the Granite City in the north-east, fronting the cold North Sea with courage and dignity; Inverness, the capital of the Highlands; Perth, the ancient royal burgh looking equally to the Highland north and the Lowland south, scene of the most terrible of all clan battles in the late fourteenth century—each of these has its own atmosphere, its own story to tell. Add to all this the wearing o' the kilt and the gay appeal of tartan, the haunting quality of bagpipe music, and the nostalgia for a lost independence which is still active in the Scottish imagination, and you get a picture that can hardly fail in its box-office appeal.

Yet Scotland, contrary to what one might sometimes be led to think,

1

is neither a stage backcloth nor a film script, but a real country with real problems. And its best known product, Scotch whisky, is not a whimsical mountain dew distilled by pixies but a spirit produced by human art and sold in vast quantities all over the world. It was not always, of course, an internationally known drink, as the pages that follow will make clear. For centuries its production and consumption was largely confined to the Highlands. For it is the Gaelic-speaking Highland clans whom we have to thank for this contribution to the joy of living. The word 'whisky' itself derives from the Gaelic *uisge beatha*, 'water of life'.

When and how the Highlanders first produced whisky we do not know. Neil Gunn, the Scottish novelist and whisky expert, has a charming fantasy of the accidental distillation of steam rising from ground and fermented barley as it boiled in a pot under the eye of some primitive clansman who proceeded at once to experiment with its consumption and to inform his friends; Gunn goes on to tell how the band of secret drinkers were surprised by the Elders, who themselves experimented with the liquor, so that knowledge of it then came to the Druid and the Chief. Gunn does not say whether his primeval discoverer of whisky was a Pict (early inhabitant of Scotland who occupied the extreme north and north-east) or a Scot. The Scots came from Ireland in the fifth century A.D., bringing to Scotland their Gaelic language and the name eventually to be adopted by the country as a whole. Was it the Scots who brought the art of distilling with them from Ireland? Douglas Young, the Scottish poet and scholar, used to maintain that whisky was invented by the Irish as an embrocation for sick mules and that once it was brought to Scotland its use was perverted from external animal application to internal human consumption. But Young was not a whisky drinker and his account is clearly an amusing invention. Nevertheless, there is reason to believe that the art of distilling whisky was developed very early in Ireland. An Irish legend says that Saint Patrick first taught the art, but it makes no mention of sick mules, so that presumably the saint intended it for human drinking. A German historian of distilling says that at one time old Irish Celtic ruins near Cashel were believed to contain the remains of bronze distilling apparatus. When Henry II of England invaded Ireland in 1172 he is said to have found the distillation of spirits from grain well established there. And since we use the term 'whisky' to denote a spirit distilled from grain as distinct from a spirit distilled from grapes or other sorts of fruit or berries, this would suggest that the Irish were drinking a form of whisky in the twelfth century.

Perhaps, then, distilling was brought from Ireland to Scotland some time in the early Middle Ages, but we cannot be certain. A second

German authority on distilling has roundly denounced the story of the origin of distilling in Ireland, and in particular of Saint Patrick's invention of it, as wholly unhistorical. All we know is that Irish whiskey (traditionally and still today distilled from a mash of unmalted barley and other grains) and Scotch whisky (distilled from malted barley only) have a history of many centuries. The first recorded allusion to a spirit distilled from barley in Scotland is found in the Scottish Exchequer Rolls for 1494, which notes the provision of 'eight bolls of malt to Friar John Cor wherewith to make aquavitae'. (*Aqua vitae*, 'water of life', is the traditional name for a distilled spirit: it is the exact Latin equivalent of the Gaelic *uisge beatha* and the French *eau de vie*.) But, of course, before a process of this kind surfaces into recorded history it is likely to have had a long run. The whole early history of distilling is still a debating ground for scholarly argument and conjecture. It seems to have been known in the Far East at a very early date. Arab chemists inherited the traditions of the Alexandrian chemists of the first nine hundred years A.D. and developed a variety of modes of distilling, though not with a view to producing potable spirits. The word 'alcohol' comes to us from the Arabic. Medieval alchemists learned something from the Arabs, and the great thirteenth-century philosopher and theologian Albertus Magnus wrote an account of how to produce by distillation what he called *aqua ardens*, 'burning water'. The thirteenth-century Spanish philosopher and alchemist Raymond Lull also studied and wrote about distilling. The distillation of wine into brandy in France was known in the thirteenth century and developed as a manufacturing industry in the fourteenth. It was also in the Middle Ages that the production of perfumes and extracts of herbs and flowers for medicinal use first developed, a process involving distillation. A variety of spirits for drinking, made both from grapes and from grain, developed throughout Europe, first as medicine and then as a drink to be consumed for pleasure: first liqueurs, made of alcohol, sugar or syrup, and flavouring matter; then brandy from France; then grain spirits whose origins we have just been puzzling over. And, as we have seen, Scotch whisky was well established in Scotland by the end of the fifteenth century.

But why Scotland and why Scotch whisky? What is so special about Scotland that it should have produced a unique spirit now known all over the world? Of course, one could point to the range of mean temperatures in Scotland and argue that any country that is liable to stay pretty chilly the whole year round requires the regular imbibing of an agreeable spirituous drink. In Scotland it does not get cold enough in the winter to encourage the periodic consumption of vast quantities of crude alcoholic spirit in order to forget the cold and the dark, such as one still sometimes finds in the more northerly parts of Scandinavian countries. The Scottish climate is never numbing, and if you walk across the heather with a fine drizzle coming down and the temperature about 55 ° Fahrenheit you will find everything round you enchantingly *fragrant*. The Scottish countryside always smells nice, whether you crush the leaves of the bog myrtle as you tramp the hillsides and inhale its lovely characteristic odour or simply receive in a more general way the varied smells of bush and flower and grass and peat and (one would be prepared to swear) of the air and the water themselves. The countryside is never dried up in Scotland; it is always damp, alive, fragrant. It is no surprise, therefore, that the traditional Scottish drink makes its primary appeal to the nose. With the climate cold enough for the national drink to have to be a warming one but not so cold as to drive people to any alcoholic expedient in order to find inner warmth or even oblivion, and with the countryside making continuously olfactory demands on the inhabitants, Scotland, one could argue, was bound to produce a spirit of rare and subtle aroma. Further, Scotland is too far north to allow the massive growing of grapes, but it has for many centuries produced barley, that most hardy of all cereal grains, so that a barley spirit ('barley bree' in the old Scots phrase) rather than a grape spirit would be the natural one. Then again, the Highlands of Scotland teem with the most beautiful clear water from stream and spring, and there are many peat bogs; so that if you need peat smoke in order to dry the barley and turn it into aromatic malt, and clear water for the further process of turning that malt into a fermented liquid before distilling it into spirit, there too Nature has laid everything on your doorstep.

What, then, *is* Scotch whisky? What is it made of, and how? These questions are not as simple as may be supposed, as a later chapter will show: a distinguished King's Counsel assisted by a bench of lay magistrates tried in vain to decide what whisky was in a famous case in 1906, and as a result of their inability a Royal Commission was set up in 1907 to settle the unresolved question, with fateful consequences for the future of Scotch whisky. But before looking at the problems created by later inventions and practices, let us consider what Scotch whisky originally, authentically and uniquely was and is. What is the distinctive spirit that only Scotland has been able to produce (in spite of honest efforts to produce it elsewhere out of the same ingredients by exactly the same process)? There are, of course, other kinds of whisky, some admirable in their own way, produced in other countries. But the whisky distilled from malted barley in the manner perfected in the Scottish Highlands

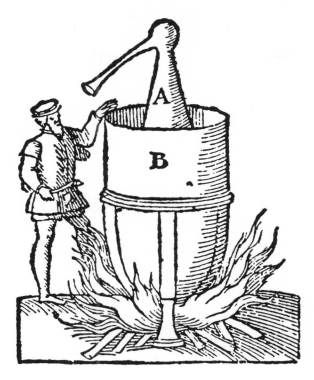

An early still

in the eighteenth century and still produced in essentially the same manner—what we call Pot Still Highland Malt Scotch Whisky—has proved to be inimitable outside Scotland. I have tasted a blended Scotch whisky produced in Canada from imported Highland malt whisky and locally produced grain whisky which was quite a respectable drink; but the true malt whiskies of Scotland remain a Scottish 'mystery' in both senses of that word. I have been told by a friend who was in the Far East during the last war that he came across a bottle labelled 'King Victoria Finest Scotchman's Whisko' allegedly made in Japan (where quantities of less eccentrically labelled whisky are certainly made and drunk today, some of it a blend of imported Scottish malt whisky and local spirit). There have been many attempts, both scrupulous and unscrupulous, to break Scotland's monopoly of Scotch. But the monopoly remains.

Barley, water and peat are what is needed to produce the malt whisky of Scotland. Though barley is not Scotland's main cereal crop, which for centuries has been oats, it is still a significant and traditional crop in Scotland. In the great whisky-producing area of Scotland, a vast rectangle immediately south of the Moray Firth in the north-east of the country, there is a coastal plain as well as valleys where barley has long been grown and where originally the distillers obtained all their barley. The combination of cold, clear streams tumbling rapidly down mountain sides with fertile valleys, of wild Highland scenery with a rich and gentle coastal plain, is characteristic of this part of Scotland. The local availability of barley, water and peat made the distilling of whisky a natural part of the rhythm of life and work, bound up with the economy of the Scottish countryside. Distilling was carried on between October and May, although today many distilleries work throughout the year, except for a few weeks in summer, used for annual holidays and necessary building or maintenance. The by-products of the process were available for use as cattle-feed during the winter months; in the summer, when there was no need of artificial cattle-feed, distillation was (and is) suspended and the distilleries cleaned and overhauled. It must be emphasized that traditionally the distilling of Scotch whisky took its place, as to a large extent it still does, as part of the normal routine of a farming community.

Barley, then, is where the process begins. Though few of us may have seen

reapers, reaping early
In among the bearded barley

most of us will have seen fields of barley with the characteristic 'bearded' tops glinting pale in the sun. Some of us may have examined more closely an ear of barley with its two longitudinal rows of grain (in the case of the common 'two-rowed' barley) and the spiky beard extending well beyond. The barley bought by the distiller is, of course, in grain form: he fills his lofts with great piles of ripe grain, each grain with its pale, wrinkled skin, shuttle-shaped and with a sweetish smell. Although originally it was always local barley that was used, some of the greatest Highland malt Scotch whiskies today use imported barley. This has been going on for some time, and it is clear that the quality of the whisky does not depend on its being made from home-grown barley. The water and the peat, however, do demonstrably contribute in large measure to the quality of the whisky, though the peat is not always local; some Highland malt distillers get their malt ready-made from Pitsligo, Aberdeenshire, or Kirkaldy, Fife, and an increasing number have given up doing their own malting. Different distilleries produce whiskies of different 'nose', body and flavour in the same way as different French vineyards, producing wine from the same variety of grape by the same process, produce quite different vintages; and this clearly has something to do with the peat and the water. There are many other factors, some quite intangible and very difficult to put one's finger on, which account both for the uniqueness of Scottish[1] pot-still malt whisky and for the differences between pot-still malt whiskies made by different distilleries in different parts of the country. A look at the actual processes involved may help to explain this.

While it is true that some of the finest Scotch whisky has for a long time been made with imported barley, it does not follow that the quality of the barley does not matter. It matters very much. The first process in making the whisky is *malting*, the turning of barley into malt. To do this properly, and to produce malt of the desired quality, the barley must be fully ripened, plump, thoroughly sound, dry and of the proper protein content. If the barley is not sufficiently dry it will go mouldy during storage. (As the barley is usually all bought at the same time of the year, in September or October during or just after the harvest, enough must be bought to provide for the year's malting, so storage is important.) Mouldy barley will not germinate properly, and germination is an essential process in malting. So after the barley has been carefully screened from impurities it is dried either on kilns in batches or in storage towers in a continuous process involving the passing of warm air over the grain.[2] The properly dry barley is stored in large bins until needed for malting.

Malt is essentially barley that has been allowed to germinate by soaking in water and has then been dried by the application of heat. Because of its high carbohydrate and protein content, malt has long been regarded as a body-builder for growing children and prescribed for what used to be called 'wasting diseases'. When I was a child, I used to be dosed with 'extract of malt with cod-liver oil' every morning after breakfast. But the part played by malt in brewing and distilling has nothing to do with its status as a symbol of strength. Unlike unmalted

---

[1] A word about 'Scotch' and 'Scottish'. In Scotland the adjective 'Scotch' is frowned on and 'Scottish' or 'Scots' preferred. But 'Scotch' is allowed for whisky. As a schoolboy in Edinburgh I was taught that 'Scotch' could only be used for Scotch whisky and Scotch broth.

[2] It is the home-grown barley especially, which contains about 20 per cent of moisture, that requires this special drying to reduce its moisture content to about 10 per cent or a little over: some imported barley is lighter and drier than the domestic barley and thus is less in need of drying.

barley, malt when ground and mashed with water converts its starch into a mixture of soluble compounds including the crystalline sugar known as maltose and by doing so makes fermentation possible. Fermentation produces a beer-like liquid and is the first stage in distilling. (Brewing is thus a process common to the making of beer, where it is the end process, and the production of whisky, where it is an intermediate process. This intermediate fermenting or brewing process in a distillery is under the supervision of the brewer, who is the most highly paid workman in any distillery.)

The first step in the malting process is to soak the barley in tanks or 'steeps' to promote germination. The period of the soaking varies according to weather conditions, the time of the year and the grade of barley; it can be as little as forty-eight hours and as much as seventy. An experienced maltster can tell whether the barley has been soaked long enough by pressing it between his thumb and forefinger, but modern distilleries also provide laboratory tests of the moisture content.[3]

After the barley has been soaked for the requisite amount of time, the water is drained off and the grain is spread out to a depth of two or three feet on a stone, concrete or tiled floor in the malting house. Here the sweet dusty smell which assails the nostrils when one visits the original barley store has given way to a distinctive smell which though not unpleasant I can best describe as a warm mouldiness. It is here on the malting floor that the germination develops, a process during which the barley 'breathes'—taking in oxygen and expiring carbon dioxide—and generates a considerable amount of heat. In order to control the rising temperature (which is highest at the bottom) the grain is regularly turned by maltmen with wooden shovels or 'skips': this process also prevents growing rootlets from becoming entangled with each other and producing a matted mess. The 'turning' of the 'piece'—to express it in technical malting language—is a somewhat stylized operation, involving tossing the grain into the air with a rhythmic movement of the skip; but I have never heard of any traditional work-songs associated with this activity. The maltmen work in silence. As a result of the daily or more often twice-daily turning, the barley is thinned out in a period of from eight to fourteen days to a level of a few inches. By this time the 'acrospire' or growing stem of the barley has grown to five-eighths of the length of the seed. Further growth must be stopped and this is done by further turning and thinning, as well, sometimes, as 'ploughing', the

---

[3] This should be 40 to 45 per cent after soaking.

BARLEY STORE　　　　　MALT BARN

Dressing machine

Barley hopper

Weighing machine

Barley steeps

Barley intake

Malting floor

actual dragging by hand of a plough through the grain. During the whole process the head maltman has been careful to maintain the temperature of the germinating grain at about 60 °F. Turning the barley in the traditional way on the malting floor is an arduous business, and some distilleries now use more labour-saving methods. Sometimes huge revolving drums are used (each holding from ten to fifty tons of barley) with cool air blown through a central inlet to control the heat produced by the germinating grain. Some distilleries use the long concrete or metal trench known as the 'Saladin box' after Charles Saladin, the French engineer who invented it. In the Saladin box revolving metal forks move slowly up and down its length to keep the grain turned and aerated.

Whether done on the traditional malting floor, or in large drums, or in Saladin boxes, the germination process is now as complete as is required and further growth is stopped. The grains are now soft and chalky. 'When you can write your name on the wall with it,' an old maltman once told Neil Gunn, 'it's ready.' The barley has been turned into 'green malt' and is ready for the drying kiln. The starch in the grain can now be converted into fermentable sugar.[4]

---

[4] In the course of germination the barley-seed develops two enzymes (an enzyme is an organic substance produced by living cells which acts as a catalyst), the enzyme cytase, which breaks down the cellulose enclosing the insoluble starch cells and so makes the starch accessible for growth, and the enzyme diastase, which converts the insoluble starch which the action of the cytase has made available into dextrin, a soluble form of starch. The diastase also changes the dextrin into maltose, a readily soluble sugar. It is the sugar which eventually produces alcohol.

Green malt is not literally green—in fact it looks very like the original malted barley grains, a pale straw colour. It contains a considerable amount of moisture, and is transferred to the kiln for drying. It is the kiln that has the 'pagoda head' which proclaims the distillery on the landscape. The floor of the kiln is of perforated iron or wire mesh. Here the green malt is spread at a depth of between one and three feet (depending on the design of the kiln) and dried in the smoke arising from a peat fire some ten or fifteen feet below. The open ventilator at the top —which is the pagoda head—draws up the hot air from the fire through the green malt on the perforated floor. The peat is of the first importance as it gives its special flavour to the malt and eventually to the mature whisky. The smell of burning peat is an agreeable domestic smell when one experiences it in front of a peat fire in a Highland cottage. But if you put your face into the kiln when the peat smoke ('peat reek' as the Scots say) is billowing you will soon feel that enough is enough. The smoke stings the eyes and catches you in the throat, and though you may recognize that this is the flavour which will one day marvellously enrich the taste and bouquet of the matured whisky, you will probably be willing to wait for your next encounter until you meet it in the glass.

In the old days, peat was the sole fuel used, but now coke or anthracite is often also used to provide heat, and peat used only to provide flavour. The drying begins in peat smoke, but after about twenty-four hours coke or anthracite is substituted and the temperature—which has been carefully regulated from the beginning, rising slowly over the peat fire—is raised further until the malt has been dried to the point of retaining only about 3 per cent of its moisture.

The traditional method of kiln drying has given way in some modern distilleries to a more rapid method of achieving the same result. Instead of using the principle of natural draught, with a ventilator at the top drawing up the hot air, these modern kilns have fans for blowing in warm, peat-flavoured air, so that the malt is dried quickly under pressure. Several distilleries now buy all or a part of their malt ready-made (and peated to the desired degree) from specialist malt producers outside their own region.

The malt is now ready—dry, crisp, friable, aromatic, very different in texture and flavour from the original barley though scarcely distinguishable in appearance. It is stored in bins to await the time when it is needed for the next processes—mashing and brewing. But before it goes on to mashing it is cleansed of the 'combings' or rootlets and any other impurities by being passed through a dressing machine. The combings used to be sold as cattle food under the name of 'malt culms'. It is then

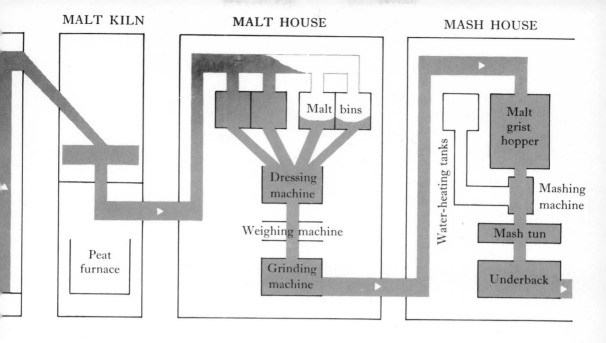

Malt bins

Dressing machine

Weighing machine

Grinding machine

Peat furnace

Water-heating tanks

Malt grist hopper

Mashing machine

Mash tun

Underback

coarsely ground in a mill. The ground malt (malt grist) then goes into the *mash tun*, which is a large circular vat of several thousand gallons' capacity. It is released into the mash tun from a hopper in carefully measured quantities (indeed, there is a great deal of weighing and measuring in the whole process of whisky production, since at each point a given quantity of raw material is expected to produce a given quantity of the product at the next stage) together with hot water. This mashing with hot water helps to complete the conversion of dextrin into maltose. The malt is extracted three and sometimes four times with hot water, each time at a different temperature, ranging from about 160 °F. for the first to over 180 °F. for the last. The resulting liquid is called *wort* (pronounced 'wurt') or *worts*. (I have heard the plural form more often than the singular in distilleries.) The wort produced by the first two washings is drained out through the bottom of the tun into the *underback* or worts receiver; the product of the later washings (*sparge*) becomes the first and second extractions of the next batch. The solids that remain after the wort is run off are known as *draff*, which (like malt culms) is used as a winter cattle food. Mashing, by the way, is a smelly process: the characteristic smell that hangs around a distillery is compounded of many factors, but the pungent smell of the mashing is central.

The thick porridge-like substance which was produced by the ground malt and hot water, when the mashing process started, was very different from the wort we now have: this is a sweet (and oddly sweet-smelling) semi-transparent liquid, not yet alcoholic. Sir Robert Bruce Lockhart recalled how as a boy on holiday at his maternal grandfather's distillery of Balmenach he 'was often allowed to taste this sugary water and found it pleasant': but I have heard of no other case of wort being used as a child's soft drink.

From the underback the wort is run into a refrigerator, because unless it is cooled (to about 70 °F.) the maltose would decompose and the yeast used in the next process, brewing, would be killed by the heat. From the refrigerator it is run into the *wash-back*, a huge vat holding up to 10,000 gallons of wort. Here yeast is added, being pumped in simultaneously with the wort, and as a result fermentation takes place. (A distillery of any size will have several wash-backs—a large one will have eight or ten.) The enzymes of the yeast then do their duty, first producing dextrose from the maltose and then converting the dextrose into alcohol and carbon dioxide.[5] It is a violent and noisy process. At first there is just the rising of faintly plopping bubbles, but gradually the activity in the liquid increases. The production of carbon dioxide causes it to froth and seethe and the brewer in charge has the responsible task of keeping it under control and seeing that it does not boil over. The wash-backs are never filled to the top, but three or four feet of space is left between the surface of the liquid and the top of the wash-back to allow for the bubbling and boiling. Even so, constant care is needed. Formerly, men with sticks of birch-wood would control the threatening liquid by beating, but for a long time now this has been done by mechanical stirrers. At the end of the process, which takes anything from thirty-six to forty hours, we have a clear liquid, known simply as the *wash*, which consists of water, yeast and a bit over 5 per cent by volume of alcohol (i.e. about 10° proof). Thus the wash, like beer, is a liquid that has been brewed but not distilled.[6]

The next process, distillation, is what actually produces the whisky. What is involved in distilling is essentially turning a liquid into vapour

---

[5] The enzymes are maltase and zymase: maltase acts on the maltose to produce dextrose (otherwise glucose, colourless crystalline soluble sugar), and zymase converts the dextrose into alcohol and carbon dioxide. Dextrose is $C_6H_{12}O_6$ and alcohol is C_2H_5OH: what happens is represented by the equation: $C_6H_{12}O_6 \rightarrow 2C_2H_5OH + 2CO_2$.

[6] It is with the stage of fermenting that the excise officer becomes interested, for according to the fall in density between the wort and the wash he will be able to work out the amount of spirit to be expected in the end. This is because the density of the wort decreases as the

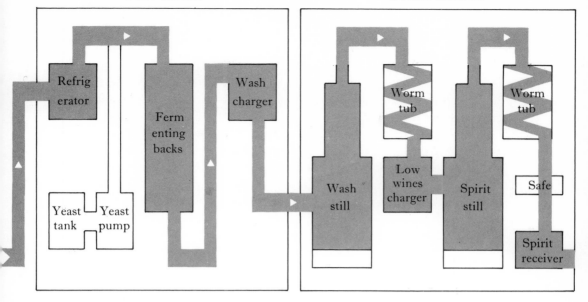

and then condensing the vapour back into liquid. If you hold a cold knife over the steam that comes from a boiling kettle, drops of water will condense on to the knife. If you heat wash in a copper pot and then condense the vapour that rises from the boiling wash by passing it in a pipe through a tub of cold water, you are going through the basic process of making whisky. Scotch whisky is a distillation of a fermented brew which has in turn been made by the addition of yeast to ground malt extracted with hot water. Though the modern method I am now describing incorporates a number of improvements, and involves operation on a larger scale, the process is essentially the same as that used in the eighteenth century and very probably much earlier than that. Highland malt Scotch whisky was and is distilled in pear-shaped copper stills ('pot stills'). Every distillery must have at least two such stills, the wash still (often with a somewhat larger neck) in which the wash is

dextrose is converted into alcohol. There will thus be a decrease in the specific gravity of the liquid from something like 1·05 (the specific gravity of the original wort) to say 0·998, the specific gravity of the wash. A decrease from a specific gravity of 1·05 to one of 0·998 represents an attenuation of 52 degrees. Every degree of attenuation in 10,000 gallons of wash represents—or should represent—at the end of the day more than twenty gallons of proof spirit. So the excise officer should know how much whisky to look for once the fermentation process is over.

first distilled to produce 'low wines', and the low wines still in which the impure dilute spirit of the low wines is distilled a second time, this time to produce whisky. Though the two stills may differ slightly in shape, each is of the same general design, bulbous at the bottom, narrow at the top, with a narrow neck extending downwards through the wall of the still house to the coiled copper pipe—the *worm*—which lies in a tank of cold water. This, then, is the simple and ancient process of distilling: the liquid is heated until it vaporizes; the vapour passes up the neck of the still and down through the worm where the lower temperature produced by the surrounding cold water causes it to condense into liquid again. The distillate from the wash goes first into the spirit safe and then into the low wines charger whence it goes to be redistilled in the low wines still. The low wines distillate is also run into the spirit safe, where it is tested until the initial highly impure samples (*foreshots*) have given way to true whisky, at which point it is run into the spirit receiver. The last part of the distillate is, like the first part, impure: this is known as *feints* and is turned into a feints receiver to be redistilled with the low wines—and with the foreshots—in the next batch.

There is no universally accepted way of heating the pot stills. Many are heated by coal fires, some by oil-fired furnaces. Some of the most recent distilleries heat by steam coils inside the still (Glenmorangie has been doing this since the 1880s). But coal furnaces with automatic stokers seem to be as far towards modernization as many Highland malt distilleries are willing to go. Some distillers insist that coal is the best fuel; the pockets of hot flaring gas—'hot points' or 'flash points'—which a coal fire produces, they maintain, assist the rise of the vapour in the still.

It is the responsibility of the stillman to test the samples so as to determine when the low wines still is producing acceptable whisky. The clear foreshot turns cloudy when water is added; when it ceases to turn cloudy with the addition of water, it is true whisky. Yet a stillman may not be satisfied with this test. I remember once watching a stillman at work at Laphroaig distillery and thinking that the tests showed that the whisky was ready. 'Not yet,' said the stillman, eyeing the sample closely, 'it's still a bit *blue*.' So we waited a further five minutes, by which time the faint blueness had gone and the distillate could be run into the spirit receiver.

The spirit safe through which the distillate is passed is rather like a large brass box or trunk with glass sides. It is constructed so that by turning the appropriate tap the stillman can pass the spirit into a vessel fitted with a hydrometer for measuring the specific gravity, or dilute it with a given proportion of distilled water. (It is important that these operations be done under glass, with the spirit not available for actual tasting, since the excise officer is responsible for checking and safe-guarding the quantity of spirit that is produced.) A handle on the outside of the safe can deflect the acceptable whisky to the spirit receiver. What is unacceptable—foreshots and feints—is run into the low wines and feints receiver for redistilling.

The precise moment at which the distillate is turned into the spirit receiver depends on the stillman's judgement, as does the moment towards the end of the process when the distillate is becoming feints and must be deflected from the spirit receiver. There are no hard and fast rules, nor is there an absolutely 'pure' whisky produced in the middle period of distilling which can be clearly distinguished from foreshots at the beginning and feints at the end. The aldehydes, esters, furfurol and other compounds of hydrogen, oxygen and carbon formed in the process of distilling the wash and known generally as *congenerics* are present in excess in the foreshots but they also give pot-still malt whisky its special bouquet and flavour, so it is not a question of eliminating them, but of nice judgement, based on long experience, of exactly when to regard the whisky as a true potable spirit and when to stop so regarding it. The making of whisky is an art, and at every stage the objective knowledge provided by the scientist must be supplemented (as historically it was anticipated) by an almost intuitive skill produced by years of practice and often by a long family tradition, for distillery workers tend to run in families. A mistake—running the foreshots into the spirit receiver by deflecting the distillate into it too soon, or waiting too long before turning the distillate away from the spirit receiver—may not be immediately noticed, but could have disastrous consequences for the flavour of the whisky many years later, when it is fully matured and all the potentialities of its bouquet and flavour are realized.

The residue of the wash, still known as *burnt ale* or *pot ale*, is removed —it is sometimes turned into fertilizer or, evaporated and dried, into animal food—and the still is thoroughly cleaned before the next distil-lation. The residue of the low wines still, *spent lees*, is little more than water, with sometimes very small amounts of copper from the still in solution: it is of no use or value and is simply run off. There is a problem of water pollution in running away the burnt ale, serious in view of the importance of trout and salmon fishing in Scottish streams and rivers. Some distilleries have their own plant for converting pot ale and draff into cattle food or fertilizer. Glenlivet distillery has joined with the Chivas distilleries in building an effluent plant to produce 'dark grains'.

Scottish Malt Distillers Ltd. (see page 104) has built seven effluent disposal plants designed for the manufacture of dark grains. These are at Aberfeldy, Aultmore, Convalmore, Dailuaine, Glenlossie, Ord and Teaninich Distilleries. An eighth, at Balmenach Distillery, will be operating by the end of 1977. The largest malt distillers' plant of this kind is the Combination of Rothes Distillers Dark Grains Plant, where four companies co-operate in running a plant which recycles the effluent of twelve distilleries: it weekly converts 1·3 million gallons of pot ale and 1700 tons of wet draff into 600 tons of dark grains. The dark grains, in pellet form, are sold for mixing with other substances to form nutritious cattle food.

Distilleries are not, as a rule, especially beautiful buildings, though some are beautifully situated and some are maintained with a sharper eye to outward appearance than others (Laphroaig, for example, with its sparkling whitewash and gay window-boxes, not for nothing the only distillery run by a woman). Nor is the lay-out always the most rational. The movement from barley store to malting floor to malt kiln to malt bins to grinding mill to grist hopper to mash tun to wash-backs to wash still to low wines still to spirit receiver would, one might imagine, normally be planned in a continuous flow in as near a straight line as possible. But in many of the older distilleries there is doubling back and a good deal of twisting and turning to accommodate everything needed in the available space. Newer distilleries, such as Tormore, are rationally planned with a lay-out which minimizes unnecessary movement.

The shape and size of the pot still affect the quality of the whisky produced. I have heard a stillman maintain that the higher the still the better, as the fewer impurities emerge in the distillate, and certainly the form of the top does influence the nature of the finished whisky. Malt-whisky distillers are conservative in many things, including the shape and size of the still: a new one is likely to be an exact replica of the old. Chemists have never been able to discover precisely what determines the special character of the product of each distillery or exactly why it is that maturing effects such an improvement in flavour. As a result, brewers and stillmen tend to have their own special mystique: theirs—to emphasize the point once again—is an art, in which instinct born of long (and often hereditary) experience plays its part. Bruce Lockhart has remarked that 'some brewers are so fearful of any change affecting their product that they will not allow even a cobweb to be swept away from the vat room'. One of the problems arises from the fact that until a whisky has matured it is impossible to be absolutely certain of its quality, though an experienced taster can hazard a shrewd guess. But we do know that the quality of the barley (even though, as we have seen, it does not have to be Scottish barley), the composition of the peat, and the quality of the water each has something to do with the quality of the finished whisky. Whiskies can be more or less heavily peated. Some have claimed that the best whisky is made from water which comes 'off granite through peat' and others that water 'off peat through granite' produces the better whisky. There is certainly a difference between the two. Heavy peating can be achieved by passing the peat smoke repeatedly over the malt in the drying kiln by means of fans. A growing number of distilleries no longer do their own malting, but buy their malt ready-made from maltsters, peated to the desired degree.

The malting process takes from nine to fifteen days; brewing and distilling together occupy one week, the first part of which is devoted to brewing and the latter part to continuous distilling. The new whisky comes from the spirit receiver at a strength of from 15° to 20° over proof (or 115° to 120° proof). At this point a digression on the nature and meaning of proof suggests itself, since I have found so many people confused about the exact meaning of the term. One of the meanings of the word 'proof' at least since the sixteenth century is 'of tried strength or quality' and it is this meaning that is involved in the phrase 'proof spirit', which simply means spirit of standard and approved strength. The problem for centuries has been what standard to require and how to define it. In earlier times the strength of a spirit was determined by very crude methods, such as dampening gunpowder with it and then applying a light to see if it would still ignite. The development of the hydrometer—a floating instrument used to determine the specific gravity (weight in relation to the weight of the same volume of water) of a liquid—led to less crude methods. After a great deal of research and calculation in a variety of countries, the British Government at the beginning of this century produced tables relating the strength of spirit to its specific gravity at 60 °F. These tables have subsequently been amended, and definition of proof is based on the amended tables. The Customs and Excise Act of 1952 gave the following definition of proof spirit: 'Spirits shall be deemed to be at proof if the volume of the ethyl alcohol contained therein made up to the volume of the spirits with distilled water has a weight equal to that of twelve-thirteenths of a volume of distilled water equal to the volume of the spirits, the volume of each liquid being computed as at fifty-one degrees Fahrenheit.' Put less forbiddingly, this means that proof spirit is that which at 51 °F. weighs twelve-thirteenths of an equal volume of water at the same temperature. The tables show how much alcohol and how much water the spirit will then contain, so that we can re-define proof, more usefully for the general reader, as spirit which contains 57·1 per cent of alcohol by volume or 49·28 per cent of alcohol by weight. Now, this is *British* proof. *American* proof is calculated differently. The standard of proof recognized by the United States is 50 per cent of alcohol by volume at 60 °F. This means that British proof spirit (i.e., 100° proof) would be 114·2° proof in the United States (or 14·2° over proof). Similarly, American 100° proof is the same as British 87·7° proof. This difference is worth noting, because Scotch whisky for the American market is bottled at 76·2° proof (or 23·8° under proof) according to the British standard, but this corresponds to 86·8° on the American standard of proof and '86·8° proof' appears on American bottles of Scotch. Though this is stronger than the 70° proof at which most Scotch whisky is bottled for the domestic market, it is not as much stronger as Americans who see '70° proof' on British bottles of Scotch and '86·8°' on bottles of Scotch exported to America generally believe, for 70° proof on the British standard is the equivalent of 80° proof on the American standard. All this may sound tediously technical, but I have deliberately not relegated it to a footnote because whisky drinkers really ought to know what proof is and what the difference between British and American proof is. I have seen more than one American knock back Scotch whisky from a British bottle marked '70° proof' under the impression that it was in fact 16 degrees lower in proof than the whisky he was accustomed to drink at home. And one's belief can colour one's actual physical sensation in drinking, so that by mis-reading the label one can really believe one is drinking a much weaker spirit than one actually is. And the results of this can be awkward.[7]

Let us now return to the newly distilled whisky, which is from 115° to 120° proof. It is colourless, extremely pungent and fiery. From the spirit receiver it is run into the spirit store, where it is reduced in strength by the addition of spring water (and here again the quality of the water is important) to about 110° proof before being run into casks to mature.

Nobody knows precisely when it was first realized that whisky improves in a spectacular fashion when matured in the wood, though French cognac distillers seem to have learned the advantages of maturing

---

[7] It has recently been announced that, with the decimalization of the British coinage and weights and measures, a new standard of British proof will be worked out.

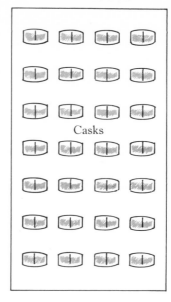

Casks

to Blenders

brandy in wood in the eighteenth century. Though I have met distillery workers who prefer the powerful new whisky straight from the still, there is no doubt at all that the characteristic qualities of a fine malt whisky require time to develop. Scotch whisky, in fact, is not (and has not been since 1915) legally Scotch whisky until it has been matured in a bonded warehouse in cask for at least three years.[8] But the whisky is still immature at three years, and five years would be a more appropriate minimum period. The rate of maturation depends in some measure on the size of the cask—the smaller the cask, the faster the maturing. Eight years in a quarter (a cask of 30 gallons or less) may be sufficient to produce

---

[8] Scotch whisky is defined in the Finance Acts 1969 as: 'Spirits which have been distilled from a mash of cereals which has been—

 i saccharified by the diastase of malt contained therein with or without natural diastases approved for the purpose by the Commissioners of Customs & Excise; and

 ii fermented by the action of yeast; and

 iii distilled at less than 166·4 degrees proof in such a way that the distillate has an aroma and flavour derived from the materials used, and which have been matured in wooden casks for a period of at least three years.'

The Act also provides that 'the expression "Scotch whisky" shall mean whisky which has been distilled in Scotland'.

a well matured malt whisky; in a hogshead of 55 to 65 gallons ten years would be a more likely bet; in a butt of 110 gallons, twelve or fifteen years. Of course one can never tell for certain in advance when a whisky is going to be at its best. Up to a point, the longer it stays in the wood the better, but after fifteen years there is always the danger of the whisky acquiring a slightly 'woody' flavour, and in a small cask it may already have acquired a woodiness by its fifteenth year. The smaller the cask, the larger the amount of whisky lost through absorption by the porosity of the wood of the cask. This wood is oak, and oak with the proper degree of porosity, for the porosity (enabling the spirit to 'breathe' without leaking) is essential for the maturing process. Not only is there a loss of volume during maturation in oak casks; there is also a loss of strength. There is a popular belief that the longer a whisky is matured the stronger it will emerge, but this is quite wrong. The degree of humidity in the warehouse where the casks lie during the maturing process also affects the degree to which a maturing whisky loses both its volume and its strength: the greater the humidity the more it loses strength and the drier the more it loses volume. It has been calculated that about four million gallons of Scotch whisky are lost each year through absorption or evaporation.

It has long been known that oak casks which have previously contained sherry give a splendid mellowing effect to the mature whisky. In 1864 William Sanderson (who later developed 'Vat 69' whisky) wrote that 'it is well-known that Whisky stored in Sherry casks soon acquires a mellow softness which it does not get when put into new casks; in fact the latter if not well seasoned, will impart a *woodiness* much condemned by the practised palate. In Sherry casks the spirit likewise acquires a pleasing tinge of colour which is much sought for.' It is the sherry, soaking back from the wood into the spirit, that traditionally has given Scotch whisky its golden colour. A cask that has held a pale sherry will impart a paler colour, and a delicate straw-coloured whisky will emerge. A cask that has held a dark sherry will impart a darker colour and a fuller flavour. (The sherry imparts a softness and sometimes, in whisky from a cask that has held dark sherry, just a whisper of sherry flavour. What is wanted, though, is not any flavour from the original sherry, rather a topping of smoothness and softness—but these are difficult things to describe.) Or one could use for a second time a sherry cask that had already been used once for maturing whisky: the 'refill' or 'second-fill' cask will impart a more delicate colouring than it imparted the first time.

Sherry casks have for long been in short supply (though as I go round the distilleries my impression is that the situation is somewhat better than it has been), and many less satisfactory substitutes have been and are being employed. Of course, whisky can be matured in plain oak casks, emerging either colourless or the palest of straw colours, and I have tasted some truly great malt whiskies matured in this way. The whole question of the nature, origin and use of casks is worth detailed consideration, and since most casks today are owned by the blending firms—who send their casks up to be filled by the individual distilleries, where they are left to mature until needed—I reserve my discussion of this topic until I come to discuss blending. The same thing goes for the artificial colouring of whisky, which as a rule is done by the blenders.

Whisky is further reduced in proof by the addition of water before bottling, the strength at which it is bottled depending on the market for which it is intended. 70° proof is now normal for the home market, though stronger bottlings of some of the best malts are available. For the United States it is 76·2° proof (86·8° proof on the American standard). For general export markets the proof is 75·8°.

Whisky does not mature in the bottle, for the porosity of the cask is a significant factor in maturation. Yet clearly *something* happens if you keep whisky in the bottle for a very long time indeed. Neil Gunn tells of finding in Caithness in the early 1930s a bottle of whisky with a seal marked 'Scrabster 1830'. He tasted it with the direct intention of finding out what happened when whisky had been in the bottle for so long, and found that 'it had matured to an incredible smoothness' yet possessed 'an attractively objectionable flavour, somewhere between rum and tar'. He concluded that some soot must have fallen into the malt (he explained how this could have happened) which, in the whisky's extreme age, had become all-pervasive. Most of us have no opportunity of carrying out an experiment of this sort. It is best to assume that whisky matures only in the wood, and to drink it after it has been so matured for at least eight years.

So far I have been describing pot-still malt Scotch whisky, the true, original whisky of Scotland. In a later chapter I shall have something to say about blended Scotch whiskies and about Lowland grain whisky which plays such an important part in modern blends. But now let us take a brief look at the different regions of Scotland where pot-still malt whisky is produced. (The reader can follow this by reference to the map on the endpapers.)

The traditional division of Scotch whisky is into Highland Malts, Lowland Malts, Campbeltowns and Islays. All are made in the manner described above, but they differ considerably in character.[9] The most famous of the Highland Malts are the Eastern Malts, most of which come from Banffshire and the areas adjoining it on the east (the western part of Aberdeenshire) and the west (Morayshire). The River Spey and its tributaries flow by some great distilleries, and Speyside has more distilleries to the square mile than any other part of Scotland. Indeed, that whole part of Scotland which lies just south of the Moray Firth—an area which, as I point out at the beginning of this chapter, includes a fertile coastal plain where barley is one of the crops grown, as well as mountains, valleys, streams and springs—is the country of the Eastern Malt. From Grantown-on-Spey to the Moray Firth coast on the north and to Huntly on the east (see the inset map) the landscape is thick with great distilleries. Glenlivet distillery, the most famous of all, lies eastward over the Hills of Cromdale from Strathspey, between the River Avon and the Livet Water, overlooking the latter, in beautiful countryside. If you go about ten miles up Glen Rinnes from Glenlivet (with Ben Rinnes on your left) you come to Dufftown, where distilleries cluster. I remember once fishing in the River Fiddich and looking across at Dufftown and seeing little else but the pagoda tops of distilleries. A little further north, on the Spey at Craigellachie, further west in Glen Rothes, and a bit north and west again around Elgin, there are further clusters of distilleries. But, though it is in these parts that we find the greatest concentration of distilleries, there are Eastern Malts somewhat further afield: further east, in Inverness-shire, across the Cromarty Firth in Ross-shire, further north still in Brora, Sutherland, and even as far north as Wick. There are also distilleries westward in Fort William and in Oban and two in the Orkney Islands which have the qualities of Eastern Malts.

The Eastern Malts vary greatly among themselves, but in general it can be said that they are subtler and sometimes lighter than the Islays and Campbeltowns. From the full and sophisticated Glenlivet to the light yet peaty Tomatin, from the quietly rich Glen Mhor to the fragrant and delicate Glenmorangie, from the mellow and fruity Clynelish to the dry yet flowery Glenfiddich, Eastern Malts cover a wide range. Yet they are all different from a typical Islay whisky, which has a characteristic

---

[9] The terminology is not consistently employed. Campbeltowns and Islays may also be regarded as Highland Malts, from which the Highland Malts produced in the north-east of Scotland are often distinguished by being called Eastern Malts.

heaviness and peatiness (which makes it important in blending). The island of Islay with its eight distilleries lies in the Atlantic opposite Kintyre, a southward-jutting peninsula west of the Isle of Arran; in Kintyre is situated Campbeltown, a town once very famous for its numerous malt-whisky distilleries. Now only two remain. Campbeltowns have in the past had something of the strength and body of Islays, and are indeed traditionally regarded as the most manly of whiskies. But of the two now distilled in Campbeltown, only one (Glen Scotia) lives up to the traditional description; the other (Springbank) is much lighter in body though agreeably full in flavour. So Campbeltowns, once a highly important category of Scotch whisky, no longer play a great part in the Scotch whisky scene. There is a single distillery on the Island of Skye, Talisker, which produces a whisky which belongs in general with the Islay and Campbeltown groups. (I have in fact seen Highland malt whisky classified simply as Eastern Malts and Western Malts, the latter including Islays, Campbeltowns and Talisker.)

Malt whisky is also distilled in the Lowlands, and has been since the eighteenth century. There are now ten Lowland malt distilleries, beside about a hundred Highland malt distilleries (including both the eastern

VIEW OF GROUND FLOOR OF BONDED WAREHOUSE, CONTAINING 6000 CASKS OF WHISKY.

WHISKY BONDED WAREHOUSES AT EDINBURGH, STORAGE CAPACITY FOR 15,000 CASKS.

PROPRIETORS, MESSRS. ANDREW USHER AND CO.

and the western). Lowland Malts are distinctly lighter than Highland or Island malts. The association of Scotch whisky with the Highlands and the fact that the greatest of malt whiskies do come from Highland distilleries should not be allowed to obscure the real merits of good Lowland Malt whisky. But I discuss the qualities of individual malt whiskies in a later chapter. All of these whiskies—Highland Malts, Islays and Campbeltowns, and Lowland Malts—must be distinguished from a much later invention, grain whisky made not by the pot-still process but in a 'patent still'. But the first thing in any inquiry into Scotch whisky is to look at the pot-still malt whisky which is the true and original spirit of Scotland and still the basis of any whisky which properly calls itself Scotch, however much grain whisky it may be blended with. It is a spirit bound up for centuries with the social history of Scotland.

We have seen the reference to Friar John Cor and his eight bolls of malt in 1494. Two centuries later we find a reference to an 'usquebaugh' (an earlier form of the word 'whisky', intermediate between the Gaelic *uisge beatha* and the modern word) in Scotland that was not made of malt at all. Writing of the Island of Lewis, in the Hebrides, about 1695, Martin Martin observed that 'the air is temperately cold and moist, and for the corrective the natives use a dose of trestarig or usquebaugh.' The cereals grown on the island were barley, oats and rye: the islanders distilled a spirit from the first two, but apparently, and perhaps surprisingly in view of the history of rye whisky in North America, not from the third.[10] Their abundance of grain, wrote Martin, 'disposed the natives to brew several sorts of liquors, as common usquebaugh, another called trestarig, *id est*, aquavitae, three times distilled, which is strong and hot; a third is four times distilled, and this by the natives is called usquebaugh-baul, *id est*, usquebaugh, which at first taste affects all the members of the body:[11] two spoonfuls of this last liquor is a sufficient dose; and if any man exceed this, it would presently stop his breath, and endanger his life. The trestarig and usquebaugh-baul are both made of oats.'

Trestarig, which comes from two Gaelic words meaning 'triple strength', is thus not the true malt whisky, and neither is usquebaugh-

---

[10] Rye was used, with barley, in the Canonmills distillery of John Haig in the 1780s. See below, p. 82.

[11] *Baul* in 'usquebaugh-baul' is the Gaelic word *ball*, meaning member, part of the body.

baul. We know very little about either of these varieties of spirit. If you look up 'trestarig' in Jamieson's *Dictionary of the Scottish Language* you will find it defined as 'a kind of ardent spirits distilled from oats' and ascribed to the Isle of Lewis; but in fact the only reference given is to the passage from Martin I have just quoted. There were clearly other spirits distilled in seventeenth- and eighteenth-century Scotland besides malt liquor. A crude spirit distilled from a mash of oats and barley was not uncommon among tenant farmers of both the Highlands and the Lowlands. Yet it is clear that by the seventeenth century whisky was already established as the characteristic Highland spirit and that in the eighteenth, in spite of continuous troubles with the Excise after the failure of the 1745 rebellion, whisky distilling flourished in the Highlands and, with its product, spread into the Lowlands.

In the seventeenth and eighteenth centuries English writers associated 'usquebaugh' or whisky with both Ireland and Scotland. John Marston's play *The Malcontent*, probably written in 1602–3, has two characters sing this song:

The Dutchman for a drunkard,
The Dane for golden locks,
The Irishman for usquebaugh,
The Frenchman for the [pox].

Dr. Johnson, who was not knowledgeable about whisky and tasted it for the first time on his Hebridean tour in 1773,[12] knew at least that the Irish and the Scotch varieties were different, though he expressed the difference rather oddly. In his *Dictionary* (1755) he defined 'usquebaugh' as 'a compounded distilled spirit, being drawn on aromaticks; and the Irish sort is particularly distinguished for its pleasant and mild flavour. The Highland sort is somewhat hotter; and by corruption, in Scottish they call it *whisky*.' The good Dr. Jamieson, whose *Dictionary of the Scottish Language* I have already cited, was moved to protest against

---

[12] 'We supped well; and after supper, Mr. Johnson, whom I had not seen taste any fermented liquor during all our expedition, had a gill of whisky brought to him. "Come," said he, "let me know what it is that makes a Scotsman happy." He drank it all but a drop, which I begged leave to pour into my glass, that I might say we had drunk whisky together.' *Boswell's Journal of a Tour to the Hebrides with Samuel Johnson*, ed. Pottle and Bennett, London, 1936, p. 348.

the older doctor's definition. *His* definition of 'whisky' reads: 'A species of ardent spirits, distilled from malt. . . . I know not how the learned lexicographer had adopted the idea of its being drawn on aromatics, unless it had been from the occasional flavour of the *peat-reek*. Perhaps Dr. Johnson meant *Bitters*, a dram much used in the Highlands as a stomachic, made from an infusion of aromatic herbs and whisky.' The 1775 enlarged edition of Nathaniel Bailey's *Universal Etymological English Dictionary* defined 'usquebeaugh' as 'a distilled Spirit made in *Ireland* and the Highlands of *Scotland* also called *Whisky*.' Bailey did not attempt to distinguish between the Irish and the Scotch varieties by flavour, nor did he make a distinction between Irish whisk*ey* and Scotch whisk*y*, which is a modern convention.

Jamieson's reference to whisky bitters reminds us that Scotch whisky was in earlier times used in ways that would make the modern connoisseur frown. Some of these ways will be discussed later, but at this point I pause only to reinforce Jamieson's conjecture about what Dr. Johnson really meant with an anecdote recorded by Sir Archibald Geikie which shows that 'an infusion of aromatic herbs and whisky' remained common in the Highlands until well into the second half of the nineteenth century. Sir Archibald was staying at a cottage in Skye, and was awakened in the morning by the eldest daughter of the house with a request that he would 'taste something before he got up', to give him an appetite for breakfast. He declined and she insisted: 'Some whusky nate? some whusky and wahtter? some whusky and milk?[13] Some acetates?' The 'acetates', Geikie decided, must have been a 'decoction of bitter roots in whisky, often to be found on Highland sideboards in the morning'.

To whatever eccentric uses the malt whisky of Scotland was sometimes put, the fact that it was a life-enhancing spirit made from barley was established in the Scottish imagination well before the seventeenth century. Burns' ballad *John Barleycorn* is, as the poet himself acknowledged, a re-working of an old folk song telling of John Barleycorn's death (when the barley is cut) and eventual resurrection as a fermented liquor; but Burns clearly saw the product as a distilled liquor, whisky. There are curious sacramental overtones in the conception:

---

[13] Whisky and milk was the breakfast drink of the American poet John Malcolm Brinnin when he entertained Dylan Thomas on his last, fatal visit to the United States.

And they hae taen his very heart's blood,
　　And drank it round and round;
And still the more and more they drank,
　　Their joy did more abound.

John Barleycorn was a hero bold,
　　Of noble enterprise;
For if you do but taste his blood,
　　'Twill make your courage rise.

Delivery of barley to Glengarioch distillery; photograph taken about 1877

Chapter Two

SOCIAL AND ECONOMIC
HISTORY TO 1823

The production of Scotch whisky early attracted the attention of tax-hungry governments, and one could write a whole history of Scotch in terms of the taxes on it, their causes and consequences. The control of the production and consumption of potable spirits by taxation can be traced at least as far back as fourteenth-century Europe with the rise of brandy consumption in France and Germany. Heavy taxation in Germany as early as 1360 in order to control the *Schnapsteufel* or brandy-devil does not seem to have achieved this object. But since then governments have continued to regard potable spirits as an obvious target for taxation on the grounds that by taxing them one can simultaneously raise revenue and lessen drunkenness. There is also the sour view that products that add conspicuously to human joy ought to be strictly controlled. 'The best things in life are free', says the song, but governments are suspicious of this view and would probably tax sex if they could. As it is, sex remains on the whole a private and untaxed pleasure, whereas Scotch whisky, from being a widely dispersed domestic industry produced in or near farms and cottages and if not actually free at least very cheap, has under centuries of government pressure become the concern of large commercial enterprises and very expensive to the consumer. This change in scale of the production of whisky from a cottage industry to an industry consisting of much larger (and much more efficient) units was a process taking place throughout the eighteenth century, with the Government devising its tax laws so as to force whisky production into fewer and larger (and so more easily controllable) units and the public resisting by dispersing illicit stills in inaccessible spots all over the country, especially, of course, the Highlands. This is part of a larger pattern of economic development throughout Britain, a pattern which becomes even more distinct in the nineteenth century, when the production of whisky becomes increasingly rationalized and commercialized. One must not get too sentimental over these changes: most of them were inevitable, many (but not all) of them resulted in the long run in the improvement of the quality of the large mass of whisky distilled and all of them helped to extend the whisky-drinking habit far beyond Scotland.

Accounts of changing tax laws are one of the more tedious kinds of history, and I do not propose to weary the reader with the details of duty levied on Scotch at different times. But the main outline of the story is of some interest, and helps to explain a great deal in the history of Scotch. An excise tax on spirits was imposed by the Scots Parliament in 1644; it was lowered under Cromwell (thus exploding any facile theory about the relation of Puritanism to drinking), lapsed after the Restoration in 1660, and was re-imposed in 1693. In 1707, the year of the Union between England and Scotland, the Board of Excise was established, and it was clear that the whisky duty was here to stay. In 1713 what was now the British Parliament (for the independent Scots Parliament vanished in 1707) decided to impose the English malt tax in Scotland, but kept it at half the English tax. In spite of this concession the new malt tax was intensely unpopular in Scotland, and caused riots in Edinburgh and Glasgow. It also both encouraged the development of illicit stills—which existed in large quantities all over the Highlands—and made certain that illicit whisky was of better quality than that legally distilled since the legal distillers, to minimize the malt tax, used a high proportion of raw grain with only enough malted barley to ensure the saccharification of the grain by the diastase of malt. Thus illegally distilled whisky was the more likely to be the genuine Highland malt Scotch whisky.

There was one famous still which remained legally tax-free until 1786. The story is well told in the elegant language of Mr. Robert Forsyth in the fifth volume of his 'clear and full account' of Scotland and her resources published under the title *The Beauties of Scotland* in 1805:

The small village of Fairntosh [or Ferintosh, in Ross-shire] only deserves notice on account of a singular privilege which its proprietor, Forbes of Culloden, long enjoyed. At the time of the revolution, in 1688, Mr. Forbes of Culloden was a zealous whig, in consequence of which his estates were laid waste, particularly the barony of Fairntosh, on which extensive distilleries belonging to him were destroyed. As a compensation, the parliament of Scotland granted to him, in 1690, freedom from excise for these lands, on condition that he should make an annual payment of 400 merks Scots. The proprietors of this estate continued extremely loyal. The son of the grantee of this privilege, in 1715, raised in arms all the men upon his estate for the

A Highland whisky still, 1827

support of the Hanoverian succession; and the succeeding proprietor, in 1745, being then Lord President of the Court of Session, contributed greatly to prevent the extension of the rebellion, and prevailed with some of the most powerful chieftains to remain quiet. The privilege was, in 1786, resumed by government, and the sum of L.20,000 was granted as a compensation to the proprietor. Before that period Fairntosh whisky was much relished in Scotland; it had a strong flavour of the smoke of the peat with which the malt of which it was made was dried; but this was considered as one of the marks of its being genuine.

It was in fact an act of 1785 (not 1786) dealing with the Scottish distilleries that abolished the Ferintosh privilege. Forbes was not satisfied with the original sum offered him by way of compensation, and the case was decided by a jury before the Scottish Court of Exchequer on 29 November 1785. Forbes's counsel, the great whig politician Henry Erskine, argued that the potential yield to the Forbes family was £7,000 a year and also that the late Duncan Forbes had spent £20,000 of his own fortune in helping to suppress the rebellion of 1745–6. The jury awarded the sum of £21,580. Forbes was happy, but young Robert Burns, as yet unknown but in the midst of an *annus mirabilis* of poetic energy and production, was not:

Thee, Ferintosh! O sadly lost!
Scotland lament frae coast to coast!
Now colic grips, an' barkin hoast   cough
          May kill us a';
For loyal Forbes' chartered boast
          Is taen awa!

Thae curst horse-leeches o' th' Excise,
Wha mak the whisky stells their prize!
Haud up thy han', Deil! ance, twice, thrice!
          There, seize the blinkers!   spies
An' bake them up in brunstane pies
          For poor damn'd drinkers.

Later on Burns himself was to become an exciseman, but here his sympathies, like those of the majority of the Scottish people, were with the illicit distillers and against the inspectors and tax gatherers. It was the aftermath of the Forty-five that did the real damage. The British Government were determined that never again should rebellion come down from the Highlands and they set about the occupation and domination of all Scotland north of the Highland line. True, after the Union of 1707 English revenue officers had appeared in Scotland to administer a system of taxation involving an obligation on the part of each distiller to produce a specified amount of whisky out of each hundred gallons of wash and a deficiency payment on the total output if this amount was not reached. But before General Wade's roads (1726–33) the Highlands were virtually impassable, and before the defeat of the Jacobite rebellion of 1745 the Highlanders, even with Wade's roads available, were still left very much to themselves. And, of course, vast areas still remained difficult if not impossible of access to those not familiar with the territory. And it was just these difficult areas—the remote glens and hillsides—which provided the best conditions for the distillation of malt whisky. The taxation of whisky in the first half of the eighteenth century was not really a serious matter; such taxation as was imposed was not savage, and it was often enough evaded by illicit distillers. It was not only in the Highlands that illicit distilling was carried on. Edinburgh in 1777 had eight licensed and, according to the excise officers, 400 illicit stills. Legal Lowland distillers (who often produced inferior whisky for the reasons explained above) complained bitterly about competition from illegal stills. Illicit Highland whisky was smuggled into the Lowlands and into England.

The Government was nonplussed by the whole situation. After innumerable reports, discussions, protests by English distillers (of gin) against the more favourable rate of taxation applied to Scotland, commissions of inquiry and debates, the Wash Act of 1784 was passed. This Act drew a formal distinction between the Lowlands and the Highlands, and in the latter duty was to be charged not on the amount of whisky produced but on the capacity of the still. In the Lowlands the tax was 5*d.* per gallon on the wash, on the assumption that 100 gallons of wash would yield 20 gallons of spirit; in the Highlands all stills had to pay a licence duty of 20*s.* per gallon of still content. The Highland line, which separated the two forms of duty, was precisely defined in the Act—the first time that a specified area of Scotland was separated from the rest as the Highlands by Act of Parliament.

But the Wash Act did not work as it was supposed to work. The Government had assumed that, by restricting the size of the Highland still, they would restrict to a predictable quantity the amount produced. But the ingenuity of the distillers found ways of speeding up the process of distilling so as to produce much more in a given period than the authorities had worked out that they would or could. The Scotch Distillery Act of 1786 applied to all Scotland; it increased the tax to £1 10*s.* per gallon of still content (considered the equivalent of 6*d.* on the gallon of whisky actually produced) and added an extra 2*s.* per gallon for whisky imported into England to bring the duty into line with the English tax of 2*s.* 6*d.* per gallon on spirits. This, of course, increased smuggling across the Border into England. It also gave a further impetus to the Scottish distillers to work out improvements which would enable them to increase their rate of production. Further increases in the rate of duty followed, in an attempt by the Government to compensate for this, but this in turn further stimulated the ingenuity of the distillers. In 1788 an additional duty of 6*d.* per gallon was imposed on whisky sent to England, and this gravely damaged the trade of the Lowland distillers, James and John Haig of Canonmills, Edinburgh, and bankrupted James and John Stein of Kilbagie and Kennetpans, Clackmannanshire, who had specialized in exports to London. (We shall hear more later of those two important whisky families, the Haigs and the Steins.)

All the time illicit distilling went on merrily in the Highlands. There, John Stein said in his evidence before the Committee on Distilleries (1798), 'the distillery is in a thousand hands. It is not confined to great towns or to regular manufacturers, but spreads itself over the whole face of the country, and in every island from the Orkneys to Jura. There are many who practise this art who are ignorant of every other, and there are distillers who boast that they make the best possible Whiskey who cannot read or write, and who carry on this manufacture in parts of the country where the use of the plough is unknown, and where the face of an Exciseman was never seen. Under such circumstances, it is impossible to take account of its operations; it is literally to search for revenue in the woods or on the mountains.' The legal distiller found it hard to compete.

To the Highlander illicit distilling was no crime. For generations he had used his barley, his water and his peat to make his national drink, and he could not see why any government should interfere. Men of the highest moral character, including highly religious men and even ministers (though some ministers deplored the consumption of whisky) regarded illicit distilling and smuggling as proper and even necessary activities. The necessity lay in the fact that since tenant farmers found their rent money from the produce of their farms, it was often only by converting their barley into whisky that they could find enough money to pay their rent. Again and again, in reading through the *Statistical Account of Scotland* (that invaluable economic and social survey of Scotland produced in the 1790s, parish by parish, by the parish ministers) we find this point made. In a final desperate measure to control distilling in the Highlands, the Government by an Act of 1814 prohibited, within the Highland line, all stills of less than 500 gallons capacity and at the same time substituted for all former duties one of 1s. per gallon of wort together with 2s. 10d. per gallon of spirit; and 18 gallons of spirit were required to be produced from each 100 gallons of wort.

The setting of the minimum size of the Highland still as 500 gallons capacity was unrealistic and indeed fantastic. 'It was evident,' wrote Colonel Stewart of Garth (the man who supervised George IV's Highland dress on the King's visit to Scotland in 1822), 'that this law was a complete interdict, as a still of this magnitude would consume more than the disposable grain in the most extensive county within this newly drawn boundary; nor could fuel be obtained for such an establishment without an expense which the community could not possibly bear. The sale, too, of the spirits produced was circumscribed within the same line,

The STILL

Carrying malt to the Bothy

the Seizure

Smuggling in the Highlands—the capture of an illicit whisky still, from an engraving of 1833

and thus the market which alone could have supported the manufacture was entirely cut off.' More than ever illicit distilling came to be the only way in which many Highlanders could sell their surplus barley in such a way as would enable them to pay their rents. The confusion resulting from the 1814 Act finally led to the much more reasonable legislation of 1823 which, as we shall see, had momentous consequences for the future of Scotch whisky.

The Reverend Mr. David Dunoon, minister of the parish of Killearnan in Ross-shire, gave a detailed account of the legal distilleries in his parish for the seventeenth volume of the *Statistical Account*, published in 1796. He concluded:

It will be asked, Why then so many distilleries? For these reasons: Distilling is almost the only method of converting our victual into cash for the payment of rent and servants; and whisky may, in fact, be called our staple commodity. The distillers do not lay the proper value on their time and trouble, and of course look on all, but the price of the barley and the fire added to the tax, as clear profit; add to these the luxury of tasting the quality of the manufacture during the process.

'The distillers do not lay the proper value on their time and trouble.' They *enjoyed* making whisky, in fact, and did not consider that they should be paid for their time while so employed. Is this one clue to the uniqueness of Highland malt whisky—that it can only be made in Scotland by people who actively enjoy making it?

The views on whisky expressed by the parish ministers who wrote for the *Statistical Account* are interestingly varied, but again and again the matter of payment of rent is mentioned. The Reverend Mr. John Downie of Urray (Presbytery of Dingwall, Synod of Ross) has this to say (volume VII, 1793):

A sense of religion and decency prevails among the people in general. One man only, within the memory of tradition, was convicted of a capital crime, and suffered for it about 50 years ago. No doubt, such a number engaged in distilling spirits, has a tendency to corrupt the morals; but the bad effects of this trade are less discernible than might be feared. Were the effects worse than they are, there is a fatal necessity of continuing the distillery, until some other manufacture be established in its stead, whereby the people will be enabled to find money to pay their rents. The worst effect of the great plenty of spirits is, that dram shops are set up in almost every village for retail, where young and idle people convene and get drunk. These tipling

huts are kept by such only as are not able to pay a fine, or procure a licence.
They are the greatest nuisance in the parish. It is a pity that no effectual
mode has yet been effected for suppressing them.

The account of the parish of King-Edward (Presbytery of Turriff,
County and Synod of Aberdeen) is, unusually, written by the parish
schoolmaster, Alexander Simpson, not by the minister. Writing in
volume XI (1794), he applauds 'the small licensed whisky stills in the
neighbourhood'. Not only do they 'afford a good market for barley', he
says, but they also supply 'us with good whisky, of a quality greatly
superior to what we have from the large stills in the southern districts,
as well as cheaper, and no less wholesome than foreign spirits'. These
stills, he concludes, 'in every point of view, are a reciprocal advantage
to the farmers, and the country at large.' Clearly the dominie's view of
the benefits of whisky is more favourable than the minister's—or is it
that the dominie can speak out more frankly on the matter?

Campbeltown, on the southern end of the peninsula of Kintyre,
Argyllshire, had thirty-two distilleries at the end of the eighteenth
century. It was for long one of the great homes of whisky, and produced
a variety of western malts of great distinction, known and distinguished
as Campbeltowns. Fifteen years ago there were only four distilleries left
there; now there are but two. But in 1794 the Reverend Mr. John Smith,
writing in the tenth volume of the *Statistical Account*, had a great deal
to say about the distilleries there:

Next to the fishing of herrings, the business most attended to in Campbelton
is the distilling of whisky; which the following is the state for the present year.

	No. of Stills	Bolls distilled	Produce in Gall.
In the town	22	5500	19800
In the country	10	2134	6350
	32	7634	26150

But the Reverend Mr. John Smith took no pleasure in contemplating
the flourishing whisky industry in his parish. 'This business is undoubtedly gainful to a few individuals, but extremely ruinous to the
community', he wrote. 'It consumes their means, hurts their morals, and
destroys both their undertakings and their health. Were it not for
preventing the temptation of smuggling, a duty next to a prohibition
would be *mercy*.' He goes on to point out that one can get completely

drunk for 2*d*. or 3*d*. But, surprisingly, he adds: 'In this place, however, very few, comparatively speaking, are given to drunkenness, as people are seldom given to excess in what is their daily fare.' No, it is not drunkenness, he continues, that is the trouble, but something else:

. . . the trade, when carried on to such an extent, is extremely hurtful to this parish in another point of view. To it we owe the want of wheat or flour of our own, which takes yearly out of the place about 2000 l.; besides the want of a sufficiency of meal to serve the inhabitants, for which we send away about as much more. Both these sums might be saved, if we could be kept from destroying so much of our own and our neighbours grain. But the prospect of enormous gain, first tempts the indigent to convert their little crop into a pernicious liquor, and then the law obliges them to drink it themselves, as it cannot be sold but where they have equal poverty and equal liberty. Thus, in the trite story, two publicans, who went alternately to each others houses, with the same twopence, drank both their cellars dry. Were we allowed to export a part, to help us pay our meal and flour, it would do us much service. We have, however, much cause to be thankful for the present law, as it stands; for it has been productive of much good to the country. It has put the business into few hands, and therefore removed from many a temptation, too strong for their feeble virtue. It has happily put an end to smuggling; and, as we must have some liquor, it makes us drink our own, and allows us to drink it better, than when it was made clandestinely and imperfectly. The revenue too has been raised since, by our collector, (Mr. Mackenzie), to full four times what it was before the act took place; and the farmer gets a better price, and better payment, for his grain.

Before we leave the *Statistical Account* (which is packed with information about whisky in late eighteenth-century Scotland), let us look at the report from a Lowland parish where highly commercialized distilling went on largely for the London market until stopped by the special tax imposed in 1788 on whisky sent to England. The Reverend Mr. Robert Moodie, minister of the Parish of Clackmannan in the County of Clackmannan, reports with expert knowledge in volume XIV (1795) on the great distilleries in his parish:

The two great distilleries of Kilbagie and Kennetpans are both in the parish of Clackmannan; and, previous to the year 1788, the manufacture of Scotch spirits was carried on at them to an extent hitherto unknown in this part of the island of Great Britain. The distillery laws have undergone various changes in Scotland. Before the year 1784, the duty was levied by a presumptive charge upon the wash (that is, fermented worts), taking it for granted, that the wash would produce one-fourth part in low wines, and that these low wines would produce three-fifths parts in spirits: hence, 100 gallons of wash was supposed to yield 15 gallons of spirits, and duty was charged accordingly; but instead of 15, 20 gallons of spirits were often drawn from the 100 of wash. In Scotland, the surplus above 15 gallons was uniformly seized, as spirits presumed to be fraudulently obtained; while in England the distiller was allowed the full exercise of his genius, and got permits for the removal of his actual produce. At this period, the quantum of duty on a gallon of spirits was more than double of what it has been ever since. But the high rate of duty afforded such temptation to smuggling, that the consumption of spirits in Scotland was chiefly supplied by the manufacture of illegal stills, and by smuggling from abroad. Great distillers could not smuggle; and being continually subjected to the surveys of the excise, the two distilleries of Kilbagie and Kennetpans depended entirely on the London market for the sale of their produce; where, previous to the year 1784, they carried on an advantageous trade: though the duty on a gallon of spirits in England was 13⅔ pence higher than in Scotland;[14] and though they had, at shipping their spirits for England, to pay down this difference on every gallon shipped. In 1784, a law was passed, rendering the duties, and mode of levying them, the same both in Scotland as in England; and at the same time reducing the rate of duty each gallon about one half of what it had been formerly; while it allowed the manufacturer a credit for 20 gallons of spirits from the 100 gallons of wash, and granted permits accordingly. The London distillers expected, that by this equalization plan, the Scotch could not continue their trade in London, and pay the duties in the same manner with themselves. But in this they were mistaken; for the trade increased. And it is the opinion of the best informed distillers, that the London distillers are not a match for the Scotch under an equal law. This mode was continued till July 1786, when the license act took place, imposing 30s. a gallon yearly on the contents of every still used for distillation in Scotland; continuing the last plan with respect to England (where the duty amounted to 2s. 6d. for the gallon of spirits), and imposing an additional duty of 2s. on the gallon of spirits sent from Scotland to England: which additional duty was to be

---

[14] The Gin Act of 1736, aimed at the peculiarly English problem of excessive gin drinking, exempted Scotland, and henceforward (until 1855) the duties on spirits distilled in England and Scotland differed. English distillers objected to the lower Scottish duty, so that an Act of 1751 imposed an equalizing duty on Scottish spirit exported to England.

*paid in London, on the arrival of the spirits in the river Thames. This act was passed as an experiment, and was to continue for two years. Under it, the London distillers expected that the Scotch could not continue the trade to London. This trade, however, still continued to increase; which increased also the astonishment of the London traders, who gave in a representation to the Treasury upon the subject. In consequence of which, and upwards of six months previous to the natural expiration of the law, another law was passed, imposing a duty of 6*d. *a gallon on all Scotch spirits sent to England, in addition to the former 2*s.*; while the duty on spirits manufactured in England was allowed to remain at the 2*s. 6*d. When this act was passed, the Scotch distilleries stopped payment. The law continued in this way till July 1788, when the license duty in Scotland was doubled, and made 3*l. *a gallon on the contents of the still; and at the same time laying the trader under such restrictions, when he worked for England, as to amount to a prohibition against his entering that market. And in July 1793, the license has been raised to 9*l. Sterling a gallon yearly. Previous to the year 1788, the quantity of corn used annually at the distillery of Kilbagie alone, amounted to above 60,000 bolls, and the annual quantity of spirits made, to above 3000 tons. The black cattle fed annually were about 7000; swine 2000. The cattle were sold to butchers, who drove them to the Edinburgh and Glasgow markets: the swine were killed and cured into bacon and pork for England. The work people employed were nearly 300. The distillery and utensils cost upwards of 40,000*l. Sterling; and when sold by the trustee for the creditors of the former proprietor, yielded about 7000*l. Sterling.*

No situation could have been more eligible for a distillery than Kilbagie; and it was erected in the most substantial manner. The buildings occupy a space of above 4 acres of ground; all surrounded by a high wall. The barns for malting are of a prodigious size, and are 4 stories in height. A small rivulet runs through the middle of the works, and drives a threshing mill, and all the grinding mills necessary for the distillery; besides supplying with water a canal, which communicates with the river Forth, of about a mile in length, cut for the purpose of conveying both the imports and exports of the distillery.

*The distillery at Kennetpans, which is advantageously situated on the very banks of the river Forth, was in proportion to that of Kilbagie, as three to five. And before these two distilleries were stopped, they paid to government an excise duty considerably greater than the whole land tax of Scotland. At present, the duty paid by both is about 8000*l. Sterling yearly. There is an engine, of Bolton and Watt's construction, at the distillery of Kennetpans; being the first of its kind that was erected in Scotland.*

One can sense the Reverend Mr. Moodie's pride as one reads his account of John Stein's two great Clackmannan distilleries, and his anger that London interests prevailed on the Government to alter the tax on Scottish spirits in such a way as to discourage exports to England. It is clear from his picture that there were relatively substantial exports of Scotch whisky from Scotland to England in the latter part of the eighteenth century, until the Act of 1788 which so damaged the Haigs and the Steins; and indeed we know this from other sources. These exports were mostly of Lowland malt whisky[15] (though I suspect that the spirit distilled at Kilbagie and Kennetpans was not always a pure malt spirit), which again in the nineteenth century was to come in quantity into the English market. But the really massive conquest of the English market, which involved quantities of quite different dimensions, was to await the invention of the Coffey still and the resulting blends of malt and grain whiskies developed by the whisky magnates of the latter part of the nineteenth century.

It is worth mentioning that whisky from the distillery at Kilbagie was well known to Robert Burns, who noted that it was 'much used as a beverage, morning, noon and night in Poosie Nansie's'. Poosie Nansie's was the pub in Mauchline where Burns set his low-life cantata, *The Jolly Beggars*. The tinker's song refers explicitly to it:

Despise that shrimp, that wither'd imp,
  With a' his nose an' cap'rin,
An' take a share wi' those that bear
  The budget and the apron!
And by that stowp, my faith an' houpe!   pot
  And by that dear Kilbaigie!
If e'er ye want, or meet wi' scant,
  May I ne'er weet my craigie!   throat

I have already suggested that I doubt whether Kilbagie consistently produced a purely malt whisky. Certainly the Haig distillery at Canonmills (and John Haig, who opened the Canonmills distillery in 1782, had learned all about distilling as an apprentice at the Kilbagie distillery, owned by his maternal grandfather John Stein) sometimes used rye and

---

[15] Scotch whisky imported into England in the eighteenth and first half of the nineteenth century was more often than not 'rectified' (re-distilled and flavoured) and turned into gin.

Dowie's Tavern, Libberton's Wynd, Edinburgh, frequented by Robert Burns

even wheat with the barley. We know this because when a hungry mob attacked the Canonmills distillery in June 1784, having heard that oats and potatoes were being used for distilling and thus were not available for food, Haig issued a statement in which he explained that he did not use these foodstuffs. 'It has unhappily taken possession of the minds of many people,' Haig's statement went, 'that all sorts of grain, wheat, oats, barley and pease, are there consumed in great quantities, and that even oat-meal and roots, such as potatoes, turnips, and carrots are made to serve the purposes of distillation; and, consequently, that the markets are really affected by this supposed consumption. Now, the genuine truth is, that no other species of grain are made use of at Canonmills but barley, rye, and sometimes such parcels of wheat as happen to receive damage, or are in quality unfit for bread; and that not a grain of oats, pease, or a particle of oat-meal, nor any potatoes, carrots, turnips or other roots, are used in the distillery in any shape.'

Burns, as every schoolboy knows, liked his dram, but he did not think much of the whisky distilled in the Lowlands. In a letter written on 22 December 1788 he thanks a friend for sending him a cask of what appears to have been Highland malt whisky, saying, 'It will bear five waters, strong; or six, ordinary Toddy.' He added: 'The Whisky of this country [i.e. region] is a most rascally liquor; and by consequence, only drank by the most rascally part of the inhabitants.' Perhaps the eighteenth-century English distillers were right to rectify the whisky they bought from Stein and Haig and turn it into gin! (No reflection, I hasten to add, on the modern blended Haig Scotch whisky, one of the most interesting of the blended Scotches.)

It was in the eighteenth century that Scotch whisky ceased to be an almost exclusive Highland drink and became increasingly popular in the Lowlands after the middle of the century. The consumption of ale diminished as that of whisky increased. Many of the parish ministers who wrote in the *Statistical Account* referred to the increase of whisky consumption at the expense of ale, and some deplored this. According to the Reverend Mr. Francis Forbes of Grange, Banffshire, the heavy excise tax on malt inevitably produced illicit distilling and smuggling and discouraged the brewing of beer (also made from malted barley).

In the earlier part of the eighteenth century English travellers noted that whisky was a peculiarly Highland drink. 'The Landlord not only sits down with you, as in the northern Lowlands'—wrote Captain Edward Burt, on General Wade's staff in the Highlands in 1724–8—'but in some little time asks Leave (and sometimes not) to introduce his Brother, Cousin, or more, who are all to drink your Honour's Health in *Usky*; which, tho' a strong Spirit, is to them like Water. And this I have often seen 'em drink out of a Scollop Shell.' In the same account (*Letters from a Gentleman in the North of Scotland to His Friend in London*, 1754) the writer gives us some idea of how whisky was transported in the Highlands:

. . . In about three Hours after my Arrival at this Hut [a 'publick Hut' which served as a primitive inn] there appear'd on the other Side of the Water a Parcel of Merchants, with little Horses loaded with Roundlets of Usky.

Within Sight of the Ford was a Bridge (as they call'd it) made for the Convenience of this Place. It was compos'd of two small Fir-Trees not squared at all, laid one beside the other, across a narrow Part of the River, from Rock to Rock. There were Gaps and Intervals between those Trees, and beneath a most tumultuous Fall of Water.

Some of my Merchants bestriding the Bridge, edg'd forwards, and mov'd the Usky Vessels before 'em; but the others afterwards, to my Surprize, walk'd over this dangerous Passage, and dragg'd their Garrons through the Torrent, while the poor little Horses were almost drown'd with the Surge.

The writer has also something to say about the quantity of whisky drunk:

Some of the Highland Gentlemen are immoderate Drinkers of Usky, even three or four Quarts at a Sitting; and in general, the People that can pay the Purchase, drink it without Moderation.

Not long ago, four English Officers took a Fancy to try their Strength in this Bow of Ulysses, against a like Number of the Country Champions, but the Enemy came off victorious; and one of the Officers was thrown into a Fit of the Gout, without Hopes; another had a most dangerous Fever, a third lost his Skin and Hair by the Surfeit, and the last confessed to me, that when Drunkenness and Debate ran high, he took several Opportunities to sham it.

They say for Excuse, the Country requires a great deal; but I think mistake a Habit and Custom for Necessity. They likewise pretend it does not intoxicate in the Hills as it would do in the low Country, but this I also doubt by their own Practice; for those among them who have any Considera- tion will hardy care so much as to refresh themselves with it, when they pass near the Tops of the Mountains; for in that Circumstance, they say, it renders them careless, listless of the Fatigue, and inclined to sit down, which might invite to Sleep, and then they would be in Danger to perish with Cold. . . . The Collector of the Customs at Stornway *in the Isle of* Lewis *told me, that about 120 Families drink yearly 4000 English Gallons of this Spirit, and Brandy together, although many of them are so poor they cannot afford to pay for much of either, which you know must encrease the Quantity drank by the rest, and that they frequently give to Children, of six or seven Years old, as much at a time as an ordinary Wine-glass will hold.*

When they chuse to qualify it for Punch they sometimes mix it with Water and Honey, or with Milk and Honey; at other times the Mixture is only the Aqua Vitae, *Sugar and Butter, this they burn till the Butter and Sugar are dissolved.*

The reference to brandy reminds us that imported (often smuggled) French brandy was also commonly drunk among Highland gentlemen, though our travelling Englishman was almost certainly wrong in suggest- ing that brandy was drunk at all by the poor. Later in the century, when whisky was becoming increasingly popular in the Lowlands, patriots exalted its claims against those of usurping brandy. The poet Robert Fergusson wrote in 1773 *A Drink Eclogue*, a dialogue between 'Landlady, Brandy and Whisky' in which Brandy attacks Whisky as a 'cottar loun' drunk by humble porters and 'chairmen' from the Highlands and asks indignantly:

Ha'e ye nae breeding, that you shaw your nose
Anent my sweetly gusted cordial dose.

Whisky laments the snobbery which makes people prefer foreign spirits:

Alake! the byword's o'er weel kend throughout,
'Prophets at hame are held in nae repute;'
Sae fair'st wi' me, tho' I can heat the skin,
And set the saul upon a merry pin,
Yet I am hameil, there's the sour mischance! home-bred
I'm no frae Turkey, Italy, or France; ...

Robert Fergusson

More than twenty years later Burns, in his poem *Scotch Drink*, praised whisky as the great native drink and attacked brandy—

Wae worth that brandy, burnin trash!

In another poem written about the same time Burns addressed 'the Scotch representatives in the House of Commons' in a complaint about the taxation of whisky, ending with a 'Postscript' which is a great paean of praise to whisky, with the famous conclusion:

Begins "ye Irish lords..."

Scotland, my auld, respected mither!
Tho' whiles ye moistify your leather,   sometimes
Till whare ye sit on craps o' heather
            Ye tine your dam,   lose; water
Freedom and whisky gang thegither,
            Tak aff your dram!

The English traveller's reference to punch is important: though Highlanders generally drank their whisky neat, and though whisky connoisseurs today like their malt whisky neat or with a little water, whisky toddy was a common drink in eighteenth-century Scotland, especially in the Lowlands from the middle of the century. The traditional recipe for toddy involves whisky, sugar and hot water. The tumbler must be heated before the lump sugar is put in and dissolved in a glassful of boiling water. When the sugar is melted, add half a glass of whisky; stir with a silver spoon. The chief use of toddy in modern times is to relieve the symptoms of a cold. There used to be an elaborate ritual in both making and drinking toddy.

Toddy was drunk by gentlemen, but in the latter half of the eighteenth century in the Lowlands—as Fergusson's poem makes clear—neat whisky was more often the poor man's drink. Claret was the great drink of the Edinburgh 'literati', and many of them drank enormous quantities of it. They might drink toddy, or rum punch (the great drink of the Glasgow merchants trading with the West Indies) late in the evening, but were not as a rule serious dram-takers. Whisky in the Highlands was always a classless drink; in the Lowlands, once it became at all common, it was the democratic drink, the people's drink ('Freedom and whisky gang thegither!'), later, amid the squalid horrors that the Industrial Revolution left in its wake, often the only comfort of the destroyed and desperate; then high taxation put it virtually beyond the reach of the common man.

Whisky in the Highlands had its ritual and sacramental uses as well as satisfying daily needs. It was the standard drink at funerals. ('The ceremony [of burial] was closed with the discharge of pistols; then we returned to the castle, resumed the bottle, and by midnight there was not a sober person in the family, the females excepted. The 'squire and I were, with some difficulty, permitted to retire with our land lord in the evening; but our entertainer was a little chagrined at our retreat; and afterwards seemed to think it a disparagement to his family, that not above a hundred gallons of whisky had been drank upon such a solemn occasion.' Jery Melford's description of an Argyllshire funeral in Smollett's *Humphry Clinker*, 1770.) Whisky is still the funeral drink in the Highlands. Sir Archibald Geikie recorded an incident from the nineteenth century: he asked a girl if her aunt, who was gravely ill, was still living, and received the reply, 'Ay. She's no deid yet; but we've gotten in the whusky for the funeral.'

But, especially in the Highlands, it did not need a funeral to produce the whisky. Elizabeth Grant of Rothiemurchus, looking back in old age on Highland customs she had observed at the beginning of the nineteenth century, remarked on the perpetual whisky drinking:

The cheer she [Mrs. Macintosh, 'a tidy guid-wife'] offered us was never more than bread and cheese and whisky . . . the whisky was a bad habit, there was certainly too much of it going. At every house it was offered, at every house it must be tasted or offence would be given, so we were taught to believe. I am sure now that had we steadily refused compliance with so incorrect a custom it would have been far better for ourselves, and might all the sooner have put a stop to so pernicious a habit among the people. Whisky-drinking was and is the bane of that country; from early morning till late at night it went on. Decent gentlewomen began the day with a dram. In our house the bottle of whisky, with its accompaniment of a silver salver full of small glasses, was placed on the side-table with cold meat every morning. In the pantry a bottle of whisky was the allowance per day, with bread and cheese in any required quantity, for such messengers or visitors whose errands sent them in that direction. The very poorest cottages could offer whisky; all the men engaged in the wood manufacture drank it in goblets three times a day, yet except at a merry-making we never saw any one tipsy.

In another passage Elizabeth Grant gives an account of the drinking habits of the loggers and their families:

The Spey floaters lived mostly down near Ballindalloch, a certain number

*of families by whom the calling had been followed for ages, to whom the wild
river, all its holes and shoals and ricks and shiftings, were as well known as
had its bed been dry. They came up in the season, at the first hint of a spate,
as a rise in the water was called. A large bothy was built for them at the
mouth of the Druin in a fashion that suited themselves; a fire on a hearth
stone in the middle of the floor, a hole in the very centre of the roof just over
it where some of the smoke got out, heather spread on the ground, no window,
and there, after their hard day's work, they lay down for the night, in their
wet clothes—for they had been perhaps hours on the river—each man's feet
to the fire, each man's plaid round his chest, a circle of wearied bodies half
stupified by whisky, enveloped in a cloud of steam and smoke, and sleeping
soundly till the morning. They were a healthy race, suffering little except in
their old age from rheumatism. . . .*

*. . . When the men met in the morning they were supposed to have
breakfasted at home, and perhaps they had had their private dram, it being
cold work in a dark wintry dawn, to start over the moor for a walk of some
miles to end in standing up to the knees in water; yet on collecting, whisky
was always handed round; a lad with a small cask—a quarter anker—on his
back, and a horn cup in his hand that held a gill, appeared three times a day
among them. They all took their 'morning' raw, undiluted and without
accompaniment, so they did the gill at parting when the work was done; but
the noontide dram was part of a meal. There was a twenty minutes' rest
from labour, and a bannock and a bit of cheese taken out of every pocket to
be eaten leisurely with the whisky. When we were there the horn cup was
offered first to us, and each of us took a sip to the health of our friends around
us, who all stood up. Sometimes a floater's wife or bairn would come with
a message; such messenger was always offered whisky. Aunt Mary had a
story that one day a woman with a child in her arms, and another bit thing
at her knee, came up among them; the horn cup was duly handed to her, she
took a 'gey guid drap' herself, and then gave a little to each of the babies.
'My goodness, child,' said my mother to the wee thing that was trotting by
the mother's side, 'doesn't it bite you?' 'Ay, but I like the bite,' replied the
creature.*

Whisky was in fact given to new-born infants in the Highlands, but
just a spoonful. Elizabeth Grant's little brother William was given at his
birth a spoonful of gin by his nurse instead, 'to test the strength of the
young heir'.

There are numerous anecdotes of illicit distilling and whisky smuggling in the eighteenth and early nineteenth centuries. Looking back in
her *Autobiography* on her summers spent at Park Hall, near Balfron,

Stirlingshire, in the years 1813–17, Mrs. Eliza Fletcher recalled:

Balfron was a most lawless village. There was a cotton mill in it, and the workers in it were among the best people there. It was illicit distillation that demoralised the district. The men of the place resorted to the woods or to the sequestered glens among the Campsie Hills, and there distilled whisky, which their wives and daughters took in tin vessels in the form of stays buckled round their waists to sell for a high price at Glasgow.

Thomas Guthrie recalled in his *Autobiography* the smugglers of his native Brechin when he was a boy there about the same time:

When a boy in Brechin [he was born in 1803], I was quite familiar with the appearance and on-goings of the Highland smugglers. They rode on Highland ponies, carrying on each side of their small, shaggy, but brave and hardy steeds, a small cask, or 'keg', as it was called, of illicit whisky, manufactured amid the wilds of Aberdeenshire or the glens of the Grampians.

They took up a position on some commanding eminence during the day, where they could, as from a watch-tower, descry the distant approach of the enemy, the exciseman or gauger: then, when night fell, every man to horse, descending the mountains only six miles from Brechin, they scoured the plains, rattled into the villages and towns, disposing of their whisky to agents they had everywhere; and, now safe, returned at their leisure, or often in a triumphal procession. They were often caught, no doubt, with the contraband whisky in their possession. Then they were subjected to heavy fines besides the loss of their goods. But—daring, stout, active fellows—they often broke through the nets, and were not slack, if it offered them a chance of escape, to break the heads of the gaugers. I have seen a troop of thirty of them riding in Indian file, and in broad day, through the streets of Brechin, after they had succeeded in disposing of their whisky, and, as they rode leisurely along, beating time with their formidable codgels on the empty barrels to the great amusement of the public and mortification of the excise-men, who had nothing for it but to bite their nails and stand, as best they could, the raillery of the smugglers and the laughter of the people. . . . Everybody, with a few exceptions, drank what was in reality illicit whisky —far superior to that made under the eye of the Excise—lord and lairds, members of Parliament and ministers of the Gospel, and everybody else.

Another Scottish minister, this time in the Borders, remembered whisky smuggling at the beginning of the nineteenth century. In his posthumous book entitled by its editors *Reminiscences of Yarrow* James Russell wrote:

About fifty years ago, smuggling was carried on to a considerable extent. It was generally counted a very slight offence to defraud the revenue in this form, and informers were not to be found. The recesses of the mountains afforded ready opportunities for the preparation of mountain-dew, *and the old corn-mill supplying the materials, the part of the river at which it stood was appropriately termed the 'maut pool'. The still was a very primitive affair, consisting generally of a hole dug in some quiet nook; the roof was formed by some strong branches covered with turf; and there was no outward indication of its whereabouts. The farmer was usually let into the secret, lest, in riding or coursing over his farm, he and his horses had come to grief.*

But it was in the Highlands that illicit distilling was most common and where the battle of wits between distillers and excisemen waxed most furious—ending, in the great majority of cases, in victory for the former. The rugged nature of the country favoured the natives, who knew every inch of it, against the intruding excise officers. Even a reward of £5 offered by the Government to anyone reporting the whereabouts of an illicit still helped rather than hindered the illicit distillers. As Sir Robert Bruce Lockhart explained in his book *Scotch*:

In those days the most expensive part of a primitive still was the 'worm', a coiled copper pipe which condenses into liquid the hot vapour from the wash-still and then passes it into the spirit-still. When their copper-pipe was worn out, the smugglers used to dismantle their still, taking good care to remove whatever might be of further use to them, but leaving the worn-out worm and other minor implements to show that a still had been there. One of the smugglers would then go to the gauger, report that he had discovered a still, and receive the £5 as a reward. With the money thus acquired the smugglers would then buy the copper for a new pipe and set up their still in another glen.

These illicit distillers were not, of course, full-time; they were farmers who distilled their own whisky in the old Highland tradition of family distilling. From the very first confrontation between Government and Scotch whisky the governmental ambition was to transform whisky distilling from a private family affair to public manufacture by professionals. And with the passing of the Act of 1823 the completion of this process became inevitable.

The 1823 Act was a final attempt by the Government to solve a hitherto insoluble problem. In that year there were 14,000 official discoveries of illicit stills (which gives some idea of the number there must have been that were not detected). It seemed impossible to prevent Scotsmen, especially Highlanders, from distilling whisky privately in small stills wherever the geographical conditions were favourable. But complaints from the legal Lowland distillers about the unfair competition from smuggled Highland whisky produced frequent debates both in the Commons and the Lords on the question of whisky control and, after more than a century of constantly shifting and uniformly unsuccessful measures, it became increasingly felt that a completely new approach to the problem was called for. It was the intervention in the House of Lords of Alexander Gordon, fourth Duke of Gordon, that proved decisive. The Duke, 'the greatest subject in Britain' as a contemporary called him, was a great landowner in Inverness-shire and Banffshire (great whisky country). He argued that you could not stop the Highlander from distilling: he was a natural distiller and whisky was his traditional national drink. If, he maintained, legislation were passed that

Thomas, Lord Wallace

would provide realistic opportunities for the legal manufacture of whisky under reasonably favourable conditions and of as good quality as the product of illicit stills, he and his fellow landed proprietors in Scotland would do their best to suppress illicit distilling and smuggling and encourage their tenants to take out licences for their stills. Largely as a result of the Duke's promise, and after a commission under Thomas Wallace (later Lord Wallace), vice-president of the Board of Trade, had sat for two years, the 1823 Act was passed. This sanctioned the distilling of whisky on payment of duty of 2s. 3d. per gallon of proof spirit and a licence fee of £10 on all stills with a capacity of 40 gallons or over. Forty gallons (rather than the 500 gallons of the 1814 Act) now became the legal minimum size.

The effect of the new Act was not immediate, and illicit distilling went on, though in diminishing quantities, for some time. It was not, in fact, until the complete commercializing of whisky production and distribution by the blended whisky houses of the latter part of the nineteenth century that illicit distilling virtually disappeared. It did not completely disappear even then, and some illicit activity went on well into the twentieth century; but by then it had long ceased to be a real problem. The 14,000 detections in 1823 diminished to 692 in 1834, 177 in 1844, 73 in 1854, 19 in 1864 and 6 in 1874. There was a short-lived revival of illicit distilling after the repeal of the Malt Tax in 1880 made it safe for the illicit distiller to engage in all the processes except the final brewing and distilling, and the Depression of the early 1930s produced another temporary revival of illicit distilling. Steadily increasing taxation of whisky after the Second World War has prevented the total disappearance of the illicit still, and it seems fairly certain that a limited amount of illicit distilling is still going on.

It was not an easy job to persuade Highland farmers to take out licences and become legitimate distillers. But the example was set by George Smith of Glenlivet in 1824. Before then, like many others in that great whisky district, he had been distilling illicitly. There were in fact 200 illicit stills in Glenlivet in 1823. Smith, an unusually well educated farmer who had been trained as an architect, had his illicit still on his farm of Upper Drumin (further up the hill from the present Glenlivet distillery). Encouraged by the Duke of Gordon, Smith rebuilt his distillery on a larger scale and took out a licence: thus in 1824 the Glenlivet distillery came legally into being, producing a great whisky which, still known as 'Smith's Glenlivet', is one of the very finest of Highland malt whiskies and indeed has a claim to be considered the champion of them all. Glenlivet had been producing excellent whisky long before this; but now the name 'Glenlivet' could be freely used and boasted about as the home of great whisky—so much so, indeed, that the word became synonymous in Scotland with good whisky. The old rhyme says:

Glenlivet it has castles three,
Drumin, Blairfindy and Deskie,
And also one distillery
More famous than the castles three.

One could fill a book with references to Glenlivet in literature, which became a legal whisky and remained legendary after it became legal. Witness the case of the valiant Macpherson of W. E. Aytoun's poem, who

      had a son
Who married Noah's daughter;
And nearly spoiled ta Flood,
    By trinking up ta water:

Which he would have done,
  I at least pelieve it,
Had ta mixture peen
    Only half Glenlivet.

Glenlivet had a reputation long before George Smith went legitimate. When George IV visited Scotland in 1822, two years before Smith's conversion, he insisted on having it. Elizabeth Grant of Rothiemurchus has a vivid account of what happened:

Lord Conyngham, the Chamberlain, was looking everywhere for pure Glenlivet whisky; the King drank nothing else. It was not to be had out of the Highlands. My father sent word to me—I was the cellarer—to empty my pet bin, where was whisky long in wood, long in uncorked bottles, mild as milk, and the true contraband goût in it. Much as I grudged this treasure it made our fortunes afterwards, showing on what trifles great events depend. The whisky, and fifty brace of ptarmigan all shot by one man, went up to Holyrood House, and were graciously received and made much of, and a reminder of this attention at a proper moment by the gentlemanly Chamberlain ensured to my father the Indian judgeship.

Earlier the King, on his arrival at Leith, had, in J. G. Lockhart's words, 'called for a bottle of Highland whisky, and having drunk his health in this national liquor, desired a glass to be filled for [Sir Walter Scott, who had welcomed him]. Sir Walter, after draining his own bumper, made a request that the King would condescend to bestow on him the glass out of which his Majesty had just drunk his health.' This is the glass that Scott, having put it into his pocket, forgot about when, on returning home, he found the poet Crabbe awaiting him; he sat down on it and it smashed to pieces, giving him a painful but insignificant scratch. There is no record of whether the Highland whisky consumed on that occasion was Glenlivet or not.

George Smith had to contend against much local opposition. Some of his neighbours, considering him the worst of blacklegs, threatened to burn down his new distillery—indeed, one distillery on Deeside was burned down in 1825. But Smith was undaunted, even though for some

George IV at Holyrood, engraved from the painting by Sir David Wilkie

years he thought it prudent to go about with 'a pair of hair-trigger pistols' in his belt, presented to him by the laird of Aberlour. In 1825 and 1826 three more legal distilleries were started in Glenlivet, but had to give up in the face of opposition from the smugglers. But in the long run the 1823 Act did work, and steadily as the century advanced legitimate distilleries emerged in the Highlands. Smith himself reaped the reward of his pioneering in legitimacy: the subsequent history of the Glenlivet distillery is told in another chapter.

Chapter Three

THE PATENT STILL
AND ITS CONSEQUENCES

In the last chapter I said something about the Stein family (who inter-married with the Haigs) and their large distillery at Kilbagie, Clack-mannanshire. The owner of Kilbagie distillery in 1826 was Robert Stein, and it was in that year that he invented a process for the rapid distillation of grain whisky, a 'patent still' that represented quite a different method from the traditional pot-still method used in making malt whisky. Stein's method was quickly introduced by his cousin John Haig at his distillery at Cameron Bridge, Fife. But it was soon superseded by an improved patent still invented in 1830 by Aeneas Coffey, formerly inspector-general of Excise in Ireland. Both Stein and Coffey had carried out some of their experiments in developing their methods of distillation at the Islay distillery of Port Ellen, built in 1825 and in 1826 taken over by John Ramsay, Member of Parliament for Stirling and a prominent Glasgow business man with a great interest in the whisky trade. Known as the Coffey still or patent still, Aeneas Coffey's invention had obvious commercial advantages over the pot still: it can produce whisky more quickly, more cheaply, in much greater quantities and in a continuous process. It is also independent of locality, in the sense that the quality of its product is not related to the local peat and water and other mysterious local factors which help to determine the individuality of the whisky produced at each pot-still malt distillery. The patent still was designed for the production of a whisky out of a mixture of malted and unmalted barley mashed with other cereals. Its product derived no peaty flavour from the malt, for the malt had not been dried over peat fires, nor did it contain the oils and aromatic substances that give malt whisky its characteristic flavour. As it is an improved design of Coffey's patent still that today produces that grain whisky with which malt whiskies are blended to give the popular blended Scotch whiskies of our time, we had better take a look at how it works. The much debated question concerning the merits of patent-still grain whisky, and indeed the question whether it can properly be called Scotch whisky at all, will be an important part of the story later.

Scottish grain whisky today is made largely from maize with a small amount of malted barley (not dried over peat fires); unmalted barley is also sometimes used with the maize. The unmalted cereal is crushed and then cooked at a temperature of 140 °C. to break up the starch before being blown off into a mash tun. Wet ground malted barley is now added (one-fifth of the amount of the unmalted cereal), then hot water, and the mixture is stirred. As with the making of malt whisky, the enzyme diastase of the malted barley converts the starch in the cereal into maltose, producing the liquid wort. The fermenting of the wort with yeast in wash-backs is done in much the same way as the fermenting of the wort in the making of malt whisky, with the same result. The wash is then pumped into the Coffey still, and henceforward the process is radically different from that employed in the making of pot-still malt whisky. The Coffey still consists of two linked copper columns, forty to fifty feet high; these are the analyser and the rectifier. Each is divided horizontally into chambers by perforated copper plates. Steam is led by a pipe into the analyser and proceeds up the analyser and then through the linking pipe into the rectifier. The wash which is all the time being pumped into the rectifier comes down the rectifier in a coiled copper pipe and then by the connecting wash pipe into the top of the analyser. It moves down, chamber by chamber, but not through the perforations (through which the steam ascends) as the rising steam prevents this so that the level of the wash rises until it reaches the entrance of the drip pipe, which is a little above the plate, and by the drip pipe descends to the lower chamber. The wash descends in this way compartment by compartment, and by the time it reaches the base of the analyser all the alcohol which it had contained has been vaporized by the steam. The alcohol vapour and the steam rise up through the analyser and go down the connecting vapour pipe (which emerges from the top of the analyser) into the rectifier. As the alcohol vapour and the steam move up the rectifier, chamber by chamber, the new incoming wash, coming down the rectifier in its winding pipe, cools them, so that condensation takes place.

The ingenuity of the process is illustrated by the fact that the vapours that heat the wash are also condensed by the wash. Another important point in the patent-still process is the progressive condensation of the alcohol vapour as it rises through the chambers of the rectifier. It is only the almost pure alcohol that gets to the top. The higher alcohols, esters and aldehydes distil first and drop out through a pipe at the bottom of the rectifier to be eventually returned to the analyser for re-distilling. Further up the rectifier column, the residual alcohol vapour distils, producing 95 per cent ethyl alcohol and water, and this is drawn off through a cooling worm to the stainless-steel spirit receivers. Like pot-still whisky, it is then reduced in strength by the addition of water before being passed into barrels for maturing. Patent-still whisky, being nearer neutral spirits than pot-still malt whisky, takes less time to mature and changes less in maturing.

What exactly is the product of the Coffey or patent still? Dr. Philip Schidrowitz, writing in the 1911 edition of the *Encyclopaedia Britannica*, hotly denied that the product was true 'silent' or 'neutral' spirits—i.e. alcohol and water. 'They possess a distinct flavour,' he wrote, 'which varies at different distilleries, and analysis discloses the fact that they contain very appreciable quantities of the "secondary" products which distinguish potable spirits from plain alcohol.' And Dr. Schidrowitz (who was not altogether disinterested in the matter, as he was a member of the Council of the Institute of Brewing and had close contacts with both the brewing and distilling industries) went on to say that as a result of 'an extensive investigation of the question' carried out by himself, it had been shown 'that the relative proportion of "secondary" products in Highland Malt, Lowland Malt and "grain" whiskies respectively, is as 3:2:1'. The informative pamphlet put out by the Distillers Company Limited (DCL) in 1962—and, as we shall see, DCL became early in the present century a tremendous force in popularizing blends of malt and grain whiskies as the standard Scotch whisky so that their view, also, can hardly be considered disinterested—calls patent-still grain whisky 'still a true Scotch whisky, but lighter in body than the malt whisky of the pot-still'. On the other hand, Neil Gunn, that great champion of pot-still malt whisky, in his stimulating if idiosyncratic book *Whisky and Scotland*, published in 1935, wrote: 'The product of the pot still contains the oils and aromatic substances that gives true whisky its body and flavour. The product of the patent still is almost pure alcohol, flavourless, and is mainly used for industrial and scientific purposes.' Bruce Lockhart expresses a more moderate view: 'Grain whisky is lighter in weight and less distinctive in taste than malt whisky. It does not improve in cask in the same manner or to anything like the same extent as malt whisky, but it is wrong to describe it as a neutral spirit.'

As we shall see, the future of patent-still grain whisky was to lie chiefly in blended Scotch whisky; its chief use today is as it has been for many years to 'lighten' the heavier malt whiskies with which it is blended. The relative merits of these blends and of single malt whiskies will be discussed in due course; all that need be said here is that it is on its merits as a blending agent that patent-still grain whisky must stand or fall. It is very rarely drunk now unblended, although it once was. Today the only available patent-still grain whisky in bottle is *Choice Old Cameron Brig*, made at Cameronbridge Distillery by Scottish Grain Distillers Ltd. and bottled and sold by John Haig & Co. Ltd. It is sold locally, where I am told it is preferred by the natives to a blended whisky. The only place in England where I have found it on sale is the Fosseway Restaurant and Hotel, Newark-on-Trent, where they have a remarkable range of Scotch whiskies on sale in the bar, including a wide range of malts. I find it clear and sharp in taste, almost antiseptic indeed, with nothing at all of what I would call whisky character. The only other grain whisky I have drunk by itself is North British, a seven-year-old sample of which was made available to me by courtesy of an Edinburgh blending firm. This has a sharp, pungent, acidy smell ('like surgical spirit', my wife remarked as I passed the glass to her, and she sniffed it). Its sharp-

ness caught me at the back of the throat as I drank. It seemed to have little or no body, but all surface flavour, and that flavour of a pungent sweet sharpness that makes one think more of a chemistry laboratory than a bar. My own experience with patent-still grain whisky, then, suggests that while it has a part to play in blends it is not a whisky to drink by itself, nor can it begin to compare as a drink with a pot-still malt whisky. But it is clearly not just 'silent spirit': indeed, it is rather noisy.

The arrival of the Coffey still produced no immediate revolution. Its use was legalized by Treasury warrant in September 1832 but it was not until 1839 that the Board of Excise issued the appropriate instructions to the Excise Officers who would have to supervise its working. There was no question yet of producing blends of Lowland grain and Highland malt whiskies for the English market. Scotch whisky—whether malt or grain—which was sent to England was not as a rule drunk as whisky; it was rectified and turned into gin. The Royal Commission which sat from 1833 to 1836 under Sir Henry Brooke Parnell (later Lord Congleton, the distinguished Whig economist and financial expert), one of many such commissions inquiring into the question of potable spirits in Britain, observed that in England there was 'scarcely any demand for whisky in the pure state in which it is prepared for consumption in Scotland and Ireland'. The Commission also put its finger on one factor that was hindering the export of Scotch whisky to England: 'There is no doubt that orders for the fine quality of malt whisky from the Highlands would be increased to a great extent both for the use of private families in England and also for ship stores, if spirits were permitted to be shipped in casks of smaller capacity than eighty gallons.' They went so far as to suggest that 'an arrangement might be made under which the exportation of Scotch spirits in bottles might be permitted in the same way as is practised with regard to foreign wines.' It was not in fact until Gladstone's Spirits Act of 1860 that this aspect of the Parnell Report was implemented and whisky was allowed to be imported from Scotland to England in bottles.

The 1823 Act, as we have seen, had an immediately beneficial effect in encouraging the development of good legal distillers of pot-still malt whisky and in lessening illicit distilling and smuggling. But further legislation and competition between grain and malt distillers changed the picture within a decade. In 1822, just before the new policy was introduced, something over two million gallons of tax-paid Scotch whisky were recorded as having been consumed; in 1825—the year of an important Consolidating Act which ironed out most discrepancies in

(*Honoured Guest at big Country-house is invited by affable Butler to walk through the Cellars.*)

Guest, " Ah! ha! So *you've* been laying in the fashionable drink, I see! The Doctors are all mad about it."

Affable Butler, "Yezzir—less hacid, they say, in good Malt Wiskey than in any form of Alco'ol. I've took to it myself. In fact, I may say *I*'ve quite given up Champagnes, Clarets, Burgundies and 'Ocks!"

the manufacture and sale of spirits in different parts of the United Kingdom—the figure was almost six million. Encouraged by this, the Government thought the time ripe to increase taxation. In 1826 they raised the tax from 2s. 4d. to 2s. 10d. per imperial gallon (the imperial gallon was now the legal measure for spirit duties in Scotland) and in 1830 to 3s. 4d. The result might have been predicted: legal consumption dropped again, and illicit distilling and smuggling rose. Government measures for prevention and detection stiffened. At the same time distillers, facing increasing competition, could not afford to let their whisky mature but for the most part sold it new. There was as yet no legislation governing the maturing of spirits. Distillers tried to solve their problems by building up exports, and slowly a small export trade was built up, chiefly from Glasgow. John Ramsay's distillery at Port Ellen, Islay, pioneered direct whisky export to the United States. From 1,500 gallons of malt whisky exported from Scotland (excluding what went to England) in 1824, the figure rose to 25,000 gallons in 1834. A tiny trickle when compared with the massive exports of a later age, but still a pointer to the future.

An act of 1848 allowed English distillers to use a great variety of raw materials (including molasses and treacle) for purposes of distilling, but the Scots were still restricted to grain, and the Scottish Lowland patent-still distiller felt that he was unfairly treated compared with his English rival. These distillers then turned to a new solution: if competition was making it difficult for them, they would try combination. The first movement in this direction came in 1856, when six of the leading Scottish patent-still distillers entered into a trade agreement, sharing the trade among themselves in fixed proportions in order to avoid over-production and its resulting slumps. The arrangement did not last and nine years later a similar association was formed. Arrangements were discussed with Irish and English distillers and much ebb and flow of proposals and counter-proposals went on among interested parties in all three countries. Finally, in 1875 it was proposed 'that the principal firms engaged in the grain distillery business should form themselves into one company under the Limited Liabilities Act'. In April 1877 six Lowland grain patent-still distillers combined to form the Distillers Company Limited with a nominal capital of two million pounds and headquarters in Edinburgh. The firms were: M. Macfarlane & Co., Port Dundas Distillery, Glasgow; John Bald & Co., Carsebridge Distillery, Alloa; John Haig and Co., Cameron Bridge Distillery, Fife; McNab Bros. & Co., Glenochil Distillery, Menstrie; Robert Mowbray, Cambus Distillery, Alloa; Stewart & Co., Kirkliston Distillery, West Lothian. These were all Lowland firms. By now the cities of Scotland—Leith (which had become the whisky capital), Edinburgh, Perth, Glasgow, Aberdeen— had become the centre of the whisky trade. And Andrew Usher & Co. of Edinburgh, who were agents for Glenlivet first for the South of Scotland and England and from 1864 for the world, had already pioneered the blending of pot-still malt and patent-still grain whiskies. One other factor was necessary to achieve the great break-through of Scotch whisky and make it a standard drink in England and throughout the world. This was a stimulus to turn people away from brandy as the fashionable English drink in favour of Scotch. It was an event across the Channel that achieved this.

Between 1858 and 1863 there was a great deal of importation into France of American vines for grafting purposes. (The native American vine east of the Rocky Mountains is very hardy, and its roots are resistant to the *Phylloxera vastatrix*, an insect which destroys growing vines by attacking their roots and leaves. The European vine, *Vitis vinifera*, which grows also in California but not east of the Rockies, is vulnerable to phylloxera.) It was the imported American plants that brought the deadly insect which invaded Europe and devastated French vineyards. It was first observed in France in 1865, and after that French wine production fell steadily year by year until the middle eighties. In the end many French vineyards had to be replanted entirely with French vines grafted on to eastern American phylloxera-resistant stocks. In the 1880s the vineyards of the Grande Champagne, the centre of the Cognac district, were terribly devastated and the production of cognac brought almost to a standstill. One of the expedients resorted to by the cognac producers in this crisis was to blend a very little cognac with other spirits made from a variety of raw materials. In the 1890s it was impossible to refill cognac stocks, and the British brandy drinker had to look elsewhere for a comparable spirit. (At least one notable port was in 1897 fortified with Scotch whisky instead of the normal brandy.) By now blends of pot-still malt and patent-still grain Scotch whisky were being vigorously marketed in England by energetic and enterprising Scottish whisky firms. It was the combination of the results of phylloxera in France, the development of blends of malt and grain whiskies in Scotland, and energetic commercial activity and brilliant salesmanship, that put blended Scotch whisky on the sideboard of the English gentleman at the end of the nineteenth century. Winston Churchill once recalled that 'my father could never have drunk whisky except when shooting on a moor or in some very dull chilly place. He lived in the age of brandy and soda.' Whisky and soda[16] began to replace brandy and soda

---

[16] Soda water, or aerated water, is water charged with carbon dioxide and was first artificially produced in England in the eighteenth century, when it was regarded as beneficial to health. Large-scale commercial manufacture was begun at Geneva in 1790 by Nicholas Paul, and it was Paul's partner, J. Schweppe, who started its commercial manufacture in London and founded the firm which still flourishes. Sodium bicarbonate was sometimes added to the water before carbonation, and originally the term 'soda water' referred only to carbonated water which also contained sodium bicarbonate. But soon it came to be used to describe carbonated

as the Englishman's drink later in the century; and as it would be criminal to add soda to a fine Highland malt whisky, it was the blending of malt with grain that made whisky and soda, like the American highball (which includes a great deal of soda and ice), a rational potation.

The blending of cognac with other spirits, resulting from the shortage of cognac caused by the ravages of phylloxera in French vineyards, was symptomatic of the general movement towards blending in the latter part of the nineteenth century. At the same time, concern was being shown in government quarters about the adulteration of potable spirits. A Licensing Act of 1872 had prohibited adulteration, but the relevant section was repealed in the 1874 Licensing Act. However, Disraeli's great Sale of Food and Drugs Act of 1875, the first truly comprehensive legislation on the subject and the principal statute until 1928, forbade ingredients which would 'render the article injurious to health', and in 1879 an amending Act took special note of the adulteration of spirits. It was under this legislation that the right of patent-still grain whisky and of blends of this with malt whisky to call themselves Scotch whisky was challenged in the new century.

Meanwhile, blended Scotch whisky flourished and the great whisky boom was on. In 1892 there were 130 working distillers in Scotland; in 1898 there were 161; new ones were built and old ones expanded. DCL, in a pamphlet of 1905,[17] congratulated itself on what had happened.

---

water both with and without sodium bicarbonate. (In the United States the term was extended to apply to any sparkling drink—hence 'soda fountain'.) Various other salts were sometimes added to carbonated water, to produce potash water, lithia water, etc. When I was a boy the standard soda water produced by the Scottish mineral-water firm of Dunbar and seen regularly on the sideboards of Edinburgh families was labelled 'potash water'.

The soda water siphon, standard in Britain but not in the United States where the individual small sealed bottle is preferred, was developed from the 'Regency portable fountain' patented by Charles Plinth in 1825. In 1837 Antoine Perpigna patented his 'vase siphoïde', which substituted for the stopcock of the Regency portable fountain a valve closed by a spring. A tube reached from the bottom of the siphon to the curved spout, and the pressure of the gas forced the soda water out when the valve was opened. This is essentially the modern siphon.

[17] The pamphlet was produced in an effort to influence opinion against a 'Sale of Whisky Bill' introduced into the Commons by Sir Herbert

'Previous to this [the blending of grain and malt whiskies] the principal whisky drinkers were confined to Scotland and Ireland. In England, wines and brandies occupied important positions as fashionable beverages. Such whisky as was consumed was largely the product of the Irish pot still, which consisted, as it does still, of a mash of from 30 to 50 per cent of malt and the remainder of unmalted wheat, rye, oats, etc. The pure Scotch malt whisky was even then admittedly too heavy for the ordinary palate, but, with the advent of the Scotch blend, being an admixture of the finest Highland malt whisky with a pure grain whisky (which latter the Scotch patent-still had now brought to a state of high perfection), the public taste all over England underwent a complete change. Irish whisky gradually lost favour, brandy and wines went out of fashion, and, led by the medical profession, the consumption of Scotch blended whiskies soon took a leading place.' DCL—which we must remember was originally an association of grain-whisky distillers who had only recently enlarged their activities by going into blending and malt-whisky distilling—had every right to be pleased. Fifteen years earlier a Select Committee of the House of Commons, looking into certain questions relating to both domestic and foreign spirits, had remarked in their report: 'They gave evidence that there was increased demand for Whisky of a milder kind and the blends of pot still and patent still Whisky were in large demand by the consumers, which thus obtained a cheaper and milder Whisky containing a smaller quantity of fusel oil and other by-products.'

Of course, these 'other by-products' were what gave pot-still malt whisky its characteristic flavour and quality. And, of course, 'mildness' is a matter of maturing the whisky properly and of reducing the proof with water. And, again of course, if the brilliant salesmanship which went into the marketing of blended Scotch whisky in England in the second half of the nineteenth century had been put at the service of the marketing of matured malt whisky instead, it might have had the same success. I confess that I am always a bit dubious about arguments from the popular palate when, in the first place, brilliant and intensive advertising and merchandising have largely created that palate and, in the second place, my own observation has demonstrated that most whisky-and-soda drinkers, even if they religiously ask for the same brand each time, do not in fact notice if they are given something

---

Maxwell. The Bill would have prevented patent-still whisky from being sold as whisky. It did not survive its first reading.

different. Indeed, I doubt whether a genuinely discriminating popular palate for something like whisky exists or ever has existed among whisky-and-soda drinkers, and I do not think that this doubt is answered by the indisputable fact that people do have their favourite brands and that some brands are more popular in some parts of the world than others. It is a question of advertising and habit. This is not to say that many blended Scotch whiskies are not admirable drinks of their kind; they are indeed, and they will be discussed in a later chapter.

So I read the report of the Select Committee of 1890–1 a little sceptically when it goes on to say: 'It is stated that public taste requires a Whisky of less marked characteristics than formerly, and to gratify this desire various blends are made, either by the mixture of pot still products, or by the addition of silent spirits from the patent still [it is interesting that patent-still whisky is here regarded simply as "silent spirits"]. In the latter case cheapness is often the purpose of the blend, but it is also stated that it incorporates the mixture of several Whiskies more efficiently.' The report did note, however, that the blends were often made 'of old spirits of various kinds' and even that these were 'frequently kept in bond for a considerable time', thus emphasizing one important virtue of the more responsible whisky blenders: they offered the public a mature spirit, not something straight from the still. Nevertheless, there was as yet no legislation compelling whisky producers to mature the whisky for a minimum period before selling it: this had to wait until 1915, and even then the compulsory period was only three years. The Select Committee of 1890–1, however, concluded 'from the evidence submitted to us, that the compulsory bonding of all spirits for a certain period is unnecessary and would harass trade.' The public, they said, 'show a marked preference for old spirits' and therefore 'it is not desirable to pass any compulsory law in regard to age, especially as the general feeling of the Trade is that such an obligation would harass commerce, and be an unfair burden on particular classes of spirits.'

The triumph of Scotch whisky in England in the latter half of the nineteenth century was not entirely the result of the three factors I have already discussed. There was a fourth, less tangible, factor which certainly must have had something to do with it. This was the development of a *mystique* about Scotland which really began with the publication of Walter Scott's narrative poem *The Lady of the Lake* in 1810. The romantic descriptions of Highland scenery in this enormously popular poem, while not the first admiring descriptions of such scenery, were certainly the first to be circulated on such a large scale and have such a remarkable effect. For Scott virtually invented the Highlands as a holiday area for English tourists, and in the wake of this tourism there developed a spate of what modern critics have disparagingly called 'tartanry'. When Queen Victoria built Balmoral Castle on Deeside, Aberdeenshire, in the early 1850s, the seal of royal approval was set on the enthusiasm for things Scottish. There was a revival of the wearing of the kilt. Scottish souvenirs, from tartan tea-cosies to miniature bag-pipes, found their way to the tea-tables and chimney-pieces of English visitors. And, of course, any Englishman of wealth and standing had to do some shooting in Scotland in the autumn and preferably also to own a shooting lodge or a house in Scotland. In Oscar Wilde's play, *The Importance of Being Earnest*, the late Mr. Thomas Cardew had three addresses: '149 Belgrave Square, S.W.; Gervase Park, Dorking, Surrey; and the Sporran, Fifeshire, N.B.' ('N.B.' = North Britain, i.e. Scotland). It was his possession of a Scottish house that put the seal on his respectability and social standing. (It would not, in fact, have been likely to be in Fife but in the Highlands.)

The image of the Scots as picturesque, romantic, noble, even primitive, goes back to Macpherson's *Ossian* of 1760, but it was only in the

Balmoral Castle, from an engraving of 1881

second half of the nineteenth century that this image became blended with a passion for tourism, the manufacture of souvenirs, and a widespread, popular desire to imitate the habits of the gentry. There was a great deal of vulgarity about this conception of Scotland, and a great deal of condescension too. It was oddly mixed with music-hall notions of the Scots as a nation of hairy-kneed, kilt-wearing consumers of whisky and haggis who sang songs about a wee hoose amang the heather. Harry Lauder was the apotheosis of this conception of Scotland. It is a view which has been violently repudiated by thoughtful Scotsmen today, who see this concept of the Scot very much as the modern Negro sees the old-fashioned picture of the happy and comic Negro of popular entertainment some fifty years and less ago. Nevertheless, it was bound up with the fashion for things Scottish which helped in the popularization of Scotch whisky in England.

The story of the great whisky blenders and merchants who made 'Scotch' a household word in England and across the seas is told in the next chapter. But in addition to the 'big five'—Haig, Dewar, Buchanan, Walker and Mackie—and other great names which have survived up to our own day, there were others who tried unsuccessfully to take advantage of the whisky boom. The most notorious failure, and one which illustrates very clearly the nature of the whisky boom, was that of Pattison's who started with a wholesale grocery firm in Leith and in the early eighties expanded into whisky blending in the hope of a quick fortune. At first the firm, which called itself Pattison, Elder and Co. and then became a limited liability company calling itself simply Pattison's Ltd., had immense success, and Robert and Walter Pattison, the two brothers who controlled it, made or appeared to have made an enormous amount of money. They built themselves a palatial house in Leith Walk, Edinburgh, and lived there in conspicuous extravagance. Robert Pattison also bought a country estate near Peebles, and it is said that on returning from it to Edinburgh he used to deliberately let himself miss the train so that he could order a private train at the cost of £5 1s. 0d. per mile. They splashed their advertising about with enormous gusto, on one occasion releasing hundreds of grey parrots trained to cry, 'Drink Pattison's whisky!' The public, eager to participate in the Pattison fortune, invested heavily in Pattison's Ltd. The firm itself got ample credits from the Scottish banks. More and more distilleries were built, whisky production went up and up. The public invested more and more. But soon it became clear that production had far outstripped demand. The Pattisons ran into trouble and after desperate but unsuccessful attempts to get further finance in order to reorganize and re-float the

company it suspended payment on 6 December 1898, with effects that reverberated through the whole whisky trade. Investors and speculators hoping for quick and easy money lost all; distilleries lost money and some had to close down; other firms were involved and seriously distressed. The Pattison brothers were tried for fraud and sentenced to imprisonment, Robert, the elder and the leading spirit, to eighteen months and Walter to eight months. Among other things, the Pattison failure demonstrated the dangers of over-production and encouraged DCL in its policy of amalgamation.

But the greatest storm of all that the booming Scotch whisky trade had to weather was the result of legal doubt as to whether blended Scotch whisky was really whisky at all. In 1904 the Borough Council of Islington had successfully brought proceedings under the Food and Drugs Act against certain public houses for offering for sale brandy (which, as we have seen, was now liable to be a blend of cognac and other spirits as a result of the devastation wrought by phylloxera) which was 'not of the nature, substance and quality of the article demanded by the purchaser'. The following year was the turn of whisky. In November 1905 summonses were taken out as test cases by the Islington Borough Council against certain publicans who were charged with selling as whisky a spirit 'not of the nature, substance and quality demanded' by a purchaser who asked for whisky. Mr. Fordham, the magistrate of the North London Police Court before whom the case was heard, gave judgement against the defendants, which meant that patent-still whisky was not true whisky and that blends containing it represented adulteration in terms of the Food and Drugs Act. The decision was an immense shock to DCL and the Scotch blended-whisky industry in general. The grain distillers encouraged the defendants to appeal, which they did. The appeal was lodged to Quarter Sessions, and in May and June 1906 Mr. W. R. McConnell, K.C., sitting with a bench of lay magistrates, heard the case. After seven sittings, it became apparent that the bench was equally divided, so that no decision was possible. So the earlier judgement stood: the grain distillers were despondent and the malt distillers jubilant. The grain distillers and blenders clearly could not let matters rest there, and after discussions it was decided that DCL should ask the President of the Board of Trade to appoint a Committee or a Royal Commission to settle the 'what is whisky?' question (as it came to be called) once and for all. The Islington Borough Council were also anxious to have an authoritative ruling on the matter, and they too approached the President of the Board of Trade. He was John Burns, the labour leader and first artisan to reach cabinet rank, no friend to the whisky trade, for he knew at first-hand the effects of drinking cheap liquor in the slums of big cities. But the joint representations of DCL and the Islington Borough Council eventually had their effect and in July 1907 Parliament agreed to Mr. Burns's request for a Royal Commission, which was set up in February 1908 under Lord James of Hereford, the distinguished Liberal lawyer, statesman and cricket enthusiast. Its terms of reference were to inquire into 'Whisky and Other Potable Spirits' with a view to determining, in the interests of consumers and of public health in general, whether restrictions should be placed on the materials or processes by means of which spirit called whisky could be manufactured in the United Kingdom, and whether a minimum period should be fixed for maturing whisky in bond.

Although the Commission included six scientific and medical experts, they all seemed to have started from scratch so far as their knowledge of whisky was concerned. They tried to learn. Revenue officials visited thirty-nine public houses in England and twenty-three in Scotland and asked for 'a glass of whisky': what they received in answer to this request they took away and analysed. In every case it was patent-still grain whisky. An important question was whether consumers who asked for whisky and received patent-still spirit knew in advance exactly what it was that they would get and in fact expected and wanted to get it. The Commission decided that they did. In an interim report issued in June 1908 the Commission recommended 'that no restriction should be placed upon the processes of, or apparatus used in, the distillation of any spirit to which the term "whiskey" may be applied as a trade description'. They further recommended 'that the term "whiskey" having been recognized in the past as applicable to a potable spirit manufactured from (1) malt, or (2) malt and unmalted barley or other cereals should not be denied to the product manufactured from such materials.' (Note that the Commission consistently spelt 'whisky' with an 'e'—'whiskey' —a spelling then regular in official Government publications on whisky but now confined to Irish and American whiskey.)

The Commission's final report was published on 28 July 1909. It had held thirty-seven sittings for the purpose of taking evidence, examined 116 witnesses, and considered various documents submitted to it. Several members of the Commission had visited distilleries in Scotland and Ireland and even some brandy distilleries and warehouses in France. They had looked into the history of whisky-drinking in Britain and in particular the development of blending. 'Blending for the English and foreign markets on a large scale', the report states in its historical survey, 'seems to have commenced between 30 and 40 years ago. Since that time the practice has gone on increasing. It has undoubtedly done very much to popularize Scotch whiskey.' They go on to point out that 'it would probably be safe to say that the majority of Englishmen who drink whiskey seldom drink anything but a blend.' They seem to have been much influenced by the popularity of blends in England and by the fact that almost two-thirds of the whisky then being distilled in Scotland was patent-still whisky. There is no evidence that the members of the Commission had themselves done any comparative tasting of different pot-still malt whiskies and patent-still whisky: they depended on analysis. 'On reference to the analyses, it will be seen that there is a very wide

John Burns addressing an election meeting in Battersea Town Hall, 1910.
By Arthur Garratt

variation between whiskies from different distilleries; and that there is
a very wide variation between whiskies from the same distilleries in
different years.' As for the difference between pot-still and patent-still
whisky, 'we have received no evidence to show that the form of the still
has any necessary relation to the wholesomeness of the spirit produced.'
And therefore 'we are unable to recommend that the use of the word
"whiskey" should be restricted to spirit manufactured by the pot-still
process.'

That was it. It was a glorious victory for the grain distillers and a
defeat for the pot-still malt distillers. The report's 'general conclusion'
was equally significant:

Our general conclusion, therefore, on this part of our inquiry is that 'whiskey' is a spirit obtained by distillation from a mash of cereal grains saccharified [i.e. turned into sugar] by the diastase of malt; that 'Scotch whiskey' is whiskey, as above defined, distilled in Scotland; and that 'Irish whiskey' is whiskey, as above defined, distilled in Ireland.

The report also refused to recommend that a declaration of the raw materials used in the preparation of whisky should be required, on the grounds that such a declaration interfered with trade and such interference could only be justified 'for the purpose of defeating fraud or semi-fraud, or to protect public health, or to prevent injurious adulteration.' They had found no evidence of fraud or injurious adulteration (note that the Commission throughout considered the 'wholesomeness' but not the taste and flavour of whisky) and gave it as their opinion that 'in the numerous distilleries existing in the United Kingdom the trade in whiskey seems to be honestly and fairly conducted.' The Commission stress on 'wholesomeness' is further evidenced in their conclusions concerning compulsory ageing. 'If compulsory bonding is considered as a means of securing the maturity and flavour, as distinct from the wholesomeness, of spirits, it must be borne in mind that spirits of different character do not mature with equal rapidity.' They were perfectly aware that 'a very much longer period is required for the maturation of a heavy pot-still malt whiskey, for example, than for a light patent-still whiskey' and that 'even in the case of spirits of the same character, differences in the condition of storage, such as the nature and size of the vessel in which the spirit is kept, the relative humidity of the place in which it is stored and climatic conditions generally, have a considerable effect in determining the rapidity of maturation.' They concluded that 'whatever period might be fixed would inevitably be open to one or two objections; it would either impose an unnecessary burden on particular classes of spirits, or it would be too short for the maturing of other classes.' Because, then, different kinds of whisky required different times to mature and the maturation rate in any case was affected by the size of the cask and by humidity and 'climatic conditions' generally, the Commission somewhat illogically concluded that no minimum period of any sort should be required. 'For the above reasons,' this section of the report concludes, 'we have come to the conclusion that it is not desirable to require a minimum period during which spirits should be matured in bond.'

It is important to note the definition of whisky given by the Commission: 'a spirit obtained by distillation from a mash of cereal grains saccharified by the diastase of malt'. As the description of the patent-still process at the beginning of this chapter makes clear, this definition will apply to patent-still grain whisky since a proportion of malted barley is always added in order to convert the starch in the cereal into maltose by means of the enzyme diastase. Patent-still grain whisky is thus clearly obtained 'from a mash of cereal grains saccharified by the diastase of malt'. So, of course, is pot-still malt whisky, though there the cereal used is always barley and all the barley is malted before mashing. Under this definition—which was reaffirmed in the Customs and Excise Act of 1952, though with the addition of the provision, first introduced in 1915, that it should be in a bonded warehouse in casks for at least three years—pot-still malt whisky, patent-still grain whisky, and blends of both, are all legally entitled to the appellation of 'Scotch whisky' if they are distilled in Scotland and have matured in bond for three years.

DCL, which had led the fight for the recognition of patent-still whisky and paid the grain distillers' costs, had triumphed gloriously. While the Commission was sitting DCL had advertised its Cambus whisky (a patent-still grain whisky made, as it still is, in the Cambus distillery, Alloa) in the *Daily Mail*, thus deliberately challenging the Islington decision and anticipating the Commission's report. The advertisement stressed the lightness and palatability of this whisky and its greater suitability for sedentary city-dwellers.[18] When the Commission's final report was issued, the advertisement disappeared. Since then Cambus has been used (so far as I know) only in blending.

This was not, of course, the end for the malt distillers, for pot-still malt whisky was and is an important ingredient of blended Scotch whisky. But it accelerated the decline of single malt whiskies and of 'vatted' malt whiskies (i.e. single malts of different ages and of different dates, though from the same pot-still distillery, blended together) as a drink readily available to the public, for the great majority of malt whiskies more and more went for blending. And it finally absolved the blenders from any obligation to state on the label of the whisky bottle what proportions of malt and grain were used. The blenders have never done this, and have indeed made a terrific mystery of their blending procedures. Writing in 1935 Neil Gunn complained that 'at the present

---

[18] This odd point about sedentary drinkers crops up again and again in the arguments of the grain distillers and the blenders. The Scotch Whisky Association's pamphlet *Scotch Whisky: Questions & Answers* (Edinburgh, 1967) repeats the ritual statement that 'pot-still malt whisky is too strongly flavoured for most people in sedentary occupations'.

time our most famous blends are mixtures of pot and patent still spirits in proportions which we do not know, but in which the preponderance is believed to be heavily patent.' He added: 'Yet the blender could very easily tell us what surely we have a right to know by stating on his label the proportions of patent and pot still and their respective ages. Nothing could be simpler. All reputable vineyards carry their vineyard and their year.' He went on, more belligerently still: 'A fine pot-still whisky is as noble a product of Scotland as any burgundy or champagne is of France. Patent-still spirit is no more a true whisky than, at the opposite extreme, is any of those cheap juices of the grape heavily fortified by raw spirit which we import from ends of the earth a true wine.'

The subject of patent-still whisky has always generated a certain amount of heat among dedicated malt-whisky drinkers, as well as among certain independent malt-whisky distillers. Shortly after the Royal Commission reported, Colonel George Smith Grant, proprietor of the Glenlivet distillery (he was a nephew of John Gordon Smith who had succeeded his father George Smith, founder of the distillery), was presented with his portrait at a large gathering of friends. In the course of the speech he delivered in making the presentation, the Duke of Richmond and Gordon expressed the feelings of his audience on the Commission's report:

Quite recently a public enquiry has taken upon itself to decide—What is whisky? [laughter] *And I regret to say that apparently anything that is made in Scotland, whatever its combination, is to be called Scots whisky. But for my part, I should prefer, and I think most of those whom I am addressing now would prefer, to trust to their own palates* [laughter] *rather than to the dogma of chemists, and to be satisfied with the whisky that is produced in Glenlivet* ['Hear, hear!'] *as against any other quality that is produced in Scotland.*

DCL, however, continued to flourish. Its first years had not been easy. It was not until 1883 that it obtained a quotation on the Stock Exchanges of Edinburgh and Glasgow while the London Stock Exchange, to which it had applied for a quotation in January 1884, did not grant it until October 1886. Afraid of a DCL monopoly, a group of independent whisky merchants and blenders set up their own patent-still distillery in Gorgie, Edinburgh, in 1885, forming for the purpose the North British Distillery Company with William Sanderson as managing director and Andrew Usher as chairman. But this competition did not seriously bother DCL. In 1889 Mr. William H. Ross became company secretary of DCL and gave it immense new impetus. It was after Ross became its chief executive that DCL became the largest producer of yeast in Britain (and, for that matter, in Europe). It was Ross, too, ever mindful of the larger interests of whisky production and distribution as a whole and of the need to stabilize prices and prevent wasteful competition, who pioneered the policy of amalgamation which eventually brought the 'Big Five' into DCL.

WHAT IS WHISKY?

Lord James of Hereford (*Chairman of the Royal Commission on Whisky*): —

"BE THOU A SPIRIT OF HEALTH OR GOBLIN DAMN'D . . .
THOU COM'ST IN SUCH A QUESTIONABLE SHAPE
THAT I WILL SPEAK TO THEE."—*Hamlet*, ACT I., Sc. 4.

Lloyd George's budget of 29 April 1909, raising the duty on Scotch whisky from 11*s*. per proof gallon to 14*s*. 9*d*., was a blow to grain and malt distillers alike. At the same time growing American exports of blended Scotch whisky were threatened by the commission appointed by President Theodore Roosevelt to determine the proper legal definition of whisky. Its report was favourable to the blenders, but President Roosevelt would not accept it. In 1910, however, President Taft, who had succeeded Roosevelt in 1909, took with grand simplicity the decision that spirit made from cereals was whisky and spirit made from molasses was rum and that was that. He did, however, insist on proper labelling to distinguish a 'straight' whisky from a blend. It was to face the problems arising from Roosevelt's commission that the Scotch whisky exporters formed themselves into a Scottish Whisky Exporters' Association.

In spite of setbacks, and in spite of the 1909 budget, the Scotch whisky trade was flourishing in the years immediately preceding the First World War. DCL acquired its own patent-still distilleries in England and Ireland, and moved into the English gin and industrial alcohol trades. The lesson of the Pattison failure had been learned, especially by DCL, who substituted amalgamation, controlled acquisition, and controlled sales and prices for the runaway overproduction indulged in by rasher spirits in the height of the whisky boom. And the great whisky magnates who made blended Scotch whisky the popular international drink it still is today continued to expand their activities in both the home market and abroad. To these magnates I now turn.

Chapter Four
GROWTH OF THE BIG FIVE

One of the many paradoxes with which the history of whisky is involved is that while Scotch whisky came down to the Lowlands from the Highlands, its true home, the oldest name in Scotch whisky is not Highland at all. It is Haig (earlier del Hage, de Haga, de la Hage), a name of Norman origin. A Norman knight of that name crossed the Channel into England in the eleventh century and soon afterwards the Haigs pushed north into Lowland Scotland, where we find them well settled by the middle of the thirteenth century. They built a Border castle at Bemersyde, Berwickshire, and the Haigs of Bemersyde have been known in Scottish history since Thomas of Erceldoune (modern Earlston, near Bemersyde), the almost legendary thirteenth-century seer and poet otherwise known as Thomas the Rhymer, prophesied:

Tide what may, whate'er betide,
Haig shall be Haig of Bemersyde.

He has been proved right so far. But old Thomas said nothing about Haig and whisky, which showed a certain lack of prophetic power. For though a Haig fought at the Battle of Stirling Bridge with William Wallace and another was killed with his King at the Battle of Flodden —and though in a later age a Haig was commander-in-chief of the British forces in France and Flanders in the First World War—the first association of the name today all over the world is with Scotch whisky.

Like most Scottish Border families, the Haigs led a turbulent life in the Middle Ages and well into the seventeenth century. Family feuding in the seventeenth century brought Robert Haig, a Haig younger son, to leave the family home and settle as a tenant farmer at Throsk, in the parish of St. Ninian's, Stirlingshire. Like many Scottish farmers of that and the next century, he carried on a certain amount of distilling on his farm. The following extract from volume I of the Session Record of St. Ninian's Parish Church tells its own story:

Januar 4, 1665.—Compeared Robert Haig being summoned for Sabbath breaking and Wm. Reid, John Croby, William Harley and Christian Eason, Witnesses. Robert Haig denied he knew any such thing as was laid to his chairge. The witnesses deponed unanimously that they saw the caldron on the fyre, and a stand reiking and that they heard the goodwife say, 'the lasse has put on the caldron and played some after-wort' and she knew not whether her caldron was befor on the fyre on a Sabbath day and had she been at home it should not have been done (for she was byt presentlie cam'd from Alloway Church). So it being only some pynts of small drink played by a servant lass naither maister nor maistresse accessarie to it upon engadgment of Christian carriage for the future, rebuked befor the Session.

This brush with the Kirk Session was obviously not serious, but it is fortunate for us that it occurred, for it gives us a glimpse into domestic distilling in the Scottish Lowlands in the seventeenth century. The Haigs continued to farm in Stirlingshire and neighbouring Clackmannanshire. They seem to have kept on distilling, too, for we find the name of Robert Haig's son Alexander in the Inland Revenue Collectors' accounts for 1699–1700 as having distilled 128 gallons six pints between 1 March and 1 June 1699. The spirit distilled was probably not a pure malt whisky: members of the Haig family had been in Holland in the seventeenth century and learned Dutch methods of distilling. Their distilling skill had not therefore come south from the Highlands. Nor had that of the Stein family (presumably of Dutch origin) who established the distilleries of Kilbagie and Kennetpans in Clackmannanshire early in the century. In 1751 John Haig, great-great-grandson of Robert Haig of St. Ninian's, married Margaret Stein, daughter of John Stein. When John Haig died at the age of fifty-three in 1773 Margaret's five fatherless sons were taken in as apprentices at their maternal grandfather's distillery of Kilbagie and there learned the art of distilling. Four of the five eventually founded their own distilleries elsewhere; but Andrew remained in Clackmannanshire and went into partnership at Kincardine with a member of what was to become the famous Irish distilling family of Jameson. It was the eldest son James who became the leading Lowland distiller after his grandfather's death. He developed the Edinburgh distilleries of Canonmills, Lochrin and Sunbury. John, after having been in partnership with James at Lochrin, established his own distillery at Bonnington, Leith. Robert went to Ireland and

Bemersyde Castle, ancestral home of the Haig family; engraved from a drawing by J. M. W. Turner

developed Dodderbank distillery near Dublin. William, the youngest, settled in Fife and thus was the first to establish the long Haig connection, still existing, with that county. He built a distillery at Seggie, near St. Andrews. Their sisters also did their bit for whisky. One married John Jameson who settled in Ireland and founded the firm of John Jameson and Son at Bow Street distillery, Dublin, in 1780, and another married John Philp, who had a distillery at Dolls, Menstrie, Clackmannanshire.

I mentioned in an earlier chapter the riots that broke out in June 1784 when a mob, believing that James Haig was using oats and potatoes in his Canonmills distillery, organized an attack on it, to which Haig replied by announcing that his distillery used only 'barley, rye, and sometimes such parcels of wheat as happen to receive damage, or are in quality unfit for bread'; this is pretty conclusive evidence that Haig used a mash of mixed cereals rather than malted barley in making his spirit. In this same statement Haig called attention to the fact that, far from consuming roots that would otherwise be available for cattle-feed, the distillery provides for cattle 'the grains or draff, and by that food alone they are fattened for the market.' The mob seem to have been placated, but James Haig continued to have his troubles, chiefly the tax problems that have already been discussed and competition from illicit distilling and smuggling, activities which were not confined to the Highlands. In 1777 400 illicit stills were said to have been discovered in the city of Edinburgh alone, compared with eight legal stills. In 1815 a most ingeniously contrived illicit still was discovered under the arch of the South Bridge, Edinburgh.

James Haig continued throughout his life to be a chief spokesman before the Government on the problems and needs of legitimate Lowland distillers in Scotland and the all-important Act of 1823 embodied several of his suggestions. His sons carried on distilling at Lochrin and Sudbury until 1849, when these distilleries closed down. His brother John's distillery at Bonnington prospered, and after John's death in 1819 it was continued by *his* sons William, George and Thomas, operating as William Haig and Company. Thomas Haig eventually settled in England and helped to build Hammersmith distillery.

Meanwhile the distillery established at Seggie by James Haig's brother William was flourishing. William became an important figure in St. Andrews, of which he was Provost for twelve years. He died in 1847, leaving two sons, John and Robert. Robert took over the management of the distillery at Seggie, but it was John who achieved the most spectacular advance in the fortunes of the Haig family. Already during his father's lifetime he had built a new distillery at Cameron Bridge, Fife (in 1824) and expanded his trade rapidly with the help of 'riders', travelling salesmen who rode all over the country drumming up business and soliciting orders. By 1877 Cameron Bridge distillery was producing 1,250,000 gallons annually. By this time he had long been using the Coffey still. He had erected a Stein still on its first invention (paying a

Plate 1 *Pouring the barley into the steep*

Plate 2 *Turning the malt on the malting floor*

Plate 3   *Grinding the malt*

Plate 4   *Inspecting the malted barley*

Plate 5 *Kiln interior*

Plate 6 *Stoking the kiln*

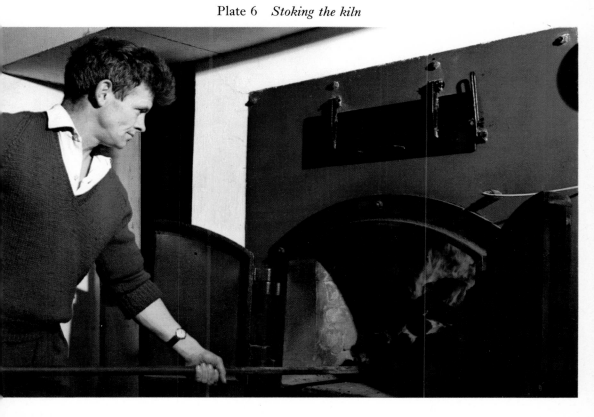

Plate 7   *A mash tun*

Plate 8   *Wash backs*

Plate 9   *Still and spirit safe*

Plate 10   *Stills*

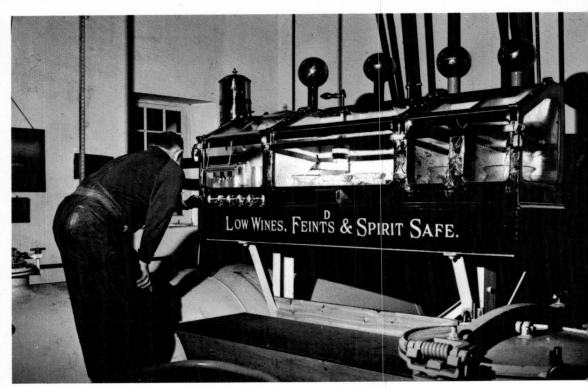

Plate 11   *Spirit safe*

Plate 12   *Spirit safe (detail)*

Plate 13   *Filling a cask with new whisky*

Plate 14   *Checking and weighing new-filled cask by excise officer*

Plate 15　*Sealing the barrels of new whisky*

Plate 16　*Whisky maturing*

royalty of one penny a gallon to Stein), and soon after Aeneas Coffey's invention of his improved model he had introduced that. Previously he had distilled mostly malt whisky ('malt aqua' as it was called in the trade), but now he produced the cheaper and more plentiful grain whisky.

John Haig of Cameron Bridge inherited his father's position as spokesman for the Lowland whisky trade before the Government, and several times discussed the question of duties on spirits with Gladstone. He was also much concerned with the whole pattern of distilling in the Lowlands, and it was because of this concern that the Cameron Bridge distillery, as we have seen, was one of the six constituent firms of the Distillers Company Limited when it was founded on 24 April 1877. DCL thus took over the proprietorship of the Cameron Bridge distillery, John Haig and his eldest son Hugh becoming Directors of the new company and a younger son William becoming Secretary. But the blending business of John Haig and Company remained independent, moving from Cameron Bridge to Markinch, only a few miles away, and, with John and his sons Hugh, William and Alexander, operating as John Haig Sons and Co.

The Haigs were thus active both in distilling at Cameron Bridge and in blending at Markinch. John Haig died in 1878 and his son William prematurely in 1884. But the firm continued to prosper. In 1882 it amalgamated with David Smith and Company of Leith in order to obtain the use of their bonded warehouse which they used until 1892 when they established their own bonded warehouse at Markinch. In 1894 John Haig and Company was floated as a limited company, registered in Edinburgh, with John Haig's eldest son Hugh as first Chairman. Hugh died in 1902 and was succeeded as Chairman by his son John.

In 1888 Hugh's brother John Alicius Haig established the separate firm of Haig and Haig Ltd., which specialized in exports to the United States between that date and the advent of prohibition in America in 1920. Haig and Haig remained inactive during the period of prohibition in America, but revived on its repeal in 1933 and resumed its American exports, so that even now, Haig whisky in America until recently had 'Haig and Haig' and not, as in Britain, 'John Haig and Co. Ltd.' on the label of the bottle, though Haig and Haig has been a wholly owned subsidiary of John Haig and Co. since 1925, six years after John Haig and Co. were acquired by DCL. In 1903 John Haig and Co. acquired the Glen Cawdor distillery to make sure of its own supply of Highland malt whisky for blending. In 1906 the firm were appointed purveyors to the House of Lords. Together with all the other whisky firms they suffered under the restrictions and high taxation of the First World War, under the high taxation of the period between the wars, under the severe restrictions and still higher taxation during the Second World War and its aftermath, and under the even higher taxation of more recent years: these are matters for a later chapter. But in spite of all setbacks the firm has continued to prosper. Like the other great whisky firms that established themselves as blenders and merchandisers of blended Scotch whisky in the latter part of the nineteenth century, Haigs were active in advertising. In the early part of the present century their slogan was 'D'ye ken John Haig?' but this gave way in the late 1920s to the familiar 'Don't be vague—ask for Haig'. At one time Haigs had a yacht which sailed up and down the south coast of England in the holiday season displaying the Haig slogan on its sails. Before the First World War Haigs advertised in Berlin with a trap pulled by two Shetland ponies driven by a Highlander in full panoply.

Facilities at Markinch were much expanded during the present century, with the provision of automatic filling and labelling machinery, additional bottling vats, a new case factory equipped with the latest plant, and other new developments. A fire at one of the stores in December 1928 destroyed old and valuable stocks, but it at least had the advantage of leading to the erection of more modern premises. By 1938, after recovery from the slump of the early 1930s, a tremendous expansion had been carried out, under the energetic managing directorship of Mr. William Reid. The new 'coronation Bond' building completed in 1938 provided storage accommodation for over 1,500,000 gallons of whisky and bottling facilities for over 1,750,000 cases annually. It was in the late 1930s, too, that Mr. Thomas Wilkinson, then Chairman of the Company, developed exports throughout the world with a vast network of Haig distributors. On the home market, it is the largest selling brand.

The export trade was carried on, under enormous difficulties, during the Second World War. It was a consignment of 2,000 cases of Haig and Haig whisky on the S.S. *Politician* that went down when the ship was wrecked off the Isle of Eriskay in the Outer Hebrides on the way to America. This was the basis of Compton Mackenzie's novel *Whisky Galore* which was made into the brilliant comic film of that title (called *Tight Little Island* in America). In the story and the film the ship was called *The Cabinet Minister*; the actual filming was done on the island of Barra.

Haig is the oldest of the 'Big Five', in one sense the most romantic, because of its long history, in another the least romantic because the

Haig story is not that of one picturesque character of enormous energy and even flamboyance creating single-handed a great new business. The great self-made men of the Scotch whisky industry are fascinating figures. Let us now take a look at them.

John Dewar was born in 1806 on a small Perthshire farm. When he was twenty-two he went to Perth at the invitation of a relative, James Macdonald, a wine-merchant in that city, to look after the cellars. Dewar was happy in Perth and prospered there. In 1837 he was made a partner in the firm, which was now renamed Macdonald and Dewar. In 1846 he decided to set up on his own, and opened a wine and spirit business in a little single-fronted shop at 111 High Street. There he flourished, soon blending his own whisky and putting it up in bottles, a hitherto unknown refinement. At first he sold principally in Perth and its environs, but gradually he extended his activities. In 1860 he employed a traveller to go further afield for orders. In 1879 he took his son John Alexander Dewar into partnership. He died in 1880, having established a very comfortable business, soundly based if limited in size and not yet looking beyond Scotland.

It was the next generation that really made whisky history. John Alexander Dewar and his younger brother Thomas Robert had both been carefully trained in the whisky business and had been apprenticed in Leith, by then the centre of the Scotch whisky trade. The two brothers (the elder was only twenty-four when his father died) decided to go for the English market. Tommy Dewar was sent to London by his elder brother, when he was only twenty-one, to get English orders. He knew nobody there: he had in fact two introductions but found on arrival that one of the two people he was to meet was dead and the other was bankrupt. But Tommy triumphed by wit and resourcefulness. In 1886 he startled the Brewers' Show at the Agricultural Hall by drowning out all other sound with the bagpipes and refusing to stop playing when requested. This brought him the initial publicity he wanted. Within a few years he had obtained orders for his bottled blended whisky from a great variety of hotels and restaurants in London. In 1894 Dewars opened a branch in Bristol. The year before Queen Victoria had granted them a Royal Warrant. And by now the firm was acquiring distilleries of its own; the brothers leased from the Duke of Atholl the distillery of Tullymet near Balinluig on upper Tayside, and in 1896 they built their own distillery a few miles away at Aberfeldy, near the croft where the original John Dewar was born in 1806. This distillery still contributes its malt whisky to Dewar's 'White Label'.

It had all been a tremendous gamble, financed by bank overdrafts.

But it paid off. In 1894 the firm became a limited liability company with a capital of £100,000, raised to £600,000 in 1897. Tommy Dewar travelled the world setting up agents for the importing of Dewar's whisky. By 1901 Dewars had passed the million-gallon-a-year mark. It was a partnership between these two very different brothers that had achieved this remarkable success. John stayed in Perth and looked after the production end; he was the administrator, while the livelier Tommy was the salesman. It was Tommy who pioneered the flamboyant and enormously successful Dewar advertising. Before 1908, when Dewar House was built in the Haymarket, Dewar's London offices were at Dewar's Wharf on the South Bank of the Thames near Waterloo Bridge, and included the old Shot Tower. On the tower Dewars displayed a huge electric sign showing a bearded Highlander periodically raising to his lips a glass of Dewar's 'White Label' while each time he raised his

Thomas Robert Dewar

glass his kilt and beard appeared to sway in the wind. The name DEWAR in enormous letters above the Highlander's tam o' shanter dominated the landscape. A once well-known Dewar advertising slogan was 'The Whisky of his Forefathers', with appropriate picture, another was the series starting with the phrase 'The spirit of . . .'.

Tommy Dewar received a knighthood in 1901 and John a baronetcy in 1907. In 1917 John was raised to the peerage as Baron Forteviot of Dupplin—the first of the 'whisky barons'. Tommy got *his* peerage in 1919, becoming Baron Dewar of Homestall, Sussex. It was not for their services to whisky that they were thus honoured—at least not ostensibly. Each had served his city with distinction. John served as Lord Provost of Perth and Tommy as Sheriff of London. John also served two terms in Parliament as Liberal member for Inverness, while Tommy served as Conservative member for St. George's in the East. Tommy was the livelier character. While Lord Forteviot loved his native Perthshire and his estate of Dupplin there, where he died in 1929, Lord Dewar set up as an English country gentleman at Homestall, Sussex. True to the traditions of the English landed gentry, he became a patron of sport and a race-horse owner. Horse-racing, indeed, became his chief hobby, and he bred some famous horses, with one of which, 'Cameronian', his heir and nephew John Arthur Dewar won the Derby in 1931, shortly after his uncle's death in 1930.

After Dewar House was built in 1908 it rapidly became, thanks to Tommy Dewar, a social centre for more than those interested in the whisky trade.[19] Tommy was a wit and a character. He never married, as one of his sayings, 'Do right and fear no man; don't write and fear no woman', suggests. Another of his well-known remarks was: 'The motor car has done away with horses, but not with the ass.'

The work of the brothers was carried on by another Dewar, who was in fact no relation—Peter Menzies Dewar, Chairman of the Company from 1930 to 1946. He was a man of immense energy and ability, who had joined the firm as a boy and was wholly dedicated to it. He did a great deal to expand Dewar's exports and also saw the firm through the difficult days of the Second World War, when their exports to America were of great economic value to the country. In 1946 Peter Dewar was succeeded as Chairman by John Arthur Dewar who was in turn

---

[19] It still is. I spent a lively and convivial few hours there recently with one of the directors, an Israeli agent, a knowing Czech and other interesting characters.

succeeded in 1954 by Henry Evelyn Alexander Dewar, third Lord Forteviot and grandson of the founder. Though Dewars joined DCL in 1925 the firm remained under the administration of the family who founded it.

When in August 1966 John Dewar and Sons were awarded the Queen's Award to Industry, the Earl of Mansfield, who made the presentation on behalf of the Queen, pointed out in his speech that the award was instituted 'in order to encourage and suitably recognize those firms and businesses who are contributing materially to the export trade of this country'. Dewars have indeed a remarkable export record: 90 per cent of all output of whisky is exported. They boast that they export to every market in the world except Albania, Rhodesia, Saudi Arabia and the People's Republic of China. They have a promising trade with Soviet Russia. They have agents throughout the world, and even where the sale of alcoholic liquor is conducted by Government monopolies—as in Turkey, Canada, Norway, Sweden, Iceland and Finland—they have agents to supervise their interests and to promote sales. In Britain there are sales offices in London, Liverpool and Glasgow to act as inter- mediaries with merchants and as shipping offices.

Dewar takes second place to John Walker in world-wide whisky sales. But sales of other of the 'Big Five' follow closely behind with 'Vat 69' making a 'Big Six'.[20]

Dewar's head office is now at Inveralmond, near Perth, where they have built one of Scotland's largest plants for blending and bottling whisky. This was opened in June 1962, replacing the former headquarters of the firm at Glasgow Road, Perth. The plant at Inveralmond occupies 24 acres, with 26 acres reserved for expansion. It is an enormous place. Approximately 700 people are employed there. The bottle store holds 3,000,000 bottles and the bottling vats hold up to 110,000 gallons. The plant can fill 350,000 bottles a day of 45 different sizes. Only blending and bottling go on at Inveralmond: it is not a distillery. But to it come for blending whiskies from a great variety of distilleries throughout

---

[20] It has been suggested to me by a well-known figure in the Scotch whisky trade that 'Vat 69' sells well on the Continent because it is regarded as a sex symbol. Dewars continues to be the best selling of DCL whiskies in America. 'J. & B. Rare' and 'Cutty Sark' (the former of which used to have a high proportion of grain whisky but has been con- spicuously improved) are the over-all best sellers among Scotch whiskies in the U.S.A. Incidentally, 'Vat 69' is *not* the Pope's telephone number.

Scotland, including, of course, Dewar's own distillery at Aberfeldy. Two blends a day are mixed in the blending vats into which compressed air is blown to 'rouse' the mixture. The blend stands for twenty-four hours in the blending vat before being put into plain oak casks to 'marry' over a minimum period of six months.

One more name must be mentioned before I conclude the Dewar story, that of Alexander John Cameron, the man who devised the Dewar's 'White Label' blend. There are various legends about the origin of blending, one of which states that the original John Dewar discovered the art by accident by mixing the remains of empty kegs. This is an invention. It was the firm of Andrew Usher and Co. of Edinburgh who began blending whiskies commercially about 1853 by 'vatting' different Glenlivet whiskies. W. P. Lowrie and Co. of Glasgow were also early in the field with blended whisky. But blending was in the air in the middle of the nineteenth century and increasing later; the French had been mixing old and new brandies for some time. There is a lot of nonsense talked about blending, and blended Scotch whisky may be anything from 80 per cent cheap patent-still whisky to a carefully balanced blend of many different malt whiskies with some 50 per cent patent-still whisky. I shall not anticipate here the discussion of blends and blending that belongs to a later chapter. But I do not want to leave the House of Dewar without recording the name of their distinguished blending expert, Alexander John Cameron, one of the pioneers of blending and one of its most remarkable practitioners.

The next great nineteenth-century whisky family to bring on to the stage is the Walkers. Most people are familiar with the advertising slogan of 'Johnnie Walker' whisky—'Born 1820, still going strong'; and it was in fact in 1820 that John Walker set up as a grocer and wine and spirit merchant in Kilmarnock, Ayrshire. But the whisky associated with his name was not born until some thirty years later. John's business was that of a modest retailer, and it was not until his son Alexander joined him in 1856 that it began to expand and to move from retail to whole-sale. In that year Walker, who had survived a disastrous flood in 1852 in which he had lost all his stock, had only one cellar, less than sixty feet long, as his warehouse; within ten years his output was 100,000 gallons of blended whisky and the firm's premises had to be greatly enlarged. This was largely Alexander's doing. He sold his whisky to ships sailing out of Glasgow, and he took advantage of Kilmarnock's reputation as a centre for Brussels, Turkey and Scottish carpets and for tweeds, blankets and shawls to familiarize the English buyers who came there with his Scotch whisky; then he followed them to England and in 1880 opened an office in London. The change from brandy to whisky that I discussed in the previous chapter was now strongly under way, and Alexander Walker arrived in London at a good time. In 1886 Alexander brought his two sons, George and John, into the firm, which now became John Walker and Sons Limited. But it was Alexander's third son Alec who became head of the firm on his father's death in 1889.

Though Alexander Walker was the real founder of the firm as blenders and exporters of Scotch whisky, it was not until long after his death, in 1908, that the brand name 'Johnnie Walker' began to be used in the now well-known slogan. It was invented to accompany a poster by Tom Browne, the painter and black-and-white artist (who also created the American comic characters Weary Willie and Tired Tim). In its earlier history the whisky had been called simply Walker's Kilmarnock Whisky. But Tom Browne's poster and the accompanying slogan, one of the most successful advertising devices ever known, soon made the name of 'Johnnie Walker' universally known: it is still the best-selling whisky in the world.

If Alexander Walker was the great character who put the Walker firm on the map, it was a local youngster called James Stevenson, who joined the firm in 1890, who played the main part in the later strengthening and expansion. Stevenson was an administrative genius who later was to do important work for munitions production in the First World War and was Surveyor-General of Supply at the War Office from 1919 to 1921; he was also chairman of the board that arranged the great British Empire Exhibition at Wembley in 1924 and 1925. But it was in the years between his joining the firm and the outbreak of the First World War that his greatest services to Walkers were rendered. Working with George and Alec Walker, he succeeded in making the firm the largest blenders and bottlers of Scotch whisky in the world. In 1893 they acquired the malt distillery of Cardow at Knockando near Craigellachie on Speyside: this distillery had been begun by John Cumming in 1824 in the same circumstances which led George Smith to go legitimate at Glenlivet in the same year, and a long history of illegal distilling lay behind it. (Cardhu, a pleasing if not world-shattering Highland malt whisky, has fairly recently become available again as a single whisky.) In 1897 the firm opened a branch in Birmingham, which Stevenson took charge of, and in 1907 they moved their London office to Dunster House, Park Lane.

Stevenson's services to the Government in the First World War won him a baronetcy in 1917 and a peerage (as Baron Stevenson) in 1924. Alec Walker never achieved the peerage and had to make do with a

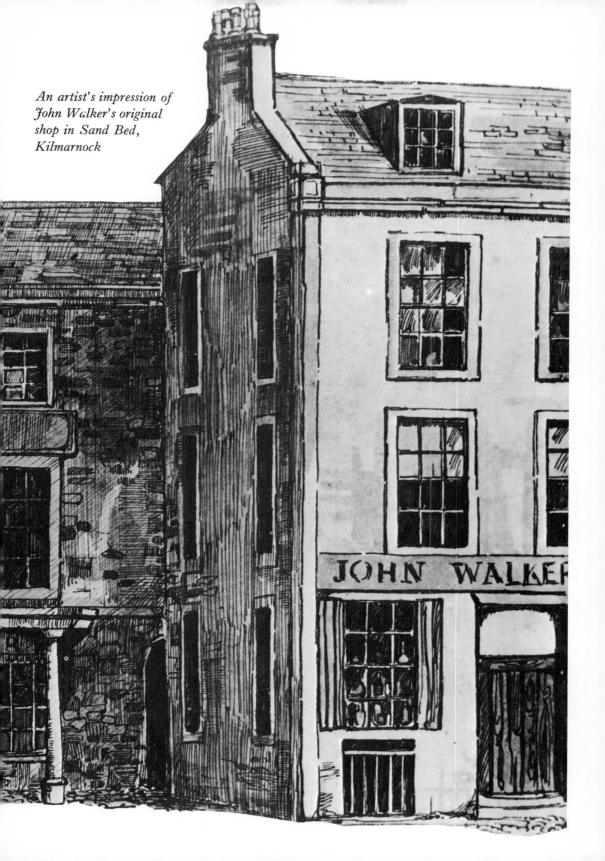

*An artist's impression of
John Walker's original
shop in Sand Bed,
Kilmarnock*

knighthood. He was not the greatest of the whisky magnates, for the pioneering work had been done by his father and the expansion in his own time was largely engineered by Stevenson. But he was an interesting character, with an enormous knowledge of whisky. His training had been both legal, with a firm of Ayrshire solicitors, and in the whisky trade, for as a young man he had been sent to work with Robertson and Baxter, Glasgow distillers and blenders. Alec's elder brother George became managing director in 1890; in 1912 George, Alec and Stevenson became joint managing directors. By this time their enormous and rapid expansion had raised the bogy of over-production. A few years earlier John Walker and Sons had entered into negotiation with two other members of the 'Big Five', Dewars and Buchanans, with a view to amalgamation in the face of rising competition from DCL and the threat of over-production, but the negotiations did not prove successful. (It was not until 1925 that Walker's, together with Buchanan's and Dewar's, merged with DCL.) The problems brought about by the outbreak of the First World War soon removed the threat of over-production. The firm has survived wars and taxation. Sir Alec Walker survived until 1950, devoting his last years to golf in the Ayrshire town of Troon to which he had retired. Lord Stevenson died in 1926 at the relatively early age of fifty-three.

Johnnie Walker's enormous export business has necessitated a re-development of their mode of operation. Their Hill Street premises at Kilmarnock were expanded in the 1950s to develop to the full all the land the company had available, and a new blending plant has recently been built on a 32-acre site near by at Barleith. Blending operations on the one hand and bottling and transportation on the other are now separated, the latter carried out at Hill Street (where as recently as 1955 a new integrated blending, bottling, warehousing and cooperage complex came into operation) and the former at Barleith. The fact that between the mid-1950s and the early 1960s the integrated functions of the new Hill Street building became too much for the space available and necessitated a great new blending plant, is evidence of the rapid strides made in the production and world-wide distribution of Johnnie Walker whisky. The two great bottling halls at Hill Street (like the Dewar bottling hall at Inveralmond) have lines which work automatically, and bottles of many different sizes are mechanically filled, corked, labelled (with different labels for different markets) and, for export to the U.S.A., provided with the strip stamp across the top demanded by the U.S. Customs (these Customs stamps have to be paid for in advance). The warehouse at Barleith can store 15,000 barrels of whisky. At Barleith, too, are the largest blending vats of their kind in the world—three 40,000-gallon stainless-steel-lined vats. In May 1975 DCL announced that the extra capacity required by Johnnie Walker because of its expanding sales would be met by the building of an additional blending and bottling complex at an estimated cost of £25 million. The plant is on a 44-acre site at Shieldhall, near Glasgow, where there is direct access to the motorways serving central Scotland and to the docks. As with Dewar's and others of the world-famous blended Scotch whiskies, the bulk of Johnnie Walker whisky is exported—over 85 per cent of the annual production.

It is always worth looking at the *Dictionary of National Biography* to see what a man's life looks like when it is distilled into a few paragraphs. For this purpose the *Concise D.N.B.* is better still. Stevenson made the *D.N.B.*; none of the Haigs, Dewars or Walkers did. Our next whisky magnate, however, was more successful. His brief entry in the *Concise D.N.B., 1901–1950* is an ironic commentary on his life and character: 'BUCHANAN, JAMES, BARON WOOLAVINGTON (1849–1935), philanthropist and race-horse owner; made a fortune as a distiller of whisky; won St. Leger (1916) with Hurry On, Derby (1922) with Captain Cuttle, and both races and Eclipse Stakes (1926) with Coronach; benefactor of British Museum, Edinburgh University, Middlesex Hospital, etc.; baronet, 1920; baron, 1922; G.C.V.O., 1931.' Philanthropist and race-horse owner! The fourteen-year-old youngster working as an office boy in the Glasgow shipping firm of William Sloan & Co. for a salary of £10 a year (rising to £15 the second year and to £20 in the third year of his initial three-year contract) would hardly have recognized *that* description. For Buchanan really was a self-made man. Born in Canada in 1849 of Scottish emigrant parents, he had been brought back to Scotland as an infant and then lived for some time with his parents in Northern Ireland. He joined the Glasgow shipping firm in 1863. After his first three years there he became a Custom House and clearing clerk, working very long hours for no increase in pay, though the normal pay for such a clerk was £60 to £70 a year. So he left, and at the age of nineteen joined his brother in his grain business in Glasgow. Here he remained for nearly ten years, gaining experience of grain that was to lead him to an interest in distilling.

In 1879 Buchanan got himself a job as London agent for the Leith whisky-merchants and blenders, Charles Mackinlay & Co. Five years later, sniffing a whisky boom in the air, he founded his own firm of James Buchanan & Co. at 61 Basinghall Street, London. He was now thirty-five years old, venturesome, ambitious, confident—and virtually without capital. He was shrewd, too, and knew of the commercial advantages involved in marketing in England a blend of malt whiskies and patent-still grain whiskies. W. P. Lowrie, chairman of W. P Lowrie & Co., a Glasgow whisky firm which had early gone into blending, supplied him with stocks of whisky. Lowrie owned the Convalmore distillery in Dufftown (still going strong), a Highland malt distillery which Buchanan himself later bought; Lowrie also owned Glentauchers distillery in Mulben, Ross-shire. (On Mr. Lowrie's retirement in 1906 Buchanan took over his firm, though it still retains the Lowrie name.) 'What I made up my mind to do,' Buchanan wrote years later as Lord Woolavington, 'was to find a blend sufficiently light and old to please the palate of the user. This I fortunately was able to do, and I made rapid headway. I need hardly say that I was on the quest for business night and day, getting introductions and getting to know people wherever I could.' In his old age Lord Woolavington wondered how he had done it: 'When I think sometimes I marvel at the supreme self-confidence that upheld me—a young man without capital and practically no knowledge of the business I was embarking in; a stranger, too, amongst strangers in the City of London. The extraordinary thing is that the possibility of failure never once occurred to me. I had it always before me in my mind that sooner or later I was bound to make a success.'

Buchanan first set about selling his product with whisky blended from stocks obtained from Lowrie. He put it in a black bottle with a white label and went about selling it with enormous panache. A gay, irrepressible, resourceful character, Buchanan reminds one a bit of Tommy Dewar, but he had even more charm and spirit than his brilliant rival from Perth. By every kind of stratagem, ranging from deliberately cultivating the acquaintance of hotel and restaurant owners to squiring the daughters of a rich whisky buyer, he got his orders. He got the contract for the supply of whisky to the London music halls and was the first whisky supplier to get a contract to supply whisky to the House of Commons bar. He called his whisky 'Buchanan's Blend'[21] at first, then put 'House of Commons' in larger letters on the label. In March 1904 the registered design of the label was altered to 'Buchanan's Special' and later in the same year he registered the name 'Black and

---

[21] Buchanan entered 'Buchanan's Blend' at the Paris Centennial Exhibition of 1889; it won the gold medal for blended whisky. At this time he had a London staff of only seven.

White' which, because of the black bottle and the white label, had already for some time been the unofficial name by which customers had asked for it. In 1898 Buchanan bought the famous Black Swan distillery in Holborn, which he rebuilt on borrowed money. Everything he touched prospered. His whisky moved about London in splendid drays

James Buchanan, founder of the firm

drawn by magnificent horses with the drivers in spectacular olde Englishe uniforms. They were one of the sights of London until they were replaced by motor vans in 1936.

In the fifteen years before the First World War broke out Buchanan's business expanded rapidly. He opened branches in England and on the Continent; he secured royal patronage from both Edward VII and George V. He exported to Europe, North and South America and New Zealand. The firm became a limited liability company in 1903, but characteristically Buchanan kept the shares in his own hands: until 1915 the firm remained a one-man show. Like the other big whisky firms, he had his difficulties during the war, and in 1915 amalgamated with Dewars as a means of solving some of these. Both Dewars and Buchanans joined DCL in 1925. Buchanans moved their head office to Devonshire House, Piccadilly, in 1953.

In the decade before the outbreak of the First World War Buchanan brought himself to public notice by his strong advocacy of military preparedness. He founded the Buchanan Rifle Club in 1905 and encouraged his employees to train. He was raised to the peerage as Baron Woolavington of Lavington in 1922. By that time he had long been widely known as a sportsman. Like Tommy Dewar, he became an English country gentleman with an estate in Sussex and took up race-horse breeding with the success referred to in the *D.N.B.* entry I began by quoting. As the *D.N.B.* says, Buchanan made a fortune out of whisky. He was a great *entrepreneur* rather than a great whisky expert. In a way he was almost a caricature of the self-made capitalist whose heyday was more in late nineteenth-century America than in Britain. But everyone who knew him agreed that he was a most attractive character. If it could not be said of him, as Dr. Johnson said of Garrick, that his death 'eclipsed the gaiety of nations', at least it could be argued that his life contributed to the gaiety of nations, not only by his production of vast quantities of whisky but by his personality and the colour and vivacity with which he conducted his business. He was almost eighty-six when he died in 1935, active until the end, in spite of having broken a thigh eleven years before. By that time his days of lively pioneering in whisky salesmanship were long behind him, and he was mourned as a great sportsman and philanthropist.

The last of the 'Big Five' whisky firms is 'White Horse' which, contrary to what some of the advertisements suggest, has no historical connection at all with the White Horse Inn in the Canongate, Edinburgh, where Boswell is erroneously supposed to have met Dr. Johnson at the beginning of the latter's Highland jaunt. The firm was founded in

The Black Swan distillery in Holborn, former headquarters of James Buchanan & Co Ltd

Glasgow by James Logan Mackie in 1883. Mackie had had experience as a distiller in Islay and he and his partner, Captain Graham, decided to make a blend of the great Islay malt whisky Lagavulin, an Eastern malt whisky from Craigellachie distillery, and patent-still grain whisky. The characteristic peatiness of the Lagavulin gave the blend a highly distinctive flavour. (Lagavulin is still used in 'White Horse', and its flavour is still discernible, but many other whiskies are also now used in the blending and the blend is not identical with what it once was.) James Logan Mackie and Co., as the firm was called, decided to call their blend 'White Horse', and it was James's nephew, Peter Mackie, who succeeded his uncle on the latter's retirement in 1890, who effectively exploited the various historical and symbolic associations of the name. James was the founder, Peter the *entrepreneur* who built up the firm into one of the great whisky firms of the world: the story is by now a familiar **one. Peter** had been trained as a distiller at Lagavulin distillery, which **his uncle** took over in 1888 (Peter bought Craigellachie distillery in 1915). **In 1891** Mackie and Co. became a limited liability company and the name **'White Horse'** was officially registered.

The story now becomes one of continuous expansion. Into the by **now** highly competitive world of blended Scotch whisky Peter Mackie brought a blend of highly distinctive flavour and pushed it with all the devices of advertising that were so characteristic of the whisky trade. He was created a baronet in 1920, and died in 1924, the year when the firm of Mackie and Co. was dissolved to be replaced by White Horse Distillers Ltd. It was shortly after the reconstruction of the company under this new title that White Horse introduced screw caps for their bottles instead of corks—a revolution in whisky bottling which sharply accelerated their sales.

Bruce Lockhart has described Peter Mackie as 'one-third genius, one-third megalomaniac and one-third eccentric'. He boasted of his Highland blood and loved to parade in full Highland dress. He was an ardent Tory politician and a great supporter of imperial preference. He loved to shoot over the moors and wrote an authoritative book on the subject. He was always full of schemes, and diversified his activities in some rather odd ways, including milling a special health-giving flour and weaving tweed. He was always very much the boss and ruled his employees with benevolent despotism. Like most of the other Scotch whisky magnates, he resisted amalgamation with DCL as long as he could and in fact kept White Horse Distillers out of DCL during his lifetime. It was only after his death, in 1927, that DCL acquired control of White Horse and William Ross's dream of seeing all the 'Big Five' inside his company was finally realized.

These, then, were the 'Big Five' of blended Scotch whisky whose activities helped to revolutionize the Scotch whisky industry in the latter part of the nineteenth and the first part of the twentieth century. There were, of course, many other firms, as there still are, playing an important part in the Scotch whisky trade. Some of these will be mentioned when I discuss the quality of some individual whiskies. One, however, really deserves a place here beside the 'Big Five' for its importance in the history of blended Scotch whisky. This is the firm of William Sanderson Ltd., founded by William Sanderson of Leith in May 1863. It was as a wine and cordial manufacturer that Sanderson started: under Gladstone's Act of 1860 he could make and sell wholesale (but not retail) any fermented liquor made from fruit and sugar for a licence fee of five guineas and he could also do his own rectifying for an additional licence fee of ten guineas. He experimented with different cordials and mixtures. The first entry in his record book reads as follows:

MIXTURE WHISKY
10 gallons Glenlivet, 10 gallons Pitlochry
5 gallons Reduced mixed Aqua [i.e., whisky], 8 gallons Grain
4 gallons water, ½ gallon aqua Shrub
8 gallons Grain Aqua

The next year, in 1864, Sanderson noted in his record book the improvement produced by maturing whisky in sherry casks, and heavily underlined the observations. He went on experimenting with a variety of mixtures—Ginger Cordial, Rhubarb Wine, Raspberry Cordial, and many others. And he tried various kinds of 'Aqua Shrub', a compounded drink made of fruit juice, sugar and whisky. He also made a 'Whisky Bitters', a drink which, as I noted in chapter 1, remained popular well into the present century. He travelled Scotland seeking buyers for his products. He began to export to the Continent. He prospered and bought himself a fine new house in Ferry Road which he called Talbot House because the Talbot Hound had been the badge of his Border ancestors. (The Talbot Hound is still impressed on the seal of every bottle of 'Vat 69'.)

William Sanderson was a friend of John Begg, who owned Royal Lochnagar distillery above Balmoral Castle on Deeside. Queen Victoria and Prince Albert had visited the distillery and sampled its product in 1848. Lochnagar was one of the main malt whiskies used by Sanderson in his mixtures. He became more and more interested in mixing (or, as we would now say, blending) whiskies and noted his experiments in a cash book headed 'Adventures in Aqua'. In 1876 he took out a licence as a spirit dealer. In 1880 he was joined in the business by his son William Mark Sanderson. It was William Mark who, taking advantage of the fact that Leith had long been noted for its manufacture of glass bottles, persuaded his father to sell his blends in bottles rather than in barrels to ensure that they were not tampered with by the retailer or publican. By this time both Sandersons were sure that the future of the firm depended on their production of blended Scotch whisky: the problem now was to fix on a suitable blend. William Sanderson was a born experimenter, and might have gone on trying out new blends for ever if (one suspects—but this is guesswork) his son had not insisted that they choose a first-rate blend and make that their principal merchandise. The

William Sanderson, founder of the firm

story goes that in July 1882 Sanderson made up nearly a hundred different blends of malt and grain whiskies, putting each into a numbered small cask or vat. Then he invited a number of expert blenders and friends to taste them and select the best. Their choice—and it was Sanderson's own as well—was unanimously the blended whisky in the vat numbered 69. And so 'Vat 69' was born.

The year 1877 had seen the birth of DCL. Worried by the competition and anxious to secure their supplies of grain whisky, William Sanderson and a number of other whisky merchants and blenders decided to form a company that would set up their own patent-still distillery. The company was formed in October 1885, with Sanderson as Managing Director, Andrew Usher as Chairman, and, as directors, John M. Crabbie, George Robertson, John Somerville, James McLennan and Alex. Murdoch. The company called itself the North British Company and their distillery opened at Gorgie, Edinburgh, in 1887.[22] In 1886 Sanderson became co-owner of the Glengarioch malt distillery, Old Meldrum, Aberdeenshire. He could thus count on the North British grain whisky, Glengarioch malt whisky, and John Begg's Lochnagar malt whisky.

For some time Sanderson kept a variety of blends on the market instead of concentrating all his efforts on 'Vat 69'. He had a blend for morning drinking called 'A.M.' and one for postmeridian drinking called 'P.M.'. He had his 'S.V.G.' or 'Specially Vatted Glengarioch', his 'I.M.' containing a high proportion of Islay whisky, his 'Special', 'Extra Special' and others. He also tried out a 'Vat 88' which had a degree of success for some time. And he produced a Whisky Bitters described on the label as 'A Drink, not a Flavouring Extract, The King of Tonic Drinks, A Pick-me-up and Appetiser. May be taken as a liqueur, or with plain or aerated water. Made with very fine Scotch Whisky of great age.' But as the firm grew, 'Vat 69' came more and more to the fore. By 1903, when William Sanderson's youngest son Arthur Watson Sanderson· joined the firm (now 'William Sanderson and Son, Distillers and Scotch Whisky Merchants'), the most exotic of the firm's activities had been allowed to dwindle, and whisky, particularly 'Vat 69', was its main output.

William Sanderson died in 1908 and was succeeded by his son William Mark. The concentration was now on exports, already considerable to Australia, South Africa and Canada and now extended to Denmark, Sweden, Germany, Belgium and France. The first consignment to America was shipped in March 1908. William Mark introduced the advertising slogan 'Quality Tells!' and 'Vat 69' continued to boom. In 1917 Sandersons took over the eighty-year-old firm of whisky-merchants Carstairs and Robertson and in 1920 the old Leith firm of wine and spirit merchants D. and G. McLaren. After the First World War, with all its problems, Sandersons resisted amalgamation with DCL and in fact held out until 1937, when amalgamation took place.

---

[22] The North British Distillery, now enormously enlarged and modernized, still operates at Gorgie. Shareholders in the company are still restricted to wholesale whisky merchants. Though none of the really big whisky firms are today what could be called family businesses, they still represent very much an 'in-group' and, rivals though they may be, they treat each other both inside and outside DCL with a generosity not commonly found among commercial enterprises.

The firm incorporated as a limited liability company in 1925 with William Mark Sanderson as Chairman. He died in 1929 and was succeeded as Chairman by his son Kenneth. In 1933 Sandersons amalgamated with Booth's Distilleries Ltd., a firm which already owned the Stromness distillery in Orkney, the Royal Brackla distillery in Nairn, and Millburn distillery near Inverness, all fine malt-whisky distilleries. Kenneth Sanderson (whose great hobby was motor racing) devoted himself to extending exports and travelled widely for this purpose. Finally, as I have mentioned, the growing rationalization of the whole Scotch whisky trade brought Booths and Sandersons into DCL in 1937. In 1962 the firm moved their London office to a new building in Stanhope Gate, by Park Lane.

The Sanderson story is an interesting family saga which really goes back to old Captain Mark Sanderson, Leith sea captain who died in 1832. The restless curiosity of William Sanderson and more single-minded business acumen of his son William Mark are both important parts of the story. None of the Sandersons has the flamboyance and extrovert charm of Tommy Dewar or James Buchanan. But we have the feeling that their interest centred genuinely on whisky (or on 'whisky mixtures') and that they were whisky men rather than financial wizards. This is not to say that the 'Big Five' were not whisky men too, but some of them were *entrepreneurs* who happened to have chosen whisky as their product and who could have done just as well with anything else. One does not get that feeling about the Sandersons.

Talking recently to a Director of one of the 'Big Five', I was interested to hear him say that the great whisky barons of the late nineteenth century not only represented a kind of individual enterprise impossible today but also pursued a way of life which if attempted now might well land the pursuer in gaol. He was not suggesting for a moment that the founding fathers of the whisky trade were crooks, but he was emphasizing that the conditions under which business firms now operate are much more hedged round with legal restrictions than they used to be. The kind of financial risks which those old boys took might easily result in involvement with the law today. He mentioned as an example the name of a would-be builder of an industrial empire who is at the moment of writing awaiting trial on complicated charges involving financial manipulation of a kind that earlier, if it eventually resulted in success, would have escaped any legal inquiry. The other important thing to remember about the 'Big Five' is that they pioneered a lively and imaginative advertising which has had a permanent influence on trade practices. As a later chapter will show, I am highly critical of some aspects of modern whisky advertising; but I cannot help admiring the gaiety, the debonair quality, the splendid dash and vigour of much of that pioneering advertising. Whisky, after all, is not like the majority of commercial products. Its primary function is to increase pleasure, and an awareness of this in the whisky trade must be what accounts for that special air of friendliness and relaxation that I have found among whisky men.

Chapter Five

WAR AND TAXES

The Scotch whisky boom of the 1890s came to an end with the Pattison failure of 1898. After that the number of working distilleries in Scotland began to decline—from 161 in 1898 to 149 in 1902 and 122 in 1910. As we have seen, the Distillers Company Ltd. (DCL), by its policy of amalgamation and controlled production, fought continuously to prevent Scotch whisky from being caught up in a boom-and-recession cycle. This policy was especially fostered by Graham Menzies, who became Chairman of DCL in 1897, and William Ross, who held the combined office of General Manager and Secretary. Ross became Managing Director in 1900, at the age of thirty-eight, and Chairman in 1925, continuing in the latter position until his retirement in 1935, in spite of a serious accident in 1917, which fractured one leg and seriously damaged the other, and the onset of total blindness in 1931 as a result of an accident on shipboard two years before. It was Ross who negotiated the formation in 1899 of the United Yeast Company Ltd. as a DCL subsidiary and so both safeguarded Britain's bread supply and enabled British distillers to survive the cutting off of yeast imports from the Continent at the beginning of the First World War. It was Ross who, just before the start of the First World War, took the lead in forming Scottish Malt Distillers Ltd., originally a concentration of the resources of five Lowland malt distillers (of which three still operate), but since 1930 the organization through which DCL controls its 45 malt distilleries in Scotland. It was Ross who fought unremittingly to bring the great blending firms into DCL and who had his reward in 1925 when Buchanan-Dewar (these two had merged in 1915) and John Walker & Sons amalgamated with DCL on the basis of an exchange of the shares of each of the three companies. It was Ross, indeed, who could without exaggeration be said to be the man who enabled the Scotch whisky trade to survive the First World War. The British Government, or at least

the Chancellor of the Exchequer, Lloyd George, was seriously considering imposing prohibition on the country after the outbreak of war in
order to prevent workers' efficiency from being impaired by alcohol.
Ross went to see Lloyd George and explained some of the facts of life
to him—the tie-up of the manufacture of yeast (necessary for the baking
of bread) with distilling, the industrial and military uses of alcohol. A
conference called by the Government in 1915 were told of the dire
necessity to conserve grain because of the growing damage to imports
done by German submarines. Distilling was, therefore, severely
restricted and spirits rationed. In the same year the Immature Spirits
(Restriction) Act was passed, prohibiting delivery of whisky for consumption in Britain unless it had matured in a bonded warehouse for
a minimum period of three years.

The Immature Spirits (Restriction) Act was intended as a wartime
measure, but in fact it has remained law, with unexpected consequences
for the future of Scotch whisky. Lloyd George saw it as a means of
restricting the consumption of whisky. But James Stevenson, the director
of John Walker & Sons who now had a high administrative position in
the Ministry of Munitions, persuaded Lloyd George (then Minister of
Munitions) to support this legislation (rather than impose prohibition
on the country) on the grounds that it was cheap, raw whisky that caused
drunkenness among workers, not mature whisky. Stevenson, in fact,
seized the opportunity to turn restrictive legislation to the benefit of
whisky. The fact is that cheap, new patent-still grain spirit had for some
time been a curse in the city. For hopeless workers in gloomy city
slums such whisky, before the war, had provided a quick and destructive
way out of misery. The availability of this cheap, raw spirit did not do
the reputation of Scotch whisky any good, and Lloyd George's Act,
whatever his intentions may have been, has done nothing but good to
the Scotch whisky trade. It was not immediately seen in this way, of
course. The immediate effect was a great increase in the price of whisky
to the consumer. Many independent firms involved in blending and
distributing whisky were forced out of business, and their valuable
stocks often came into the hands of DCL or their associates. The total
cessation of distilling in 1917 further weakened the independent firms
and strengthened the case for amalgamation. Further, while the grain
distilleries in the DCL group produced industrial alcohol for war purposes, the independent malt distillers did not, and had to close. Thus
weakened, these distilleries were in no position to cope with the difficult
position of the immediate post-war years, and so a great number
of them agreed to amalgamation proposals by DCL. However we look

at the picture, it is clear that the First World War and its consequences accelerated the drive towards amalgamation in the Scotch
whisky industry and provided new opportunities for DCL. But it was
the genius of William Ross that enabled DCL to take advantage of these
opportunities. After the great Buchanan-Dewar and John Walker merger
with DCL, White Horse Distillers Ltd. came in in 1927. William
Sanderson and Son Ltd. ('Vat 69') came into DCL in 1937; A. & A.
Crawford (a distinguished Leith blending firm whose 'Three Star' and
'Five Star' whiskies have long been highly esteemed blends) in 1944,
and John Crabbie and Company Ltd. (an old-established blending firm,
originally grain-whisky distillers and one of the original six in the 1856
trade arrangement of patent-still distillers) in 1963.

Meanwhile, the duty on whisky kept going up. At the beginning of the
First World War the price in the United Kingdom of a bottle of one of
the proprietary brands of blended Scotch whisky was between 4s. and
4s. 6d., with the excise duty standing at 14s. 9d. per proof gallon. In 1918
the duty was raised to 30s. per proof gallon, and the retail price of whisky
rose from 8s. to 9s. 6d. per bottle. In 1919 the duty rose again to 50s. and
the retail price to 10s. 6d. From 1920 until the outbreak of the Second
World War in September 1939 the duty was 72s. 6d. per proof gallon
and the retail price 12s. 6d. per bottle. In September 1939 the duty went
up to £4 2s. 6d. and from then it has climbed steadily—to £6 17s. 6d.
in 1942; £7 17s. 6d. in 1943; £9 10s. 10d. in 1947; £11 11s. 11d. in 1961;
£12 17s. 6d. in 1964; £14 12s. in 1965; £16 1s. 3d. in 1967; and
£17 2s. 9d. in 1968. In November 1968 it was raised to £18 17s., which
made the duty on a standard bottle of blended Scotch whisky £2 4s. (or
£2.20 in the decimal currency introduced into Britain in 1971).

The introduction of Value Added Tax in April 1973 (initially at 10
per cent) involved a reduction of excise duty to £15.45 per proof gallon,
which meant that the duty on a standard bottle was £1.80 plus 10 per
cent of the retail price. In March 1974 the duty per proof gallon was
raised to £17.01, making the duty on a bottle of £1.98 plus 10 per cent of
the retail price. In July 1974 VAT was reduced to 8 per cent. The excise
duty is paid only once, when the whisky is withdrawn from bond,
whereas VAT is charged as a percentage of the price charged by the
distiller or blender to his first customer and again at each subsequent re-
sale. (As with all VAT taxation, at each stage the vendor passes on to
Customs and Excise the amount of VAT he charges the purchaser, less
the amount of VAT he himself has paid to his supplier.)

The combination of excise duty and VAT now included in the price of
a bottle of whisky, with each calculated and paid in a different way,

makes it difficult for the ordinary retail purchaser in Britain to know how the price he pays is made up. In March 1975 the lowest price for a bottle of blended Scotch whisky was £2.55, and sometimes one saw a special offer of a few pence less even than that. But with excise duty £1.98 a bottle and VAT at 8 per cent of the combined purchase price and duty, even a retail price of £2.55 would not have been profitable. Most whisky in Britain left the producer at about 42 pence a bottle: add to this the duty of £1.98 and 8 per cent VAT on the resulting retail price of £2.40 and you got a final retail price of £2.59, which meant that a retail price of £2.55 was a 'loss leader'. (And this assumes that there is no intermediate price rise between the producer and the retailer: the retailer is indeed often a large chain of grocery shops or wine and spirit merchants, sometimes associated with other firms in a powerful group, which buys direct from the blender.) No wonder that there was a demand in the trade for an increase in the price for the domestic market. Increase in cereal prices, and a huge increase in fuel costs after the Middle East crisis of October 1973, together with industrial action by some distillery workers in 1974 to secure additional pay in the face of rapidly rising inflation, all pointed to a higher price for whisky in Britain. 'The present price,' said Mr David Grant of William Grant and Sons Ltd. ('Standfast' and 'Glenfiddich' and 'Balvenie') in December 1974, 'is suicidal to an industry which employs 23,000 people in Scotland and earned £260m. abroad last year.' After making the necessary applications to the Price Commission, DCL announced rises in its gross home trade prices in January, April, July and October 1975, totalling 28·4 pence per bottle of their whiskies over the year. And on 16 April 1975 the Chancellor announced a massive increase in excise duty (59·25 pence per bottle), to which he added a duty increase of 29·6 pence in April 1976 and 28·7 pence in January 1977. Three months later, DCL companies increased the gross home trade prices of their brands by 12 pence per bottle, so that with VAT at 8 per cent levied on the consumer price, a bottle of whisky on the domestic market in August 1977 cost at least £4.20.

The Second World War inevitably brought serious problems to the Scotch whisky trade. The Ministry of Food informed the distillers that the production of whisky would cease at the end of 1939. The six month's stocks of cereal held by DCL for distilling were requisitioned. Three short periods of distilling were allowed up to 1944, when a restricted supply of home-grown cereals were allocated for the manufacture of Scotch whisky for export. Rationing of Scotch whisky for the home market began on 1 March 1940—each wholesaler was allowed a

percentage of what he had bought in the year ending 29 February 1940.
In 1940–1 the percentage allowed was 41; it was reduced to 20 in
1948–50. The reason for the severe restriction after the war was over
was the desperate need to export. The exports of whisky went on, under
most difficult conditions, throughout the war: they were especially high
in 1940, reaching £10,470,000. After the 'lend-lease' agreement with
America the need to export to pay for needed imports was not quite so
desperate and there was a slight decline.

After the end of the Second World War the Ministry of Food continued to allocate cereals for distilling, but the amount gradually
increased. There is a famous minute of Mr. Churchill's in April 1945:
'On no account reduce the barley for whisky. This takes years to mature,

and is an invaluable export and dollar producer. Having regard to all our other difficulties about exports, it would be most improvident not to preserve this characteristic British element of ascendancy.' The characteristic British element was preserved, and whisky exports flourished while the consumers at home had to make do with the allocation allowed by an agreement between the Ministry of Food, the Board of Trade and the Scotch Whisky Association[23] which, from 1947 to 1953, specified what proportion of the output of Scotch whisky annually should go for export and what should be made available at home. The sort of proportions involved is indicated by the fact that in 1953 11,000,000 proof gallons was set as the export objective (actually exceeded by more than 2,000,000 gallons) and 2,750,000 for the home market. It was not until 1954 that the quota system for domestic consumers was discontinued, but even then stocks had been run down to such an extent that it was 1959 before whisky rationing for the home market (by the whisky trade now, not by the Government) was completely discontinued.

According to DCL statistics issued in May 1977, the sales of the whole Scotch whisky industry for the years 1970 to 1976 were as shown in the table below.

Stocks of whisky have been steadily building up, and by 1976 they reached 1,084,500 proof gallons.

The USA is by far the largest importer of Scotch whisky. In 1976 the USA imported 32,520,000 proof gallons. Japan, which imported 348,000 proof gallons in 1964, expanded its imports rapidly to become the second largest importer of Scotch whisky after America in 1973, and in 1976 it imported 8,948,000 proof gallons. In 1976 France came next with 4,272,000 proof gallons, then Italy with 3,835,000 and West Germany with 3,263,000. The major proportion of the Japanese imports was of malt whisky in bulk for blending with Japanese whisky.

A tour of Highland malt distilleries in October 1967 showed many of them working a seven-day week, round the clock. Old distilleries had been modernized, distilleries long out of commission had been put back to work (e.g. Port Ellen distillery, Islay, closed in 1930 and reconstructed in the 1960s; Benriach, Elgin, closed between 1903 and 1965, then re-opened; Caperdonich distillery, Rothes, closed in 1901, re-opened in

---

[23] This is an association of all the principal firms of distillers and blenders producing or blending Scotch whisky: it has over 140 members, and its head office is in Edinburgh.

Calendar year	Production (in thousands) of proof gallons)	%
1970	142,853	+ 7·7
1971	149,399	+ 4·6
1972	167,638	+12·2
1973	181,541	+ 8·3
1974	183,582	+ 1·1
1975	151,932	−17·2
1976	139,601	− 8·1

Home and export sales (in thousands of proof gallons)

Calendar year	Home	%	Export	%	Total	%	EEC Nine
1970	10,535	+14·1	62,010	+18·3	72,545	+17·7	
1971	11,087	+ 5·2	70,328	+13·4	81,415	+12·2	
1972	12,583	+13·5	68,752	− 2·2	81,335	− 0·1	
1973	15,347	+22·0	78,449	+14·1	93,796	+15·3	28,651
1974	17,370	+13·2	87,605	+11·7	104,975	+11·9	32,030
1975	16,343	− 5·9	90,279	+ 3·1	106,622	+ 1·6	32,301
1976	18,694	+14·4	91,832	+ 1·7	110,526	+ 3·7	35,534

1965, and then enlarged and modernized); new distilleries were built (e.g. Tormore at Advie, Morayshire; on the Island of Jura; Loch Lomond distillery, a £1,000,000 complex of distillery, warehousing, bottling plant and cooperage, opened in September 1967, at Alexandria, Dunbartonshire); great new bottling halls and blending warehouses had been built (in addition to those of Dewar and Johnnie Walker, already described, there is Arthur Bell and Sons' vast new one near Broxburn, West Lothian).

The expansion continued into the 1970s. In 1972 DCL opened a new Highland malt distillery, Mannochmore, with an annual capacity of one million proof gallons. It adjoins the company's Glenlossie distillery at Birnie, Morayshire, but draws its water from a different source. DCL also built a new malt whisky distillery at Brora, Sutherland, adjoining Clynelish distillery (it is called simply Brora). Caol Ila distillery on Islay has been rebuilt. Major mechanical maltings have been built, at Ord distillery, Beauly, and Hillside distillery, Montrose, with a slightly smaller one at Port Ellen, Islay, to serve three Islay distilleries (Port Ellen, Caol Ila and Lagavulin) run by Scottish Malt Distillers Ltd.,

The Whisky War in Ohio, 1874—ladies laying siege to a drinking saloon

which since 1930 has run all the malt distilleries owned by DCL companies. In 1973 DCL's new subsidiary, The Distillers Company (Bottling Services) Ltd., opened a major blending and bottling complex in Leven, Fife, where the brands of minor companies in the DCL group are mostly blended and bottled. Other developments include a £14m. expansion of its Scotch whisky interests announced at the end of 1974 by Distillers Corporation–Seagrams, to include a new bottling complex on 250-acre site at Darnley, to the south of Glasgow, and a new distillery, Allt-A-Bhainne, as well as expansion of their existing recently built distillery Braes of Glenlivet. Other new distilleries have been opened at Auchriosk (International Distillers and Vintners, Rothes), Pittyvaich (A. Bell & Sons Ltd., Dufftown) and at Ledaig (Ledaig Distillery (Tobermory) Ltd., Mull), although this last distillery closed down in 1976.

The hundreds of millions of proof gallons of whisky now stocked represent, of course, an enormous investment. Everything must be planned ahead. The whisky that is being distilled now will not come on to the market for some years; but the amount distilled now determines what will be available then. If distillers expand production, as they are doing, it means that the big firms who blend and sell the whisky are demanding this: a distillery does not fill casks 'on spec'; for the most part it fills casks sent to it by the blenders, who keep the whisky maturing in the distillery until they want it (occasionally they will sell it to another blender who is short of that particular whisky for his blend: whisky firms are generous in helping each other out in this way). When malt distillers shorten their summer shut-down and work a seven-day week (instead of the traditional Monday to Saturday) they do so in order to fill specific orders. Those orders in turn are based on forecasts (and hopes) by the firms who blend and sell the whisky. To make these forecasts come true, high-powered selling campaigns (especially in America) are necessary and in addition new areas for export have to be found.

Although the bulk of whisky distilled in the great distilleries is now done to order, a small amount is bought by speculators whose aim·is to sell it at a profit to a blender in.sudden need of it. There are also whisky brokers, important middlemen who hold stocks of whisky and mediate between distillers and blenders so as to provide the latter with what they want when they want it. For blenders cannot always foresee their needs as they would like to. It is still open to private individuals to buy whisky in the cask as an investment, as periodical advertisements in *The Times* make clear. One holds it until it matures and hopes to be able to sell it to a blender at a profit. But it can be dangerous to people not brought up in the whisky trade to get involved in it, and some notable investors in whisky have had their fingers burnt.

Although expansion of distilling and the building of blending and bottling facilities continued into the 1970s, by the beginning of 1975 the picture had begun to change. In December 1974 the Chairman of DCL (which, it must be remembered, is responsible for about six of every ten bottles of Scotch whisky sold throughout the world), after referring to problems caused by unofficial strikes in support of pay claims, other disputes curtailing the transport of materials inwards and of cased goods outwards, and a shortage of bottles and other packaging materials, went on to observe that with the long-term capital market virtually closed, the company had to keep its forward planning within the resources available. 'It will be necessary therefore,' he said, 'to reduce distillation of Scotch whisky in 1975. Hitherto production levels have been designed to cover projected increases in the volume of sales resulting from the continuing expansion in the demand for Scotch whisky together with substantial reserves of stock to meet possible eventualities. A reduction in distillation can therefore be effected whilst maintaining stocks at a level which is entirely adequate to support the forecast increase in demand for our major brands.'

While the increasingly heavy taxation of whisky in the home market has had the effect of holding down domestic consumption, the fact remains that the home market takes more Scotch whisky than any single foreign country except the United States, as the figures which are given on page 110 show clearly. Still, what has kept the Scotch whisky trade flourishing is its massive exports. Scotland no longer keeps its great spirit to itself. Among the marginal notes written by the actress Ellen Terry in a special interleaved copy of *Macbeth* prepared by Henry Irving for the Irving-Terry production of the play in 1888 there is this comment on Lady Macbeth's line: 'But in them Nature's copy's not eterne' (III. ii. 38). Lady Macbeth is replying to Macbeth's complaint that Banquo and his son Fleance, potential rivals for the throne, are still alive, and is suggesting that they might both be murdered. Or at least that is how most people would construe her observation. But Ellen Terry interpreted the line to mean this: 'Don't trouble so, for they cannot live for ever—that fellow Banquo may die any day—*why not!* and the boy may have whooping cough in such a climate as this—we keep all the whisky to ourselves —I lock up the cupboard every night.' In 1888 Ellen Terry assumed that of course the Macbeths would have had whisky in the palace and that it would have been a good cure for whooping cough. Her reference to whisky reflects the growing awareness of it in the 1880s but also suggests

A Scottish inn

that it was still regarded by many people as primarily medicinal in function (like the 'whisky bitters' still common in the nineteenth century). The medicinal properties of whisky were debated in the House of Commons during the Second World War, and it was agreed that if it did not cure colds it undoubtedly helped the sufferer to endure one in greater comfort. It is certainly good for certain cardiac conditions and helps to prevent coronary thrombosis. But the part of Ellen Terry's comment to which I want to draw attention is her parenthetical 'we keep all the whisky to ourselves'. This was presumably advice given by Lady Macbeth to her husband for sinister power purposes. But it is precisely the fact that the Scots have not kept all the whisky to themselves that has determined its history since Ellen Terry's day.

Chapter Six

WHISKY AS A WORLD DRINK

The Distillers Company Limited began in 1877 as a combination of six Lowland patent-still distilleries. Although the company built its first malt distillery in the 1890s (at Knockdhu, Banffshire) it was not until the present century that it moved significantly into the fields of blending and of malt-whisky distilling, largely in response to the difficulties faced by the Scotch whisky trade in the First World War. We have seen the important part played by Mr. W. H. Ross of DCL in founding Scottish Malt Distillers Limited in 1914. In 1915 DCL and John Walker jointly acquired Coleburn distillery (south of Elgin) and in 1916 Dewar, DCL, W. P. Lowrie (the firm from which James Buchanan originally obtained his stocks of whisky, subsequently bought by Buchanan) and Walker jointly bought the company which operated the malt distilleries of Dailuaine (on Speyside) and Talisker (in Skye). About the same time DCL bought the Glasgow blending firms of John Begg and John Hopkins and the old-established Edinburgh firm of J. & G. Stewart (with which the firm of Andrew Usher, a pioneer of blending, is now incorporated) in order to develop its export trade in blended whisky which it had been conducting on a small scale as an inheritance from Kirkliston distillery, one of the original six in DCL. The opening of the North British grain distillery in 1887 spurred DCL to further efforts in the export field: the company built a blending and bottling warehouse at South Queensferry and marketed 'King George IV' and 'Highland Nectar' through its Export Branch and, later, through the Distillers Agency Ltd. But all this was still on a small scale until the take-overs and mergers that began during the First World War enabled DCL to increase steadily its blending, marketing and exporting activities.

The progressive amalgamation of the Big Five with DCL has already been described, as has the enormous part played by DCL in the Scotch whisky trade during the last fifty years. Today it is a vast concern, owning over forty distilling and blending firms,[24] forty-five of the just over one hundred malt distilleries now in operation and five of the ten grain distilleries, administered by its subsidiary company Scottish Grain Distillers Ltd. in the same way as its malt distilleries are administered by Scottish Malt Distillers Ltd. Finally, in the words of DCL's own publication, Scottish Grain Distillers Ltd. 'also produces, at Caledonian, Cambus, Carsebridge and Port Dundas Distilleries, substantial quantities of carbon dioxide, in liquid and solid form, to meet the needs of the soft drinks, brewing and ice-cream industries, as well as for specialised use in foundry work and as a coolant by the Atomic Energy Authority.'

The growth and success of DCL is closely associated with the growth and success of blended Scotch whisky. And that in turn depended originally on Aeneas Coffey's invention of the patent still. Has the world-wide reputation of Scotch whisky been won at a cost? Are Aeneas Coffey, the great whisky *entrepreneurs* of the latter half of the nineteenth century and William Ross of DCL villains as much as heroes? There are some dedicated devotees of single malt whiskies who say that they are. But this is to take a melodramatic and unrealistic view. The reputable blended Scotch whiskies are sound and pleasant drinks, if not as interesting, as individual or as flavoursome as a pure malt whisky. If—as Neil

---

[24] DCL owns the following Scotch whisky distilling and blending firms: Ainslie & Heilbron (Distillers) Ltd., Baird-Taylor Ltd., John Begg Ltd., Benmore Distilleries Ltd., John Bisset & Co. Ltd., James Buchanan & Co. Ltd., Bulloch Lade & Co. Ltd., A. & A. Crawford Ltd., D. Crawford & Son Ltd., Dailuaine-Talisker Distilleries Ltd., Peter Dawson Ltd., John Dewar & Sons Ltd., Distillers Agency Ltd., Donald Fisher Ltd., John Gillon & Co. Ltd., John Haig & Co. Ltd., J. & W. Hardie Ltd., J. & R. Harvey & Co. Ltd., John Hopkins & Co. Ltd., Low, Robertson & Co. Ltd., W. P. Lowrie & Co. Ltd., D. & J. McCallum Ltd., Macdonald Greenlees Ltd., John McEwan & Co. Ltd., Macleay Duff (Distillers) Ltd., John Robertson & Son Ltd., Wm. Sanderson & Son Ltd., Torphold Ltd., John Walker & Sons Ltd., James Watson & Co. Ltd., White Horse Distillers Ltd. Among DCL's subsidiary companies are also the following gin distillers and rectifiers: Boord & Son Ltd., Booth's Distilleries Ltd., Charles Tanqueray & Co. Ltd., Tanqueray Gordon & Co. Ltd. and numbers of yeast distributing firms and bakers' suppliers, chemical and industrial product manufacturers, a variety of miscellaneous companies and twelve overseas distilling companies (including two in the U.S.A.).

Gunn once maintained—the large drinking public on whom the Scotch whisky trade depends for its sales really prefer 'a tasteless alcohol' and go for the blended Scotch that approximates most closely to it, then in the long run Scotch will have to cede to vodka. But the evidence does not support Gunn's view, though it is true that in America there is a real demand for spirits of little characteristic flavour. Gunn's attack on the blenders was made in 1935, when the situation did indeed look desperate and the number of Highland malt distilleries at work was steadily diminishing. It looked, too, as though blending might do permanent injury to the production of the finer malts. 'If the pot-still product is too fine, too delicate,' wrote Gunn, 'in other words if it is a highly desirable single whisky, it will not communicate in sufficient measure to a waiting vat of patent spirit the characteristics of a Highland malt whisky; but, on the other hand, if it contains these characteristics in excessive degree, making it pungent and rather objectionable as a single whisky, it then achieves perfection for blending, on the principle that a little of it goes a long way.' But the situation described by Gunn has changed radically. The number and variety of pot-still malt distilleries now working and selling their product to the blenders makes it clear that there is no threat from the blenders to the finer malts. It is indeed quite wrong to suppose that the reputable blends today use a very little heavy and pungent malt whisky and avoid the lighter malts—the reverse is rather the truth. And the demand from the blenders for a range of good malt whiskies has been growing steadily. This is not to say that there is not a case against blended Scotch whisky, or at least against some blended Scotch whiskies. But before deciding on the merits of the issue we had better take a look at the nature and process of blending.

As I have already mentioned, and as anybody investigating the state of Scotch whisky today very quickly discovers, the Scotch whisky trade is unanimous in refusing to reveal the proportions of malt and grain whiskies that go into any given blend. While one can understand a refusal to reveal the precise nature and proportions of the different malts and grains that make up the blend, I have long felt that it is reasonable to expect to be told the proportions of malt and grain. Any given blend will still remain secret even if that information is released. One is indeed forced to suspect that a refusal to reveal these general proportions (which, to repeat, does not involve the revealing of the formula for the blend) is based on an underlying and perhaps sub-conscious desire to prevent the public from knowing that a large proportion of blended Scotch whisky is not pot-still malt whisky at all. In booklets and films blending houses will again and again explain and

CANDID.

Tam (very dry, at door of Country Inn, Sunday Morning). "AYE, MAN, YE MICHT GIE ME A BIT GILL OOT IN A BOTTLE!"

Landlord (from within). "WEEL, YE KEN, TAMMAS, I DAURNA SELL ONYTHING THE DAY. AND FORBYE YE GOT A HALF-MUTCHKIN AWA' WI' YE LAST NICHT (AFTER HOORS TAE); IT CANNA BE A' DUNE YET!"

Tam. "DUNE! LOSH, MAN, D'YE THINK A' COULD SLEEP AN' WHUSKEY I' THE HOOSE?!"

show in great detail the romantic, traditional process of making pot-still malt whisky; they have much less to say about patent-still grain whisky. Once, after seeing an advertising film on the production of Scotch whisky made for a distinguished blending house, and finding that it dealt exclusively with the making of pot-still Highland malt whisky, I rose from my place in the audience after the performance and asked the representative of the firm who was showing the film what proportion of the whisky in his firm's blend was actually made in that way, and why nothing had been shown of the making of patent-still whisky. It was not a question I was supposed to ask. It is true that the skill of the blender is played up enormously in whisky advertising; at the same time much of this advertising refers back to dates long before there was any blending of malt and grain whiskies. 'There are more than three centuries of affection and conviction behind our blend', says an advertisement in an American magazine of Haig's 'pinch bottle'; 'established 1742' says the sign under the white horse and 'the white horse cellar' legend; an American advertisement of 'King William IV' whisky claims that it has been produced since 1817; and there is, of course, the famous 'Born 1820—still going strong' slogan of 'Johnnie Walker'. My point is simply that in the advertising of blended whiskies the impression is given that the blends go back to dates long before blends existed and before the patent still was in fact invented. Further, how often do we find patent-still grain whisky mentioned in descriptions of blends? 'Rich Islay whiskies. Smooth whiskies from Falkirk and Campbelltown. Mellow Keith whisky, and the fragile whisky of Speyside.' That is from an American advertisement of '100 Pipers', a blend marketed by Seagrams, a relative newcomer to Scotland. Not a single patent-still grain whisky is mentioned. (The whisky from Falkirk is presumably Rosebank, a DCL Lowland malt distillery.) I could cite many other similar examples. It is almost as though the blenders are afraid to mention patent-still grain whisky. Of course, in the more technical information booklets issued by DCL and by the Scotch Whisky Association patent-still grain whisky is described (in as complimentary a way as possible). But in general the patent still is kept in the background.

So the blenders have only themselves to blame if one has to guess at the proportion of malt to grain in their whiskies. Of course, one's guesses can be helped out by other sources. Individuals in blending firms, while keeping quiet about the proportions in their own blend, will, on convivial occasions, risk a generalization about the proportions adopted in the trade generally. And one can use one's eyes. In visiting malt distilleries, for example, one can observe the colours of the ends of the casks in the warehouses: each blending house uses its own colour, so it is not difficult to see at a glance which blends use which malts. Indeed, managers of malt distilleries are not, in my experience, reluctant to tell you to what blenders they sell their whisky. But that is only part of the story. One may be able to form a pretty shrewd idea of the different malts in a blend without knowing what proportion of the blend is made up of malt whisky at all.

My own view is that in what one might call the standard blend of Scotch whisky today the proportion is 60 grain to 40 malt, and that the proportion of grain has risen since the earlier days of blending, when it was more likely to be 50:50.[25] I also believe that the 'light' whiskies being extensively pushed in the American market today (and increasingly in the home market too) are liable to have a significantly less proportion of malt than the 40 per cent of the standard blends. In the standard blends there is a basic distribution of malts, with Islays together with Eastern Malts of varying degrees of quality and maturity. Dewars claim that there are forty different whiskies in their blend; there are seventeen in the Glenlivet Distillers' 'Queen Anne' whisky. I have recently seen an advertisement for 'Johnnie Walker Black Label' claiming that 'over 40 Scotch whiskies' go into it. 'White Horse' claims 'thirty selected malt whiskies' in their blend. Some blends claim many more than this. I have no reason to question these claims, which are borne out by what one observes at distilleries. But nobody talks about the patent-still grain whiskies that make up the larger proportion of the blend. It is, further, the quality as well as the proportion of malt whisky in the blend that matters. There is no necessary gain in having an enormous range of malts if many of them are less mature or simply less good and the total proportion of malt remains small.

That there are inferior blends with a proportion of patent-still grain whisky of 80 per cent and even more can hardly be denied. But DCL's blends and those of well-known independent firms (some of which will be discussed later) are good and stable blends to which a great deal of careful thought has been given. Some independent firms produce superior blends which do not necessarily consist of a higher proportion of malts but may instead use more matured and better quality malts. This is also true of the higher priced 'quality' versions of some standard DCL blends, such as 'Johnnie Walker Black Label' or Dewar's 'Ancestor' (a whisky, incidentally, which is not advertised in Britain, because it is felt that the promoting of a superior Dewar blend might have adverse effects on the sales of their regular blend).

The actual blending process is not complicated. The whiskies to be blended, having been assembled from the various distilleries, are run through blending troughs (now often of stainless steel) into large vats.

---

[25] My latest information is that some blends are moving back to a 50:50 proportion.

The whiskies in the blend can be 'roused' either by the modern method of running compressed air into the vats (as at the Dewar plant at Inveralmond) or by the older method of mechanical rousers. The blended whisky is then stored in oak casks for at least six months. Some blenders 'marry' the malts and the grains separately and bring them together only in bottling.

It is after blending and before bottling that artificial caramel colour is added. The blenders will tell you that this is to maintain evenness of colour, which the public expects. Whisky itself is colourless, and when matured in casks that have held sherry absorbs some of the sherry colour. But even if all whisky were matured in sherry casks (which is no longer so) the colour of each cask would be liable to come out differently. The public, it is argued, seeing one bottle of its favourite brand one day of a lighter colour than it had been before, will suspect the barman of watering it. The use of artificial colouring thus—the argument runs—reassures the public and maintains confidence.

I think this is nonsense, and contributes to the rubbish about whisky colour that is perpetuated in whisky advertising. The argument about the public's attitude could be disposed of very quickly: a six months' advertising campaign by the Scotch Whisky Association could educate the public as to the significance (or lack of significance) of colour in whisky and the campaign would be paid for by the saving in spectrometers, colorimeters and tintometers and their expert handlers which so many blending houses employ. I have seen a skilled tintometer operator carefully working out the amount of caramel colouring that goes into an eight-year-old (a very light colour this), a twelve-year-old (somewhat darker) and a twenty-year-old (darker still), blend, colouring the whisky according to its age[26] to fool the consumer into believing that the darker it is the older. They say that the sweet, gooey caramel stuff that goes into the whisky is in too insignificant proportions to affect the taste, but in the case of the darker coloured whiskies I am not so sure.[27]

---

[26] It is important to realize that by law the age on a bottle of blended Scotch whisky is the age of the *youngest* whisky in the blend.

[27] I put my argument against the artificial colouring of whisky to a Director of one of the 'Big Five' recently, and he would not accept it. He pointed out that with the continued expansion of Scotch whisky sales all over the world it would be impossible to convince everybody, including many who had just begun to drink Scotch whisky, that variation in colour did not mean variation in quality. Still. . . .

Many of the blending firms now put less caramel colouring into their whisky that is exported to America because of the American mystique about lightness and paleness. This is a very odd thing. The American drinker seems to associate lightness in body, lightness in colour, and less likelihood of the consumer becoming intoxicated. Anyone who has drunk colourless 119° proof whisky straight from the still will know how ridiculous this is. But lightness is a powerful word in whisky advertising in the United States, and there is scarcely a Scotch whisky advertised there that doesn't use the word somewhere in the description of the whisky's quality. Some blenders have put on the market two versions of their whisky, one, sold as 'lighter', with less artificial colouring than the other, the only real difference being visual. I am told that this experiment has not gone well, and I confess that I am glad. If by a 'light' Scotch whisky one means a blended Scotch with a higher proportion of patent-still grain whisky in it, then in my view a 'light' Scotch is an inferior Scotch. If by a 'light' Scotch whisky one means a whisky light in colour, then the consumer who prefers this should be given a whisky matured in plain oak casks (which might be of any quality, any degree of body, and any strength). If by a 'light' Scotch whisky one means one of less alcoholic content, then it is a question of reducing proof and colour has nothing to do with the matter at all. My complaint is that the artificial colouring of Scotch whisky is un-necessary and misleading and also that the confusion of different kinds of lightness in whisky advertising misleads the public. Indeed I will go further and say that much whisky advertising, especially in the United States, the greatest single importer of Scotch whisky, is calculated to confuse the public as to what Scotch whisky is and how it can be recognized. By all means let people drink what they prefer; if they really want their whisky sharp and bodiless and not full and subtly flavoured let them have it that way; but don't fool them about the meaning of colour or tell them fairy stories about the ancient Scottish tradition of blending when you are selling them a whisky which bears very little relation to what Scotch whisky was before the development of blending in the latter part of the last century. As for 'lightness', the only use of the term that is at all helpful in discussing whisky refers to the kind of difference between, say, the delicate and fragrant Glenmorangie and the full-bodied, peaty Laphroaig—a difference, that is, in body and peatiness.

There is a further paradox involved in this business of lightness. One 'light' blend of Scotch is alleged to have been invented at the end of Prohibition to appeal to an American palate destroyed by bath-tub gin and similar monstrosities and totally incapable of appreciating the body and flavour of malt whisky. A blend of this kind, with a high proportion of patent-still grain whisky, is *sharp* both to the nose and to the palate. Yet lightness also seems to be aimed at the ladies, who are assumed by some manufacturers and advertisers to prefer a spirit as *bland* and tasteless as possible. Hence the present popularity in the United States of vodka and its use in a great variety of cocktails. American whisky, too, especially blended whisky, is increasingly presented as light and smooth (i.e., bland), which means with less definite taste and nose. But I repeat that some of the heavily advertised 'light' Scotches are not bland at all, but possess the sharpness that comes from the very high percentage of grain whisky. It is as though the sharpness is accepted as a guarantee that this really is an alcoholic spirit but that in all other respects the whisky is expected to be as tasteless, odourless, bodiless and even colourless as possible.

Incidentally, it is not only whisky that has been affected by popular myths about colour and lightness. Beer-drinking habits in England have been changing in accordance with the same beliefs. Mr. J. A. P. Charrington, President of Bass Charrington, the large British brewing firm, discussed in a recent article the effect of increasing standardization of all kinds of consumer goods on changing tastes in beer as reflected by demand in English pubs. 'Beer is no exception to this overall standard-ization,' he wrote, 'and there is evidence that the public is moving from the highly hopped bitter beers to a smoother and blander palate. Young people particularly seem to prefer this kind of beer, and their popularity has been boosted by the strange belief that light coloured beers are alcoholically weaker and therefore safer with the breathalyser[28] threat.' Mr. Charrington also referred to the replacement of the traditional criterion of taste by the new criterion of stability and appearance in the customer's choice of beer. I suspect that this is happening over a wide variety of foods as well as drink; it seems to me to be a sad development.

Whisky matures in the cask and not in the bottle, and the kind of cask in which it matures is, of course, important. The practice of maturing malt whisky in sherry casks still goes on, though not universally: malt distilleries get sherry casks when they can and mature at least some of

---

[28]The breathalyser is a device for measuring the amount of alcohol consumed and is now regularly employed by the police in Britain in determining whether a motorist is unfit to drive through drink.

Steel torpedoes, filled with Scotch malt, found aboard the schooner
Rosie MB, New York 1926

their whisky in them. The single whisky they bottle (those that do bottle their single malts) may be 'vatted' in the sense of made up of the same whisky, perhaps of different ages, matured in different casks, some sherry and some plain. Only recently I saw a noble collection of sherry butts (casks of 110 gallons) that had just arrived at Glenmorangie distillery, but not all Glenmorangie whisky is matured in sherry wood.

Sherry casks are used again and again, and repaired by the insertion of new sections from casks too far gone to be usable, so that there are casks in use which are partly original sherry casks and partly made from other casks or from new wood. There is thus a gradual and progressive introduction of new casks, with the new wood mixed in bit by bit and old casks being 'cannibalized'. In the cooperage at Dewar's huge plant at Inveralmond—as at other such plants and at numerous distilleries throughout Scotland—you can see the cooper at work in the old traditional way, repairing or re-building casks. Of course, there are also independent cooperage firms who supply the whisky distillers and blenders—Speyside Cooperage Ltd. of Craigellachie, for example, who manufacture new casks and repair sherry casks and refill casks for a great variety of distillers. Though distillers and blenders use sherry casks when they can, for at least a proportion of their maturing whisky, plain oak casks that have been 'wine treated' or 'charcoal treated' are sometimes also used.

The best oak for maturing whisky is 'American white oak' (*Quercus alba*) from the United States. Many whisky casks are now imported direct from America. (Sherry casks, too, were often made from Arkansas oak and so came to Scotland from America via Spain: now they more and more come direct.) Casks that have held American bourbon whisky are imported in collapsed form and re-built with bigger ends into 55-gallon hogsheads. This is done for economic reasons: blenders own their casks which they send to particular distilleries for filling and may leave there for some time to mature before taking delivery. They pay for the whisky at the time of filling, and then have to pay rent to the distillery for as long as they leave the whisky there. The rent is so much for each cask below 80-gallon capacity, so much for each cask above 80-gallon capacity. The scale of charges is such that rental on small casks proves uneconomical. On the other hand, the bigger the cask the longer the period necessary for maturing, so the loss involved in having to wait a longer time till the whisky is ready must be balanced against the gain in having to pay a smaller rent.

Maturing is a less significant (and shorter) process for patent-still grain whisky: the most important part of the maturing process in a blended whisky is that which the malts in it have undergone before blending. Whisky once blended is kept at least six months in the cask (generally plain oak) to 'marry'. 'Vatted' whiskies—blended from malts of different distilleries—are now uncommon, but it is interesting that Dewars have recently put on the market a fine twelve-year-old 76° proof vatted malt whisky made up of matured malts they use for their luxury 'Ancestor' blend.

The proportion of single malts to blends consumed, even in Scotland, is very small; but there is nevertheless a steady rise in the availability and the consumption of single malts both in Britain and in certain overseas countries. I have seen a variety of single malt whiskies in a shop window in Venice, and in April 1975 I learned that a five-year-old Glen Grant was the best-selling whisky in Italy. At a large liquor supermarket in Berkeley, California, I found some years ago, among an enormous variety of blended Scotch whiskies, both Glenlivet and Laphroaig (the former the twelve-year-old whisky bottled by the distillery in the familiar buff label), and the manager told me, somewhat to my surprise, that Laphroaig was the more popular, though the sales of neither compared to the sales of the blends. It was, incidentally, the same manager who told me that American whisky drinkers demanded a 'light' whisky but were confused as to whether this meant light in colour, light in body, or with less alcohol content. This was far from the first or the last time that I heard this.

Few single malt whiskies are advertised: they apparently make their way by verbal recommendation from the knowing to the less knowing. One occasionally sees them well displayed in the windows of wine merchants in Scotland: notable examples are Muirhead's in Edinburgh (owned by Macdonald and Muir, who own Glenmorangie and Glen Moray distilleries) and two Elgin wine and spirit merchants who themselves bottle a large number of malt whiskies—Gordon & Macphail and A. Campbell Hope and King, the former having a number of associated companies which export, blend, bond and distribute whisky. Some (but far from all) hotels in Scotland carry a wide range of single malts, though I must confess that some years ago when I asked what malts they had at the bar of a well-known hotel in Stirling, the barman told me that they only had Canadian Club! I suspect that the situation has changed now. The Staff Club at Edinburgh University is famous for the range of single malts it carries. Glenfiddich is the only single malt Scotch whisky that has advertised consistently over a period of years; more recently Arthur Bell and Sons have been advertising their Dufftown and Blair Athol malt whiskies and their third malt, Inchgower, is also now available. I have found, in certain academic circles in America, an awareness and appreciation of single malts, and when dining recently with the distinguished American bibliographer Professor Fredson Bowers at Charlottesville, Virginia, I was offered a choice of Glenlivet and Talisker. As long ago as 1950, when I was teaching at Cornell University, I introduced American friends to Mortlach, available at Macy's in New York, and they took to it with enthusiasm. Perhaps the fact that it was matured in plain oak and was virtually colourless was held to be in its favour. I remember that I was asked to give a talk at the University on Scotch whisky, and in the course of my remarks I observed that one of the 'best buys' in pot-still Highland malt whisky was the Mortlach available at Macy's. The next time I went to Macy's to re-stock for myself I was told that they were out of stock. When I expressed astonishment, the assistant said: 'Some damn fool professor at Cornell has been telling all his students to buy it, and we've run out.'

Single malt whiskies bottled and supplied in the United Kingdom by the DCL group are Aultmore, Cardhu, Clynelish, Glendullan, Lagavulin, Linkwood, Ord and Talisker, and also Rosebank, a Lowland malt. Some others of their malt whiskies are available in certain overseas markets. Among available single malt whiskies from distilleries outside the DCL group are Aberlour, Bowmore, The Glendronach (available in England since 1971), Glenlivet, Glen Grant, Glenfiddich, Glenmorangie, Glen Moray (since 1974) and Highland Park.

It has been suggested that there is a connection between the increased availability of single whiskies and the pushing of the 'lighter' blends with a greater proportion of grain; for the higher the proportion of grain whisky the less malt whisky will be used. As I have already mentioned, the blending firms will not themselves admit that these 'lighter' blends include a higher proportion of grain, though my own experience both in tasting and in talking to people working in blending firms is that the trend to a higher proportion of grain whisky in at least some blends is a real one. Anyway, we can at least observe what Cyril Ray has called the 'odd coincidence: the growing popularity of the whiskies at opposite ends of the scale of taste—the light blends that seem, at any rate, to incline more in character towards the grain whiskies, and the heavy unblended malts.'

So the 'self whisky' has survived the great international popularity of the blends and, in spite of some sticky moments, Aeneas Coffey's invention has not proved to be the end of the true pot-still malt whisky. It is not easy to predict the future. Some have seen the temptation 'to market blends of cheap grain whisky flavoured slightly with very young malt whisky' (in Professor McDowall's words) as a threat to the future of quality Scotches. The minimum age of three years (which many believe, as I do, ought to be increased to five) applies only to whisky sold on the home market, not to whisky exported, though if exported under three years old it must be described as spirit, not as whisky. There is a considerable export of fairly young whiskies in cask to America, where they are blended in some odd ways and given some odd names. Of course, many reputable blends are shipped to the U.S.A. in cask, which saves the Americans tax. And in spite of my objections to the way in which some blended whiskies are advertised, I can testify from my own knowledge to the integrity, efficiency and co-operativeness of DCL, whose distilleries are always clean and attractive and whose malt whiskies are produced in the traditional manner. Still, the expanding international consumption of Scotch whisky is bringing a great many new firms into the act, some of them more interested in selling their product than in maintaining quality. After all, the selling of Scotch whisky is one of the major businesses in the world, and I have myself spoken to people in the Scotch whisky trade (and not newcomers either) who seem willing to do pretty well anything to their whisky if they can produce it more cheaply and sell it in larger quantities. The danger of any alcoholic drink is that it can always be sold to those who simply want an alcoholic kick from it and have no interest in its quality and flavour.

Whisky, even if it is not Scotch whisky, is also being produced in increasing quantities in countries other than Scotland. Whether any other country will ever be able to produce a 'Scotch-type' whisky which is really comparable to genuine Scotch whisky in nature and quality remains doubtful. But if they don't it won't be for lack of trying. If such attempts outside Scotland are accompanied by a cutting of corners on the part of Scotch whisky distillers (speeding up and cheapening the process to produce less good whisky more easily) the future of Scotch whisky may well be in jeopardy. It is in the last analysis the great blending firms who determine what goes on in the whisky industry, and it is to be hoped that their sense of responsibility for maintaining quality will not be allowed to diminish. The only thing that the consumer can do in order to ensure that quality is maintained is to cultivate his palate, to learn to drink his Scotch whisky with true appreciation and discrimination. The scattered observations on different whiskies to be found in the next chapter are meant as one man's somewhat impressionistic contribution to that learning process.

Chapter Seven
INDIVIDUAL DISTILLERIES

In this chapter I propose to say something more about individual distilleries and blending companies to show the situation as it is today. In chapter 2 I talked about the prestige of Glenlivet whisky even before George Smith decided to go legitimate in 1824. That prestige did not diminish after Smith's re-built and improved distillery began a new phase of its history. The distillery was at Upper Drumin, thirty-five miles partly over difficult country to the coast of the Moray Firth, and the whisky was sent by horse and cart to Garmouth and Burghead on the Firth whence it went south by boat. In 1863 the extension of the railway to Ballindalloch, about seven miles from the distillery, eased the transport problem somewhat. By this time Smith's son, Colonel John Gordon Smith, was in partnership with his father, and succeeded him on the latter's death at an advanced age in 1871. The Upper Drumin distillery had originally a capacity of only 50 gallons a week, which was increased to 200 gallons in 1839, but even this increase proved insufficient to meet the growing demand for Glenlivet. George Smith—who was an enterprising and pioneering farmer and cattle breeder as well as a distiller, and a great reclaimer of waste ground—had kept increasing the acreage he farmed, and in 1840 had taken the farm of Delnabo, above Tomintoul, where he had built another, smaller, distillery, the Cairngorm. But he and his son were still dissatisfied with their production of whisky: in 1858 they built a new and larger distillery on the farm of Minmore, which George Smith had first leased in 1840. The other two distilleries were scrapped, for the new Glenlivet distillery produced 600 gallons a week. Two new stills were put in in 1896 and the warehousing capacity has been much expanded since John Gordon Smith built four bonded warehouses in the 1860s. Until recently there were two still houses, each with one wash still and one spirit still, and ten wooden wash-backs. Although the Faemussach moss, with its great peat deposits, lies near

129

The Glenlivet distillery from an engraving 1890

the distillery, it has not done its own malting since 1966. Until 1972 the stills were heated by coal fires.

Such was the prestige of Glenlivet by the middle of the nineteenth century that other distilleries, not actually situated in Glenlivet but in that general part of Scotland, began to call themselves Glenlivet. It came to be said that Glenlivet was the longest glen in Scotland, so many distilleries were apparently situated there. In 1880 John Gordon Smith decided to go to law to protect the name of his whisky. The court's decision was that only Smith's Glenlivet was legally entitled to the name Glenlivet without any qualification. Other distilleries which used the name must hyphenate it with the true name of the particular distillery. Thus a large number of Eastern malt distilleries decided to hyphenate the word 'Glenlivet' with their name: Aberlour-Glenlivet, Aultmore-Glenlivet, Balmenach-Glenlivet, Balvenie-Glenlivet, Benromach-Glenlivet, Coleburn-Glenlivet, Convalmore-Glenlivet, Cragganmore-Glenlivet, Craigellachie-Glenlivet, Dailuaine-Glenlivet, Dufftown-Glenlivet, Glenburgie-Glenlivet, Glendullan-Glenlivet, Glen Elgin-Glenlivet,

Glenfarclas-Glenlivet, Glen Grant-Glenlivet, Glen Keith-Glenlivet, Glenlossie-Glenlivet, Glen Moray-Glenlivet, Glenrothes-Glenlivet, Imperial-Glenlivet, Longmorn-Glenlivet, Macallan-Glenlivet, Miltonduff-Glenlivet, Speyburn-Glenlivet, Tamdhu-Glenlivet. These are fine whiskies, some of them splendid. DCL does not now use the name 'Glenlivet' in the titles of any of its distilleries, and this makes sense, since none in the above list really needs this designation to prove its merit. The only whisky which can call itself 'The Glenlivet', or just Glenlivet, is 'Smith's Glenlivet'.

Only 5 per cent of Glenlivet is today bottled as a single whisky: the rest goes to the blenders, and virtually all the important blenders take some Glenlivet. The distillery itself bottles (though not at the distillery) only a twelve-year-old, which is splendid, though I have tasted admirable older Glenlivets bottled by Berry Bros. & Rudd. Other bottlers bottle it at different ages: Gordon & MacPhail of Elgin bottle a variety of ages, each with a differently coloured label. If I had to single out one classic of malt whiskies it would be the twelve-year-old Glenlivet.

But to return to the history of Glenlivet. John Gordon Smith died in 1901 and was succeeded by his nephew, Colonel George Smith Grant, son of Margaret Smith (who was the daughter of the original George Smith) and William Grant. Colonel Smith Grant kept up the Glenlivet tradition of farming as well as distilling. He was a great stock breeder, and had a notable Aberdeen-Angus herd. He was succeeded in 1918 by his younger son William Henry Smith Grant, after the death in the war in May of that year of his elder son John Gordon Smith Grant. In March 1951 the firm became a private company with Captain William Smith Grant as Chairman and in 1952 it joined with another distinguished distilling firm, J. & J. Grant, Glen Grant Ltd., to form a public company, The Glenlivet & Glen Grant Distilleries Ltd.

In 1972 the hitherto independent blending firm of Hill Thomson merged with the Glenlivet and Glen Grant Distilleries to form The Glenlivet Distilleries Ltd. Glenlivet Distillery has seen many changes in recent years. They now have three pairs of stills (three wash stills, three spirit stills) in the same building and in 1972 they introduced gas (LPG) firing. Nothing, however, is changed in the actual method of distilling. There has been no speeding up, even though this would be possible with gas heating, for this might affect the quality of the whisky. They built a new mash house in 1972 and a new still house in 1973. Their new mash tuns are all covered (this is becoming standard practice in distilleries), and this keeps everything cleaner. Three mashes are produced every twenty-four hours. They have three double-size washbacks,

The Smugglers' Cave.

each holding 14,200 gallons. They now use condensers instead of the traditional worm-and-tub for cooling, which is much more efficient and is also becoming more and more common in distilleries. There has been no cut-back in production. The distillery works 168 hours a week, with a staggered shut-down for cleaning. The gas firing of the stills means that one man now looks after six stills whereas previously two men looked after four. Automatic controls make the work lighter and more precise, thus increasing rather than threatening the effectiveness of the traditional mode of distilling.

Glen Grant distillery was founded by John and James Grant who in 1840 moved their distillery from Dandaleith, where they had been distilling whisky since 1834, two and a half miles north to Rothes (between Craigellachie and Elgin). Legend has it that well before 1834 they were whisky smugglers in Glenlivet. But we do know for certain that James Grant, who may well have known George Smith, studied law in Edinburgh and in 1829, at the age of twenty-eight, set up as a solicitor in Elgin. But law did not satisfy him, and he moved to a number of other activities including distilling. By March 1842 a writer in *The Second Statistical Account of Scotland* was able to talk about 'one of the most extensive distilleries in the North . . . established in Rothes by Messrs. J. and J. Grant, in which establishment between

30,000 and 40,000 gallons of whisky are annually made.' With the distillery producing 1,500 gallons of whisky a week it is not surprising that James Grant became interested in railways: transport has always been a problem for Highland malt distillers. He worked hard and successfully to get a railway laid between Lossiemouth and Elgin and between Elgin and Rothes, and served as Provost of Elgin for fifteen years. James Grant was succeeded in 1872 by his son, Major James Grant, who died in 1931 at the age of eighty-three and was succeeded by his grandson, Mr. Douglas Mackessack, who is now managing director of both Glen Grant and Caperdonich distilleries.

Glen Grant distillery at Rothes was considerably enlarged in 1865, seven years before James Grant's death. In 1897 Major James Grant built a second distillery. At the insistence of the excise authorities, the whisky from the new distillery had to be pumped to the original distillery, where the two whiskies were mixed. The whisky was pumped through a pipe which crossed the main street of Rothes and was known locally as the 'Whisky Pipe'. But the end of the whisky boom which followed the Pattison failure in 1898 made it increasingly difficult to keep the new distillery going, and it had to close down in 1901. However, the steady expansion of whisky exports which has led to the present prosperity of the whisky industry led Grants to reopen the second distillery in 1965. It is now called Caperdonich distillery and was completely modernized in 1967. Before 1967 it operated with its two original stills, one wash still and one spirit still. Now it has two new stills (one wash still and one spirit still) heated by steam coils and it also has a remarkable system of automatic controls. Any process can now be operated by button-pushing from a central position. The grinding of a specific quantity of malt, the charging or discharging of the stills, the starting of conveyors and the opening of elevators—all this can be done from a central control. Neither Glen Grant nor Caperdonich now does its own malting; they buy their malt ready dried from Robert Hutchison & Co. Ltd. of Kirkcaldy and other suppliers. This is increasingly the practice with distillers.

Caperdonich distillery and Glen Grant distillery use water from the same burn, but, of course, the two whiskies are not identical. A five-year-old Caperdonich was sold in Italy for a short period, to supplement the five-year-old Glen Grant for which the demand exceeded the supply, but when Hill Thomson were absorbed in Glenlivet Distilleries they wanted it all for their luxury blend 'Something Special' and so none was left for bottling as a single whisky. Most of Glen Grant, too—at least 95 per cent—goes to the blenders; as with Glenlivet it is taken by every one of the important blenders. But fortunately, again as with Glenlivet, it is also available as a single whisky. Some is matured in sherry casks, and a smaller quantity in plain oak. A variety of ages are available; I should say that the fifteen-year-old shows the whisky at its best, but the ten-year-old is a fine whisky and the eight-year-old is eminently drinkable. The Glen Grant label, by the way, has remained unchanged for generations: it is a splendid example of Victorian design.

Glen Grant distillery has a new still house, with two new stills and space for four more. Four stills are coal-fired; the two new ones are fired by LPG gas. There has been an increase of 63 per cent over the capacity of the original two coal-fired stills, with a projected increase of 163 per cent when the four new stills are finally introduced. There are four new wash-backs.

There are about fifty Highland malt distilleries situated near enough to the Spey valley for their product to be considered Speyside whisky. Over twenty of these, as we have seen, hyphenate 'Glenlivet' to their name. In spite of common features possessed by all Speyside whiskies, each has its own distinctive quality: some are discussed below. Each distillery, too, has its characteristic customs and methods, though all use the traditional pot-still process. Many have been modernized in recent years, but new stills have always scrupulously copied the shape of the old. The small but numerous low wines stills of Glenfiddich distillery, for example, strike the observer's eye: on one side there are five low wines stills of 1,100 gallons capacity and two wash stills of 2,000 gallons, and on the other side three low wines stills and two wash stills. Glenfiddich is one of the growing number of distilleries that buy their malt. Longmorn, the distillery near Elgin that was founded in 1894, for long used coal fires. Its four wash stills are still fired by solid fuel but its four spirit stills are now heated by steam cones (not coils), which give a very fine control. Of the eight stills, three use worm tubs for cooling and five use condensers. Longmorn still does some of its own malting, but this represents a small proportion of the malt it uses. Its new wash tuns are covered, as at Glenlivet. Altogether Longmorn, with its recently increased capacity and new automatic controls, gives the impression of a distillery that faces the future with complete confidence. It has more than doubled its production of whisky in recent years. Its sister distillery of Benriach, almost next door, which was reopened in 1965 after a long period of idleness, uses steam coils. (Both these distilleries belong to the same company.) Benriach now produces a light-bodied malt whisky, which goes entirely for blending. Some stillmen claim that coal fires have something to do with the quality of the whisky produced, others do not think so. In the bright new distillery of Tormore, where the eight wash-backs are of steel and are cleaned by an automatic device known as 'Sputnik', their four stills (two wash stills of 4,050 gallons capacity and two low wines stills of 3,000 gallons) are heated by coal fires, automatically stoked.

One could pick out examples of varying practices and varying beliefs from a great range of Highland malt distilleries. To look further north than Speyside, Glenmorangie distillery has unusually high stills—both the wash stills and the low wines stills are of the same height, the former of 3,500 gallons capacity and the latter of 2,000 gallons—and they attribute the quality of the whisky partly to the height of the stills, which have long been heated by steam coils. In some distilleries the low wines stills are distinctly smaller and of a slightly different shape from that of the wash stills; in others they are about the same. In Lagavulin distillery, Islay, the stills are heated by coal fires. In nearby Laphroaig Distillery, the stills are heated by steam coils; there are two wash stills of 2,000 gallons capacity each and three low wines stills of 800 gallons. They also do their own malting, and the last time I was there they were using Australian barley. Laphroaig is the only distillery in Scotland with a woman as chairman—Mrs. Wishart Campbell, who combines a brisk efficiency with charm.

One could go on rambling round the malt distilleries, picking out characteristics of each, but enough has probably been said to give some idea of their differences as well as their common features. Of the ninety-five Highland malt distilleries (including eight in Islay and two in Campbeltown) now operating, forty-five are in the DCL group and are operated by Scottish Malt Distillers Ltd. Of the ten Lowland malt distilleries now functioning, DCL through SMD operate three (Glenkinchie, Rosebank and St. Magdalene). Among the DCL Highland malt distilleries are twenty in the Speyside area (Aultmore, Benrinnes, Benromach, Balmenach, Cardow, Coleburn, Convalmore, Cragganmore, Craigellachie, Dailuaine, Dallas Dhu, Glendullan, Glen Elgin, Glenlossie, Glentauchers, Imperial, Knockdhu, Linkwood, Mortlach and Speyburn), two in the Moray Firth area (Banff and Royal Brackla), three near the east coast (Brechin, Glenury and Hillside), one on Deeside (Lochnagar), two in Central Scotland (Dalwhinnie and Aberfeldy), one in Inverness (Millburn), one not far away at Beauly (Ord), one at Fort William (Glenlochy), one at Oban (Oban), one on the Cromarty Firth (Teaninich), and two (Clynelish and Brora) in Sutherland. In 1972, by buying complete control of Mackinlays & Birnie, DCL acquired Glen Albyn and Glen Mhor distilleries. The Islay distilleries of Caol Ila,

The Lagavulin distillery, Isle of Islay

Lagavulin and Port Ellen are also in the DCL group, as is Talisker, on the Isle of Skye. Five distilleries are owned by the Highland Distilleries Company, Limited, a company which dates back to 1887. They are the Islay distillery of Bunnahabhain, Glen Rothes-Glenlivet, Tamdhu-Glenlivet, and Highland Park, the last being one of the Orkney distilleries of which the other is Scapa, acquired by Hiram Walker in 1965 and run by Taylor & Ferguson. The ownership of the other Highland malt distilleries is indicated in the accounts of the rise of the various blending companies either above in chapter 4 or below in this chapter. Some are still family businesses or run by private limited companies. Macallan-Glenlivet (it is now dropping the 'Glenlivet' from its label) is owned by R. Kemp-Macallan-Glenlivet Ltd.; Glenfarclas-Glenlivet is owned by J. & G. Grant Ltd.; Tomatin is owned by Tomatin Distillers Ltd., a public company; Longmorn-Glenlivet and nearby, Benriach are owned by the Glenlivet Distilleries Ltd. The attractive little distillery of Edradour near Pitlochry is owned by the firm of William Whitley & Co. of Leith (a nineteenth-century firm which has since 1922 been a subsidiary of Glenforres Distillery Company, a large and active

136

company which produces a great variety of blends, including 'House of Lords' and 'King's Ransom'). Of the two Campbeltown distilleries Glen Scotia has been owned by A. Gillies & Co. (Distillers) Ltd. from 1955 to 1970, when it was absorbed in Amalgamated Distilled Products Ltd., and Springbank, which was built by the Mitchell family in 1823, is owned by J. & A. Mitchell & Co. Ltd. The Islay distillery of Bruichladdich, attractively situated on the shores of Loch Indaal, is owned by Invergordon Distilleries Ltd. Bowmore distillery, opposite Bruichladdich on the other side of the loch, is owned by Sherriff's Bowmore Distillery Ltd., whose principal Director is S. P. Morrison of Stanley P. Morrison Ltd., Glasgow whisky brokers. Ardbeg distillery, a little up the east coast of Islay from Lagavulin, Laphroaig and Port Ellen, is independently owned. The Islay distilleries are all picturesquely situated on the seashore.

I do not know how many blends of Scotch whisky there are now on the market, but I do know that I am continuously being surprised at discovering new blends I had never heard of before. Not long ago the manager of a very large liquor store in the United States showed me his 'bin book', and the number of different blended Scotches listed there astonished me. The quality of course varies greatly. One is liable to find more inferior blends abroad than at home, because blenders abroad can do what they like with whiskies of different ages and qualities imported in cask. Unscrupulous traders can also re-fill labelled bottles with whisky not of the quality described on the label. In some South American countries whisky must be sold in bottles which have special tops which allow the contents to be poured out but do not allow anything to be poured in: I have seen such tops on bottles being filled for the South American market at Dewar's bottling plant at Inveralmond. There does not appear to be any significant variation in quality—that is, in the proportion of well-matured fine Highland malts in the blend—among the great number of standard blended Scotches put out by firms in DCL, though there are clearly discernible differences in body, sweetness, peatiness, sharpness to the nose, and other aspects of taste and smell. Many of these differences are not, however, discernible to the casual drinker and only become apparent if one has learned to know a particular blend very well (drinking it neat or with water) and then tries a different one. A trained taster can, of course, tell differences at once, and by smell only. But I repeat a point I have made before: most drinkers of whisky and soda (and *a fortiori* of whisky and ginger ale or whisky with any highly flavoured mixer) who ask for a particular brand would not know the difference if given a brand other than the one they ordered if it came out of a bottle which bore the label of the brand demanded. It is not unknown for a barman to say, on being asked for a particular blend, 'We've run out of it here; I'll just bring some from the other bar,' and return with a glass allegedly of the requested blend but actually of some other one. In the great majority of cases he gets away with it. Nor is it unknown—I am speaking of experiences in Britain which I can vouch for—for barmen simply to serve a different whisky from the one demanded on the (generally justified) assumption that the drinker will not taste the difference. In

Bunnahabhain distillery, Isle of Islay

such a case he has his back to the customer when pouring the whisky and arranges that the customer does not see what bottle it comes from.

But in fact most Scotch whisky drinkers, in Britain at least, do not ask for a blend by name, but simply ask for a 'whisky' or a 'Scotch'. The blenders, who after all spend a great deal of effort in getting their blend right, resent this, and I think it is true to say that most of them would prefer to have customers ask for a specific blend even if it is not their own: it is the habit of specifying the blend that they want to encourage.[29] The increasing take-over of pubs and hotels in England by breweries has led to a restriction in the number of blends available, for the brewers understandably prefer to push the blends of the firms with which they have a business connection. The ramifications are often complicated. 'Queen Anne', a blend previously produced by Hill Thomson but now produced by The Glenlivet Distilleries Ltd. which absorbed Hill Thomson in 1972, is now sold in the 6,000 pubs owned by the brewing firm of Courage, because Courage is a subsidiary of Imperial Group (best known for its cigarettes and tobaccos) which has acquired $27\frac{1}{2}$ per cent of the shares in Glenlivet Distilleries. (11 per cent of the shares in Glenlivet Distilleries are owned by the largest Japanese distillery group, Suntory.) In December 1977 it was announced that Seagram Investments Inc., a wholly-owned U.S. subsidiary of the Canadian group Seagram, had made a successful bid for Glenlivet Distilleries with an offer of 510p a share. In 1970 the brewery firm of Bass Charrington took over the UK marketing of 'Vat 69', so that blend became the 'pouring whisky' of Bass Charrington's 10,000 pubs.

In an earlier chapter I discussed the 'Big Five' of DCL—Haig, Dewar, Walker, Buchanan, Mackie (White Horse)—and a sixth who really belongs with them, Sanderson. But, of course, there are many admirable smaller firms in DCL, some of them long established. D. & J. McCallum Ltd. of Edinburgh, for example, goes back to 1807 when the brothers Duncan and John McCallum established themselves as wine and spirit merchants and innkeepers. Their inn, popularly known as the 'Tattie Pit', was a well-known Edinburgh rendezvous. The brothers' wine and spirit business expanded, and on their death (they had both remained bachelors) it was taken over by their nephew Duncan Stewart, who developed McCallum's 'Perfection' blend. McCallums own Glenlochy distillery in Fort William. The firm merged with DCL in 1953. McCallum's head office is at 4 Picardy Place, at the east end of Edinburgh's 'New Town', a handsome Georgian house with fine Adam interior decoration and fireplaces. McCallum's 'Perfection' is one

---

[29] As a Director of one of the 'Big Five' blending firms said to me the other day: 'After all, nobody would think of simply asking for a packet of cigarettes or an ounce of tobacco, without specifying the brand.' Incidentally, 70 per cent to 80 per cent of Scotch whisky sales in Europe are over-the-counter sales and not bar sales.

of the few whiskies to call itself on the label 'Scots whisky' rather than 'Scotch whisky'. It is exported to more than sixty countries, with especially important markets in Australia and New Zealand.

John Begg was one of the many Scotsmen who took advantage of the 1823 Act to build a legitimate distillery. He built Lochnagar distillery, near Balmoral, in 1825, and Queen Victoria visited it, with Prince Albert, the Prince of Wales, Prince Alfred and the Princess Royal on 12 September 1848. John Begg recorded the event in his journal. He asked Prince Albert if he would like to taste a dram. 'H.R.H. having agreed to this, I called for a bottle and glasses (which had been previously in readiness) and, presenting one glass to Her Majesty, she tasted it. So did His Royal Highness the Prince. I then presented a glass to the Princess Royal, and to the Prince of Wales, and Prince Alfred, all of whom tasted the spirit.' As a result of this visit, Lochnagar distillery was allowed to call itself 'Royal'. (The only previous granting of the appellation 'royal' to a distillery had been to Captain William Fraser of Brackla distillery by King William IV in 1835. As an advertisement in the *Morning Chronicle* put it at the time: 'His Majesty, having been pleased to distinguish this "by his royal Command to supply his Establishment", has placed this Whisky first on the list of British Spirits. . . .' The Royal Brackla distillery is now owned by John Bisset.) A single malt from the Lochnagar distillery is not, unfortunately, now available except to privileged visitors to the distillery. It almost all goes for blending—to Sanderson for 'Vat 69' as well as to 'John Begg' itself, a well-established blend and the only whisky I know of which once, in a Glasgow Jewish newspaper, advertised in Yiddish, translating its erstwhile advertising slogan 'Take a peg of John Begg' into 'Nem a schmeck fun Dzon Bek'. John Begg has been in DCL since 1916.

Other blending companies in DCL include Bulloch, Lade, which has owned the Islay distillery of Caol Ila since 1857 and merged with DCL in 1927: its de luxe blend, 'Old Rarity', is highly esteemed by many who like a light-bodied whisky bottled at a slightly higher proof than is normal. Its regular blend is 'BL Gold Label'. There is also the Leith blending firm of A. & A. Crawford, dating from 1860, which joined DCL in 1944. They have two long-established blends, 'Three Star' and, a de luxe blend, 'Five Star', both well thought of. There are other blending houses with excellent reputations within the DCL group; my present purpose, however, is not to provide a catalogue of all such firms but merely to give some idea of their range and variety.

The range of DCL blended Scotch whiskies is wide, from the full-flavoured 'White Horse' with its discernible Islay component to the sweeter, less peaty 'Vat 69'. In the middle of this spectrum I would place Dewar's,[30] a sound blend leaning neither to smokiness on the one hand nor sweetness on the other, together with 'Black and White' and 'Johnnie Walker'. 'Haig' has a bit more fullness than these: Professor McDowall has spoken of its 'delicious after-flavour which lingers on the palate', but, while I find it a thoroughly agreeable blend, I cannot say that I myself have been struck by this after-taste. Which goes to show the extraordinarily personal quality of whisky appreciation. Not only do some drinkers prefer a flavour which others positively dislike (the distinctive flavour of 'White Horse', for example, makes it a whisky which people who really taste the whisky they drink either insist on or avoid), but some actually taste or smell elements which others cannot discover at all. I have already declared my interest: I am normally a drinker of single pot-still malt whiskies, though there are a considerable number of blends which I drink with pleasure in the appropriate circumstances.

All of the DCL blended Scotch whiskies are conscientiously produced blends of good quality, but this does not mean that some independent firms do not produce admirable blends. Matthew Gloag and Son of Perth, a small but long-established firm which was bought by Highland Distilleries in 1970, produce in their 'Famous Grouse' whisky a very fine blend, full and round, containing an unusually high proportion of matured malts. Personally, I would put 'Grouse' whisky very near the top of my list of blended Scotches. There are also larger and more widely known firms outside the DCL group who produce fine blends. I can discuss only a few of these, but would emphasize that this book makes no claim to provide a full list of producers of good blended Scotch whisky: there is bound to be an element of arbitrariness in the selection I mention.

One of the oldest as well as one of the largest independent Scotch whisky firms is that of Arthur Bell & Sons Ltd., whose history begins in Perth in 1825. In that year a distiller named T. R. Sandeman opened a shop on the south side of the ancient church of St. John and began to trade as a whisky-merchant. Some years later the business was operated by James Roy and shortly before the middle of the nineteenth century it

---

[30] Dewar's is known as 'White Label' in the United States and in most foreign countries. It is, however, known as 'Dewar's' in Canada, Australia and New Zealand as well as in Great Britain. Dewar's de luxe blend, 'Ancestor', is on sale in Canada as 'Ne Plus Ultra' but as 'Ancestor' elsewhere throughout the world.

was known as Roy and Miller. Arthur Bell joined the firm in 1851 and for a time it was known as Roy and Bell. It was Bell and Sandeman between 1862 and 1865, in which year Arthur Bell took over sole control. In 1895 he was joined by his two sons, Arthur Kinmond Bell and Robert Bell, and the firm assumed the name of Arthur Bell & Sons. Bell's became a limited company in 1922, shortly after opening its present headquarters in Victoria Street, Perth. A. K. Bell (widely known as 'A. K.') became Chairman and Managing Director of the limited company: the original Arthur Bell had died in 1900. 'A. K.' was a notable figure in Perth, and is remembered for his establishment of the Gannochy Trust which has done so much for the amenities of the city.

Lochnagar

There is now no longer a Bell among the company's directors. The present Chairman and Managing Director is Mr. W. G. Farquharson, who took over on A. K. Bell's death in 1942.

The firm was not, of course, originally a blending firm. It purchased pot-still malt whisky from farmer-distillers and stored it in its warehouses in Perth before sale. It was the blending boom of the last three decades of the nineteenth century that brought Bell's into blending, at first on a small scale, buying whiskies from different distilleries. In 1933, during a period of depression for Scotch whisky, when many distilleries found it hard or impossible to carry on, Bell's bought the Blair Athol distillery, Pitlochry, and the Dufftown-Glenlivet distillery, Dufftown, and in 1936 they bought Inchgower distillery (near Buckie on the Moray Firth). In the eighteenth century the area around Pitlochry had been noted for illegal distilling, and Blair Athol distillery, taking advantage, like George Smith of Glenlivet, of the new Act of 1823, 'went legitimate' in 1825. Inchgower distillery had been built in 1871 and Dufftown in 1887.

Bell's still maintains its head office in Perth. They have bonded warehouses at Perth, Edinburgh, Halbeath (near Dunfermline, Fife) and Auchtermuchty (Fife). In 1967 they opened a £1,000,000 bottling and blending plant on an eighteen-acre site at East Mains Industrial Estate near Broxburn, West Lothian. This includes a huge bottling hall with six loading tables and provision for an additional three to be installed later. The bottling is automatic, with an electronic console controlling the flow of whisky to each bottling line. Some blending is still done at the firm's older premises at Leith.

Bell's advertising slogan is 'Afore ye go', which appears at the base of the neck of each bottle. It is the largest selling whisky in Scotland, fairly light in body, slightly sharp to the nose, but with an agreeable after-taste of Eastern malts. Bell's has 11 per cent of the total United Kingdom Scotch whisky market, coming equal with Teacher's Highland Cream after Haig (15 per cent) and Johnnie Walker (12 per cent).

Another old-established blended whisky outside the DCL group is 'Long John', with a history also going back to 1825, when John Macdonald, known as Long John because of his great height, took advantage of the 1823 Act and built Ben Nevis distillery at Fort William. Long John died in 1856, and his son took over the distillery. But the firm did not remain in the Macdonald family. The name 'Long John' was sold in 1911 to W. H. Chaplin & Co. Ltd., London wine and spirit merchants, by which time the whisky was no longer the Highland malt whisky it had originally been, but a blend. In 1935 Long John

The Tormore distillery

Distilleries Ltd., as the firm had by now become, was taken over by Seager Evans, originally established in 1805 as gin distillers in London. Long John had in 1927 built the Strathclyde distillery in Glasgow, a patent-still grain distillery, and in 1937 the firm acquired the Highland malt distillery of Glenugie, near Peterhead, which had been built in 1875. In 1956 Seager Evans was bought by Schenley Industries, Inc. of the United States. Schenleys brought new capital and vigorous new expansion into the production of 'Long John'. Mr. John Mackie, a Scot who had spent twelve years working with Canadian Schenley Ltd., returned to his native country to be chairman of Seager Evans and to pursue the policy of expansion. In 1957 Long John Distilleries built the Lowland malt distillery of Kinclaith near Glasgow and in 1958–9 built their splendid new Tormore distillery, designed by Sir Albert Richardson, past President of the Royal Academy. Tormore is now one of the show malt distilleries on Speyside, and has recently bottled its own eight-year-old single malt whisky. At the same time Long John has enormously expanded its warehousing facilities and is planning as a long-term project a great new complex of distilleries, warehouses, and bottling plant at Westthorn Farm, Glasgow, where they already have a warehousing and blending depot and where the building of a great new bottling plant has already commenced. It is some time since I have tasted 'Long John', but I remember it as a whisky somewhere in the middle of the spectrum, lacking that metallic taste which I sometimes detect in blends.

Seager Evans and Co. changed its name to Long John International in 1971. They have available for their 'Long John' whisky two Highland malt distilleries (Tormore and Glenugie), a Lowland malt distillery at Kinclaith and a grain whisky distillery at Strathclyde. In addition, they have the distinguished Islay distillery of Laphroaig, run by the Johnston family from 1815 to 1954 and owned by D. Johnston & Co. Ltd. since 1950: in 1962 D. Johnston & Co. merged with Seager Evans. The story of 'Long John' whisky thus involves a pattern of amalgamation and expansion reminiscent of that of DCL itself. Long John Distilleries Ltd. still exist as a working entity, and the name will be found on bottles of 'Long John' and of Tormore. Laphroaig is bottled under the label 'D. Johnston & Co. (Laphroaig) Ltd.', as is 'Islay Mist', a blend of Laphroaig and other whiskies. Seager Evans also put out 'Black Bottle', a blend, through Gordon Graham & Co. of Aberdeen.

Another important independent firm is William Grant & Sons Ltd., whose brand name 'Standfast' (from the Grant clan battle cry, 'Stand Fast!') is over seventy-five years old. The original William Grant of Glenfiddich worked for some years in Mortlach distillery before building Glenfiddich distillery, which began operations in 1887. It is said that the first salesman for Grant's whisky made 500 calls before he sold a case; but they have come a long way since then. The firm built Balvenie distillery, Dufftown, in 1871, and in 1955 greatly enlarged their original Glenfiddich distillery. In 1962 they opened a £1,250,000 grain distillery at Girvan, Ayrshire, and a vast blending and bottling plant at Paisley, with four automatic bottling lines. They have also recently opened Ladyburn Lowland malt distillery at Girvan. 'Standfast' is one of the notable blends, and is exported to 154 countries as well as enjoying a comfortable share of the home market. Grant's also bottle their Glenfiddich as a straight malt whisky, the first straight malt to be publicized in a national advertising campaign. In 1973 they put their other single malt whisky, 'Balvenie', on the market. Both are characteristic eastern malts, 'Glenfiddich' slightly the less peaty of the two but both are light on peatiness. I personally prefer either of these malts to 'Standfast', but the latter is a well-balanced blend of distinctive character.

An Edinburgh blending firm whose history goes back to 1793 is Hill Thomson & Co. Ltd., whose 'Queen Anne' whisky is well known (although not, at the time of writing, doing as well in the United States as it deserves). William Hill set up business as a wine and spirit merchant in Rose Street Lane (behind Princes Street) in 1793, and six years later moved to 45 Frederick Street, an elegant Georgian house where the firm still has its head office. On William Hill's death in 1818 his two sons continued the business under the name of Messrs. William and Robert Hill; but they both died relatively young and a third brother George took control of the business on Robert's death in 1837. William Thomson was taken into partnership in 1857 and the firm became Hill Thomson & Co. It was William Shaw, an energetic young man who entered the business in 1883, who produced the blend 'Queen Anne' and developed the export trade. Since then the Shaw family have been prominent in the firm. William Shaw's sons, W. D. and J. N. Shaw, became partners in 1919, and in 1936, six years after their father's death, formed a limited company, Hill Thomson & Co. Ltd., with themselves as joint managing directors. Since then sales have been further developed abroad, notably in Europe, the Middle and Far East, and South Africa. In addition to 'Queen Anne' (a distinctive blend with a predominantly Speyside after-taste), the firm produces an extra quality whisky, 'Something Special', and they export two other of their blends, 'Hilltop' and 'St. Leger'. They also bottle an 83° proof gin (94·8° American proof), 'Old Gentry'.

The firm of W. and A. Gilbey represents a different pattern of growth. Walter and Alfred Gilbey set up as wine-merchants in London in 1857 and then went into the distillation of gin. The ravages of phylloxera in the French vineyards in the 1880s led them to expand into the whisky trade: in 1887 they bought Glen Spey distillery, Rothes, and in 1904 Knockando distillery, Cardow, both of which Highland malt distilleries the firm still owns in addition to Strathmill distillery, Keith. They went in only for malt whisky at first, but the blending boom proved irresistible:

Gilbey's 'Spey Royal' has long been an established blend with a distinct Speyside malt flavour. The firm has since 1962 been part of the very large firm, International Distillers and Vintners, among whose constituent companies is the old-established firm of London wine-merchants Justerini and Brooks (hence 'J. & B. Rare' blended Scotch whisky). In 1972 International Distillers and Vintners was bought by the brewery firm of Watney Mann, which was then in turn taken over by Grand Metropolitan Hotels. This is now a large empire which includes Peter Dominic's, the chain of retail wine and spirit merchants.

A firm which is increasingly coming into public notice is Whyte & Mackay Ltd., 'an independent company established 1844' as their advertising claims, though James Whyte and Charles Mackay did not enter on their partnership until 1882. In that year they took over the firm of Allan and Paynter, which certainly does go back to 1844. They produce three blends, their 'Special', which they rightly describe as 'one of the oldest proprietary brands' since it dates from the beginning of the Whyte and Mackay partnership; 'Supreme', a fuller whisky with a

higher proportion of malts; and '21 Years Old'. Whyte & Mackay merged in 1960 with Mackenzie Brothers, proprietors of Dalmore distillery, Ross-shire, a Highland malt distillery which goes back to 1839 and with which the Mackenzie family have been associated since 1867. In 1972 Dalmore Whyte & Mackay were taken over by Scottish & Universal Investments.

One of my favourite pot-still malt whiskies is 'Glenmorangie', produced at Glenmorangie distillery, Tain, which is one of two distilleries (the other is Glen Moray-Glenlivet, north of Elgin, whose single malt whisky was made available in 1973) owned by Macdonald & Muir Ltd., whisky blenders of Queen's Dock, Leith. 'Glenmorangie' has become increasingly popular, in England as well as Scotland, and the assignment of its distribution in England and Wales to Dent & Reuss Ltd. (the wines and spirits subsidiary of the cider firm of Bulmer) in July 1974 made it more readily available. Macdonald & Muir began in 1893; their blend is 'Highland Queen', which contains 'Glenmorangie' among other whiskies, and they also produce a fifteen-year-old blend, 'Grand 15'. Macdonald & Muir also blend and export 'Martin's V.V.O.' of three different ages, eight, twelve and twenty years old; other of their whiskies, perhaps less well known, are Muirhead's (Gold Label, Silver Label, and 'Rare Old Maturity' twelve years old) and 'Glen Moray '93', a de luxe whisky described with engaging *bravura* as 'of tremendous stature, yet full of grace'. (This description comes from the wine list of Charles Muirhead & Sons Ltd., an attractive Edinburgh retail firm owned by Macdonald & Muir. It is so far as I know the only place in the United Kingdom where 'Martin's V.V.O.', virtually unobtainable in Britain because it is blended almost entirely for export, can sometimes be bought.)

I must emphasize again that in this section of the book I am picking out a number of firms representing different types and categories and not making any attempt to cover the whole field or even to discuss a substantial selection. There are many good blends that are not mentioned here. But I cannot conclude this account of some different types of blending houses outside the DCL group without saying a word about that well-known blend 'Teacher's Highland Cream', produced by a firm which goes back to 1830 and remained in the family until 1923. Since 1949 the firm has been Teachers (Distillers) Ltd. The name 'Highland Cream' was first used in 1884, and the blend was originally based on malt whisky from Ardmore distillery, Kennethmont, Aberdeenshire, which William Teacher built in 1891 and which the firm still owns. In 1962 the firm acquired Glendronach distillery, originally built in 1826; in the same year they built a great new blending and bottling plant in Craig Park, Glasgow.

I must mention, too, the two important Canadian firms who have entered the Scotch whisky field. Hiram Walker of Ontario first aquired interests in Scottish bonding and distilling companies in the early 1930s, and followed this up by acquiring George Ballantine & Sons of Dumbarton and the Miltonduff-Glenlivet distillery near Elgin. They had already taken over the firm of James & George Stodart Ltd., owners of Glenburgie-Glenlivet distillery, Forres, Morayshire. In 1955 they acquired another Stodart distillery, Pulteney distillery in Wick, whose admirable 'Old Pulteney' malt whisky is discussed below. By this time they also had their own Lowland malt distillery of Inverleven, Dumbarton, and went on to build a great grain distillery also at Dumbarton. They also acquired Glencadam distillery, Brechin, and Scapa distillery, Kirkwall, Orkney, both in 1954. They have a large blending and bottling plant at Dumbarton, where they also now have a second Lowland malt distillery, Lomond. (This is not the same as Loch Lomond distillery, the highly automated Highland malt distillery owned by the Littlemill Distillery Co. Ltd. and opened in 1966.) Hiram Walker (Scotland) Ltd., with its numerous distilleries and its facilities for blending and warehousing, is thus in a position to put out a great variety of blended Scotch whiskies, though none bears the name of Hiram Walker. It is in fact (like DCL) a group of associated companies which, though under the general umbrella of Hiram Walker, maintain their identity and compete with each other. 'Ballantine's' is probably the best known of the blends put out by the Walker group and is highly esteemed among connoisseurs of blends; among the nineteen others are 'Old Smuggler' (which I have seen a great deal in the United States), 'Ambassador' (a de luxe blend) and 'Thorne's' (also well known in America).

The other Canadian firm that has come to Scotland is Seagrams. In 1928 Samuel Bronfman,[31] who had already developed his own distilling company in Montreal, bought the Canadian firm of Joseph Seagram

---

[31] The career of Sam Bronfman, who emigrated to Canada from Eastern Europe (where his family had long been involved in distilling) and who went through some rather stormy times during the prohibition era in the U.S.A., is worth a book by itself. One of his rivals in those stormy times was Joseph Kennedy, father of the late President of the United States.

& Sons, and later became president of the giant Distillers-Seagrams Ltd. Seagrams is a well-known Canadian rye whisky. But Mr. Bronfman also had a nose for Scotch, and in 1950 he took over the old-established Aberdeen firm of Chivas Brothers. In the same year Chivas acquired the distillery of Milton, Keith, changing its name to Strathisla-Glenlivet. Under Mr. Bronfman's control—he took a great personal interest in this —Chivas developed, with their Strathisla-Glenlivet and other whiskies, their rich and mellow luxury blend, 'Chivas Regal'. Seagrams also built the Glen Keith-Glenlivet distillery, on the other side of the town from Strathisla, so Chivas now have these two malt distilleries in Keith. Seagrams have also developed a number of other blends of Scotch whisky, including '100 Pipers' and 'Passport'.

Sam Bronfman died in 1971 and was succeeded by his son Edgar. The firm, which changed its name to The Seagram Co. Ltd. in 1974, claims to be the 'world's largest liquor company'. In December 1974 Mr Edgar Bronfman announced an investment of £14m. in expanding its Scotch whisky interests. With its enormous stocks of mature and maturing whisky, the DCL group can afford to cut distillation of new whisky in the immediate future, but Seagrams, which only seriously came into the Scotch whisky scene in the 1950s, needs to build up its stocks to cope with the expansion of its brands. Seagrams also sends Scottish malt whisky to its new distillery in Japan, which it jointly owns with the Kirin brewing group. There it is blended with local grain spirit to make Japanese whisky. Seagrams have recently made a successful take-over bid for Glenlivet Distilleries.

Chapter Eight
INDIVIDUAL WHISKIES

Knowledge about the equipment of distilleries and the history of blending firms is no necessary help to discriminating drinking. How should whisky be drunk? Is it a crime to drink it with soda, ginger ale or lemonade? Are whisky cocktails indecencies? How old should whisky be before it can be properly enjoyed? Is it mere snobbery to prefer a single malt whisky to a blend?

The first thing to be said about the drinking of whisky is that all traditions, customs, fashions, rules and snobberies which do not help a given individual to enjoy his whisky are so much nonsense as far as that individual is concerned. The rule is simple: what you enjoy best is best. The real question is whether what you casually or lazily think you enjoy best is what you really do enjoy best or would enjoy best if you experimented more widely and paid more attention to what you drink when you drink it. The trouble with any alcoholic drink is that it can be drunk by people who dislike the taste and who are simply out for the alcoholic kick. It used to be standard practice in Hollywood films for actors to indicate when they were taking an alcoholic drink by the grimacing gulp which accompanied its rapid ingestion, the implication clearly being that it tastes horrible but you drink it for social reasons or because it makes you feel good. There are, of course, social reasons for drinking whisky, and it does enhance your sense of well-being, but the main reason for drinking whisky rather than any other form of spirit is (or so it seems to me) its taste and flavour. That is one reason why I am prejudiced against those 'lighter' blends which seem to be designed to please the palate of those who do not like the characteristic taste of Scotch whisky. Rather than serve up as Scotch whisky a blend so made up that it has lost most of the aroma, flavour and body that really distinguishes Scotch whisky from other potable spirits, I would have such blends marketed under a quite different name. There is nothing improper in people preferring these blends; but surely people ought to be helped to know what to look for as characteristic qualities of the spirit traditionally and uniquely distilled in Scotland.

Having said this, I go on to announce my tolerance. Do Americans like a Scotch 'highball' in a tall glass with soda and lots of ice? Scotch and soda, with or without ice, is an excellent hot-weather drink, and I enjoy it myself under the proper conditions. And if I were drinking Scotch and soda I would certainly drink a good blend and not a single whisky. 1 find that the grainy[32] taste that comes, as it were, off the surface of a blended Scotch whisky if drunk straight, is either lost when the whisky is mixed with soda or combines with the effervescence of the soda in a way that satisfies the desire for a refreshing long drink. That grainy taste, by the way, I find in almost all blends as a first, surface flavour; the malt in the blend comes out as an after-taste—indeed, one of the best ways to distinguish between blends is to 'listen' for that after-taste, and even assist it by letting the flavour out of your nose just after you have swallowed. It is logical that blended Scotch whisky should have been developed largely for English palates used to brandy and soda. Under the right temperature conditions, I consider the traditional Scotch and soda an excellent drink.

But it would be a mistake to add soda to a single malt whisky. Any whisky, single malt or blended, can be savoured neat or with plain water, but with a single malt neat and with plain water are the only alternatives. And no ice. The reason for this can easily be demonstrated by anyone for himself. Ice sharply diminishes the availability of all the subtle flavours in a malt whisky that are provided by the 'congenerics'. Soda, too, kills much of the characteristic flavour of a malt whisky, or at least disperses it in an intolerable way. If whisky is to be diluted, it is best of all to dilute both malt and blended whisky with the local water that is used either in making it or in reducing it for maturing. I have drunk twelve-year-old Glenlivet at the distillery qualified with the water from the local wells where they get the water they use in making the whisky, and there is no doubt that it tastes better than the same whisky drunk with just any old water. I have proved this again and again while 'taking a dram' in a distillery manager's office. This goes for blended whisky too.

---

[32] 'What do you mean by "grainy taste"?' I have been asked. It is my term for that characteristic grain-spirit taste, sharpish and slightly metallic, that hits the nose as soon as that organ is assailed by a glass of neat blended Scotch whisky.

When I drank Dewar's at their Inveralmond plant qualified with water from Loch Ordie which they use in reducing the strength of the whiskies they receive at about 117° proof from the distilleries, it tasted better than the same whisky mixed with tap water. Of course, a lot depends on which tap water it is. Water has taste, and some household water supplies are chlorinated (sometimes, in America, very heavily) or may have any of a great variety of flavours from a great variety of sources. This is why, for diluting blended whisky, there is a good case for preferring soda to water unless the water is spring water or from some other known and approved source. I myself, when I am not lucky enough to be drinking whisky at the distillery with the same water the distillery uses in making it, dilute my whisky (when I do dilute it) with Schweppes Malvern water.

As we have seen, whisky is reduced to 70° proof (for the home market) before bottling, and one might think that it made no difference to the taste whether one drank it from the bottle at 70° proof or got it at a much higher proof at the distillery and diluted it to 70° or so in the glass at the time of drinking. But the fact is that it tastes better in the latter case. Time and again I have found that a dram in the distillery manager's office, broken down with their own water on the spot, tastes better than the identical whisky broken down before maturing and bottling. I don't quite understand why this should be so. But it must be remembered that the local water is the most important single factor in determining the special characteristics of an individual Highland malt whisky. It is more important even than the peat, as is indicated by the fact that some great Highland malt distilleries get their ready peated malt from outside the region. (But even if you get the water right you can't necessarily make good whisky. Once in Australia they discovered a stream whose water was chemically identical with that which is used at Glenlivet distillery. They proceeded to make malt whisky, using that water and imported Scottish peat. When it was quite new, just off the still, it might have been the real thing. But on maturing it was terrible. This suggests that the climate is important in the maturing process. Temperature and humidity certainly affect the rate and quality of maturing.)

How much water should one add to one's whisky? This is very much a question of personal taste. I have known some real experts who drink single malt whisky with the same amount of water added, which seems a lot. Of course, much depends on the strength of the whisky and on when you are drinking it. With a normal 70° whisky I myself would add just a little Malvern water if drinking it before dinner and none at all if drinking it after dinner. A really well-matured Highland malt whisky of high proof—say a fifteen-year-old 100° Macallan, a bottle of which happens to catch my eye as I write—really needs the addition of some water, which serves to open out the flavour. I find that if I want to savour fully a whisky of this age, strength and quality, a few drops of water bring out its nose and 'release the natural oils'; one may want to add some more water after this initial tasting. The nose, incidentally, is the prime organ for determining the flavour of whisky. With a whisky of high proof, a good way is to rub some on the palms of both hands and then sniff your hands. I have done this with 119° malt whisky straight from the still, and it is amazing how precisely the flavours come through. First the flavour of the peat, and then, as the spirit evaporates on your hands, the flavour of the malt, with which you are left at the end. Professional tasters use this method and also use the 'nose glass', a tall tulip-shaped glass, rather like an outsize copita, in which the nose can be buried as the taster sniffs. The nose of a professional is a remarkably sensitive organ, though often its possessor may not be able to put into words exactly what he is looking for. One expert blender was once asked, as he went about sniffing samples of malt whisky from different distilleries, exactly what he was looking for. 'The smell of pear drops,' he replied. This is not as absurd as it may sound. Although I have not sucked a pear drop since my childhood in Edinburgh, I recollect now that the smell and flavour of that particular sweet is reminiscent of the first aroma that comes off a fine Eastern malt when sniffed.

How old should a whisky be? It is difficult to give a precise answer. The rate of maturing is affected by the atmospheric conditions of the warehouse in which the cask is stored as well as by the size of the cask. But in general I do not think a malt whisky should be drunk at under five years old. Though even five years is young—too young according to some whisky experts—I must say that I have had several eminently drinkable whiskies at that age. Whisky loses both strength and volume as it matures (it tends to lose strength in a humid atmosphere, whereas in a dry atmosphere there is more loss of bulk through absorption into the wood of the cask), and the Excise people allow a loss by evaporation and absorption of 2 per cent per year. (The loss of whisky in the cask during the maturing process is known as 'ullage', which is the difference between 'original' gallonage, the amount originally put into the cask, and 'regauge' gallonage, the amount remaining at a later date.) It is thus an expensive business keeping whisky in the wood for a long time. But it pays off in terms of improved flavour and quality up to, say, fifteen years. It is impossible to determine the optimum age for whisky in general terms; so much depends on the individual case. I recently drank, at Longmorn distillery, whisky from a cask that was filled in April 1899 and broached in 1967. By all the rules it should have gone 'woody'—and indeed, it should have evaporated, because a loss of 2 per cent per annum over sixty-eight years should yield less than nothing. But in fact it was not woody at all: it had lost strength and body, but it was mellow and pleasant though (surprisingly perhaps) without the character of a much younger Longmorn. Some whiskies are at their best at twelve years old: the managing director at Glenlivet distillery told me that in his view the twelve-year-old Glenlivet bottled by the company is as good as it can get. There is no doubt that some whiskies keep on improving, up to fifteen, twenty, twenty-five years or even longer. But it is possible to make too much of a fuss about mere age. I would rather have a superior whisky eight years old than an inferior twelve years old. As a general rule, I would say that ten years is a good drinking age for a single malt whisky, but some will be excellent a year or two younger and others will improve noticeably if left longer in the cask. As for blends, it will be remembered that the age (if any) stated on the label is the age of the youngest whisky in the blend. A blend labelled 'eight years old' is liable to contain some malts considerably older. The age of the malt whiskies in a blend is, of course, of first importance in determining the quality of that blend. It must be realized that all the greatest pot-still malt whiskies go largely for blending, and some go entirely for blending; and since most blends contain more than 50 per cent patent-still grain whisky, the quality of the malt whisky must be high if the resulting body and flavour is to reflect the malt content. Though for drinking neat or with water I personally prefer a single malt whisky, I must stress that all the reputable blends contain a proportion of some of the finest well-matured malts.

Whisky is a drink that can be taken before, with or after a meal. An Eastern malt with a little water before a meal, a good blend with quite a lot of water or soda with a meal, and a full, fruity malt drunk neat (as one would drink brandy) after a meal—this, to my taste, is the best way of taking it. Some foods, however, demand neat whisky. Haggis, for example, should be consumed with neat whisky, and in fact a blended Scotch whisky goes quite well with it. With fresh Scotch salmon whisky (to my taste, a single malt) with quite a lot of water goes very well. But, of course, I would not insist on whisky with everything. A variety of dry white wines go admirably with salmon, and I am certainly not going to recommend that one should replace wine as a dinner drink with whisky. Each has its part to play in a well-ordered meal. But I do want to stress the versatility of Scotch whisky and its suitability for a great variety of occasions.

Here again one must consult one's own taste and the important thing is to give one's own taste a chance by experimenting freely and really paying attention as one drinks. Whisky is not a drink to be swilled. I need hardly say that, like all spirits, it must be drunk in moderation. Whisky to be savoured must be drunk in small quantities: the palate soon loses its power of discriminating and relishing if too much is drunk at once. I confess that in tasting whiskies in order to make up my mind about their quality I cannot go on for long without my palate becoming dulled (even if I do not swallow but spit out after tasting). Professional tasters have told me that the best time to taste whisky is in the morning before breakfast, before the palate has lost its edge after food has been taken or after smoking. One old stillman claims that at six o'clock every morning he takes a tumbler of neat whisky to 'clean out the tubes', but this is not a practice I would recommend. For the layman whisky is certainly not a pre-breakfast drink. I myself do not normally drink whisky before evening, though I have some glowing recollections of memorable exceptions to this rule. The knowing whisky drinker will surely appreciate lots of other drinks besides whisky. I do not normally drink before lunch on a working day, but if I do a dry sherry in winter and a campari and soda in summer is very likely to be my choice. On a damp, chilly day in Scotland, on the other hand, whisky is the right drink at almost any hour. And there can be special social occasions at any time when whisky is appropriate. Otherwise, 6 p.m. seems to be the earliest time when one's thoughts might well turn to a pre-prandial whisky. A malt whisky with a little Malvern water seems to me the best before-dinner drink in the world, and another drunk straight in a tall tulip-shaped wine glass (which enables you to savour the 'nose') at room temperature is a perfect after-dinner drink.

Blended Scotch whisky with ginger ale is now a very common drink, and so (in Scotland, surprisingly) is whisky and lemonade. I suspect that many people who drink these mixtures do so in order to give an alcoholic kick to their ginger ale or lemonade, in which case it seems rather a pity to use Scotch whisky at all. But there must also be many people who genuinely like the taste of the combination of Scotch and ginger ale or Scotch and lemonade. If they do, then more power to them. So long as they are not just drowning their Scotch whisky with some other flavour because they do not really like the taste of Scotch but feel that they ought to drink it for social reasons, and so long as they are not just adding alcohol for the kick, then nobody can object to their preferring

Grand procession of the Gorbals Temperance Society, at Dumfries, 1852

the combination of flavours that pleases them. This goes for whisky cocktails too. Though conservative in my own whisky tastes, I am no purist in these matters. Just as I remain sceptical about all the mumbo-jumbo that goes with the drinking of wine and maintain that a man has a perfect right to drink any wine with any food if he is really tasting what he is drinking and genuinely likes it that way, so my only plea to Scotch whisky drinkers is that they attend to what they drink and base their preference on a decision deliberately made from a number of alternatives on the basis of genuine gustatory enjoyment.

Taste is notoriously difficult to describe, and the taste of a good Scotch whisky is so subtly compounded of bouquet, the actual taste on the palate, the after-taste, and the pleasing intellectual and physical glow that accompanies its consumption, that one man's account of his experience in drinking a given whisky may be very different from that of another who enjoys it equally. If, therefore, I now proceed to give some account of my experience of different pot-still malt whiskies, it is on the understanding that the reader will bear these reservations in mind. About blended whiskies I will add nothing to the scattered remarks I have made throughout this book, except to say once again that the drinker should select his brand thoughtfully and not drink merely out of habit or convention. And let him test the claims of advertisers on his own palate.

Let me make it clear at the outset that I do not believe it possible to arrange Highland malt whiskies in a simple order of merit. This is not only because an individual whisky will vary from year to year—not so much as a wine from a single vineyard will, but still perceptibly—and according to its age. There is also the question of individual taste and the time, mood and circumstances in which the whisky is drunk. There are times when I have felt like a full, peaty Islay whisky and other times when I have preferred a more delicate and fragrant Eastern malt. I have found, too—and I am sure that my experience cannot be unique here—that my actual palate is not constant: when I first tasted Clynelish, for example, it seemed to me a rich, full, robust yet gentle whisky with a mellow fruity quality quite different from the characteristic 'medicinal' fullness of, say, Laphroaig. Yet later, tasting the identical Clynelish, I could perceive a definite relationship with the Laphroaig kind of peatiness. As for Laphroaig itself, perhaps the most distinctive of all Scotch whiskies, sometimes I feel that its special quality (which I have heard described by a novice on his first drinking it as suggestive of iodine) is exactly what I am in the mood for—a whisky idiosyncratic enough to stand up to other strong flavours that one may have been tasting, admirable for rounding off a meal which has included highly seasoned food. At other times again I prefer my Laphroaig in the blend 'Islay Mist', which retains the fullness of Laphroaig but with only a touch of its strong 'medicinal' flavour, very soft and mellow. (I myself would not use the term 'medicinal' to describe the flavour of Laphroaig, but I know what people mean when they use it and I cannot think of a really descriptive term that fits. Some say they can taste seaweed, and it may well be that the characteristic Islay peat does contain sea vegetation, which explains this.) 'Islay Mist' contains Laphroaig, Smith's Glenlivet and Glen Grant, blended together with grain whisky. It is one of the very best blends.

The Laphroaig I have enjoyed as an after-dinner drink in the suitable conditions described is ten years old and 75° proof, bottled by the distillery; the 'Islay Mist' is eight years old and 70° proof. (Perhaps I ought to remind American readers once again that British proof is calculated differently from American and that I am using British proof percentages: British 70° proof is American 80° proof.) The Clynelish which sometimes seems to me to bear a similarity in its kind of fullness and body to Laphroaig but at other times seems softer and less pungent, is twelve years old, 70° proof, bottled by Ainslie and Heilbron. I always find it, whatever the state of my palate, a splendid whisky, especially when drunk neat after dinner. I have tried George Saintsbury's recipe of mixing half Clynelish with half Glenlivet, and the result is a very fine drink indeed.

If I feel like an Islay whisky but do not want its Islay features to be quite so pronounced as they are in Laphroaig, I drink Lagavulin bottled by White Horse Distillers at 75° proof (no age is given on the label). This is an admirable robust whisky with just enough of the Islay kind of peatiness to give it distinctive character. I have drunk an even better Lagavulin at the distillery on a wet and windy day when one realized how appropriate to the climate of the island Islay whisky is.[33] Of the other Islay whiskies, I have tasted Bowmore at the distillery and more recently bought a bottle at the duty-free shop at Heathrow; quite some time ago I bought a bottle of Ardbeg at a licensed grocer's in Crieff, bottled by D. & J. MacEwen of Stirling. Each has its own version of the Islay taste. Of the other island whiskies, Talisker, the Skye whisky,

---

[33] In presenting this discussion of Scottish malt distilleries geographically I hope I will not weary or confuse the reader with no knowledge of or interest in the geography of Scotland. The fact is that I associate the taste of different pot-still whiskies with the localities where they are made, and to me part of the pleasure of drinking a pot-still whisky is associating the flavour with the scenery in which the distillery is set. It is taken for granted by knowing wine drinkers that they should relate any discussion of a given wine to the specific place where it is produced. Scotch whisky is equally a *local* product, and I should like to encourage discriminating Scotch whisky drinkers to take an interest in the localities from which their favourite whiskies come. Wine connoisseurs make pilgrimages to French vineyards. Perhaps some day a small proportion at least of the visitors to Scotland will want to make a special whisky pilgrimage.

is the best known. This is available at a number of ages and strengths: the best I have tasted is the 100° proof bottled by Gordon & Macphail (no age on the label). If you breathe the flavour out of your nose immediately after swallowing, you get an aftertaste of a kind of oily smokiness which I find extremely agreeable. Talisker is not perhaps to everybody's taste, nor is it an all-purpose whisky; but it is a whisky of great character and certainly the whisky to be drunk in Skye itself when a light rain is falling and the mist is on the hills. And, of course, one does not need to go to Skye for this appropriate situation to present itself.

Across the water from Islay are the two Campbeltown distilleries, Springbank and Glen Scotia. In Springbank distillery the foreshots and the feints are redistilled in a second, separate still (instead of being run back through the feints receiver to be re-distilled with the next batch of low wines in the low wines still). This may account for Springbank's special kind of mellowness and lightness. It is a rich yet not at all a heavy whisky, soft, fragrant, not peaty, and quite unlike the traditional heavily peated and very full-bodied Campbeltown. I have recently drunk an 80° Springbank, bottled by Eaglesome Ltd. 'over twelve years old'; it is a beautifully smooth and gentle whisky that has perhaps more finish than individuality. Very different is Glen Scotia, full bodied and heavily peated, with a rich 'nose' and a fine robustness of flavour. A. Gillies & Co. (the owners) bottle an eight-year-old at 75° proof.

It was an accident of illustration that made me start this tasting tour with Islay whiskies. The more obvious thing to do would be to begin with Glenlivet and then work north and west. But since I have been talking of the whiskies of Islay and Skye, perhaps I had better stay with the islands before moving back to the mainland and go on now to Orkney, where Highland Park is an outstanding whisky. (I have never tasted Scapa, the other Orkney whisky, as a single whisky, nor have I spoken to anyone who has.) Highland Park is regularly bottled at 75°. It is a rich, heavy whisky with a peaty nose. The 100° proof bottled by Gordon & Macphail is even better: the full yet subtle flavour seduces the nose as soon as it approaches the glass. The 100° proof reduced with water just after being poured from the bottle tastes more full-flavoured than the 75° proof reduced with water to the same strength, just as the 100° proof poured from the bottle and reduced with water to 75° proof tastes better than that bottled at 75° and drunk neat. This is a phenomenon I have noted before. It does not apply to all whiskies, but it does so noticeably to Highland Park.

Let us now cross the Pentland Firth and come to the mainland of Scotland. The most northerly distillery on the mainland is Pultney, which produces 'Old Pultney'. This is a whisky I have known about ever since I read Neil Gunn's book on whisky in 1935, but it was only in 1967 that I was able to get some (bottled at 85° proof, eight years old). It has a splendid fruitiness (as distinct from a peatiness), the tasted flavour fulfilling most interestingly and complexly the promise of its 'nose'. At the moment I am preaching it with all the enthusiasm of a convert, and I hope that the distillers, or Hiram Walker who are now the parent company, will make more of it available as a single whisky. Coming down the Caithness coast into Sutherland, one comes to Clynelish distillery. Let me once again raise my hat to Clynelish, that fine, full, mellow whisky, before moving down into Ross and Cromarty and the distilleries of Balblair, Glenmorangie and Dalmore. Balblair is a pleasing light-bodied whisky of distinctive flavour. Glenmorangie, only a few miles away, is very different: it has a special kind of floweriness, a delicate yet unmistakable fragrance, that I find extremely attractive. It is bottled at 70°, ten years old, and is not too difficult to get, at least in Britain. Glenmorangie is what I would call an all-purpose whisky. It is equally good as a pre-prandial and as a post-prandial drink, and I confess I have drunk it at many other times as well. There is a Glenmorangie which I have drunk at the distillery which is older and more full-bodied than that which is available bottled, possessing more richness and less delicacy than the latter. It goes for blending, of course, but anyone lucky enough to get a dram of it at the distillery will have a memorable experience. Dalmore is a heavier whisky altogether, peatier, full-bodied and—one doesn't want to over-use this word, but it is inevitable here—robust. I have some bottled at 70° proof by Duncan Macbeth & Co. of Invergordon. William Cadenhead of Aberdeen bottles both a twelve-year-old and a twenty-year-old at 75° proof. It is an excellent after-dinner drink.

Continuing south from Ross-shire to Inverness-shire we come to Glen Mhor distillery at Inverness. Glen Mhor is one of the truly great post-prandial whiskies, full, rich and mellow, slightly less peaty than Dalmore and with a smoother finish. Glen Mhor is a 'bigger' whisky than a characteristic Speyside whisky, but it has some of the qualities of a Glenlivet.

Going north-east from Inverness to Elgin and then south from Elgin we approach the great heartland of Highland malt whisky. I can only pick out some of the many fine malt whiskies produced in this region and discuss those I know best. On the south side of Elgin is Linkwood, a fairly light-bodied whisky with a 'nose' not (it seems to me) unlike Glenlivet, though less full. It has a pleasing light fragrance: I would class it as an all-purpose whisky. Some miles south of Elgin there is Longmorn, the distillery where I once drank a sixty-eight-year-old whisky from a newly broached cask. Longmorn is a full, virile whisky with a fine 'nose', admirable when drunk neat after dinner but also most agreeable with a little water pre-prandially or indeed at any time. It is bottled at 70° proof by William Cadenhead of Aberdeen.

Continuing down to the road from Elgin to Craigellachie (and ignoring perforce some excellent distilleries) we come to Glen Rothes-Glenlivet distillery, whose whisky is bottled at 80° proof, ten years old, by William Cadenhead. Glen Rothes has a strong, peaty 'nose'; if not the subtlest it is one of the fullest of the Eastern malts, a whisky of real character. Then on through Craigellachie to the great cluster of Speyside distilleries. Glenlivet I have already discussed at length, but I will add just a word about its distinctive qualities to the palate. At its best, Smith's Glenlivet combines a teasing subtlety of flavour with a distinctive 'nose' and fullness. These are not always sufficiently in evidence when it is bottled too young, but the firm's own bottling, twelve years old at 80°, gives one everything that could be desired in this noble whisky. I have tasted a Glenlivet put in cask in 1941 and bottled (by Berry Brothers & Rudd) in 1958, and the only note on it which I entered in my whisky scrap-book after the first glass was simply 'a superb whisky'. But later experience of comparing different ages and proofs leads me to believe that additional age over twelve years does not add all that much in quality, and (within limits of course) a twelve-year-old at a higher proof tastes better than an older whisky at a lower proof. But the twelve-year-old is decidedly better than anything younger. I have on my desk as I write an eight-year-old Glenlivet at 70° and the distillery's twelve-year-old at 80° proof. The eight-year-old is a good whisky, it is true, but its 'nose' is less subtle (in the twelve-year-old the sweetness mingles with the peatiness and the fullness in a most intriguing way, while in the younger whisky the flavours seem less integrated) and it is less smooth and less rounded in flavour. All the same, if an eight-year-old Smith's Glenlivet is all you can get, then seize it: it is a very good dram.

How does Glenlivet compare with Glen Grant? In general character they are not dissimilar: each has that smooth integration of peatiness, softness and full sweetness (or almost sweetness) that needs age to bring out. Like Glenlivet, Glen Grant is conspicuously better at ten or, better still, twelve years old than at, say, five (and it is available at five years old). There is a sharpness about a young Glen Grant that belies its true potential. I once compared a seventeen-year-old Glen Grant with a ten-year-old, and I noted in my whisky scrap-book that it was not the first sip of each that showed the real difference, 'but after steady comparative sipping the superior mellowness of the seventeen-year-old as against the ten-year-old became evident.' A well-matured Glen Grant has a splendid smoothness: it is not, perhaps, such a complexly patterned whisky in the combination of 'nose', taste and after-taste that is found in Glenlivet at its best, being a more single-minded whisky, as it were. At one time I used to drink a twelve-year-old Glen Grant matured in plain oak as my favourite whisky. But I have grown to like the finish given by maturing in sherry wood, and I have also outgrown any belief that I have a single favourite malt whisky. I pay my respects equally to those two whisky classics, Glenlivet and Glen Grant. The latter, by the way, is readily available in a variety of bottlings.

Moving north-west of Glenlivet to Dufftown, we come to Mortlach distillery, one of the many clustered in that area. I have a special fondness for Mortlach, because it was the all-purpose whisky I drank regularly during the five years I lived in Ithaca, N.Y. and taught at Cornell University. I used to get it sent up from Macy's in New York. It is a fine, full Eastern malt, with a rich but not a specially peaty flavour. Glenfiddich and Dufftown, two nearby distilleries, produce excellent whiskies too; the former has a pleasing dry fragrance and the latter is the more peaty. Macallan distillery in nearby Craigellachie produces a Speyside whisky of great individuality. The 100° proof bottled by Gordon & Macphail has a powerful 'nose' which proclaims very accurately the flavour to the palate, which I find difficult to describe as its special kind of richness is neither peaty nor flowery but something in between. On the other side of the Spey from Macallan distillery is Aberlour-Glenlivet founded in 1879 and controlled by the Campbell Group of Companies in Glasgow. Campbells bottle an eight-year-old 100° proof Aberlour-Glenlivet, a light-bodied malt of individuality: it is now fairly readily available in England (and at the duty-free shop at Heathrow). In Keith (the third in the triangle of whisky towns of which the other two are Dufftown and Craigellachie) Strathisla distillery produces a whisky with a full, fragrant flavour which seems to come somewhere between Glenlivet and Mortlach. Further to the south-west, near Ballindalloch on the Spey, Glenfarclas distillery produces a somewhat peatier whisky, full-bodied and assertive. (This was another whisky I used to drink in Ithaca, New York: it was the only Highland malt sold by the local liquor store that I dealt with, and very satisfying it was.) I would regard it as a post-prandial rather than an all-purpose whisky.

Once again I must point out that I am picking out some of the whiskies that I know best; those I have discussed do not represent all the good single malt whiskies. But I must add, before I conclude this somewhat impressionistic survey, two Lowland malts that I know. One is Rosebank, now available as a single whisky bottled at 70° proof, a pleasant, smooth whisky, sharper to the nose than to the palate, and the other is Glenkinchie, which so far as I know is not available as a single whisky but of which I have a sample bottle from an Edinburgh blending firm. This too is a very agreeable whisky, slightly sweeter and perhaps just a trifle sharper than Rosebank. The third is Auchentoshan, a well-rounded if not very individual whisky. 1 should like to beat the drum a bit for Lowland malts. They have been overshadowed in the literature on whisky and in the esteem of single whisky drinkers by Highland malts, which have more romance in their story and the best of which, it is true, are whiskies of greater character and grander flavour. But a well-matured Lowland malt is—especially for those who do not prefer a heavily peated whisky—a pleasant and civilized drink of distinctive quality and makes a good all-purpose whisky.

Scotch whisky is one of Scotland's great contributions to the good life. Like any alcoholic drink, it is capable of abuse, but the best guarantee against abuse is knowledge and discrimination. As we look back on its long story, remembering the farmer-distillers of the seventeenth and eighteenth centuries, the proud smugglers of the days when the Government was desperately fumbling for ways of taxing and controlling whisky production, the invention of the Coffey still and its momentous consequences, the flamboyant *entrepreneurs* of the latter part of the nineteenth century, and the world-wide reputation of Scotch whisky today, we cannot but marvel at the way in which a spontaneous Highland activity which fitted in so well with the rhythms of the agricultural year has become over the years a vast industry. And I have my more personal memories: celebrating a wedding anniversary with fresh-caught salmon and a bottle of Glen Grant in the kitchen of a little house by the Moray Firth; landing up in a little Banffshire pub after a wet day's trout-fishing to warm myself with the spirit distilled all around me; talking with fellow writers and poets on a summer evening in a Rose Street pub in Edinburgh with drams of a variety of Highland malts standing on the bar between us; sipping Clynelish after dinner at home with a few academic friends as we planned the development of the University of Sussex; arriving at the house of a friend in New Jersey to find that he had ordered in some Mortlach because he knew I was coming and had heard that I liked that particular whisky; celebrating Hogmanay sitting on a bed in a hotel room in Agra with two friends and a bottle of Glenlivet after visiting the Taj Mahal by moonlight; drinking a nameless but obviously authentic blended Scotch from a lemonade bottle full of the liquor supplied by a friendly clerk at Belgrade airport as I waited a weary time for the airport to be cleared of the top brass and security officers awaiting the arrival of President Tito; drinking with courteous distillery managers at distilleries all over Scotland; and innumerable occasions, domestic, convivial, celebratory or merely casual, gratifying the palate and warming the spirit with this great drink. The proper drinking of Scotch whisky is more than indulgence: it is a toast to civilization, a tribute to the continuity of culture, a manifesto of man's determination to use the resources of nature to refresh mind and body and enjoy to the full the senses with which he has been endowed. And so I conclude with Robert Burns' great hail to the barley from which Scotch whisky derives:

Let husky wheat the haughs adorn	meadows
An' aits set up their awnie horn,	bearded
An' pease and beans, an e'en or morn,	
Perfume the plain:	
Leeze me on thee, John Barleycorn,	blessings on
Thou king o' grain!	

To which we may add:

Freedom an' whisky gang thegither,
Tak aff your dram!

Robert Burns

165

Select Bibliography

ALFRED BARNARD, *The Whisky Distilleries of the United Kingdom*. Newton Abbot, 1969. (Originally London, 1887.)

NEIL M. GUNN, *Whisky and Scotland*. London, 1935.

SIR ROBERT BRUCE LOCKHART, *Scotch: The Whisky of Scotland in Fact and Story*. London, 1951.

R. J. S. McDOWALL, *The Whiskies of Scotland*. London, 1967.

J. M. ROBB, *Scotch Whisky: An Illustrated Guide*. London and Edinburgh, [1950].

S. W. SILLETT, *The Whiskies of Scotland*. London, 1967.

ROSS WILSON, *Scotch Made Easy*. London, 1959.

DCL and Scotch Whisky. The Distillers Company Ltd., London, 1966.

Scotch Whisky: Questions and Answers. The Scotch Whisky Association, Edinburgh, 1967.

Glenlivet, being the Annals of the Glenlivet Distillery. The Glenlivet Distillery, 1964.

JAMES LAVER, *The House of Haig*. Markinch, 1958.

ROSS WILSON, *The House of Sanderson*, 1963.

The North British Distillery Company Limited 1885–1960. Edinburgh, n.d.

R. J. FORBES, *Short History of the Art of Distilling*. Leiden, 1948.

GEORGE SAINTSBURY, *Notes on a Cellar-Book*. London, 1920.

[CAPTAIN EDWARD BURT], *Letters from a Gentleman in the North of Scotland to his Friend in London*, 2 vols. London, 1754.

J. G. FYFE (ED.), *Scottish Diaries and Memoirs 1746–1843*. Stirling, 1942.

SIR ARCHIBALD GEIKIE, *Scottish Reminiscences*. Glasgow, 1908.

ELIZABETH GRANT OF ROTHIEMURCHUS, *Memoirs of a Highland Lady 1797–1827*, revised and edited by Angus Davidson. London, 1950.

HENRY HAMILTON, *An Economic History of Scotland in the Eighteenth Century*. Oxford, 1963.

SIR JOHN SINCLAIR, BART., *Statistical Account of Scotland Drawn up from the Communications of the Ministers of the Different Parishes*, 21 vols. Edinburgh, 1791–99.

Index

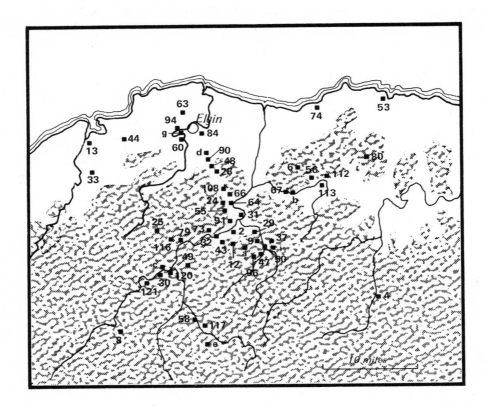

THE DISTILLERIES OF SCOTCH WHISKY

1	Aberfeldy	28	Coleburn-Glenlivet	62	Glenmorangie	94	Miltonduff-Glenlivet
2	Aberlour-Glenlivet	29	Convalmore-Glenlivet	63	Glen Moray-Glenlivet	95	Moffat
a	Allt A'Bhainne	30	Cragganmore-Glenlivet	64	Glen Rothes-Glenlivet	95	*Moffat*
3	Ardbeg	31	Craigellachie-Glenlivet	65	Glen Scotia	96	*Mortlach*
4	Ardmore	32	Dailuaine-Glenlivet	66	Glen Spey	97	*North British*
5	Auchentoshan	33	Dallas Dhu	67	Glentauchers	*h*	*North of Scotland*
b	Auchroisk	34	Dalmore	68	Glenturret	98	North Port
6	Aultmore-Glenlivet	35	Dalwhinnie	69	Glenugie	99	Oban
7	Balblair	36	Deanston	70	Glenury-Royal	100	Ord
c	Ballindaloch	37	Dufftown-Glenlivet	71	Highland Park	*i*	Pittyvaich
8	Balmenach-Glenlivet	*38*	*Dumbarton*	72	Hillside	*101*	*Port Dundas*
9	Balvenie-Glenlivet	39	Edradour	73	Imperial-Glenlivet	102	Port Ellen
10	Banff	40	Fettercairn	74	Inchgower	103	Pulteney
11	Ben Nevis	*41*	*Girvan*	75	*Invergordon*	104	Rosebank
11	*Ben Nevis*	42	Glen Albyn	76	Inverleven	105	Royal Brackla
d	Benriach	43	Glenallachie-Glenlivet	77	Jura	106	St Magdalene
12	Benrinnes	44	Glenburgie-Glenlivet	78	Kinclaith	107	Scapa
13	Benromach-Glenlivet	45	Glencadam	79	Knockando	108	Speyburn-Glenlivet
14	Ben Wyvis	46	Glendronach	80	Knockdhu	109	Speyside
15	Bladnoch	47	Glendullan-Glenlivet	81	Ladyburn	110	Springbank
16	Blair Atholl	48	Glen Elgin-Glenlivet	82	Lagavulin	*111*	*Strathclyde*
17	Bowmore	49	Glenfarclas-Glenlivet	83	Laphroaig	112	Strathisla-Glenlivet
e	Braes of Glenlivet	50	Glenfiddich	84	Linkwood-Glenlivet	113	Strathmill
f	Brora	51	Glenfyne	85	Littlemill	*114*	*Strathmore*
18	Bruichladdich	52	Glengarioch	86	Loch Lomond	115	Talisker
19	Bunnahabhain	53	Glenglassaugh	87	Lochnagar	116	Tamdhu-Glenlivet
20	*Caledonian*	54	Glengoyne	88	Lochside	117	Tamnavulin
21	*Cambus*	55	Glen Grant-Glenlivet	*88*	*Lochside*	118	Teaninich
22	*Cameronbridge*	56	Glen Keith-Glenlivet	89	Lomond	119	Tomatin
23	Caol Ila	57	Glenkinchie	90	Longmorn-Glenlivet	120	Tomintoul-Glenlivet
24	Caperdonich	58	Glenlivet, The	91	Macallan-Glenlivet	121	Tormore
25	Cardow	59	Glenlochy	92	Macduff	122	Tullibardine
26	*Carsebridge*	60	Glenlossie-Glenlivet	*g*	Mannochmore		*Italic denotes*
27	Clynelish	61	Glen Mhor	93	Millburn		*Grain Whisky Distilleries*

INTRODUCTION

Almost everyone can now become a **good** programmer.

It is time our ability to use computers caught up with the capabilities of the computers themselves. This is the first popular (elementary) book to present a step-by-step method for creating the best computer program possible every single time for every kind of need — in any language, on any machine. It is written for the novice who has just acquired a knowledge of his or her first programming language as well as for the veteran who has been programming electronic machines for as long as they have existed.

The Warnier/Orr Method presented here not only supports easy and accurate analysis of a software problem but also leads to the creation of the most maintainable software conceivable. In a world where the vast majority of programmers' time is devoted to revising existing programs, data processing personnel are obligated to insist on this quality.

Dave Higgins represents the third generation in the modern age of information handling analysis and design. The techniques have been developed, tested, and modified and they are now ready for presentation in book form. Mr. Higgins has taught the methodology to major data processing departments around the country. His experience gives rise to this publication.

Mosch Virshup
December, 1982
Denver, Colorado

TABLE OF CONTENTS

PREFACE

Building Better Programs

Structured programming has been around for a number of years
now, even though very few people know what it actually
means. To some it means that a program is "organized" or
"well-constructed," while to others it means "no GOTO statements," or perhaps even "modular." It has come to the point
in the data processing industry where a good idea cannot be
put forth without it being called structured. This is an
easy bandwagon to jump on because, after all, if you are not
structured then you must be unstructured, and who wants to
be that? The term has become meaningless of late, and worse
than that, it has been grossly overused to the point that it
means many different things to different people. When most
people speak of structured concepts these days, they are
using the term as a loose synonym for "good." This book is
really not about designing structured programs for their own
sake, but is about designing good programs.

Good programs seem to be a relative rarity in the
real world. Everyone seems to know endless horror stories
about bad programs, but stories in praise of well-designed
and well-built software are few and far between. This is
not really unusual. If you examine traditionally-designed

programs and rank them on a scale of very bad through very good, I suspect you will find a bell-curve distribution: very few programs are all that terrible or all that good, the vast majority of them being simply mediocre.

This is unacceptable in a world whose dependence upon computers is so high. The cost of creating and maintaining poor or mediocre programs is too high to be tolerated. If you think about it for a while, you will realize that no other profession engaged in building things puts up with builders that produce as shoddy results as data processing people often do. This is not to fault the programmers and analysts who have built poor software in the past; they did the best job they could with the limited knowledge they had about the nature of design. We never intended the programs we wrote to be bad, they just somehow ended up that way.

We are smarter today than we were ten or twenty years ago, and we must take advantage of that. Jean-Dominique Warnier, a pioneer in the field of data structured program design, calls what we do in data processing **informatics**, and thus we are **informaticians** —— engineers of information systems. As informaticians, we have a responsibility to do a better job of designing programs and systems than we have done in the past, and we must continue to improve our skills and our knowledge as time wears on.

About the Book

The Warnier/Orr Structured Program Design (SPD) method has been in existence in much the same form you see here for the last four years. It has been presented to dozens of organizations and hundreds of students in that period, with an outstanding success ratio. The approach is simple to learn and simple to use, and the results people can accomplish are amazing indeed. More than that, most people seem to genuinely **like** the technique, which is an important hurdle to clear for any improved-productivity aid. The best method in the world will not be successful if people dislike it or find it hard to use.

The method presented in this book is applicable to all types
of programming applications, from business applications to
scientific applications. Although the examples in the
physical design portion of the book are oriented towards the
commercial programmer in a COBOL environment, the concepts
and tenets presented can (and have been) extended into all
areas of programming.

I urge you to try the techniques presented in this book,
even if you are already familiar with some other structured
design method. I am not a believer in unnecessary change;
there is no value in change for the sake of change.
However, change for the better is something to be pursued.
I sincerely believe that this program design methodology is
the best one in existence today. I think if you try it you
will believe it, too.

Acknowledgements

There are many people who deserve mention for their help in
making this book possible. First of all, I would like to
thank my wife Monica for her support and her patience while
this was being written. Also I would like to thank my
parents and grandparents for their continuing enthusiasm.
On the professional side, I would like to thank my business
associates Karl Dakin and Gioia D'Amanti for their work in
keeping things going while I wrote and traveled. Also thank
you to Mosch Virshup, who helped me edit the book and remove
the nagging inconsistencies. Without their efforts this
book could not exist. I would also like to thank my friends
and colleagues that have developed and taught this
methodology over the last few years: Georgia Alley, Kirk
Hansen, Jim Highsmith, Rick Messinger, Morris Nelson, Judy
Noe, Ken Orr, Stiles Roberts, and Linda Swirczek. They have
all contributed ideas which found their way into this book.
Thanks also to all the support people at EduCo and at Ken
Orr & Associates for the help provided.

Finally, a special thank you to Mssr. Jean-Dominique
Warnier, without whose work we would all be doing something
else.

David A. Higgins

Chapter 1 DESIGN PRINCIPLES

Building Better Programs

People have been trying to perfect methods for building better computer software for almost as long as there have been
computers. Everyone knows that there are countless poor
ways to create and maintain programs; this is evidenced by
the many poor programs that exist today. Unfortunately,
good methods for building software are far fewer in number
than poor ones, and are much harder to come by.

Improving programming productivity (i.e., building consistently better software) began to be a popular topic for
discussion in the late 1960s when a technique called
structured programming was first discovered and introduced.
The traditional "stir until done" approach for building
programs — coding a program, running it on the computer,
and then fixing it until it worked properly — didn't
seem to be working well and was costing organizations
millions of dollars and thousands of hours of time trying to
keep pace with the increasing demands for new programs and
enhancements. Structured programming, when it began, was an
attempt to apply some rigor to the logic used in programs.
It had been recently proven that only a handful of different
kinds of program control structures were necessary to be
able to create any kind of software. By using only these

1

few control structures in programs, people seemed to be able to create simpler and more consistent programs than they could before. These "structured programs" could also be easier to read, more reliable, and more maintainable than traditional ones.

They could also end up being much worse than some traditional programs, however. Structured programs could be badly fragmented, be nearly impossible to follow, and have severe performance problems. Also, the technique only seemed to work well in the higher-level languages like PL/I and COBOL, and not in languages like FORTRAN and Assembler. In fact, many people tried "structured programming" and failed so miserably that they went back to the traditional methods; to this day there are organizations where "structured" is a dirty word not mentioned in polite company.

At the time many people felt, perhaps intuitively, that there were still better and more reliable methods for developing programs that were yet to be discovered. After years of investigation, a new technique did finally emerge. It is really a third-generation software design method, incorporating the features present in the best of the "natively good" programs and in good "structured programs." The programs created with this design technique end up being structured, but not because it is a goal of the method; it is a naturally occurring by-product of correct design.

This third-generation approach is called **data structured design** and is based upon some very simple principles that will be presented shortly. It was developed and explored by three groups of researchers headed by Jean-Dominique Warnier (pronounced "warn'-yay") in France, by Michael Jackson in England, and by Ken Orr in the United States. It is the most reliable software design method ever discovered, and has been successfully employed in literally hundreds of organizations in data processing shops worldwide.

Fundamental Principles

In the long run, the Warnier/Orr approach to software design is probably one of the easiest techniques to learn and to apply well. That is because it is based upon only three fundamental observations about the nature of good design. These basic tenets of good design are individually neither new nor particularly exciting, but when combined become quite powerful.

- Design should be **output-oriented.**
- Design should be **logical before physical.**
- Design should be **data-structured.**

These three principles color all that is done in the Warnier/Orr software development technique, and although quite simple on the surface, they have important and far-reaching consequences. It is more than worth the space of a few paragraphs to discuss their meanings and ramifications before examining the Warnier/Orr method itself.

Output-Oriented Design

The first and probably most important of the three Warnier/Orr design principles states that software design should be "output-oriented." That phrase may also be described as "goal-oriented" or "result-oriented" development. Put simply, it suggests that good software design must begin with a clear and complete understanding of the output that the intended program is to produce.

This seems like an almost trivial observation on the surface, but failure to be output-oriented is the primary reason that data processing people have had so many problems with software in the past; it is also the reason that we wind up with so many poor programs. Failure to well understand what kind of output a program is to produce is tantamount to, for instance, not knowing what kind of building you are going to build before you pour the concrete foundation. As someone once put it, "if you don't know for sure where you are going you are apt to end up somewhere else." We will be discussing output-oriented design more in the later chapters of the book.

Logical Before Physical Design

The second fundamental principle, that design should be logical before physical, is a tenet present in every other engineering discipline. Restated in less precise language, this
tenet suggests that we concern ourselves in design with
what to do before we worry about **how** to do it.   It gives
us the ability to focus our attention first on the most
important aspects of the problem, before worrying about the
less important ones.

We are probably unfortunate to be saddled with the terms
"logical" and "physical;" their everyday connotations sometimes cloud the issues involved. Stating that a part of
software design should be "logical" often implies that
another part will be "nonlogical" or even "illogical." That
is not the case. In the Warnier/Orr development method, the
two words have very precise meanings: "logical" refers to
the aspects of the software design that are hardware-indepen-
dent; "physical" refers to aspects that are specific to the
hardware environment.

Every problem that we must solve with a program is really a
problem in information handling, and as such many aspects of
the solution are quite independent of having a computer
around to perform it; information processing can be done
quite nicely (albeit slowly and imprecisely) by a clerk with
a typewriter and a calculator. The data that must be output, the data required as input, and the processing required
to transform the input into the output must be understood no
matter what computer we will be working with or what programming language will ultimately be used. The mechanics of the
solution — what language will be used, what computer
will be used, what peripheral devices will be used — are
aspects of the design that should be examined only after the
logical solution is understood.

The reason that such emphasis is placed on logical before
physical design is really twofold. First, the physical
environment that software resides in is highly changeable;
computer hardware changes, file access methods change, files
get reorganized, output devices change, even the programming
languages change. If a program design is too closely tied to

the physical operating environment, a change can make the
software completely obsolete . If, however, a program
design is based upon a physically independent solution to
the problem, a change of environment will be relatively easy
to respond to. The second reason is more subtle; examining
logical before physical requirements of a design tends to
limit the scope of investigation. We need not worry about
all aspects of the problem all at once. Limiting the scope
of an investigation is really just an extension of the
so-called KISS (Keep It Simple, Stupid) philosophy
recommended to designers of all kinds. The temptation to
design a program with physical constraints in mind too soon
tends to overly complicate and unnecessarily restrict a
project. By postponing physical design for as long as
possible, one finds that most of the programming problems
foreseen at the beginning have been designed away.

Data-Structured Design

The third and final fundamental principle, that design
should be data-structured, is one that was discovered apparently independently by both Warnier and Jackson. Both were
using graphic forms of representation to investigate the
structure of natively good programs — ones that were
easy to get and to keep running — and both came to the
same conclusion: the organization of the best programs was
the same as the organization of the data that they
processed. In the Warnier/Orr method, this observation has
been turned into an axiom: **if the organization of the data
can be discovered and represented, then the organization of
the programs necessary may be wholly derived.**

The soundness of this last principle is unfortunately not
intuitively obvious, and hence we will not try to further
explain or justify it at this point in the book. The reason
for this third tenet will become obvious as the Warnier/Orr
development method is presented in the subsequent chapters
of the book.

Summary

These three principles of design are the springboard for the discussion of the Warnier/Orr software development methodology. They provide the basis for all that we shall examine in the remainder of the book. Understanding them and learning to apply them well will provide you with the basis for designing and building consistently good data-structured programs.

Chapter 2 WARNIER/ORR DIAGRAMS

Basic Constructs

Everyone that has ever learned programming has been told at
one time or another that a program should be designed before
it is built. This design/construction dichotomy is an
important feature found in all engineering disciplines. In
construction there are both blueprints and buildings; in
electronics there are both schematics and circuitry. In
software design, there are many different ways of representing the logic before writing the program. Perhaps the most
familiar of these ways is the flowchart, but other ways
include hierarchy charts, Nassi/Schneiderman/Chapin charts,
pseudocode, decision tables, and HIPO diagrams.

The diagramming form that we will be using in this book is,
at its most basic form, a kind of "super flowchart" that enables one to depict the organization of a process (or a set
of data) in a compact and understandable form. It is called
a Warnier/Orr diagram after its two principle proponents,
Jean-Dominique Warnier and Ken Orr. Warnier/Orr diagrams
are quite easy to learn and to use because there are only a
handful of different diagramming constructs needed. We
shall introduce in this chapter the four basic Warnier/Orr
diagramming constructs necessary for program design. Two
slightly more advanced constructs will not be introduced in

this book, as they will not be directly needed for program design.

The four basic constructs are called **hierarchy, sequence, repetition,** and **alternation.** With just these four forms of representation we can represent the organization of any process or any set of data, and they will be quite sufficient for our initial work in program design. (The two more advanced constructs are called **concurrency** and **recursion,** and are needed to express certain kinds of systems relationships that cannot be expressed with any combination of the basic four.)

Hierarchy

The first and most fundamental construct needed for program design is called hierarchy; it provides us with the ability to show that a data set* is made up of simpler data. By expressing a data set hierarchically, one can achieve a "parts explosion" effect for a complicated data set; it can show how large or complicated data sets can be broken down into successively simpler and less complex data sets. Conversely, a hierarchy allows us to show how simple data can be compounded together to form more complicated data. To put it in simpler language, the use of hierarchy allows us to break big problems into little ones.

In the figure given on the next page is a simple example of how a Warnier/Orr diagram can be used to depict a level of hierarchy.

---

*Please take note of two important points: (1) The term "data set" is used here to mean a group of related data (however large or small) and is not to be confused with a similar term used to denote a physical data file in some data base management systems. (2) All comments made in this section about representing data sets apply equally well to the representation of sets of actions, i.e., processes or procedures. For instance, "hierarchy provides the ability to show that a process is made up of simpler processes." Since the Warnier/Orr philosophy is data structured, we shall introduce the diagrams in terms of data organization instead of in terms of processing or "programs."

```
                                      ⌠Employee Name
           Employee Record            ⎨Employee Address
           (1)                        ⎩Employee Pay Rate
```

Figure 2.1: Hierarchy

On this chart there are several features that you should
take note of. First of all, notice that the bracket* that
encloses the names of the data fields is the way that we
shall denote a level of hierarchy. The simplicity of this
form of representation lends itself naturally to the understanding of this diagram, even for people not familiar with
the rules of the diagramming form; the meaning of the relationship expressed by the chart seems self-evident. However, one skill that is well worth cultivating is the ability to translate a Warnier/Orr diagram into ordinary English.
This ability serves two important purposes: (1) The act of
translation often allows one to self-edit one's own work (if
the diagram doesn't make sense when translated, then it
probably isn't right). (2) Translating the diagrams into
English gives one the means to explain the relationships
described by the diagram to someone else unskilled in the
form.

A good way to read this kind of diagram is to replace the
bracket by the phrase "consists of" or "is composed of."
Thus, the diagram shown in Figure 2.1 would be translated
"One Employee Record **consists of** an Employee Name, an
Employee Address, and an Employee Pay Rate."

There are two terms that are used to describe features of a
Warnier/Orr diagram that are important to take note of. The
name which appears to the left of a bracket — in this

---

*To be technically correct, the symbol "{" is a brace, while
the symbol "[" is a bracket. Warnier's braces are more
squarish than the rounded ones we shall use in this book,
and more closely resemble a true bracket. The term "bracket" to describe a "{" has become widespread among the users
of the Warnier/Orr diagrams, so we will use it in this text.

first diagram "Employee Record" — is called a **univer-sal,** a term borrowed from a branch of mathematics called **set theory.**

Each bracket on a Warnier/Orr diagram must have a name, since each defines **a set** (a set is simply a collection of related things). The names appearing on a Warnier/Orr diagram which do not break down — in this diagram "Employee Name," "Employee Address," and "Employee Pay Rate" — are called **elements**, again a term taken from set theory. Thus, every name appearing on a Warnier/Orr diagram is either a universal (something which is further defined) or an element (something which is not further defined).

Elements appearing in one version of the diagram can, in turn, become universals if more details are depicted. An example of this is shown in Figure 2.2. In this diagram we have further broken down the Employee Name and the Employee Address into their component pieces.

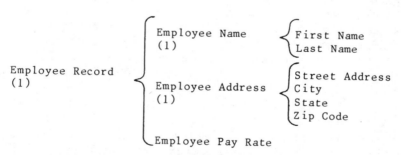

Figure 2.2: Two Levels of Hierarchy

We can use the same translation rules given earlier to describe this diagram as well: "One Employee Record consists of one Employee Name, one Employee Address, and an Employee Pay Rate. One Employee Name consists of a First Name and a Last Name. One Employee Address consists of a Street Address, a City, a State, and a Zip Code."

As you will see with the other constructs, the words used to describe the diagram correspond well with the visual

impression. A listener not looking at the diagram should be
able to understand the relationships being described with no
difficulty.

Sequence

The second basic construct needed for program design is
sequence — the ability to show that one thing occurs
after another in serial order. Sequence is the simplest of
the four constructs, and in fact has already been presented
on the two diagrams already introduced. In the diagram of
Figure 2.1, we depicted an Employee Record consisting of
three data elements by listing them from top to bottom
within the bracket. This was not just to identify the elements found on the record, but also to suggest the order in
which they would be present: the Employee Name first on the
record, the Employee Address second, and the Employee Pay
Rate last. On a Warnier/Orr diagram, sequence is always
implied within a level of hierarchy by listing features in
the proper order from top to bottom. Again, for the purposes of translating the diagrams into English, the construct
of sequence may be expressed by using the word "then" or the
phrase "followed by" between sequential features. Thus, the
diagram of Figure 2.1 would be more precisely translated
"One Employee Record consists of an Employee Name **then** an
Employee Address **then** an Employee Pay Rate" or "One
Employee Record consists of an Employee Name **followed by**
an Employee Address **followed by** an Employee Pay Rate."
Again, the description corresponds well with the visual
representation.

Repetition

The third construct needed is called repetition — the
ability to show that something occurs repeatedly within a
level of hierarchy. An example is shown in Figure 2.3.

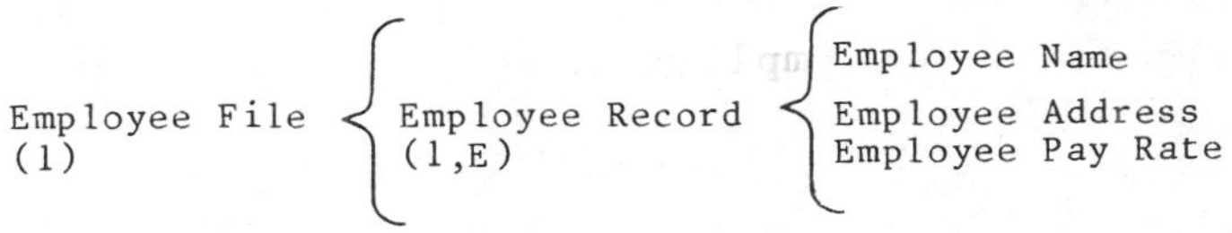

$$
\text{Employee File} \left\{ \begin{array}{l} \text{Employee Record} \\ (1,E) \end{array} \right. \left\{ \begin{array}{l} \text{Employee Name} \\ \text{Employee Address} \\ \text{Employee Pay Rate} \end{array} \right.
$$
(1)

Figure 2.3: Repetition (the DOUNTIL)

This diagram indicates that within the Employee File there is at least one and possibly many Employee Records, each one of which contains Employee Information. When we wish to indicate that a universal occurs some number of times other than just once, we will place a range of numbers representing the fewest and the most number of occurrences within parentheses beneath it. We may translate this diagram this way: "One Employee File consists of **from one-to-many** Employee Records. One Employee Record consists of an Employee Name, an Employee Address, and an Employee Pay Rate." Notice that since the maximum number of Employee Records on file is unbounded (possibly 10, 34, 298, or whatever), a placeholder letter is used to stand for some whole number greater than or equal to one. By convention, the letter chosen for the maximum bound in a repetition is the first letter of the repeating universal.

Were we to implement such a "(1,n)" structure in a program — make some process repeat at least once and possibly many times — we would have a form of a loop that has been classically identified as a **DOUNTIL** (do until) loop. The DOUNTIL was one of two forms of repetition identified and used by the proponents of structured programming. The other is called a **DOWHILE** (do while) loop, and it is different from the DOUNTIL loop in that the minimum bound is zero instead of one. If, for example, it was possible for the Employee File to be empty, we could depict its organization with the Figure 2.4.

```
                  {                       { Employee Name
Employee File     {  Employee Record      { Employee Address
(1)               {  (0,E)                { Employee Pay Rate
                  {                       {
```

Figure 2.4: Repetition (the DOWHILE)

This diagram may also be translated in a manner similar to the last: "One Employee File consists of from zero-to-many Employee Records. One Employee Record consists of ...."

For reasons that will be explained later in the book, Warnier does not allow the use of the "(0,n)" repetition, instead substituting a compound structure that will be given

later.   DOWHILE loops also cause some problems when building
process structures, and although we shall employ them to
begin with, we will eventually eliminate them in favor of
the compound construct Warnier prefers.

Alternation

The last construct needed is called alternation — the
ability to depict a universal which is partitioned into two
or more mutually exclusive alternatives. Alternation has
also been known as selection or CASE structure.

For an example of alternation, look at the diagram given in
Figure 2.5.   In this diagram we have further broken down the
Employee Pay Rate of the Employee Record we have been examining.   In this case, though, we find that the Employee Pay
Rate can be either an Hourly Rate or a Monthly Salary,
depending on whether the employee is hourly or salaried.
The "zero or one" number of times beneath the two kinds of
employees indicates that any one Employee Pay Rate may or
may not be for that particular kind of employee. The two
kinds of employees, Hourly Employee and Salaried Employee,
are alternative universals; either one or the other is
present at that level of hierarchy. The symbol between
them, the " ⊕ ", is the symbol for the **exclusive or**, and
it indicates that there is a special relationship between
the alternative universals that it separates; it indicates
that when one is present the other will not be.

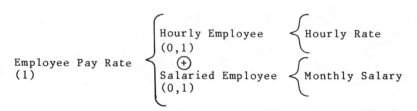

Figure 2.5: Simple Alternation

This diagram may be translated as follows: "One Employee Pay
Rate consists of **data for either** an Hourly Employee **or a**

Salaried Employee.   Data for an Hourly Employee consists of
an Hourly Rate.   Data for a Salaried Employee consists of a
Monthly Salary."

In Figure 2.5, we have suggested that an Employee is either
an Hourly Employee or a Salaried Employee, and further that
those two kinds of Employees are mutually exclusive (if they
are one they would not be the other).   This may well be
true, but depicting alternatives this way may lead to impre-
cision; the two cases may be mutually exclusive but not
exhaustive.   In other words, we must be certain that all
employees fall into one of those two categories.   If the possibility exists that an employee may be something other than
hourly or salaried, then our diagram is incomplete.   Another
form of representing alternation that guarantees both mutually exclusive and exhaustive cases appears in Figure 2.6.
This is called a **complementary alternative**, and the line
above the second case represents the negation of the first
alternative.   It is translated "not", "none", or "no".

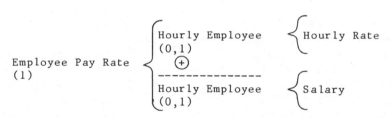

Figure 2.6: Complementary Alternation

This diagram indicates that an Hourly Rate will be found for
hourly employees, and that for employees who are not hourly
(all others) a salary will be present.   Since all employees
will fall into one of those two categories, the alternation
is exhaustive as well as mutually exclusive.

The complementary form of alternation is presented here
again out of deference to Warnier.   In this text we will
only rarely use the complement of an alternative on a
diagram, even though it is technically more precise.   If an
alternative is not exhaustive with just two cases, then we
shall depict all possibilities in the following fashion.
This is called a **complex alternation**, and it shows that

there may be three mutually exclusive (and presumably exhaustive) cases.

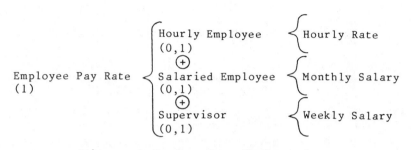

Figure 2.7: Complex Alternation

Structure

Before moving on to the application of the Warnier/Orr diagrams to program design, there is one more important concept that remains to be introduced. Ken Orr calls the concept "structure." Structure is defined to be a **hierarchy and/or sequence of repeating and/or alternating sets.** It is quite a simple idea once you get used to it.

Structures abound in the real world. One everyday example of the concept can be found in the odometer of a car: the "tenth-mile" wheel on the far right must mark off ten tenths before the "mile" wheel turns over once. It, in turn, must mark off ten miles before the "ten mile" wheel turns over, and so on. This is a simple example of what is meant by structure — having repeating or alternating levels of hierarchy which "nest" neatly inside one another.

Another structure that everyone is familiar with is to be found within the various levels of the calendar that we use. As a first example, let us develop a representation of the structure of a calendar Year with a Warnier/Orr diagram. We begin by drawing a bracket and labeling it with the name of the set that we wish to detail.

Year
(1)

Figure 2.8: Beginning a Structure

We then ask the question "What groups or chunks does a Year break down into?" or, more precisely, "What subsets does a Year consist of?" We are looking for the levels of hierarchy that fit neatly within a Year. Probably the largest subset of a Year, especially for a business concern, is the subset Quarter.

Year   Quarter
(1)   (4)

Figure 2.9: Adding a Level of Hierarchy

There are exactly four Quarters found within one Year, therefore we can create the diagram found in Figure 2.9. (Notice that "(1,4)" beneath the Quarter universal would be incorrect; it would suggest that a Year could consist of as few as one Quarter.)

Within the set Quarter we may now depict the subsets that repeat or alternate within **one** Quarter. Traditionally, a Quarter is broken down into three Months.

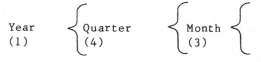

Year   Quarter   Month
(1)   (4)   (3)

Figure 2.10: More Structure

Notice that all of the repeating universals shown on this diagram are singular and not plural: Quarter instead of

Quarters, Month instead of Months. Even though there are
four Quarters per Year, within the bracket called Quarter we
will be describing what one Quarter or what each Quarter
looks like. It is important when building structures that
the universal names chosen be appropriate. You should be
able to add the words "for one" or "for a(n)" above all
universals and still have the diagram make sense. If you
cannot use the implied phrase as is shown in Figure 2.11,
then the name that you have selected for the universal is
inappropriate, and a different one should be chosen.

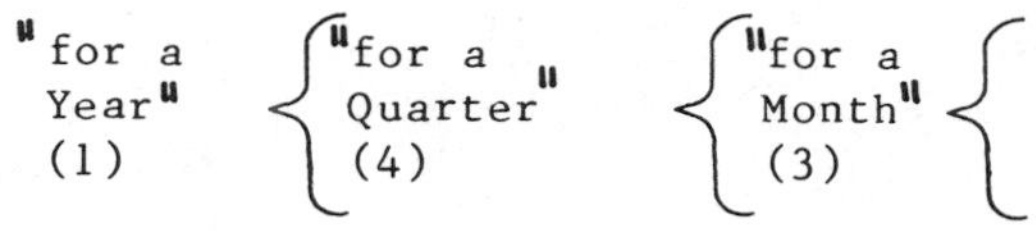

"for a
Year"
(1)
{
"for a
Quarter"
(4)
{
"for a
Month"
(3)
{

Figure 2.11: Repetitive Universals Translated to English

Another bit of terminology associated with Warnier/Orr diagrams is the concept of a **level of hierarchy.** In this
structure so far there are three levels of hierarchy: a Year
level within the Year bracket, a Quarter level within the
Quarter bracket, and a Month level within the Month bracket.
If we wish to show that something occurs monthly, we will
place it on the structure at the Month level; if something
occurs quarterly at the end, we can place it on the structure at the end of the Quarter level, i.e., physically
underneath the universal Month.

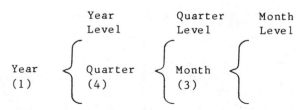

Figure 2.12: Level Names In a Structure

Now, let us get back to the structure. The next level of hierarchy is a bit tricky. The natural inclination is to say that each Month is subdivided into a number of Weeks, but unfortunately that is not correct. Weeks are not subsets of a Month, since they are not wholly contained within a Month; a week can begin in one Month and end in another. Since weeks are not a subset of a Month, we cannot show them on this hierarchy.

Since weeks do not fit neatly inside Months, the next biggest subset is a Day. Since not all Months contain the same number of Days, we will show beneath the Day universal the fewest and the most number of Days possible within a Month.

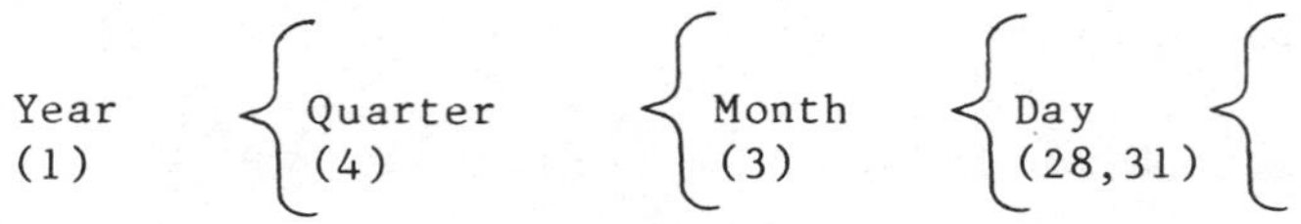

Figure 2.13: More Structure, Still

How many Days any given Month will have is dependent upon what Month and sometimes what Year it is, but the number will always be at least 28 and at most 31. Again note that the notation "(1,D)" under Day would be inappropriate.

We can continue to break this structure down into smaller and smaller subsets as has been done in Figure 2.14.

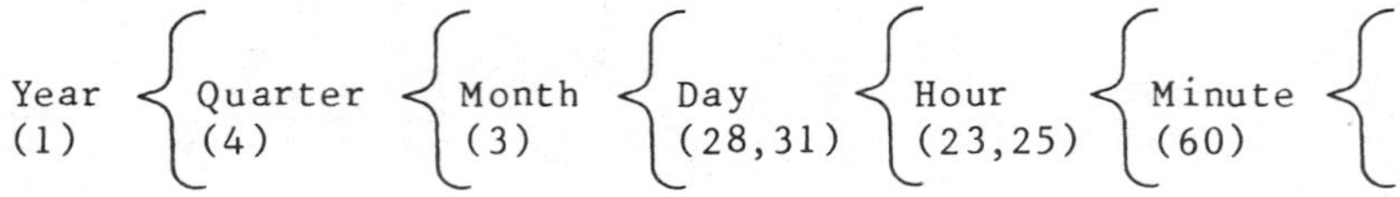

Figure 2.14: A 5-level Structure

This structure indicates that a Day consists of from 23 to 25 Hours (to be able to get into and out of Daylight Savings Time), and further that each Hour consists of 60 Minutes. We could continue on down into the structure by showing that Minutes consist of Seconds which consist of Milliseconds which consist of Microseconds, and so on, but we shall stop here.

How deeply one breaks down a structure is based upon the frequency of occurrence of elements we wish to depict. If the elements which interest us are occurring at most daily, then the structure given in Figure 2.13 is sufficiently detailed. If the elements occur more frequently than that, we would need more levels.

Summary

The use of the four constructs introduced in this chapter, along with the concept of a structure, will provide us with all of the necessary tools to create workable program designs. How one goes about creating correct program designs using the Warnier/Orr software development method is a topic taken up in the next chapter on the Warnier/Orr methodology.

Chapter 3 THE WARNIER/ORR METHODOLOGY

Background

The techniques that we begin to present in this chapter were
first developed by Jean-Dominique Warnier and his group at
CII Honeywell-Bull in Paris. Warnier calls the part of his
methodology that pertains to program design the **Logical Construction of Programs** or **LCP** for short. Apparently in
development since the late 1950s, LCP may very well be the
most widely used program design method in the world, outside
of the United States. Its use is widespread in Europe, Africa, and Japan (Warnier says that there are entire countries
in Africa where one is not allowed to be a programmer
without first learning LCP).

Warnier's LCP method, published in 1974 as <u>Les Procedures
de Traitment et leurs Donnes</u>, attracted the attention of
Kenneth T. Orr and his group working in the United States.
Orr has since used and extensively modified Warnier's concepts, and has applied them to not just program design, but
also to the design of entire systems and data bases. (To be
fair, Warnier also developed a systems analysis and design
approach called the Logical Construction of Systems (LCS)
before Orr.) Ken Orr calls his hybrid methodology **Data
Structured Systems Development (DSSD)**, and the part of DSSD
applying to local program development **Structured Program**

Design (SPD). SPD draws extensively from Warnier's LCP, but is quite different in many important respects. SPD also draws upon some of the work of Michael Jackson in the area of physical program design.

In this book we will primarily be discussing the hybrid Warnier/Orr Structured Program Design method, although occasional references to Warnier's LCP and Jackson's methods will be made.

Mappings

The basic philosophy behind Structured Program Design is a simple one, and is generally credited to Warnier.

All of data processing may be thought of as an extension of the branch of mathematics called set theory.

It is not the case, however, that a degree in mathematics or a thorough knowledge of set theory is necessary to understand the Warnier/Orr design method. A knowledge of some of the terms found in set theory and some of the more rudimentary concepts will be useful, though.

As was mentioned earlier in the book, a **set** is defined to be a collection of related things. In a very real sense, all of the collections of data that we keep and work with are sets, and all programs are basically a transformation rule designed to turn one set into another. Such a transformation is called a **mapping**.

```
=============================
      Physical Input Data
=============================


       Process (Mapping)


=============================
      Physical Output Data
=============================
```

Figure 3.1: Traditional Program Model

This view of programming is not new; as a matter of fact the traditional view of programming is also one of a mapping of one set into another. The old "input, process, output" view of programming has been around for a very long time.

The only problem with this philosophy is that the mapping represented in Figure 3.1 is not usually a simple nor easy one. When transforming input to output, there are four fundamental kinds of mappings which may be necessary. They deal with the relationship of the amount of input to the amount of output. Three of these mappings are relatively simple, and are shown in Figure 3.2.

Type 1: One to One (Identity)

I ————————— 0
I ————————— 0
I ————————— 0
I ————————— 0

Type 2: One to Many (Relation)

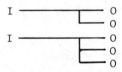

Type 3: Many to One (Function)

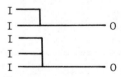

Figure 3.2: Simple Mappings

The simplest of all possible mappings is called a **one-to-one** or an **identity** mapping. Each and every record of input is transformed into one and only one record of output. The other two simple mappings are a bit more complicated, but not much. There is a **one-to-many** mapping, also called a **relation**, where one record of input

generates two or more records of output. There is also a
many-to-one mapping, also called a **function**,* where two
or more records of input are combined into just one record
of output.

All of these simple mappings represent problems that are
natively easy for most programmers to deal with. If all
programs were simply an exercise in defining one of these
kinds of mappings, then a need for an improved programming
method would probably never have arisen. However, most
"interesting" programs are not of any of these varieties.
Most programs fall under the fourth category of mapping,
shown in Figure 3.3.

Type: Many to Many (Complex)

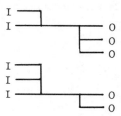

Figure 3.3: Complex Mapping

A complex mapping, as indicated by the figure, is where
several records of input are collected and used to generate
several records of output. The more input collected and the
more output generated, the more complicated the mapping is
likely to be.

The problem with complex mappings is that in practice they
can be excessively difficult if not impossible to deal with.

---

*The term "function" is used here in the mathematical sense,
and should not be confused with the usual data processing
connotation of the word as a synonym for a process or a
procedure.

No matter how natively intelligent a program designer is,
there comes a point where the complexity of a mapping is too
big to solve intuitively.

Therefore, the primary objective of both Warnier's LCP and
Orr's SPD is quite obvious: figure out some way to break one
complicated process into several simpler processes. To put
it precisely, the objective of the remainder of this book is
to find a way to resolve a complex (many-to-many) mapping of
data sets into a series of simple (one-to-one, one-to-many,
or many-to-one) mappings.

The Logical Mapping

In Structured Program Design, the technique for resolving
the complex mapping represented by a program is a many-step
process (more about that in a little bit). Principally, it
examines a series of three mappings, all of them simple, in
place of one complex one. Instead of dealing with the
transformation of the real (physical) input into the real
(physical) output in one fell swoop, the focus of SPD is on
the transformation of ideal (logical) input into ideal
(logical) output — the mapping of a simple form of the
input into a simple form of the output.


```
==================================
         Logical Input Data
==================================

         Logical Process (Mapping)

==================================
         Logical Output Data
==================================
```

Figure 3.4: Central (Logical) Mapping

Once this central transformation is understood, two subsidiary mappings are designed, one to translate the actual input

into the logical form and one to translate the logical output into the actual output. Therefore, the "big picture" of
a program designed using the Warnier/Orr method may be represented as in Figure 3.5.

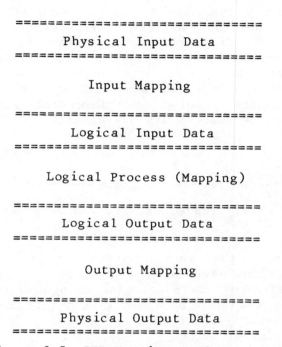

================================
Physical Input Data
================================

Input Mapping

================================
Logical Input Data
================================

Logical Process (Mapping)

================================
Logical Output Data
================================

Output Mapping

================================
Physical Output Data
================================

Figure 3.5: SPD Mappings and Data Sets

Ultimately in SPD we must investigate all four data structures and all three mappings shown in this figure. To begin
with, though, we will examine the central or logical mapping
and the data sets it will operate on: the logical output
data and the logical input data.

Building Software

Before getting into the mechanics of the Warnier/Orr program
design method, it is important to take note of the overall
context in which program design resides. Software does not

spring into being for no reason; it is a product developed
by an organization in response to some need. The process
whereby needs become programs has often been called the
information systems life cycle, and it is very much like a
product development cycle for a manufacturing concern.

Under many traditional methods, software creation was viewed
quite differently than it is today. When little was known
about software design, each new program created was an exercise in research and development; programming was a craft or
an art and programmers were craftspersons or artists. Like
crafts or artworks, there were just two basic stages of
development that a program went through, as suggested by
Figure 3.6. Each program was developed once, and then
maintained for the rest of its useful life.

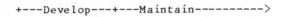

Figure 3.6: Traditional Program Development

This is the mode that many programs are in today. This is
not, however, the environment to build new programs into.
Nearly all "advanced" methodologies recognize that a program
is not simply developed once and then maintained thereafter.
A more realistic and practical approach would be that
appearing in Figure 3.7.

```
+---Develop Version 1---+---Develop Version 2---+---etc.--->
```

Figure 3.7: SPD Development

This is a more workable approach to managing changing software requirements; at some point the requirements of the program are pinned down, and version 1 of the software is
designed and built. As new requirements come in, they are
collected and eventually incorporated into the design and
construction of version 2 of the software, and so on. Under

this scheme, the quality of a particular piece of software
would not naturally degrade over time as more and more patches were applied. A program in its "nth" version should
appear to someone exactly the way that a new program
designed with the same requirements would.

Within a version of the software, there are four predictable
phases that may be detailed. A high-level picture of these
phases appears in Figure 3.8.

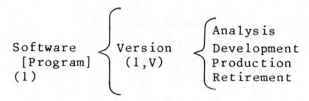

Software
[Program]
(1)

Version
(1,V)

Analysis
Development
Production
Retirement

Figure 3.8: Software Life Cycle

Software is a product, whether manufactured strictly for use
within an organization or for use by other organizations.
As such, it will proceed through four major stages called
analysis, development, production, and retirement. These
four phases can be further broken down into even finer subphases.

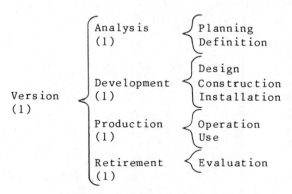

Version
(1)

Analysis
(1)

Planning
Definition

Development
(1)

Design
Construction
Installation

Production
(1)

Operation
Use

Retirement
(1)

Evaluation

Figure 3.9: Version Life Cycle

At this level a total of eight subphases are evident. Each one has a specific objective and result which is explained briefly below.

- Planning: a stage where problems and needs are evaluated and solutions selected.

- Definition: a stage where the desired outputs of a proposed software product are selected and specified.

- Design: a stage where the architecture of the software is detailed.

- Construction: a stage where the detailed designs are translated into a physical realization (a program) and tested for completeness.

- Installation: a stage where the constructed software is installed in its operating environment.

- Operation: a stage where the software is executed to produce informational results.

- Use: a stage where the results produced by the software are utilized to make decisions and take actions.

- Evaluation: a stage where the software is judged on its performance, user satisfaction, etc., as a feedback for improvement in the next cycle.

The parts of the life cycle that will concern us in this book are the phases of definition, design, and construction as they pertain to individual program design. In this text, we will not deal with all of the software life cycle, nor worry about so-called "systems" or "data base" concerns. Furthermore, the Design stage will be detailed as we have already seen — Logical Design first, Physical Design second. Further still, the Logical Design is subdivided into Data Design and Process Design.

Summary

In a nutshell, the program design method we shall present will go from **definition through construction** by the following steps:

1) Get the specifications for the actual output of the program (Actual Output Definition).

2) Establish the data specifications of the actual output (Logical Output Definition).

3) Figure out the logical output requirements (Logical Output Design).

4) Figure out the logical input requirements to support the output (Logical Input Design).

5) Develop the mapping to transform the logical input requirements into the logical output requirements (Logical Process Design).

6) Augment the Logical Process Structure with code level details (Physical Process Augmentation).

7) Design the physical output mapping (Output Mapping Design).

8) Design the physical input mapping (Input Mapping Design).

9) Translate the detailed mappings into code (Coding).

10) Test the completed program (Testing).

Steps 1 and 2 fall into the Definition phase, steps 3, 4, and 5 into Logical Design, steps 6, 7, and 8 into Physical Design, and steps 9 and 10 into Construction (see Figure 3.10). In the next chapter we will start to trace in detail the steps in the method outlined above.

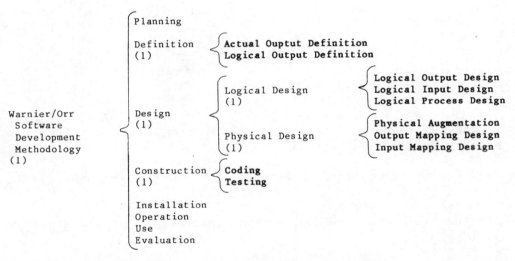

Figure 3.10: Chapter 3 Summary Diagram

Chapter 4 LOGICAL OUTPUT
DEFINITION AND DESIGN
PART 1
LOGICAL OUTPUT
STRUCTURES

Output Orientation

The final goal of the Warnier/Orr Structured Program Design methodology is a working and correct program. However, as suggested by the fundamental principles presented in Chapter 1 and the outline for program design presented at the end of the last chapter, we will not begin by creating code; if done well, the creation of code will be the next to the last step, and should be almost a trivial exercise.

In this chapter we will begin to explore a method for investigating the intended output of a program. Since the information content of the output is not dependent upon the language that we intend to code in, the computer that we intend to use, or the output device we will use, this is a step that falls into the category we have called "logical." The step is called Logical Output Definition, and the Warnier/Orr diagram that will be created is called a **Logical Output Structure.**

The Logical Output Structure (LOS) is a diagram which will depict the detailed requirements of an output: the data appearing on it and the organization with which it appears. It serves two important purposes. First, it is an excellent tool for achieving a detailed understanding of an output and

for verifying that understanding with the user requesting
it. The second purpose is equally important, though not
immediately obvious. By developing a diagram of the structure of the output, we will obtain much of the information
necessary to create the central transformation discussed in
the previous chapter — the mapping of the logical input
into the logical output.

Since all that will be done in design is based upon what is
learned about the output in this step, it is vitally important to learn how to investigate outputs well, and depict
what has been learned in a clear and understandable manner.

Output Definition

Recall from Chapter 2 the Warnier/Orr definition of the term
"structure" — a hierarchy and/or sequence of repeating
and/or alternating sets (or hierarchies). Just as the
calendar Year investigated in that chapter had a discernible
structure, so do all outputs. The outputs that we will
investigate through the first part of this text will be
represented as printed reports, but that is simply for
convenience. We can and will, later, investigate outputs
other than printed reports in the same manner: magnetic tape
output, punched card output, microfiche output, screen
output, disk output, etc. We will examine simple output
structures to begin with, and work on successively more
complex examples as we proceed.

Examine the output layout shown in Figure 4.1. We shall be
using this form of output representation to begin with. It
identifies the name of an output field only at its first
occurrence, with the repetitions of that data shown as just
a solid field of x's.

On this output layout there are three data fields represented: Attorney Name, Amount Billed, and Firm Total Billed.

One excellent way to find the structure of an output is to
think of it in terms of the data fields that would be
transmitted to an output device — what fields would be
sent and in what order.

```
xx Attorney Name xx        xx Amount Billed xx
xxxxxxxxxxxxxxxxxx         xxxxxxxxxxxxxxxxxx
xxxxxxxxxxxxxxxxxx         xxxxxxxxxxxxxxxxxx
xxxxxxxxxxxxxxxxxx         xxxxxxxxxxxxxxxxxx
xxxxxxxxxxxxxxxxxx         xxxxxxxxxxxxxxxxxx
                     xx Firm Total Billed xx
```

Figure 4.1: Output #1 Layout

The examination of such a serial stream of data will likely
show us the groups (and groups of groups) of data elements
that repeat on the output, and thus give us the structure.
Such a **data stream** for the output shown above might look
something like that shown in Figure 4.2 below.

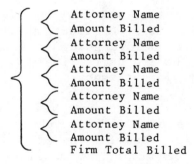

```
        Attorney Name
        Amount Billed
        Attorney Name
        Amount Billed
        Attorney Name
        Amount Billed
        Attorney Name
        Amount Billed
        Attorney Name
        Amount Billed
        Firm Total Billed
```

Figure 4.2: Output #1 Data Stream

Notice that there are patterns which are evident. The group
"Attorney Name, Amount Billed" repeats, with the element
Firm Total Billed appearing just once at the end. This
would indicate that there are two levels of hierarchy on
this output, as is shown by the spans of the brackets shown
on the data stream.   All that remains is to find the names
of the two levels.

Two candidates for names would be "Report" for the highest level, and "Detail Line" for the interior level. Although truthful, these names are relatively uninteresting. They would not tell us much about what logical groups the data is being shown for, only the physical packaging of the data. A better hierarchy would be developed if we were to ask the questions; "Who or what does each line of data represent information about?" and "Who or what is the data on the report for?" It would seem that the data on each line is data for an Attorney, while the data shown on the report is data for the whole Firm. These are much better logical names for the levels present.

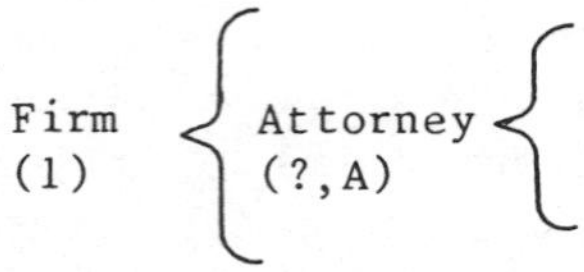

Firm   {   Attorney {
(1)   (?,A)

Figure 4.3: Structure of Output #1

In this figure we have made some assumptions about the nature of the output; we have assumed that the output is for only the one Firm and that Attorney may repeat many times. **Anytime an assumption is made about an output, it must be verified with the user before going on with the design.** If we fail to do this, we are quite likely to develop something for a user that they did not want.

Also notice that the minimum bound has been left as a question mark. There are basically two choices for this minimum bound, "0" or "1," and choosing one of the two automatically guarantees we will be making an assumption. Showing that Attorney repeats from "(0,A)" times for the Firm insinuates that the output for the Firm may have **no Attorneys shown**; just a Firm Total Billed of zero for a period with no billing. Showing that Attorney repeats "(1,A)" times indicates that the output always has **at least one** Attorney's worth of data on it, suggesting that this output is not produced for a period with no billing.

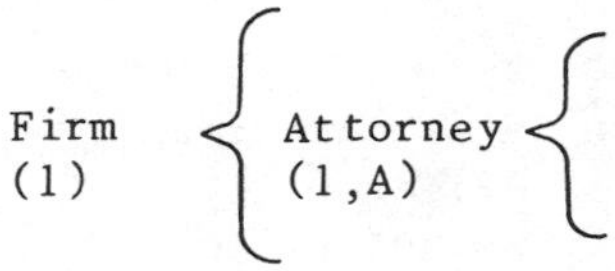

```
Firm        {  Attorney  {
(1)         {  (1,A)     {
```

"for the Firm there will be at least
one Attorney shown on the output."

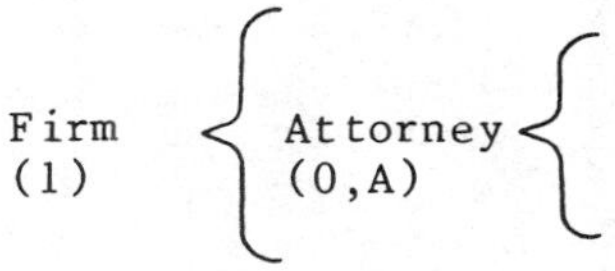

```
Firm        {  Attorney  {
(1)         {  (0,A)     {
```

"for the Firm, there may be no
Attorneys shown on the output."

Figure 4.4: Possible Lower Bounds for Output # 1

In the case in Figure 4.4, we shall assume (with the same
comment that was made earlier about assumptions) that this
output is only to be produced for a period with billing.
Thus, the "(1,A)" designation would be appropriate.

```
xx Attorney Name xx     xx Client Name xx     xx Amount Billed xx
xxxxxxxxxxxxxxxxxxx     xxxxxxxxxxxxxxxx     xxxxxxxxxxxxxxxxxxx
xxxxxxxxxxxxxxxxxxx     xxxxxxxxxxxxxxxx     xxxxxxxxxxxxxxxxxxx
                                            xx Attorney Total Billed xx
xxxxxxxxxxxxxxxxxxx     xxxxxxxxxxxxxxxx     xxxxxxxxxxxxxxxxxxx
xxxxxxxxxxxxxxxxxxx     xxxxxxxxxxxxxxxx     xxxxxxxxxxxxxxxxxxx
xxxxxxxxxxxxxxxxxxx     xxxxxxxxxxxxxxxx     xxxxxxxxxxxxxxxxxxx
xxxxxxxxxxxxxxxxxxx     xxxxxxxxxxxxxxxx     xxxxxxxxxxxxxxxxxxx
                                            xxxxxxxxxxxxxxxxxxxxxxxxxxxx
                                            xx Firm Total Billed xx
```

Figure 4.5: Output #2 Layout

This technique for finding the structure of an output works
even for more complicated outputs. Take for example the
output layout shown in Figure 4.5. This output is a bit
more complicated than the first, but still quite simple as
outputs go. This output can also be thought of as a data
stream being passed to an output device.

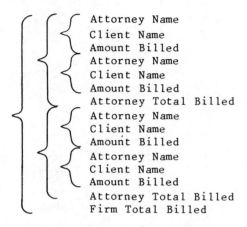

Figure 4.6: Output #2 Data Stream

This data stream suggests that in this output there are three levels of repetition: a high level just having the Firm Total Billed once at the end, an intermediate level having just an Attorney Total Billed once at the end, and an interior level containing an Attorney Name, Client Name, and Amount Billed. As before, we must choose appropriate logical names for the three levels. In this case, Firm, Attorney, and Client appear to be good names.

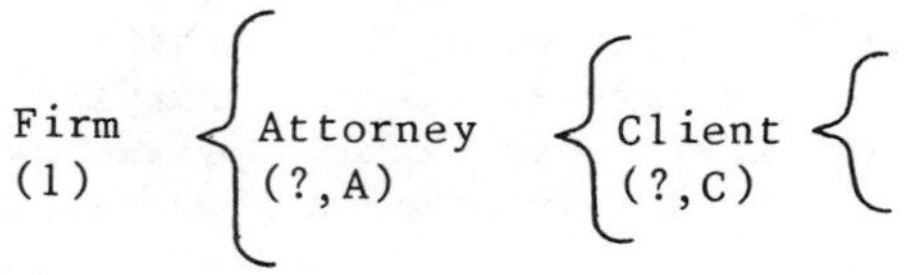

Firm   Attorney   Client
(1)   (?,A)   (?,C)

Figure 4.7: Structure of Output #2

Another way to find the structure of an output is the one recommended for everyday use. The act of listing a data stream becomes very cumbersome for a large or deeply **nested** output. The method described below works well for even complex outputs.

To begin with, notice that the structure that interests us here represents the groups (and groups of groups) of data elements which repeat on the output. Therefore, we might get some useful information by examining the data elements appearing on the output. A list of the data elements which appear on this output is given below.

```
No. Data Element
==================
 1   Attorney Name
 2   Client Name
 3   Amount Billed
 4   Attorney Total Billed
 5   Firm Total Billed
```

Figure 4.8: Output #2 Data Elements

We might then go through the list and examine the number of times or the **frequency** that each element appears on the output. The Firm Total Billed, for instance, appears just once for the Firm on the output; the Attorney Total Billed appears once for each Attorney shown; and the Attorney Name, the Client Name, and the Amount Billed all appear once for each Client for an Attorney. The names of the levels necessary for the structure will be the names of the different frequencies found: Firm, Attorney, and Client. All that remains is to line them up in the proper order, with Firm highest, Attorney within Firm, and Client within Attorney, and document our assumptions about the appearance of each level. When completed, our data element list will have grown into an **Output Definition Worksheet**, and will look something like that shown in Figure 4.9.

From the Output Definition Worksheet shown in Figure 4.9 we can more easily derive the structure shown back in Figure 4.7. The Logical Output Structure that we will produce incorporates **both** the **structure** and the **data elements**.

```
No. Data Element                Appears:
========================================
1    Attorney Name              1/Client
2    Client Name                1/Client
3    Amount Billed              1/Client
4    Attorney Total Billed      1/Attorney
5    Firm Total Billed          1/Firm
----------------------------------------
```
The output is for just one Firm.
At least one Attorney's data is shown for the Firm.
At least one Client's data is shown for an Attorney.

Figure 4.9: Output #2 Output Definition Worksheet

If we look at the structure, we can identify on it five different element areas representing five different output frequencies. The five areas are shown in Figure 4.10. The areas labeled {1} through {5} represent, respectively, the beginning of the Firm level, the beginning of the Attorney level, the Client level, the end of the Attorney level, and the end of the Firm level. To complete the Logical Output Structure we must place the data elements appearing on the worksheet onto the structure in the appropriate positions.

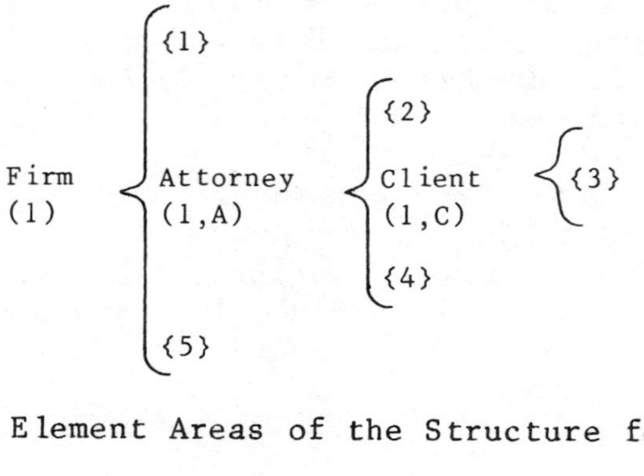

Figure 4.10: Element Areas of the Structure for Output #2

From the analysis already done, we know that the Firm Total
Billed appears once for the Firm. It must therefore go onto
the structure at the Firm level. The only choice is between
the beginning and the end of the Firm. Clearly it occurs at
the end of the Firm level, after all Attorneys, or in the
area labeled {5} on the above Figure. Similarly, we can
determine that the Attorney Total Billed should appear at
the end of the Attorney level, or area {4}, and that the
remaining elements all appear at the Client level, or area
{3}. The beginning of the Firm level and Attorney level,
areas {1} and {2}, are empty in this case, since no data
appears there on the output.

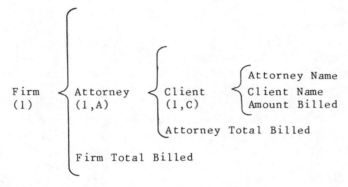

Figure 4.11: Logical Output Structure for Output #2

With the data elements all placed onto the structure at the
appropriate points, we have completed a diagram which is
probably the Logical Output Structure for this output. All
that remains is to translate the diagram back into English
to see if it does indeed describe the output. The diagram
may be read "the output for the Firm consists of output for
one-to-many Attorneys, followed by a Firm Total Billed. Output for an Attorney consists of output for one-to-many
Clients, followed by an Attorney Total Billed. Output for a
Client consists of an Attorney Name, a Client Name, and an
Amount." Since that translation does indeed seem to
describe the output as we know it, this is indeed the
correct Logical Output Structure.

Both Warnier's LCP method and Orr's SPD method create such a
diagram at the beginning of a design, only Warnier calls
this a logical output file. The Logical Output Structure is
the first step towards the production of a reliable program
design. It represents the requirements of the output in a
fashion that most people find comfortable to look at and
easy to understand. If differs from some other diagramming
forms in that in addition to being well organized it is also
fairly dense; even rather large and cumbersome outputs can
usually be represented easily on a single letter-sized sheet
of paper. In fact, an argument can be made that an output
whose LOS cannot be represented on a single sheet is
probably too complicated to be very useful; breaking it down
into two or more simpler outputs would be a very good idea.

Because of the extreme usefulness of the Logical Output
Structure and because of its importance to the program
design process, the definition, purpose, and a list of steps
to build an LOS is presented for your reference in Figure
4.12. There is a word of caution, however, that must also
be presented with this list; it should be thought of as a
guide or a suggestion for studying an output, and not as an
infallible standard. Anytime a process is as finely
detailed as this one, there is a real risk that the steps
will lapse into dogma — rote steps followed blindly and
without question. No procedure is infallible, including
this one.

```
==========================================================================
Logical Output Definition: Creating The Logical Output Structure (LOS)
==========================================================================
Purpose: to make explicit the implicit requirements of an output.
Definition of LOS: a picture of the logical output requirements.
--------------------------------------------------------------------------
Steps to build a Logical Output Structure:
1) Data Elements Definition:  Make a list of the Data Elements appearing
             on the output.
2) Element Frequency Definition:  Discover the frequency that each
             element appears on the output by creating an Output
             Definition Worksheet.
3) Universals Mapping:  Build a structure from the output frequencies
             found.
4) Elements Mapping:  Place the output elements onto the structure.
5) Logical Output Definition Testing:  Translate the structure into
             English to check the picture's accuracy.
==========================================================================
```

Figure 4.12: Building a Logical Output Structure

Of the steps given here, the most important one is the last. If you cannot justify that the translation of the diagram represents an accurate reflection of the output require- ments, then the diagram is not a correct Logical Output Structure no matter how it was produced.

Just as in mathematics or engineering, it is more important to learn the principles underlying the step, rather than the formulas. Memorized formulas are no good for solving prob- lems that don't fit them; understanding the principles involved will enable one to solve even odd problems that don't quite fit into what we know.

Physical Considerations

So far in our discussion of Logical Output Structures we have been fairly informal about the requirements for the names of universals. That is about to change. Not all out- put hierarchy names are useful for the LOS. In represen- ting the appearance frequencies of data elements, we will wish to restrict those frequencies to **logical** ones and **not physical.** For an example of what is meant by this examine the output shown in Figure 4.13.

```
                    "Attorney Time Report"
              "For the Month of:"    xx Month Name xx

xx Attorney Name xx
      xx Category Name xx      xx Hours Worked xx    xx Hours Billed xx
      xxxxxxxxxxxxxxxxxxxx     xxxxxxxxxxxxxxxxxxx    xxxxxxxxxxxxxxxxxxx
      xxxxxxxxxxxxxxxxxxxx     xxxxxxxxxxxxxxxxxxx    xxxxxxxxxxxxxxxxxxx
 "Total for Attorney:"        xx Atty Hrs Wkd xx     xx Atty Hrs Bld xx

xxxxxxxxxxxxxxxxxxxx
      xxxxxxxxxxxxxxxxxxxx     xxxxxxxxxxxxxxxxxxx    xxxxxxxxxxxxxxxxxxx
      xxxxxxxxxxxxxxxxxxxx     xxxxxxxxxxxxxxxxxxx    xxxxxxxxxxxxxxxxxxx
 "Total for Attorney:"        xxxxxxxxxxxxxxxxxxx    xxxxxxxxxxxxxxxxxxx

 "Total for the Firm:"        xx Firm Hrs Wkd xx     xx Firm Hrs Bld xx
```

Figure 4.13: Output Layout #3

Notice some slightly different fields on this output from those examined to this point. The fields appearing in quotes are **label** elements; they are present on an output not for their informational content, but simply as labels of groups of data that appear. On this output, there are labels found in the heading and in the total lines. Thus, when we list the data elements on this output, we will give a name to each of the label elements and include them: the Report Title Label, the Report Period Label, the Attorney Total Label, and the Firm Total Label.

Also notice that the identification of the appearance frequencies is not as straightforward as it was in the earlier example.

In addition to having elements that appear at the end of the Firm, at the end of each Attorney, for each Category, and at the beginning of each Attorney, there are three elements which appear once per **Page** on the output: the Report Title Label, Report Period Label, and the Month Name.

This would seem to be a problem. If we try to build a structure with a fourth level called Page in with Firm, Attorney, and Category, we quickly run into difficulty. Page will not fit neatly. Trying to fit Page in with the other hierarchies identified presents us with the same kind of problem mentioned back in Chapter 2 when we tried to put Week within Month on the calendar structure. Attorney is not a subset of Page, since an Attorney can begin on one Page and carry on over to another, and Page is not a subset of Attorney either.

It turns out there are two kinds of hierarchies that one is likely to discover when analyzing output frequencies: "logical" frequencies such as Firm, Attorney, and Category which are independent of the hardware involved, and "physical" frequencies like Page, Line, Report, Record, File, Screen, etc., which are dependent upon the output device being used. **Logical and physical hierarchies tend to be mutually incompatible;** like oil and water they do not naturally mix. For that reason we shall adopt a convention that will allow us to ignore physical hierarchies for the purposes of logical design.

Consider for the moment the production of a multivolume tape
file as an output. Under most mainframe operating systems,
a programmer building such a tape need not be concerned with
sensing the end of a tape, rewinding it, mounting a new
tape, and creating its header record. The operating system
is "intelligent" enough to do that automatically. Thus the
program building the tape file believes that it is writing
on one infinitely long tape.

It does not require a big leap in intellect to suppose that
there might be an operating systems similarly "intelligent"
for a printer (or any other kind of device you want to
name). Under such an operating system, a program would not
need to worry about pagination of a report; the operating
system would be smart enough to sense the end of one page
and then automatically eject and print a new heading. With
an operating system like this, the hierarchy Page ceases to
be visible; the Logical Output Structure would indicate that
the page heading was sent to the operating system just once
at the beginning of the Firm level, and would let the system
do the rest. Thus, the conflict between logical and physical would not come up.

**For the purposes of building a Logical Output Structure,
one always assumes that an "intelligent" operating system is
being used.** This way the completed LOS is independent of
output device. Resolving the problem of paging (and other
device-dependent processing) is a topic that will be
addressed later in the book. Those problems are part of the
mapping from logical output into physical output that was
mentioned in the last chapter.

The completed Output Definition Worksheet and the Logical
Output Structure for this output are shown in Figure 4.14.
One new notational device is introduced in this LOS: the
use of a period (".") as a qualifier for an element. A
period on a Warnier/Orr diagram is simply a way of
indicating that the name of the level is to be appended to
the element shown.

The ".Name" at the beginning of the Attorney Level is
shorthand for the element Attorney Name, while at the
Category level it is shorthand for Category Name. The
".Hours Worked" at the end of the Firm level stands for Firm
Hours Worked, etc. The period is used very much like a hori-
zontal ditto mark. It saves writing when creating an LOS
without detracting from its readability.

```
Output Definition Worksheet
No. Data Elements                    Appears
============================================
1    Report Title Label              1/Firm
2    Report Period Label             1/Firm
3    Month Name                      1/Firm
4    Attorney Name                   1/Attorney
5    Category Name                   1/Category
6    Category Hours Worked           1/Category
7    Category Hours Billed           1/Category
8    Attorney Total Label            1/Attorney
9    Attorney Hours Worked           1/Attorney
10   Attorney Hours Billed           1/Attorney
11   Firm Total Label                1/Firm
12   Firm Hours Worked               1/Firm
13   Firm Hours Billed               1/Firm
--------------------------------------------
The output is for just one Firm.
At least one Attorney's data is shown for the Firm.
At least one Category's data is shown for each Attorney.
```

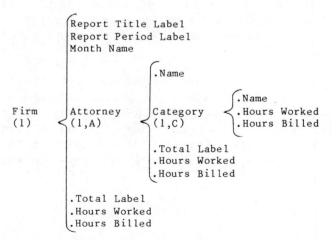

Figure 4.14: Output #3 Worksheet and LOS

Sequential Hierarchies

In the first three outputs examined, all of the repeating
subsets nested neatly inside one another. There is another
relationship possible for repeating subsets other than a
hierarchical one; repeating hierarchies may appear
sequentially (one after the other) within a larger level of
hierarchy. For an example of this kind of output, look at
Figure 4.15 given below.

```
                        "Attorney Billing"
    "Attorney"
    xx Attorney Name xx
          "Corporate Clients"          "Billed"
          xx Company Name xx           xx Amount Billed xx
          xxxxxxxxxxxxxxxxxx           xxxxxxxxxxxxxxxxxx
          "Total"             xx Total Corporate Billed xx
          "Personal Clients"
          xx Client Name xx             xxxxxxxxxxxxxxxxxx
          xxxxxxxxxxxxxxxxxx            xxxxxxxxxxxxxxxxxx
          "Total Personal"    xx Total Personal Billed xx
          "Attorney Total"    xx Attorney Total Billed xx
    xxxxxxxxxxxxxxxxxxxx
          "Corporate Clients"          "Billed"
          xxxxxxxxxxxxxxxxxx            xxxxxxxxxxxxxxxxxx
          xxxxxxxxxxxxxxxxxx            xxxxxxxxxxxxxxxxxx
          "Total"             xxxxxxxxxxxxxxxxxxxxxxxxxxxxx
          "Personal Clients"
          xxxxxxxxxxxxxxxxxx            xxxxxxxxxxxxxxxxxx
          "Total Personal"    xxxxxxxxxxxxxxxxxxxxxxxxxxx
          "Attorney Total"    xxxxxxxxxxxxxxxxxxxxxxxxxxx
    "Firm Total Corporate"    xx Firm Corporate Billed xx
    "Firm Total Personal"     xx Firm Personal Billed xx
    "Firm Total"                 xx Firm Total Billed xx
```

Figure 4.15: Output #4 Layout

In this Attorney Billing report, we see information grouped
by Attorney within the Firm level as before.

Within an Attorney there are two repeating levels of hierarchy; we list all of the Corporate Clients for an Attorney before all the Personal Clients, if any. Thus, the structure of this output is as appears, simplified, in Figure 4.16. It has two repeating hierarchies within Attorney, one sequentially before the other.

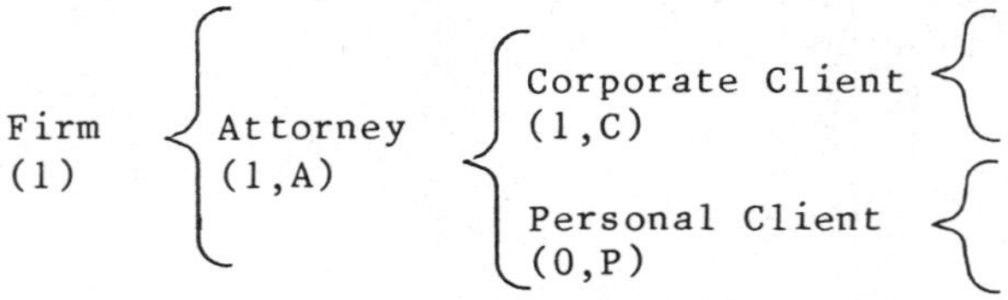

Figure 4.16: Simplified Output Structure for Output #4

The Output Definition Worksheet for this output will not be presented as an example in this text as it is very straightforward; from this point on the only worksheets that will be shown are those that have some interesting or new aspect not seen before.

The Logical Output Structure for this output is given in Figure 4.17. Notice that there are assumptions about the output inherent in this LOS; it assumes that at least one Attorney is shown on the output for the Firm, that each Attorney always has at least one Corporate Client, and that an Attorney may have no Personal Clients. If the true output requirements were discovered to be different from these assumptions (which should be documented on the worksheet), then the LOS would have to be changed accordingly.

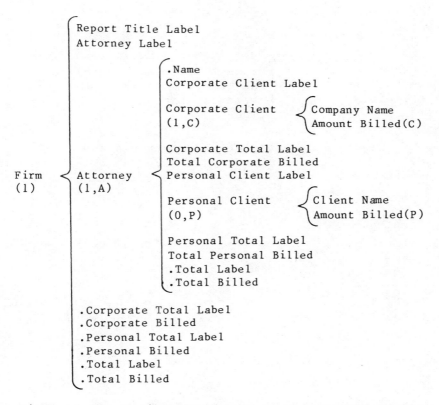

Figure 4.17: Logical Output Structure for Output #4

Summary

The diagram in Figure 4.18 depicts the ideas in Figure 4.12.
We define the logical output by creating a Logical Output
Structure.   The outputs examined in this chapter have been
outputs with only repeating elements.   Elements which may or
may   not   be   present   within   a   level   of   hierarchy   are
indicative   of   alternative   structures   which   will   be   examined
in the next chapter.

```
                                   ⎧ Data Elements Definition
             Logical              ⎪ Element Frequency Definition
               Ouptut             ⎨ Universals Mapping
             Definition           ⎪ Elements Mapping
             (1)                   ⎩ .Testing
```

Figure 4.18: Chapter 4 Summary Diagram

Chapter 5 LOGICAL OUTPUT DEFINITION AND DESIGN PART 2 ALTERNATION

Output Samples

The outputs that we worked with in the last chapter were all represented as data layouts, very similar in form to a traditional "printer spacing chart." Beginning with this chapter, actual samples of the data to be shown will be used as examples rather than just the names of the data fields. The reason for this goes back to the first fundamental principle of Warnier/Orr design: design should be output-oriented.

Remember that being "output-oriented" requires that the output be understood **as completely as possible** before proceeding with the design. This, as was mentioned earlier, seems natural to most designers; it seems a waste of effort to do detailed programming when one is not sure of just what it is that will be produced. The necessity of going to the trouble to build an actual sample output is not obvious to many, but is intimately related to the reason that many poor programs get built.

It is a curious fact of life in data processing that no one ever **intentionally** creates a bad program. A programmer may suspect that a particular piece of software will be poor by the time it is finished, but creating it poorly is not a

design goal. Most programs end up being poor when completed
because the requirements of the program were not well understood; constant changes and patches were being made to the
program during its creation as additional requirements were
uncovered.

One of the things that data processing people have classically been faulted for is not building a model of the
finished product before going out and building something.
Traditionally, users have often been asked to "sign off" on
printer spacing charts, much like the data layouts we worked
with in the last chapter. The problem with this strategy is
the one that has already been mentioned: designers must make
assumptions about what the user wants on the output. The
problem is that the designer almost never gets all of the
assumptions right (you would think that if there were ten
assumptions to be made, by sheer luck you could get five of
them right; somehow that never works out.) This leads the
user to think that the designer really does not know what he
or she is doing.

Often, the first time that a user actually sees what is to
be present on the output is when it is delivered the first
time, the program already written and debugged. A short
conversation ensues.

>   User: What's this? This isn't the output I wanted.
>   DP: It's your fault. You didn't tell us you wanted
>   something else!
>   User: No, it's your fault! You didn't ask!

As the information processing professional, it is the
software designer's responsibility to ask. If software
designers   fail to ask, it is then their responsibility to
make the software right at their own expense, and not that
of the user. This is no different than any other
engineering discipline. An architect would not put up a
couple of floors of a new building before calling in the
user to see if that is what he or she had in mind. We could
build buildings that way, but it would be incredibly
expensive in the long run and the quality of the finished
products would be highly suspect.

Alternative Universals

In Chapter 2 a "structure" was defined to be a hierarchy
and/or sequence of repeating and/or alternating sets. The
Logical Output Structures that were examined in the last
chapter all had structures consisting of only repeating sets
of data. In this chapter, we will examine outputs with
alternation present. It turns out that their Logical
Output Structures can be derived in the same fashion as
before.

Alternation on a structure is indicated when an element or a
group of elements is present "randomly" —— present
sometimes and not present at other times. For example, look
at the output sample represented in Figure 5.1.

                    Accounts Receivable Summary
                    For the Month of January 1983

```
Client #   Name                                   Balance Owed
1021       Allen, Kenneth A.                            12.35
1128       Burnham Realtors         Corporate          312.11
1267       Carpet World             Corporate          145.23
1346       Davis, John                                 96.45
1411       Hughes, Phil                                25.00
...etc....
2933       Young & Smith, Inc.      Corporate        1,947.90

Total Receivables                                    5,132.93
```

                Figure 5.1: Output #5 Sample

At first this output looks quite simple: two levels of hierarchy, with the headings and Firm total information output
once per Firm, and the Client Number, Name, and Balance Owed
output once each Client. However, the Corporate Label (the
word "Corporate") does not appear with each Client. It
appears on some Client lines and not on others.

The way that is most tempting to represent this on a Logical
Output Structure is shown in Figure 5.2. It is not quite
correct.

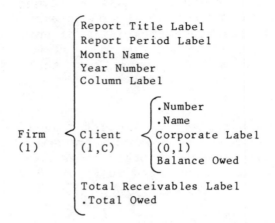

<pre>
                    ┌ Report Title Label
                    │ Report Period Label
                    │ Month Name
                    │ Year Number
                    │ Column Label
                    │   ┌ .Number
                    │   │ .Name
      Firm   │ Client   │ Corporate Label
      (1)   │ (1,C)   │ (0,1)
                    │   └ Balance Owed
                    │
                    │ Total Receivables Label
                    └ .Total Owed
</pre>

Figure 5.2: Incorrect LOS for Output #5

This LOS falls into the category "truthful but uninteresting". It is also a bit ambiguous; is just the element Corporate Label present zero or one times, or are all of the
elements Client Number, Client Name, and Corporate Label present zero or one times? This incorrect LOS also exhibits a
property not seen to this point. It has an **element** with
an associated number of times; all elements represented on
any other LOS were present just once within a level of hierarchy.

The solution to this problem may be found back in the output
worksheet. Recall that to find the LOS, we may list the
elements to be output and their output frequency. Further,
this output frequency must be **once per some logical set**,
or the correct output level is not seen. (We could list
that the Client Name, for instance, appears "1,n/Firm",
which is truthful, but not the level that we need to see.)
This "once per some logical set" convention will always
serve to find the correct level for the LOS. In this case,
the correct level is shown in the completed worksheet in
Figure 5.3.

```
Data Element                    Appears
=====================================
Report Title Label              1/Firm
Report Period Label             1/Firm
Month Name                      1/Firm
Year Number                     1/Firm
Column Label                    1/Firm
Client Number                   1/Client
Client Name                     1/Client
Corporate Label                 1/Corporate Client
Balance Owed                    1/Client
Total Receivables Label         1/Firm
Firm Total Owed                 1/Firm
---------
The output is for one Firm
At least one Client for the Firm is shown
The Corporate Label appears only for Corporate Clients
```

Figure 5.3: Output Definition Worksheet for Output #5

The Corporate Label is **not** output each Client, as the other Client elements are, but is only output for a particular **kind** of Client — a Corporate Client. Thus, Corporate Client is a logical set name or a universal on the correct LOS. It is not a repeating set, though, it is an **alternating set** — present either zero or one times for any given Client. Thus, the correct Logical Output Structure for this output will have three universals on it: Firm is the highest level, Client repeats within Firm and Corporate Client alternates within Client. (See Figure 5.4.)

This LOS is unambiguous. It is clear that the Client Number, Client Name, and Balance Owed are present for each Client, while the Corporate Label is present only for a Corporate Client. It also has the same properties as the other Logical Output Structures seen — each data element is present only one time within some level of hierarchy. This must always be the case; **universals on an LOS always have a number of times designation** while **elements never do.** This is because an element is always present just once

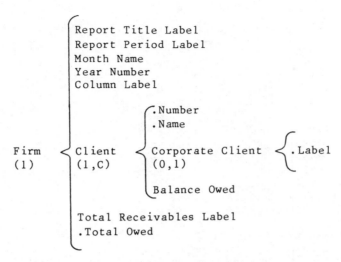

Report Title Label
Report Period Label
Month Name
Year Number
Column Label

Firm   Client   Corporate Client   .Number
(1)   (1,C)   (0,1)   .Name
                                                   .Label

Balance Owed

Total Receivables Label
.Total Owed

Figure 5.4: Correct LOS for Output #5

within a universal. An element with a number-of-times designation is **always** a clue that there is a level of hierarchy missing on the Logical Output Structure. On the other hand, an LOS "universal" with only a "(1)" designation is actually just an element and the designation should be removed and the incorrect universal should be replaced by "its" elements; the exception is the highest level universal which must only occur one time.

The DOWHILE Construct

On the output just examined, the assumption was made that at least one Client was to appear each time this output was produced, implying that some other output is produced when there are no Clients to report. If the output requirements were found to be different, a somewhat different Logical Output Structure must be derived.

As an example, let us consider the structure of the output if it **is** to be produced even when there are no Clients to report. Such an output would appear as in Figure 5.5.

Accounts Receivable Summary
For the Month of January 1983

Client # Name   Balance Owed

Total Receivables   0.00

Figure 5.5: Alternate Output Requirement for Output #5

For a month with no activity, the output just shows the headings and the Firm total information, with a Firm Total of
zero. The LOS given in Figure 5.4 is incorrect if this
output is what the user would like to see for a month with
no activity. It suggests that at least one Client will
appear on the output, and for this example that is no longer
true.

There are two ways to express the structure of the output
when this requirement is present. The two ways are shown in
Figure 5.6. The structure on the top is the DOWHILE form of
repetition mentioned back in Chapter 2. It says that there
may be from zero-to-many Clients shown for the Firm. The
"(0,n)" designation is a convenient way of expressing the
output requirements here, although in the long run it is
less precise than the structure shown below it.

In the second structure, which is the one Warnier prefers,
there is an alternative shown at the highest level. For a
month with activity, always at least one Client is shown.
For a month with no activity (the complement), no special
output is required, and the word "Skip" is inserted to
indicate an empty set. Warnier does not recognize the
"(0,n)" designation and does not allow its use. In this
text, however, we will favor the top structure over the
bottom, realizing that it is less precise but more practical
when there is no special output to be produced for a period
with no activity. In cases where a message is to appear
when there is no detail, like "There are no Clients to
report this Month," Warnier's structure **is** required, with
the message as an output element in the No Activity set.

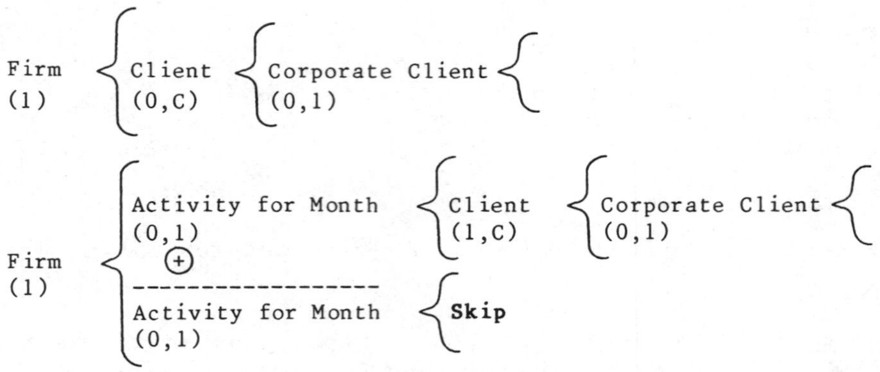

```
         ⎧        ⎧                          ⎧
Firm     ⎨ Client ⎨ Corporate Client        ⎨
(1)      ⎩ (0,C)  ⎩ (0,1)                    ⎩


         ⎧ Activity for Month  ⎧           ⎧
         ⎪ (0,1)               ⎨ Client    ⎨ Corporate Client  ⎧
         ⎪   ⊕                 ⎩ (1,C)     ⎩ (0,1)             ⎩
Firm     ⎨ ------------------
(1)      ⎪ Activity for Month  ⎧ Skip
         ⎩ (0,1)               ⎩
```

Figure 5.6 Equivalent Simplified Output Structures for
Output #5

The Exclusive OR

On the last output, there was just one alternative set present. However, there can be any number of mutually
exclusive data sets. Take, for instance, the output sample
shown in Figure 5.7.

                    Aged Accounts Receivables
                   For the Month Ended 12/31/82

Client Invoice	Date Due	Current	Overdue	Total
1134 Condon Enterprises				
10982	11/31/82		24.87	
11003	12/31/82	100.00		
11078	01/15/83	153.90		
Client Total		253.90	24.87	278.77
1214 Davis Realty				
10789	11/15/82		198.00	
Client Total		0.00	198.00	198.00
...etc...				
Company Totals		1,398.67	478.34	1,877.01

Figure 5.7: Output #6 Sample

On this output there are two alternative data sets. For an
Invoice, either Current Amount or an Overdue Amount is
listed, in addition to the other Invoice elements. The
Current Amount is output, not with each Invoice, but only
for a Current Invoice. The Overdue Amount is listed only
for an Overdue Invoice. Further, an Invoice can be either
one or the other, never both and never neither. Thus, the
Logical Output Structure for this output would be
represented as in Figure 5.8.

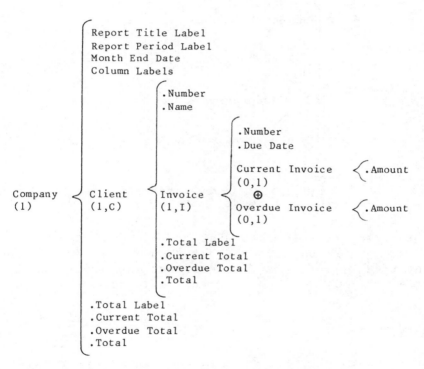

Figure 5.8: Logical Output Structure for Output #6

Again notice the presence of the alternative universals at
the Invoice level. Also note that they are shown as being
mutually exclusive; for an Invoice **either** data for a
Current Invoice **or** an Overdue Invoice will be shown. The
"Exclusive Or" sign, the " ⊕ ", **applies only to the alternative universals it separates,** and not to any elements or

other sets outside of the alternative sets; the Invoice
Number and Invoice Due Date appear at the beginning of each
Invoice, not for just Current Invoices.

For an output where Invoices were categorized into, say,
four categories instead of just two, there can be multiple
alternatives that are mutually exclusive. An example is
shown in Figure 5.9.

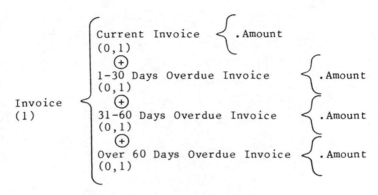

Figure 5.9: 4-way Alternation

This diagram suggests that just one field of a possible four
will appear for an Invoice: for Current Invoices a Current
Amount will appear; for Invoices that are from 1 to 30 Days
Overdue, a 1-30 Days Overdue Amount will appear, and so on.

Summary

Alternative structures are used when sets may or may not be
present within a level of hierarchy in a logical output. If
a single set is merely either absent or present we use the
"(0,1)" number-of-times designation. If there is more than
one possible alternative, we use the number-of-times
designation **and** the "Exclusive Or" sign to define the
different alternatives.

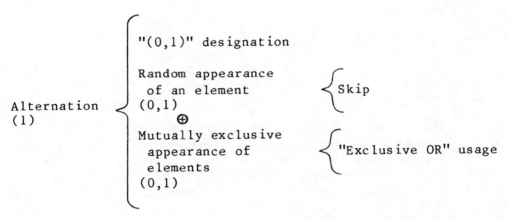

Figure 5.10: Chapter 5 Summary Diagram

Chapter 6 LOGICAL INPUT DESIGN: LOGICAL DATA STRUCTURES

Input Requirements

Developing a Logical Output Structure is the critical first step in the creation of a Warnier/Orr program design. Before we develop a diagram of such a program, however, there is one other data structure in addition to the LOS that is ultimately important to the design process. It is called a Logical Data Structure (LDS), and it represents the data needed as input to be able to produce a given output.

The Logical Data Structure **is not** a representation of the **actual** input to be used by a program; that step is done later in physical design. Rather, the Logical Data Structure is built **from** a knowledge of **output requirements only,** and is a representation of the minimal input necessary to be able to build a particular output.

Logical Data Structures are relatively easy to derive from Logical Output Structures, with only a couple of pitfalls to avoid. To begin with in this chapter, consider the output sample shown in Figure 6.1. This is a simple report of the Clients receiving Invoices from a Company, arranged by Attorney. Its Logical Output Structure is shown in Figure 6.2.

```
                           Billing Summary
                        For the Run of 10/31/83

Attorney               Client                    Invoice#   Due Date      Amount
101 John A. Baker

                       1011 Adams Construction    1123      12/01/83      679.29
                       1036 Condon Enterprises    1146      12/16/83      156.11
                       1097 Olander Corporation   1186      12/01/83     1123.07
                                                                        --------
                       Total For John A. Baker                           1958.47

110 George V. Harkness
                       1015 Armstrong, J.K.       1124      12/01/83      100.00
                       1021 Bartlett, O.L.        1134      11/15/83      213.57
                                                                        --------
                       Total For George V. Harkness                       313.57
...etc...
                                                                       ---------
Total For This Billing                                                 11253.43
```

Figure 6.1: Output #7 Sample

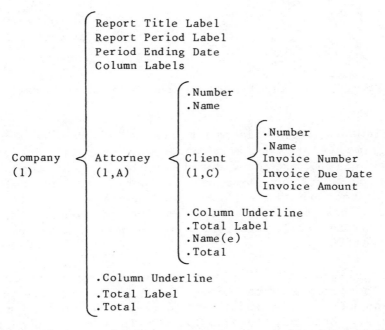

Figure 6.2: Logical Output Structure for Output #7

Creating a Logical Data Structure, a diagram of the minimal input to produce this output, can be derived in small stages, just as is the LOS. To create a diagram of the minimal input requirements, examine the elements which are output and eliminate those **not necessary** as input. Probably the easiest elements to eliminate are the label elements. Therefore on the Worksheet for this output, we can begin a new column called "Type" and identify those elements that are labels for data as type "L". Seven label elements are identified in Figure 6.3.

No.	Data Elements	Appears	Type
1	Report Title Label	Company	L
2	Report Period Label	Company	L
3	Period Ending Date	Company	
4	Column Labels	Company	L
5	Attorney Number	Attorney	
6	Attorney Name	Attorney	
7	Client Number	Client	
8	Client Name	Client	
9	Invoice Number	Client	
10	Invoice Due Date	Client	
11	Invoice Amount	Client	
12	Attorney Column Underline	Attorney	L
13	Attorney Total Label	Attorney	L
14	Attorney Name(e)	Attorney	
15	Attorney Total	Attorney	
16	Company Column Underline	Company	L
17	Company Total Label	Company	L
18	Company Total	Company	

Figure 6.3: Label Data Elements Noted on Worksheet

Label elements are those which are not needed by a program at any time before actually producing output. Notice that underlines, too, are considered labels here as they do not need to be input or computed, either. Notice, also, on this worksheet that the "once per" designation ("1/") used previously has been dropped from the appearance frequency column, since all elements must appear "once per some logical set."

The next elements to identify are those whose contents are readily computable from other data shown on the output. These include totals which are derived by adding up other data (e.g., Attorney Total, Company Total) and non-numeric information which appears earlier in the output (e.g.,

Attorney Name(e)). These get a "C" in the "Type" column and additional information under a new column called "Calculation Rules". Attorney Total and the Company Total, have two calculations each: an initializing calculation where they are set to zero, and a subsequent calculation where they are accumulated into. A computable element can have from one-to-many calculation rules; sums or totals usually have two.

```
No.   Data Elements              Appears   Type Calculation Rules
==========================================================================================
1     Report Title Label         Company   L
2     Report Period Label        Company   L
3     Period Ending Date         Company
4     Column Labels              Company   L
5     Attorney Number            Attorney
6     Attorney Name              Attorney
7     Client Number              Client
8     Client Name                Client
9     Invoice Number             Client
10    Invoice Due Date           Client
11    Invoice Amount             Client
12    Attorney Column Underline  Attorney  L
13    Attorney Total Label       Attorney  L
14    Attorney Name(e)           Attorney  C    1)Set Attorney Name(e) to Attorney Name
15    Attorney Total             Attorney  C    1)Set Attorney Total to Zero
                                                2)Add Invoice Amount to Attorney Total

16    Company Column Underline   Company   L
17    Company Total Label        Company   L
18    Company Total              Company   C    1)Set Company Total to Zero
                                                2)Add Attorney Total to Company Total
```

Figure 6.4: Computable Data Elements Noted on Worksheet

The other computable element is Attorney Name(e). Notice the addition of "(e)" for "end" to the second appearance of the attorney's name. Since it appears at a different place on the output, it is a different output element and thus has a separate name from Attorney Name above. Its calculation rule is of a type called a **logical substitution**, which has the general form "set A to B." Although it may seem strange to call a manipulation of letters a calculation, it nonetheless is.

The reason that the calculation rules are listed on the worksheet is twofold: (1) the calculations identified will be used later when a program design is created for this output, and (2) elements that are never output, but are required as input to support a calculation, may be identified. Any such elements are called "hidden" data, and none are evident in these calculations. (Technically, zero is an element, not output, but required as input for the

calculations shown; however zero and one are easily
manufactured, and thus may be ignored from an input
standpoint.) We will see hidden data present in the second
example for this chapter.

When all label elements and all computable elements have
been identified, the data elements remaining are those
required as input in some form. In other words, these are
the elements that must be provided as input or the output
cannot be produced. We will flag the required input
elements with an asterisk "*" in the "Type" column so they
will be easy to spot.

The analysis for the creation of the Logical Data Structure
has been nearly completed at this point. To find the structure of the data necessary as input, one need only analyze
the frequency with which the required elements need to be
provided as input. To produce this output, the Period End
Date must be provided once at the highest level (Company).
The Attorney Number and Name must be provided as input at
the beginning of each Attorney. The remaining required elements, the Client Number and Name and the Invoice Number,
Due Date, and Amount, must all be provided for each Client
for an Attorney. Thus, the completed worksheet is shown in
Figure 6.5. Notice that the column of the worksheet in
which calculation rules are shown can double as a column for
documenting the required input frequencies. Also notice that
this frequency is labeled "Changes" because in reality we
are documenting the "change" frequency for the element. We
are interested here in how often the data element's contents
are different; this is the same as asking: "How often is the
data required as input?"

The structure of the required input is, in this case, the
same as the structure of the Logical Output Structure:
Client within Attorney within Firm. This is not always the
case. The structure of the required input has no inherent
relationship to the output structure; the required input
structure can be radically different from the output
structure. It can have fewer, more, or quite different
levels from the output structure.

```
No.    Data Elements                 Appears   Type  Calculation Rules/Changes
=============================================================================================
1      Report Title Label            Company   L
2      Report Period Label           Company   L
3      Period Ending Date            Company   *     Company
4      Column Labels                 Company   L
5      Attorney Number               Attorney  *     Attorney
6      Attorney Name                 Attorney  *     Attorney
7      Client Number                 Client    *     Client
8      Client Name                   Client    *     Client
9      Invoice Number                Client    *     Client
10     Invoice Due Date              Client    *     Client
11     Invoice Amount                Client    *     Client
12     Attorney Column Underline     Attorney  L
13     Attorney Total Label          Attorney  L
14     Attorney Name(e)              Attorney  C     1)Set Attorney Name(e) to Attorney Name
15     Attorney Total                Attorney  C     1)Set Attorney Total to Zero
                                                     2)Add Invoice Amount to Attorney Total
16     Company Column Underline      Company   L
17     Company Total Label           Company   L
18     Company Total                 Company   C     1)Set Company Total to Zero
                                                     2)Add Attorney Total to Company Total
--------------
One Company on the output
At least one Attorney shown as output
At least one Client shown for an Attorney
```

Figure 6.5: Completed Worksheet for Output #7

All that remains to be done to complete the Logical Data Structure is to map the required input data elements onto the required input structure. (See Figure 6.6.)

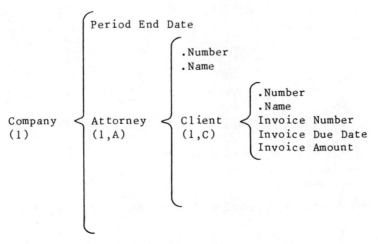

Figure 6.6: Logical Data Structure for Output #7

Just as with the LOS, we can translate this diagram back
into English to see if it describes the input requirements
for the output: This diagram states that input for this output must be provided in order by Client within Attorney for
the Company. Further, the Period End Date must be provided
at the beginning of the Company level, the Attorney Number
and Name must be provided at the beginning of each Attorney,
and the Client Number and Name, Invoice Number, Due Date,
and Amount must be provided for each Client. This seems
consistent with what we know about the output; therefore
this is a correct Logical Data Structure.

A good way to think about the Logical Data Structure is in
terms of what data on the output could be put back if it
were removed. For instance, if the output originally shown
in Figure 6.1 were instead provided to you as shown in
Figure 6.7, with certain fields x'ed out, could you replace
the x's with the appropriate data? Yes. The labels can
come from an output "template" that is the same each time
the output is built, and the other fields can be derived by
simple calculation. If you draft a Logical Data Structure
of the data left on this version of the output, you will
generate the very same LDS already identified in Figure 6.6.

```
                        xxxxxxxxxxxxxxx
                        xxxxxxxxxxxxxx 10/31/83

xxxxxxxx              xxxxxx                     xxxxxxxx   xxxxxxxx      xxxxxx
101 John A. Baker
                     1011 Adams Construction       1123     12/01/83     679.29
                     1036 Condon Enterprises       1146     12/16/83     156.11
                     1097 Olander Corporation      1186     12/01/83    1123.07
                                                                        xxxxxxxx
                     xxxxxxxxx xxxxxxxxxxxxx                             xxxxxxx

110 George V. Harkness
                     1015 Armstrong, J.K.          1124     12/01/83     100.00
                     1021 Bartlett, O.L.           1134     11/15/83     213.57
                                                                        xxxxxxxx
                     xxxxxxxxx xxxxxxxxxxxxxxxxx                         xxxxxx
...etc...
                                                                       xxxxxxxxx
xxxxxxxxxxxxxxxxxxxxxxx                                                 xxxxxxxx
```

Figure 6.7: Required Input Data Set for Output #7

Notice that the data found on the last figure is the minimum data that need be provided; no fewer data elements can be provided and still be able to produce the output. It is also sufficient for the output; no more data is required to be able to produce the output. In mathematical terms, the LDS represents the **necessary and sufficient** data requirements for an output.

Also notice that in this case, the Logical Data Structure is simply a **subset** of the Logical Output Structure — just the LOS with the computable and label elements removed. **Not all outputs have this property.** Outputs that do are called **well-behaved** outputs, since they are very easy to work on. Outputs that do not have this property are termed **ill-behaved**, and can be difficult to work with. Ill-behaved outputs are those whose LDS has either different elements and/or different levels from the LOS. In practice, they are more common than well-behaved outputs, and present the designer with subtle traps to watch out for.

Ill-Behaved Outputs

Examine the output given in Figure 6.8. This is a list of Transactions by Client for a Company. The Transactions are one of two kinds: either Debits, which add to the Client's Balance, or Credits, which subtract from it. On the output, subtotals are shown for each Client, with totals shown at the end of the Company.

```
                           Client Activity Report
                         For the Month of August 1983

     Client
          Date      Description      Atty#     Debit    Credit    Balance
     101 Abrams, John J.
          08/10    Consultation       103      60.00              160.00
          08/11    Will               206     140.00              300.00
          08/11    Filing Fee         206      20.00              320.00
          08/19    Consultation       103      60.00              380.00
          08/19    Payment Received                      100.00   280.00
          Total For Abrams, John J.           280.00    100.00    280.00

     110 Adams Construction Co
          08/01    LD Phone           211       2.30              312.30
          08/01    LD Phone           211       4.65              316.65
          08/01    LD Phone           211      11.30              327.95
          Total For Adams Construction Co      18.25      0.00    327.95
     ...etc...
     Total For August                       16211.13  14920.16   6732.73
```

Figure 6.8: Output #8 Sample

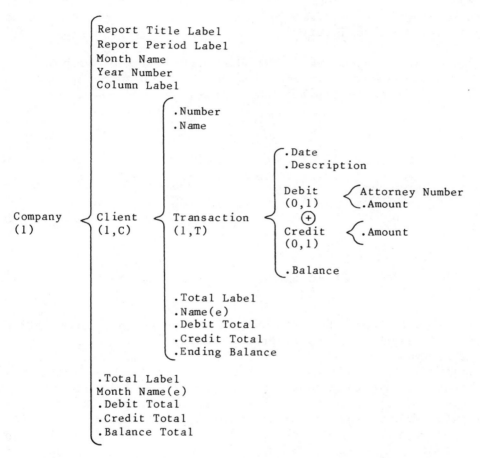

Figure 6.9: Logical Output Structure for Output #8

The Logical Output Structure for this output is shown above
in Figure 6.9. It is fairly simple.

When creating a Logical Data Structure for this output, some
problems crop up. Again as a first step, we may identify
the elements which are computable. The Company totals are

all computable, as are the Client totals and the Month
Name(e). The question that arises deals with the Transaction Balance: Is it computable? Not always, it appears.
The Transaction Balance appears to be a running balance of
the amount owed by a Client, with debits added in and
credits subtracted out. In that sense it seems computable.
But what about the first balance for each Client? It seems
to be required as input.

This is an example of a **"hidden" data element** such as was
discussed earlier. Transaction Balance is computable, with
the calculation rules that are shown in Figure 6.10.

```
No.   Data Elements              Appears   Type Calculation Rules/Changes
===============================================================================================================
13    Transaction Balance        Trans.    C    1)Set Transaction Balance to Client Balance Forward
                                                 2)Add Debit Amount to Transaction Balance
                                                 3)Subtract Credit Amount from Transaction Balance


24    Client Balance Forward      -------   *    Client
```

Figure 6.10: A "Hidden" Data Element

This element has three calculation rules, one initializer
and two cumulative actions. Initially, the Transaction
Balance must be set to the Balance Forward for a Client;
thereafter we will be adding in Debit Amounts and
subtracting out Credit Amounts. The Client Balance Forward,
however, is not an element that appears explicitly on the
output, although it is required as input. Therefore we will
add it to the end of our element list as shown. It has no
appearance frequency, since it is not output, but is
required as input once each Client.

Another subtle problem to watch out for is called a
"hidden" hierarchy. It is a level of hierarchy appearing
on the Logical Data Structure that does not appear on the
Logical Output Structure. A hidden hierarchy is present
**whenever data is output more frequently than it is required
as input.** There is an example of such a hierarchy on the
output sample shown in Figure 6.11.

```
No.   Data Elements              Appears   Type Calculation Rules/Changes
==========================================================================================
8     Transaction Date           Trans.    *    Day
9     Transaction Description     Trans.    *    Trans.
```

Figure 6.11: A "Hidden" Sort Hierarchy

Notice that the Transaction Date is repeated on each Transaction line. Thus it appears at the Transaction level on the LOS. However, **if Transactions are in order by date**, the Transaction Date would not have to be provided as input each Transaction; the Date would be the same for many Transactions, hence it would not need to be provided as input more than once for a group of Transactions which all occurred on the same Day. In particular, the Transaction Date need only be provided once each Day shown for a Client.

Note that this is only true if it is a requirement that Transactions are to be output in order by Date. If Transactions are to appear in some other order within a Client, then the Transaction Date does not change with a predictable frequency, and there would be no hidden Day hierarchy. This is also the reason that the Transaction Description does not represent a hidden hierarchy; it does not participate in the sort sequence of the output. Even though it is the same sometimes from one Transaction to the next, that is an **accident** and not the result of a requirement.

The completed worksheet for this output is shown in Figure 6.12, and the Logical Data Structure appropriate appears in Figure 6.13.

```
No.    Data Elements              Appears   Type Calculation Rules/Changes
==================================================================================================
1      Report Title Label         Company   L
2      Report Period Label        Company   L
3      Month Name                 Company   *    Company
4      Year Number                Company   *    Company
5      Column Label               Company   L
6      Client Number              Client    *    Client
7      Client Name                Client    *    Client
8      Transaction Date           Trans.    *    Day
9      Transaction Description     Trans.    *    Trans.
10     Attorney Number            Debit     *    Debit
11     Debit Amount               Debit     *    Debit
12     Credit Amount              Credit    *    Credit
13     Transaction Balance        Trans     C    1)Set Transaction Balance to Client Balance Forward
                                                  2)Add Debit Amount to Transaction Balance
                                                  3)Subract Credit Amount from Transaction Balance

14     Client Total Label         Client    L
15     Client Name(e)             Client    C    1)Set Client Name(e) to Client Name
16     Client Debit Total         Client    C    1)Set Client Debit Total to Zero
                                                  2)Add Debit Amount to Client Debit Total
17     Client Credit Total        Client    C    1)Set Client Credit Total to Zero
                                                  2)Add Credit Amount to Client Credit Total
18     Client Ending Balance      Client    C    1)Set Client Ending Balance to Transaction Balance
19     Company Total Label        Company   L
20     Month Name(e)              Company   C    1)Set Month Name(e) to Month Name
21     Company Debit Total        Company   C    1)Set Company Debit Total to Zero
                                                  2)Add Client Debit Total to Company Debit Total
22     Company Credit Total       Company   C    1)Set Company Credit Total to Zero
                                                  2)Add Client Credit Total to Company Credit Total
23     Company Balance Total      Company   C    1)Set Company Balance Total to Zero
                                                  2)Add Client Ending Balance to Company Balance Total
24     Client Balance Forward     -------   *    Client
       -----------------
One Company on the output
At least one Client is shown on the output
At least one Transaction is shown for a Client
Transactions are sorted by Date within Client
```

Figure 6.12: Completed Worksheet for Output #8

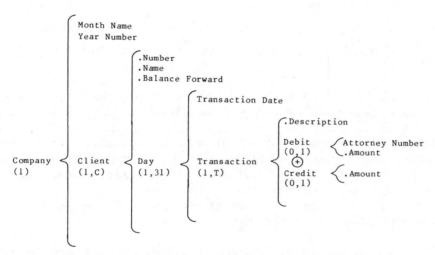

Figure 6.13: Logical Data Structure for Output #8

Again, this Logical Data Structure can be thought of in
terms of the data that remains on the output after all of
the unnecessary data has been removed. Such a view of the
output appears in Figure 6.14. Notice that a Client Balance
Forward must be added to the output at the beginning of each
Client, and that the duplicate Transaction Dates may be eliminated. The data shown in this figure is the necessary and
sufficient data to build the required output.

```
                        xxxxxxxxxxxxxxxxxxxxxx
                        xxxxxxxxxxxxxxxx August 1983

    xxxxxx
         xxxx        xxxxxxxxxxxx      xxxxx      xxxxx    xxxxxx    xxxxxxx

    101 Abrams, John J.                                             100.00
         08/10      Consultation       103        60.00            xxxxxx
         08/11      Will               206       140.00            xxxxxx
         xxxxx      Filing Fee         206        20.00            xxxxxx
         08/19      Consultation       103        60.00            xxxxxx
         xxxxx      Payment Received                      100.00   xxxxxx
         xxxxxxxxx xxxxxxxxxxxxxxx               xxxxxx   xxxxxx    xxxxxx

    110 Adams Construction Co                                       310.00
         08/01      LD Phone           211         2.30            xxxxxx
         xxxxx      LD Phone           211         4.65            xxxxxx
         xxxxx      LD Phone           211        11.30            xxxxxx
         xxxxxxxxx xxxxxxxxxxxxxxxxxxxx            xxxxx    xxxxx   xxxxxx
    ...etc...
    xxxxxxxxx xxxxxx                           xxxxxxxx xxxxxxxx   xxxxxxx
```

Figure 6.14: Data Requirements for Output #8

The Logical Data Structure, in addition to providing information about the necessary input requirements, is also a good
tool for improving the quality of outputs. The LDS just
developed for the second output sample indicates that there
is hidden data and a hidden sort hierarchy present. That
makes the output, by definition, ill-behaved. Changing the
output slightly so that the output would be well-behaved
(having the LDS simply a subset of the LOS) would probably
improve the quality of the output.

The hidden data element Client Balance Forward can be made
to appear on the output quite easily; simply output a line
at the beginning of the Client's output that states "Balance
Forward of 100.00." Thus, the Client Balance Forward would
not be hidden at all, but would appear on the output and on
the LOS.

The hidden hierarchy is similarly easy to remove; just
change the output so that subsequent repetitions of the
Transaction Date are blanked out, so it is only output once
for a Day's worth of Transactions. The modified output
sample would then appear as in Figure 6.15.

```
                          Client Activity Report
                       For the Month of August 1983

      Client
            Date       Description        Atty#     ·Debit    Credit     Balance
      101 Abrams, John J.                      Balance Forward of         100.00
            08/10     Consultation        103      60.00                  160.00
            08/11     Will               206     140.00                   300.00
                      Filing Fee         206      20.00                   320.00
            08/19     Consultation        103      60.00                  380.00
                      Payment Received                        100.00      280.00
            Total For Abrams, John J.            280.00       100.00      280.00

      110 Adams Construction Co                 Balance Forward of         310.00
            08/01     LD Phone           211       2.30                   312.30
                      LD Phone           211       4.65                   316.65
                      LD Phone           211      11.30                   327.95
              Total For Adams Construction Co    18.25         0.00       327.95
      ...etc...
      Total For August                        16211.13    14920.16      6732.73
```

Figure 6.15: Improved Output #8 Sample

This is probably a better output than the original; now some-one can manually cross-check the Balances if something looks wrong, and find, say, the third Day's worth of Transactions for a Client without scanning each Transaction line.

When possible, it is always a good idea to suggest changes to an ill-behaved output so that it is well-behaved. This not only makes life easier on the program designer, but also generates a better-quality output for the user. If such changes are not possible, or are rejected, then the output will remain ill-behaved, and the Logical Data Structure will look different from the Logical Output Structure. In gener-al, the more different the LDS from the LOS, the worse the quality of the output.

Building the LDS

The rules for generating Logical Data Structures can be
documented in the same fashion as the rules for creating
Logical Output Structures given in Chapter 4. (See Figure
6.16.)

```
=============================================================================
Logical Input Design: Creating the Logical Data Structure (LDS)
=============================================================================
Purpose: to identify required input for an output
Definition of LDS: a picture of an output's minimal input requirements
-----------------------------------------------------------------------------
Steps to build a Logical Data Structure:
1) Data "Type" Identification:  Identify the type of each data element
            on the worksheet: C = Computable, L = Label, * = Required as
            Input.
2) Calculation Description:  List the calculation rule(s) for each
            Computable element.
3) "Hidden" Data Definition:  Add any "hidden" elements to the list
            of Data Elements.
4) Frequency Identification:  List the frequency of changes for each
            Required element.  Watch for "hidden" sort hierarchies.
5) Hierarchy Mapping:  Build a structure from the required input
            frequencies.
6) Elements Mapping:  Place the required elements onto the structure.
7) Logical Input Design Testing:  Translate the structure into
            English to check the picture's accuracy.
=============================================================================
```

Figure 6.16: Building a Logical Data Structure

The same comment made about fallibility with reference to
the steps to build Logical Output Structures also appears
here; these are guidelines, not hard and fast rules. There
can occasionally be data required as input that will not be
discovered using this list of steps. A very common problem
people run up against is data required as a sort field that
does not appear on the output. Such sorting data is a
subcategory of "hidden" data, and should be shown in some
form on the LDS. For instance, the first output in this
chapter, Output #7, was a list by Client within Attorney for
a Company. If this output is to be sorted by Client Number
within Attorney Number, then there is no hidden sort data;
both fields used in sorting appear on the output. If,

however,   the Client lines were to appear in order within
Attorney by the "size" of the Client, with the biggest
Client first and the smallest Client last, there is a hidden
sort field.   This field may be documented on the Logical
Data Structure as is shown in Figure 6.17.

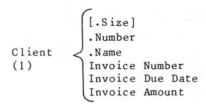

```
                        ⎧ [.Size]
                        ⎪ .Number
             Client     ⎨ .Name
              (1)        ⎪ Invoice Number
                        ⎪ Invoice Due Date
                        ⎩ Invoice Amount
```

Figure 6.17: Hidden Sorting Element

The Client Size appears within square brackets because the
form that it takes is not known; it could be some kind of
code, some numeric field, some position in a file, etc.
Since the form it takes is not known from the output requirements, it is not properly application data, but is something
called **structural data**: data present in a system for posi-
tioning, sorting, selecting, relating, etc., and not for
reporting or calculating.

Summary

The most common mistake that people make with the Logical
Data Structure is assuming too much about the "real" input
to a program.   Remember that the Logical Data Structure is
derived **only from a knowledge of output requirements** and
is not a picture of the actual input used by the proposed
program.   The form of the actual data that is stored or used
as input will not affect the LDS in any way.

Logical
Input
Design
(1)
{
Data "Type" Identification
Calculation Description
"Hidden" Data Definition
Frequency Identification
Hierarchy Mapping
Elements Mapping
.Testing

Figure 6.18: Chapter 6 Summary Diagram

Chapter 7 LOGICAL PROCESS DESIGN
PART 1
LOGICAL PROCESS
STRUCTURES

Review

So far in this text we have examined the technique for creating two data structure diagrams: a Logical Output Structure
and a Logical Data Structure. The Logical Output Structure
(LOS) is a pictorial view of the requirements of an output;
the Logical Data Structure (LDS) is a pictorial view of the
data required as input to support an output. In this
chapter and the next, we will examine the process of generating the mapping from a simple form of the required input
into a simple form of the required output. This mapping is
the **central transformation** mentioned in Chapter 3, and
will take the form of a Warnier/Orr diagram, a slightly
different kind of Warnier/Orr diagram, though. The Logical
Output Structure and Logical Data Structure examined so far
are diagrams of data; the Logical Process Structure (LPS) we
will create in this step of the design will be a diagram of
the structure of a **procedure.** The LPS will be a
high-level blueprint for a program.

For the output for which we will first develop a Logical
Process Structure, examine the sample shown in Figure 7.1.

This is a straightforward output, very similar to ones that
have been examined in earlier chapters. It is a report of

Invoices generated for a Company, arranged by Customer
within Salesperson. The output also shows subtotals of
sales and profit for each Customer and for each Salesperson,
in addition to the Company totals.

```
                          Monthly Sales Report
                       For the Month Ended 11/30/83

Salesman        Customer              Invoice     Date      Sales Amt   Profit
J.A. Johnson
                Armstrong Carpets
                                       2311     11/13/83      118.30     46.20
                                       2319     11/16/83       82.70     19.96
                                       2321     11/21/83      763.52    174.68
                            Total For Armstrong Carpets       964.52    240.84
                Miller Appliances
                                       2310     11/13/83     2376.95    463.76
                            Total for Miller Appliances      2376.95    463.76
                Total for J.A. Johnson                        3341.47    704.60
L.B. Newman
                Hilmers Hardware
                                       2314     11/13/83      185.20     45.04
                            Total for Hilmers Hardware        185.20     45.04
                Total for L.B. Newman                         185.20     45.04
...etc...
Total for the Month                                         12874.32   3423.26
```

Figure 7.1: Output #9 Sample

The completed worksheet, the Logical Output Structure, and
the Logical Data Structure are shown in Figures 7.2, 7.3,
and 7.4, respectively. Familiarize yourself with this
partial design, as elements from all three will be used to
generate the Logical Process Structure.*

---

*For all references to Output #9, the genderless form
"Salesperson" will be used in the text, while the term
"Salesman" will be used in the figures to save space.

```
No.    Data Element              Appears   Type   Calculation Rules/Changes
==============================================================================================
1      Report Title Label        Company    L
2      Report Period Label       Company    L
3      Month End Date            Company    *      Company
4      Column Label              Company    L
5      Salesman Name             Salesman   *      Salesman
6      Customer Name             Customer   *      Customer
7      Invoice Number            Invoice    *      Invoice
8      Invoice Date              Invoice    *      Invoice
9      Sales Amount              Invoice    *      Invoice
10     Profit Amount             Invoice    *      Invoice
11     Customer Total Label      Customer   L
12     Customer Name(e)          Customer   C      1)Set Customer Name(e) to Customer Name
13     Customer Sales Total      Customer   C      1)Set Customer Sales Total to Zero
                                                   2)Add Sales Amount to Customer Sales Total
14     Customer Profit Total     Customer   C      1)Set Customer Profit Total to Zero
                                                   2)Add Profit Amount to Customer Profit Total
15     Salesman Total Label      Salesman   L
16     Salesman Name(e)          Salesman   C      1)Set Salesman Name(e) to Salesman Name
17     Salesman Sales Total      Salesman   C      1)Set Salesman Sales Total to Zero
                                                   2)Add Customer Sales Total to Salesman Sales Total
18     Salesman Profit Total     Salesman   C      1)Set Salesman Profit Total to Zero
                                                   2)Add Customer Profit Total to Salesman Profit Total
19     Company Total Label       Company    L
20     Company Sales Total       Company    C      1)Set Company Sales Total to Zero
                                                   2)Add Salesman Sales Total to Company Sales Total
21     Company Profit Total      Company    C      1)Set Company Profit Total to Zero
                                                   2)Add Salesman Profit Total to Company Profit Total
----------
One Company on the output
At least one Salesman for the Company is shown
At least one Customer is shown for each Salesman
At least one Invoice is shown for each Customer
```

Figure 7.2: Worksheet for Output #9

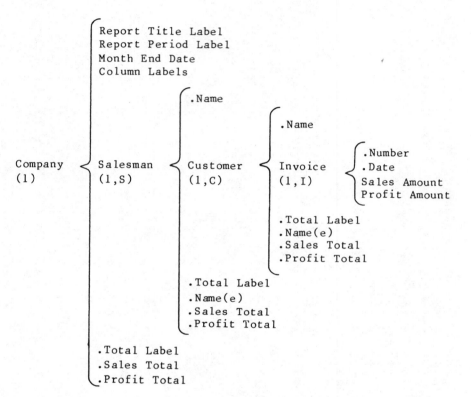

Figure 7.3: Logical Output Structure for Output #9

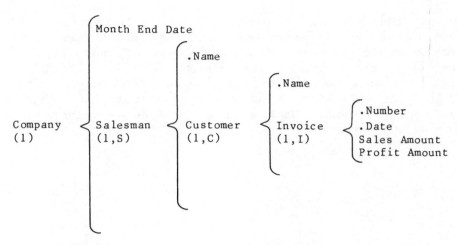

Figure 7.4: Logical Data Structure for Output #9

The Ideal File

Let us examine for a moment the Logical Data Structure shown in Figure 7.4. It shows that we must be able to get the Month End Date at the beginning of the Company level, a Salesperson Name at the beginning of each Salesperson, a Customer Name at the beginning of each Customer, and an Invoice Number, Date, Sales Amount, and Profit Amount for each Invoice. Recall that this diagram represents the **minimal** data requirements; if those data elements cannot be provided with the structure indicated, then the output **cannot** be produced. It does not necessarily represent a picture of the actual input that is available for our program's use. The LDS just says that any input that is provided will have to contain at least that information in those quantities and with that structure.

In actuality there are many different ways that the data could be stored physically so that it could be rebuilt into the LDS. Salesperson Names, for instance, might be kept in a file by themselves and read in when needed. Or perhaps the Salesperson Names may be compiled into a table in the

program and simply looked up. Or, the Salesperson Name
could be present on each Invoice record, and would not have
to be looked up.

For the sake of this discussion, let us say that the data
were stored in the **simplest possible form.** The simplest
form to store data in is a single, sorted, sequential file
with only one record type — a so-called "flat" data
file. The data needed for this output could be kept in such
a file, if we didn't mind having duplicate data from one
record to the next. Such a file could be represented as is
shown in Figure 7.5.

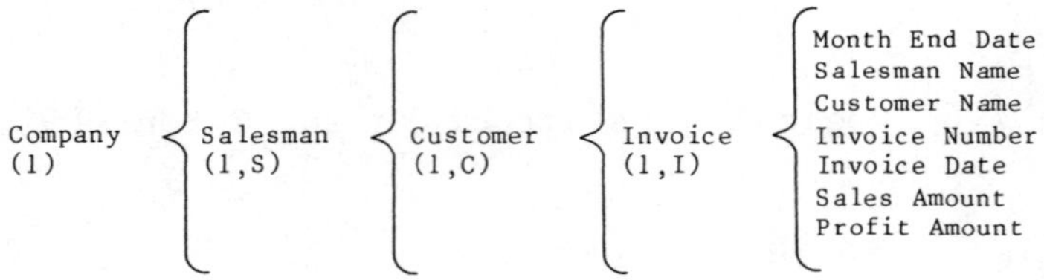

```
                                                      Month End Date
                                                      Salesman Name
                                                      Customer Name
    Company     Salesman      Customer      Invoice   Invoice Number
    (1)         (1,S)         (1,C)         (1,I)     Invoice Date
                                                      Sales Amount
                                                      Profit Amount
```

The Ideal File is sorted by Salesman Name, Customer Name, Invoice Number

Figure 7.5: The Ideal Input File Structure for Output #9

The simplest possible file to keep the data needed for this
output would contain a record for each Invoice sent during
the period, arranged by Customer within Salesperson for the
Company. Each Invoice record would have on it the Month End
Date, the Salesperson Name, the Customer Name, the Invoice
Number, Date, Sales Amount, and Profit Amount. As the
figure indicates, this representation of the data is called
the **Ideal File;** it is ideal because it is the very
simplest form that the necessary data can take. It contains
all and only the records needed in precisely the correct
order for the production of the output. (See Figure 7.6.)

```
11/30/83   J.A. Johnson   Armstrong Carpets   2311   11/13/83    118.30    46.20
11/30/83   J.A. Johnson   Armstrong Carpets   2319   11/16/83     82.70    19.96
11/30/83   J.A. Johnson   Armstrong Carpets   2321   11/21/83    763.52   174.68
11/30/83   J.A. Johnson   Miller Appliances   2310   11/13/83   2376.95   463.76
11/30/83   L.B. Newman    Hilmers Hardware    2314   11/13/83    185.20    45.04
...etc....
```

Figure 7.6: An Ideal File Sample for Output #9

Processing Actions

Having selected a possible representation of the input data
as a starting point, we are ready to develop an understanding of the process to transform this Ideal File into the
output we desire. We will begin by making a list, this time
of processing activities necessary for the mapping. There
are only three fundamental kinds of processing activities
that must take place in the central mapping: output
activities, calculations, and input activities. Each of the
three types of actions can be derived from information
already gathered in the design.

As far as output instructions, we must have an output action
for each **logical group** of data elements shown on the Logical Output Structure, a logical group being **one or more elements that are all output together.** In looking at the LOS,
we find that there are seven logical groups of elements to
be output: the elements output at the beginning and at the
end of the Company, Salesperson, and Customer levels, and
the elements output for an Invoice. Thus, we would wish to
list seven output instructions.

The calculations required for our processing can be lifted
directly off of the completed output worksheet. There are a
total of 14 calculations to be listed.

The input activity is quite simple; we must direct someone
to get a record from the Ideal File.

Thus, a complete list of the logical processing actions necessary for this output (in no particular order) is shown in Figure 7.7.

```
Output Actions:
        Print Company Heading Information
        Print Salesman Heading Information
        Print Customer Heading Information
        Print Invoice Information
        Print Customer Total Information
        Print Salesman Total Information
        Print Company Total Information
Calculations:
        Set Customer Name(e) to Customer Name
        Set Customer Sales Total to Zero
        Add Sales Amount to Customer Sales Total
        Set Customer Profit Total to Zero
        Add Sales Amount to Customer Profit Total
        Set Salesman Name(e) to Salesman Name
        Set Salesman Sales Total to Zero
        Add Customer Sales Total to Salesman Sales Total
        Set Salesman Profit Total to Zero
        Add Customer Profit Total to Salesman Profit Total
        Set Company Sales Total to Zero
        Add Salesman Sales Total to Company Sales Total
        Set Company Profit Total to Zero
        Add Salesman Profit Total to Company Profit Total
Input Actions:
        Get An Ideal Record
```

Figure 7.7: Logical Processing Actions for Output #9

As before with the LOS and the LDS, we will now want to analyze the frequency that each instruction on this list must be executed in the logical process. For instance the instruction Print Company Heading Information must be done once for the Company; Set Salesperson Sales Total to Zero must be done once each Salesperson; etc. The only tricky instruction is the input action. Get an Ideal Record must be done once each Invoice, plus one extra time; the input file must be read one more time than there are records to get to know that there aren't any more. The completed list of actions and frequencies is shown in Figure 7.8.

```
Output Actions:                                                  Frequency
        Print Company Heading Information                        1/Company
        Print Salesman Heading Information                       1/Salesman
        Print Customer Heading Information                       1/Customer
        Print Invoice Information                                1/Invoice
        Print Customer Total Information                         1/Customer
        Print Salesman Total Information                         1/Salesman
        Print Company Total Information                          1/Company
Calculations:
        Set Customer Name(e) to Customer Name                   1/Customer
        Set Customer Sales Total to Zero                        1/Customer
        Add Sales Amount to Customer Sales Total                1/Invoice
        Set Customer Profit Total to Zero                       1/Customer
        Add Sales Amount to Customer Profit Total               1/Invoice
        Set Salesman Name(e) to Salesman Name                   1/Salesman
        Set Salesman Sales Total to Zero                        1/Salesman
        Add Customer Sales Total to Salesman Sales Total        1/Customer
        Set Salesman Profit Total to Zero                       1/Salesman
        Add Customer Profit Total to Salesman Profit Total      1/Customer
        Set Company Sales Total to Zero                         1/Company
        Add Salesman Sales Total to Company Sales Total         1/Salesman
        Set Company Profit Total to Zero                        1/Company
        Add Salesman Profit Total to Company Profit Total       1/Salesman
Input Actions:
        Get An Ideal Record                                     1/Invoice + 1
```

Figure 7.8: Processing Actions and Frequencies for Output #9

These frequencies are familiar; they are in fact the same frequencies that were found earlier in the output and input data structures. This is the manifestation of the third fundamental principle given back in Chapter 1: design should be data-structured. It turns out that the best structure to use for processing is the same as the structure of the data being processed. (There are other processing structures other than data-structured ones possible. We will examine the difference between data-structured and non-data-structured designs later in the book.) Thus, the framework for this Logical Process Structure is Invoice within Customer within Salesperson for the Company.

Working level by level, we may place the instructions identified onto the structure at the appropriate points. Examine the partial diagram shown in Figure 7.9.

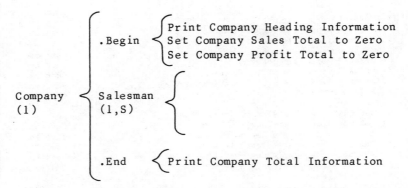

Figure 7.9: Company Level Processing for Output #9

Notice that on a Logical Process Structure we add some **placeholder universals,** here named Company Begin and Company End, to more clearly identify the instructions to be done at the beginning and at the end of the Company level. At the beginning of the Company level, the Company Heading must be printed and the Company totals must be initialized to zero. At the end of the Company level, the Company totals must be reported. In between the beginning and the end of the Company level, we must process from one-to-many Salespersons.

The processing for each Salesperson for the Company is shown in Figure 7.10.

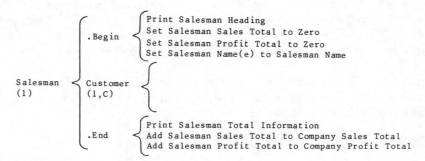

Figure 7.10: Salesperson Level Processing for Output #9

At the beginning of each Salesperson, the Salesperson
Heading must be printed, the Salesperson totals must be
initialized to zero, and the Salesperson Name to be output
at the end of the Salesperson must be initialized to the
Salesperson Name that is current. At the end of a
Salesperson, the Salesperson totals must be reported, and
then added to the Company totals. Again between the
beginning and the end of a Salesperson, we must process from
one-to-many Customers.

The processing for each Customer within a Salesperson is
very similar to the Salesperson level processing; the
heading must be printed at the beginning, along with the
initialization of the totals, and the totals must be
reported at the end and added into the Salesperson totals.
In between the beginning and end of a Customer, one-to-many
Invoices will be processed. (See Figure 7.11.)

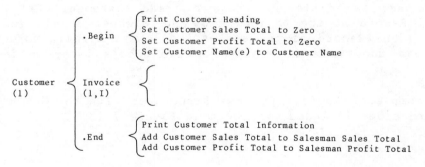

Figure 7.11: Customer Level Processing for Output #9

The processing for an Invoice is quite simple; print the
Invoice information and add the two Invoice amounts to the
Customer totals. In fact, the Invoice level does not even
need to be subdivided into a beginning and an end; since
there is no processing within an Invoice other than simple
sequence, the beginning and the end run together as just one
continual process. (See Figure 7.12.)

```
                  ⎧ Print Invoice Information
     Invoice      ⎨ Add Sales Amount to Customer Sales Total
      (1)         ⎩ Add Profit Amount to Customer Profit Total
```

Figure 7.12: Invoice Level Processing for Output #9

The only instruction excluded from this processing so far is the input instruction Get An Ideal Record. Since it must be done once each Invoice plus one time, apparently it must be done at the Invoice level. Getting a record each Invoice will take care of all of the read's except one, and there are only two places on the structure that a read statement can be placed and be done just one time: at the beginning or the end of the Company level. The end of the Company level is probably too late, so the final Get Record instruction must go at the beginning of the Company level. In reality there are two different kinds of read statement: Get First Ideal Record at the beginning of the highest level, and Get Next Ideal Record at the end of the lowest level. More will be said about the necessity for two read's later on in the text.

The completed Logical Process Structure, with the Get Record instructions included, is shown in Figure 7.13.

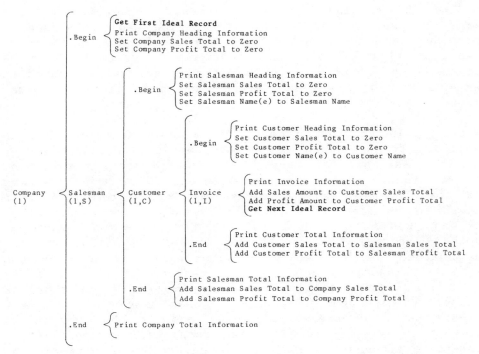

Figure 7.13: Logical Process Structure for Output #9

This is a very important diagram. It depicts the logical processing which must take place to transform the ideal input file into the logical output that was required. It also is a high-level blueprint for the program we will eventually write.

The Logical Process Structure is not quite at a level where one could directly code from it; it isn't specific to any one computer system or language yet. However, it is interesting and useful to trace the operation of the process depicted here.

The first group of activities that would be performed if one traced the execution of this process would be those found at the beginning of the Company level: the first record would be read, the heading would be printed, and the Company totals would be cleared. Then we would begin to process the

first Salesperson for the Company by printing his or her
heading and setting his or her totals to zero. Then the
first Customer for the first Salesperson would be begun by
printing the heading and setting his or her totals to zero.
Then the first Invoice for that first Customer would be
processed by printing its information, adding its amounts to
the Customer totals just zeroed, and then getting another
record.

After getting another record, there is a decision that is
implied: If the record is another Invoice for this Customer
for this Salesperson, then the Invoice process is repeated;
if not, then there are no more Invoices for this Customer
and the Customer ending process may be performed. Again
after performing the Customer ending process, another
decision would be made based on whether or not there is
another Customer to process for this Salesperson. If so,
the Customer process would be begun again. If not, the end
of the Salesperson would be processed. Following this,
would be another decision based on whether or not there is
another Salesperson to process. When there are no more
Salespersons to process then the end of the Company is
processed, and the procedure has completed its run. If we
wished, a flowchart depicting the operation of this diagram
may be created. It is shown in Figure 7.14.

The flowchart in the figure has some interesting properties.
It is called a Warnier flowchart, since it is a direct
translation from the data-structured process. (Warnier
actually builds such a flowchart in LCP. Orr's SPD does
not.) It is much more organized than a normal flowchart;
none of the lines of control cross one another. On a
Warnier flowchart, the lines will never cross, which is by
the way where the root of the term "structured" lays; an old
style "structured program" was one whose flowchart had no
overlapping lines. It is easy to see that such a control
structure could be built into a program in **any** computer
language.

This flowchart also illustrates the native modularity of the
Warnier/Orr design method. The processing for the Company
level (the whole flowchart) has only one entry point and one
exit point. The processing for all Salespersons for the
Company (between the Company Begin and Company End blocks)

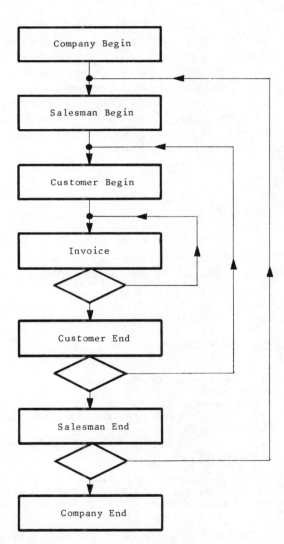

Figure 7.14: Warnier Flowchart for Output #9

has only one way in and one way out. So does the processing
for all Customers for a Salesperson, and all Invoices for a
Customer, as does each individual block of activities.
(Warnier calls such blocks **logical sequences** — a group
of zero-to-many instructions all done the same number of
times or under the same conditions.) Thus, sections of this
flowchart could be lifted out and replaced if necessary.

Also notice that the Logical Process Structure shown in
Figure 7.13 has another interesting property; it is an
optimal processing structure for a sequential processor
(for a concurrent processor there is an even faster version
of the LPS). There is no way to remove any of the instructions shown, nor do them any fewer times than they are
shown. Certainly there are less than optimal ways of translating this diagram into code, but it is nice to know what
the minimal required logical processing is.

```
================================================================================
Logical Process Design: Creating the The Logical Process Structure (LPS)
================================================================================
Purpose: to identify required logical processing
Definition of LPS: a picture of the process for mapping the ideal
        input file into the logical output.
--------------------------------------------------------------------------------
Steps to build a Logical Process Structure:
1) Logical Action Definition:  List the logical actions necessary for
        the LPS:
    ● the Output Actions needed (from the LOS),
    ● the Calculations needed (from the LDS),
    ● the Input Actions needed (Get 1st, Get Next Ideal).
2) Frequency Identification:  Identify the frequency with which each
        action must be performed.
3) Hierarchy Mapping:  Build a structure from the frequencies found.
4) Placeholder Mapping:  Add ".Begin{" and ".End{" to each level of the
        structure that is subdivided (all but the lowest levels).
5) Logical Action Mapping:  Place the logical actions onto the structure.
6) Logical Process Design Testing:  Translate the structure into English
        to check the picture's accuracy.
================================================================================
```

Figure 7.15: Building a Logical Process Structure

Summary

Remember that the Logical Process Structure is a picture of
a logical mapping — one that is independent of hardware,
language, data retrieval method, etc. It assumes that an
Ideal File is available for input, and that it is running
under an operating system intelligent enough to handle page
heading breaks. Detailing this diagram with instructions
specific to the actual physical operating environment moves
us out of the realm of logical design and into physical
design. That topic will be taken up in Chapter 9. In the
following chapter, we will examine the logical design of a
problem a bit different than the ones discussed to this
point.

```
                         ┌ Logical Action Definition
        Logical          │ Frequency Identification
        Process          ┤ Hierarchy Mapping
        Design           │ Placeholder Mapping
         (1)             │ Logical Action Mapping
                         └ .Testing
```

Figure 7.16: Chapter 7 Summary Diagram

Chapter 8   LOGICAL PROCESS DESIGN
PART 2
SCIENTIFIC APPLICATIONS

Scientific Programs

The Warnier/Orr program design methodology not only works well for business applications, such as those discussed so far in the book. It also works very well for so-called "scientific" applications —— programs that are more algorithm- or calculation-intensive than output-intensive. Although the output of a scientific program may be quite simple, perhaps just a value that has been computed, the analysis methods discussed to this point — the LOS, LDS, and LPS —— can serve as a valuable aid to the understanding of these "number crunching" programs as well.

Take as a simple example the output shown in Figure 8.1. This is the intended output of an interactive program to compute the square root of a given number. It uses a method discovered long ago called **successive approximation** whereby two rough guesses are made as to the correct value sought and then refined to the desired level of accuracy. This kind of algorithm is generically known as a "pinching" algorithm, since it narrows down closer and closer on an answer with each guess.

The algorithm for this program begins by selecting two guesses as to the square root of the target number, one

```
Enter a number to find the square root of: 5
Iteration  High Guess  Low Guess     Guess      Result
0          5           1             3          9
1          3           1             2          4
2          3           2             2.5        6.25
3          2.5         2             2.25       5.0625
4          2.25        2             2.125      5.51563
5          2.25        2.125         2.1875     4.78516
6          2.25        2.1875        2.21875    4.92285
7          2.25        2.21875       2.23438    4.99243
8          2.25        2.23438       2.24219    5.0274
9          2.24219     2.23438       2.2828     5.0099
10         2.23828     2.23438       2.23633    5.00116
11         2.23633     2.23438       2.23535    4.9968
12         2.23633     2.23535       2.23584    4.99898
The square root of     5.000 is     2.236
```

Figure 8.1: Output #10 Sample

which is obviously too high and one which is too low. The
actual square root must therefore be somewhere between the
high and low bound. The algorithm then computes the arithmetic average between the two guesses. By multiplying the
average by itself, the high and low bounds can be refined.
If the squared average is bigger than the target number,
that means that the average is bigger than the true square
root, and it becomes the new high guess; if the squared
average is less than the target number, then that means the
average is smaller than the true square root, and it then
becomes the new low guess. The process is then repeated with
the new high and low guesses until the desired accuracy is
reached; any degree of accuracy may be achieved by simply
making more guesses.

As before, we begin the design process by analyzing the
output elements and the appearance frequencies.

The data element list (Figure 8.2) suggests that the Logical
Output Structure for this output (Figure 8.3) is two levels
deep; there are elements output for the target Number and
for each Guess.

No.	Data Element	Appears
1	Entry Prompt Label	Number
2	Target Number	Number
3	Column Label	Number
4	Iteration Number	Guess
5	High Guess Value	Guess
6	Low Guess Value	Guess
7	Guess Value	Guess
8	Result Value	Guess
9	Answer Label	Number
10	Target Number(e)	Number
11	Answer Value	Number

Figure 8.2: Data Element List for Output #10

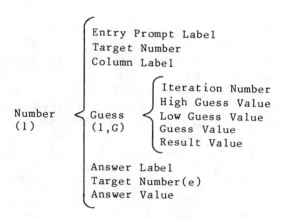

Figure 8.3: Logical Output Structure for Output #10

Next, the output elements can be analyzed to find which are Computable, which are Labels, and which are Required. The labels are those found in the entry prompt, the column heading, and the answer line. These elements can be identified as labels and then effectively dropped from further consideration.

The next step in design, the analysis of the computable
elements on the output, will yield valuable information for
our process. The Iteration Number may be computed by
initially setting it to zero, and then adding one for
successive values. The High Guess Value is computable by
setting it initially to the Target Number, and thereafter
setting it to the Guess Value at the appropriate times. The
Low Guess Value is computable by initially setting it to one
and then setting it to the Guess Value when necessary. The
Guess Value is computable as the average between the High
and Low Guess Values. The Result Value is computable by
multiplying the Guess Value by itself. The Target Number(e)
is computable by setting it to the Target Number. Finally,
the Answer Value is computable by setting it to the final
Guess Value. These computations are shown in the completed
output worksheet of Figure 8.4.

```
No.    Data Element           Appears  Type  Calculation Rules/Changes
====================================================================================================
1      Entry Prompt Label     Number   L
2      Target Number          Number   *     Number
3      Column Label           Number   L
4      Iteration Number       Guess    C     1)Set Iteration Number to Zero
                                             2)Add One to Iteration Number
5      High Guess Value       Guess    C     1)Set High Guess Value to Target Number
                                             2)Set High Guess to Guess Value
6      Low Guess Value        Guess    C     1)Set Low Guess to One
                                             2)Set Low Guess to Guess Value
7      Guess Value            Guess    C     1)Set Guess Value to
                                                (High Guess Value + Low Guess Value) / Two
8      Result Value           Guess    C     1)Set Result Value to Guess Value * Guess Value
9      Answer Label           Number   L
10     Target Number(e)       Number   C     1)Set Target Number(e) to Target Number
11     Answer Value           Number   C     1)Set Answer Value to Guess Value
```

Figure 8.4: Completed Worksheet for Output #10

This worksheet suggests that the only element required as
input is the Target Number. Thus, the Logical Data
Structure for this output is quite simple. (See Figure
8.5.)

Number
(1)   Target Number

Figure 8.5: Logical Data Structure for Output #10

Developing the Logical Process Structure for this output proceeds in the same manner as LPS in the last chapter; a list of the logical activities can be made and the frequency of execution of each action analyzed. As before, there are three types of logical actions: output, calculation, and input activities.

```
        Output Actions
                Print Number Heading Information
                Print Guess Information
                Print Answer Information
        Calculations
                Set Iteration Number to Zero
                Add One to Iteration Number
                Set High Guess Value to Target Number
                Set High Guess Value to Guess Value
                Set Low Guess Value to One
                Set Low Guess Value to Guess Value
                Set Guess Value to (High Guess Value +
                        Low Guess Value) / Two
                Set Result Value to Guess Value * Guess Value
                Set Target Number(e) to Target Number
                Set Answer Value to Guess Value
        Input Actions
                Get First Ideal Record
```

Figure 8.6: Logical Instruction List for Output #10

On this list (Figure 8.6) is an output action for each group of elements output (there are three), the calculation rules for each element that is computable (there are ten calculations for seven computable elements), and an input action for the Ideal File (in this case the Ideal File would contain just one record with one field on it, thus no "get next ideal record" instruction is necessary).

The frequency with which each instruction must be executed can now be listed. (See Figure 8.7.) The output instructions are easy; Print Number Heading Information must be done once for the Number, Print Guess Information must be done once each Guess, and Print Answer Information must be done just once for the Number.

```
Output Actions                                              Frequency
        Print Number Heading Information                    1/Number
        Print Guess Information                             1/Guess
        Print Answer Information                            1/Number
Calculations
        Set Iteration Number to Zero                        1/Number
        Add One to Iteration Number                         1/Guess
        Set High Guess Value to Target Number               1/Number
        Set High Guess Value to Guess Value                 1/Guess is too High
        Set Low Guess Value to One                          1/Number
        Set Low Guess Value to Guess Value                  1/Guess is too Low
        Set Guess Value to (High Guess Value +
            Low Guess Value) / Two                          1/Guess
        Set Result Value to Guess Value * Guess Value       1/Guess
        Set Target Number(e) to Target Number               1/Number
        Set Answer Value to Guess Value                     1/Number
Input Actions
        Get First Ideal Record                              1/Number
```

Figure 8.7: Instruction Frequencies for Output #10

The input instruction, Get First Ideal Record, must be done just once for the Number. The calculations, except for two, are also relatively easy. At the beginning for the Number, the following calculations must be done: Set Iteration Number to Zero, Set High Guess to Target Number, Set Low Guess to One, Set Target Number(e) to Target Number. At the end of the Number, the Answer Value must be set to the last Guess Value. For each Guess, the Iteration Number must be incremented, the Guess Value and the Result Value must be computed.

The instructions "Set High Guess Value to Guess Value" and "Set Low Guess Value to Guess Value" must also be executed in the process, but not simply once for the Number nor once each Guess. The two instructions are only done under certain conditions: "Set High Guess Value to Guess Value" is to be done only when the Guess Value is too high, while "Set Low Guess Value to Guess Value" is to be done only when the Guess Value is too low. Since each Guess is not always too high nor too low, some kind of alternative structure is suggested. The conditions under which these two instructions are done, "Guess is Too High" and "Guess is Too Low," are names of two alternative universals which must be present on the Logical Process Structure. They are mutually exclusive.

The Logical Process Structure appropriate to this output
will have four universals; Number will be the highest level,
with Guess repeating within Number, and Guess is Too High
and Guess is Too Low alternating within Guess. As before,
we will add to this process structure ".Begin" and ".End"
universals to the levels that are subdivided —— the
Number and the Guess levels. Then, the logical actions can
be placed onto the structure at the appropriate points.

```
                             ┌ Get First Ideal Record
                             │ Print Number Heading Information
                  .Begin    ┤ Set Iteration Number to Zero
                             │ Set High Guess Value to Target Number
                             │ Set Low Guess Value to One
                             └ Set Target Number(e) to Target Number

                                      ┌ Set Guess Value to
                                      │     (High Guess Value + Low Guess Value) / Two
                             .Begin   ┤ Set Result Value to Guess Value * Guess Value
                                      └ Print Guess Information

                             Guess is Too High ┤ Set High Guess Value to Guess Value
                             (0,1)
  Number    Guess            (+)
  (1)       (1,G)            Guess is Too Low  ┤ Set Low Guess Value to Guess Value
                             (0,1)


                             .End  ┤ Add One to Iteration Number



                    .End  ┤ Set Answer Value to Guess Value
                          └ Print Answer Information
```

Figure 8.8: Logical Process Structure for Output #10

The completed Logical Process Structure for this output is
shown in Figure 8.8. It also can be translated into the
Warnier flowchart given in Figure 8.9. Notice that the LPS
does not indicate how many Guesses are taken, nor how one
knows that a particular Guess is too High or Low. The
actual tests indicated by the decision diamonds on the
Warnier flowchart will be documented later in physical
design. The LPS just says to do the things found within the
Guess bracket for each Guess (however many there are) and
the things within the Guess is Too High and Guess is Too Low
bracket whenever the guess is too high or low (however you
know that it is).

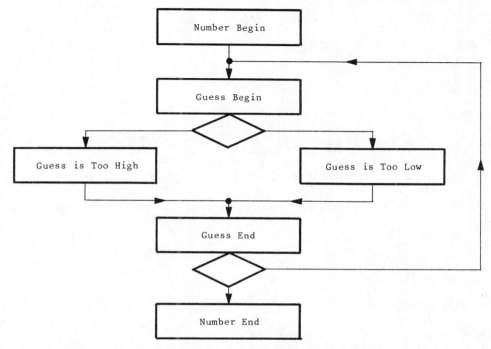

Figure 8.9: Warnier Flowchart for Output #10

Again, the Warnier flowchart shown here is not a step in Orr's hybrid Structured Program Design, although it is in Warnier's original Logical Construction of Programs. It is presented here just as a visual aid to the understanding of the processing represented by the LPS.

Also note that the algorithm provided for in this LPS will only work for Target Numbers greater than or equal to one: for numbers between zero and one, and for negative numbers, a slightly different algorithm must be designed.

Summary

It is a myth that different kinds of environments require intrinsically different approaches. Structured Program Design may be applied with the same procedural steps regardless of the nature of the programming problem.

Chapter 9 PHYSICAL PROCESS AUGMENTATION

Detailed Design

The Logical Process Structure can easily be a high level
blueprint for a program. However, it is not sufficiently
detailed to become a program just yet; by definition, an LPS
is a hardware- and language-independent view of processing.
It represents the processing necessary no matter what
language or what machine is used. Any computer program must
be specific to a particular kind of computer and a particular language. In this chapter we will begin the process of
transforming the Logical Process Structure into a program
design. That procedure is known as **physical design.**

To begin with, we must decide what hardware and language
environment we must work in. After all, the details
peculiar to a COBOL program are different than the details
of a FORTRAN or BASIC program. In this text we will be
detailing examples for use in a COBOL environment, since
COBOL is by far the most commonly used application language.
The principles described in the following sections, however,
are the same no matter which language environment is chosen.

Let us return to the Logical Process Structure first
developed for the Monthly Sales Report investigated in
Chapter 7. The LPS constructed is repeated in Figure 9.1.

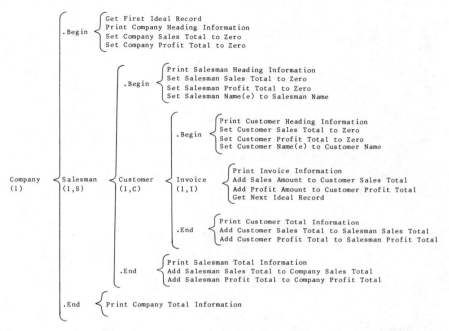

Figure 9.1: Logical Process Structure for Output #9 (Repeat)

In this chapter, we wish to explore the detailing necessary to bring this logical view of the processing down to a **code level** — where each activity expressed on the diagram is translatable into one and only one statement in the source language we have chosen. We will do so by adding specific COBOL-level details to the diagram shown in Figure 9.1. Once such details are added, the diagram ceases to be a Logical Process Structure. It begins to become a program design.

Control Structure

The first bit of physical detailing that we should do has to do with the **physical control structure** of the finished program, in other words, the program's "logic." Recall that the logic expressed on the LPS could be represented as a Warnier flowchart, which also was shown earlier.

Company Begin

Salesman Begin

Customer Begin

Invoice

Customer End

Salesman End

Company End

Figure 9.2: Warnier Flowchart for Output #9 (Repeat)

The first details we will add to the Logical Process Structure are those associated with the decision diamonds depicted in the flowchart in Figure 9.2. The LPS suggests that
there is processing to repeat for each Salesperson for the
Company; it doesn't say anything yet about how such a loop
should be controlled in a program.

It turns out that every repeating or alternating universal
on a Warnier/Orr diagram has a **physical test** associated
with it. Such tests will be used in the finished program to
control branching, and therefore should be spelled out in
detail on the program design we create.

Rather than add the physical tests directly on the program
design, we will reference them via a series of footnotes.
Beside each "number of times" designation on the diagram, we
add a question mark and a reference number to a particular
test. The actual tests, then, may be placed in a table at
the bottom of the page on which the diagram appears.

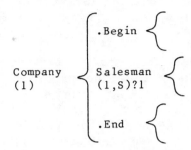

Tests: ?1-No More Salesmen = True

Figure 9.3: Documenting Test #1 for Output #9

In Figure 9.3, we have shown that the repetition of the Salesperson process is controlled via the test "No More Salespersons = True". Getting into a loop in a program is not a problem; getting out is the trick. Therefore for repeating universals, we will document the test to be made in the program to stop doing the Salesperson process. The above diagram indicates that the Salesperson routine is to be repeated over and over again until some indicator we have named No More Salespersons becomes True (more about this indicator in a moment). Documenting the tests in this fashion will allow us to translate the control structure seen here into executable code without too much effort. Just this much of the design can be translated as is shown in Figure 9.4.

```
PROCEDURE DIVISION.
COMPANY-PROCESS.
      PERFORM COMPANY-BEGIN.
      PERFORM SALESMAN-PROCESS
          UNTIL NO-MORE-SALESMEN = TRUE.
      PERFORM COMPANY-END.
      STOP RUN.
```

Figure 9.4: Translated Design of Test #1 for Output #9

Actually, because of the way COBOL works, this code **is not** a faithful rendition of the logic indicated by the diagram of Figure 9.3; we will introduce the appropriate translation rules later on in Chapter 12. However, you can see that building the finished program is very easy when the design is sufficiently detailed.

The No More Salespersons indicator named in the test shown is a switch whose status allows the program to know when to make an appropriate branch. As long as it is False, the program is to execute some branch back to the beginning of the Salesperson process; when it becomes True, the program is to fall through to the Company End process. Because they allow the program to know the status of the data being processed, such data fields are called **state variables,** a term taken from the work of Michael Jackson mentioned earlier in the book. The No More Salespersons switch is to remain False until there is no more data to process for any Salespersons, thus it must be set False at the beginning of the Company level, and set True whenever the input data is exhausted. (This must be a function of the "Get Next Ideal Record" instruction, which will be examined in detail in Chapter 11. For now, we will assume the switch is automatically set True when the input file is empty.)

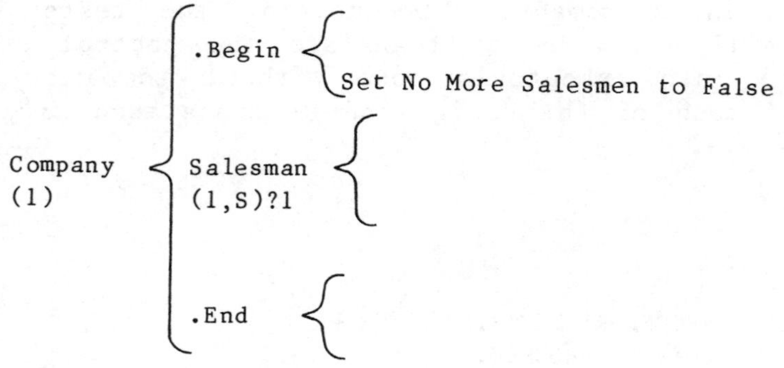

```
                  ⎧ .Begin ⎧
                  ⎪         ⎩ Set No More Salesmen to False
                  ⎪
       Company   ⎨  Salesman ⎧
        (1)       ⎪  (1,S)?1  ⎩
                  ⎪
                  ⎪  .End ⎧
                  ⎩
```

Tests: ?1-No More Salesmen = True

Figure 9.5: Initializing the State Variable for Test #1
for Output #9

Setting the No More Salespersons switch False at the point
indicated in Figure 9.5 is cause for alarm for some programmers. After all, the argument goes, the No More Salespersons
switch is the "end of file" indicator; you have to initialize it **before** the first "read" statement or the program
will "blow up" if the file is empty. Many programmers have
been told to always write a program so that it will still
execute even if there is no data to process. Is it acceptable to create a program that will "blow up" if there are no
records on the input file? Yes, on one condition — if
this program can be kept from running when there is no data.
That level of intelligence can be built into some operating
systems. In others an analogous level may be installed in
the program above the logic being detailed here. In such a
program, this logic represents the part of the program to be
invoked when there is data present to be processed. Therefore it is perfectly acceptable to design this process as if
there will always be at least one record on the input file.

In addition to detailing the code-level processing instructions necessary for our program, it is also important to
keep track of the physical names that the program will use
for data elements. As we add more detailed instructions,
the data elements referenced can be documented in a **Physical Data Dictionary**. This is simply a list of the data
fields that will have to be defined somewhere in the program; in COBOL they will become the entries in the working
storage section of the data division. (See Figure 9.6.)

```
             Physical Data Dictionary
             ========================
             State Variables
                   No More Salesmen
             Truth Values
                   True
                   False
```

Figure 9.6: Starting the Physical Data Dictionary
                  for Output #9

Keeping such a Physical Data Dictionary will allow us to retain control over the names used in the physical design. If the same data is referred to in many places in the design, the same name may be used.

Level Breaks

The No More Salespersons state variable controls the highest level Salesperson repetition. Within the Salesperson process there is another layer of repetition; the Customer process is to be repeated for all Customers of that Salesperson. Controlling the Customer loop also calls for the introduction of a state variable.

Probably the easiest way to control the Customer loop is to keep track of the Name of the Salesperson being processed. Whenever we come across input data for a different Salesperson, we will know that there are no more Customers for the current Salesperson, and the Customer loop may terminate. The test, therefore, for controlling the Customer loop is dependent upon the Name of the Salesperson being processed. (See Figure 9.7.)

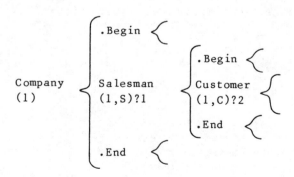

Tests: ?1-No More Salesmen = True
       ?2-Salesman Name is not = Old Salesman Name
          or No More Salesmen = True

Figure 9.7: Documenting Test #2 for Output #9

We may quit repeating the Customer process for a Salesperson whenever the Salesperson's Name on the record just read is different from the Name of the Salesperson that was being processed, or the No More Salespersons switch becomes True. The Old Salesperson Name state variable must therefore be initialized at the beginning of each Salesperson, as is shown in Figure 9.8.

```
                    .Begin

                                .Begin
                                              Set Old Salesman Name to Salesman Name
    Company         Salesman    Customer
    (1)             (1,S)?1     (1,C)?2

                                .End

                    .End
```

    Tests: ?1-No More Salesmen = True
           ?2-Salesman Name is not = Old Salesman Name
              or No More Salesmen = True

Figure 9.8: Initializing the State Variable for Test #2
for Output #9

The test for recognizing the end of the Invoice loop to be executed within each Customer is controlled in a similar fashion. (See Figure 9.9.)

Notice that **the tests compound as the levels increase.** The test for quitting the Invoice loop includes not only the comparison of the incoming Customer Name with the saved one, but also a comparison of the incoming Salesperson Name with the compared one, and a test of the No More Salesperson indicator. This is to avoid missing a "level break" — a change in the hierarchy of the input data. If the Invoice test just checks to see if the Customer Name has changed on the input record, then two Invoices for the same Customer but from different Salespersons will not be recognized as a change in the hierarchy of the data, and the output will be incorrect.

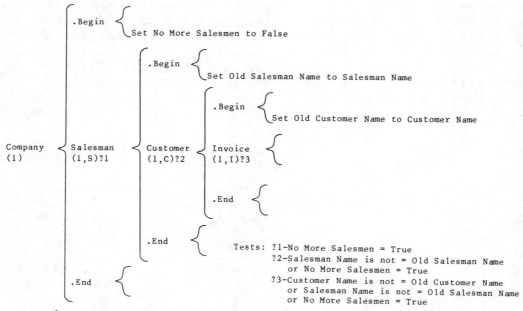

Figure 9.9: Physical Control Structure for Output #9

The physical data dictionary that was started earlier can be
augmented with the names of the additional data elements
shown in Figure 9.10. As the physical design progresses,
the new physical data being referenced will be added to this
list, although it will not be shown as an example from this
point on.


```
          Physical Data Dictionary
          =========================
          State Variables
               No More Salesmen
               Old Salesman Name
               Old Customer Name
          Truth Values
               True
               False
          Ideal Input Record
               Salesman Name
               Customer Name
```

Figure 9.10: Expanding Physical Data Dictionary
for Output #9

Since there are no further repeating or alternating universals present on the Warnier/Orr design, this part of the augmentation process is complete.

Additional Detailing

Once the control structure has been physically detailed, we may now explore the actions depicted on the diagram. Any actions not at a code level should be expanded into more detail. For instance within the Invoice process, the statement "Print Invoice Information" is not sufficiently detailed for a COBOL program. In COBOL, an Invoice line must be built before it can be printed. Therefore the statement should be expanded so that each instruction shown represents only one COBOL statement, as has been done in Figure 9.11. Notice that the actions detailed need not be actual executable COBOL statements, although they could be without much trouble. As long as they are at a code level, the actions are sufficiently detailed.

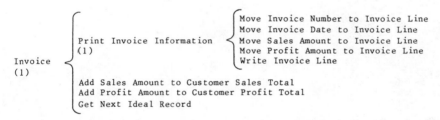

Figure 9.11: Detailing Output Information for Output #9

In practice, one need not redraft the original diagram with the new level of detail incorporated. An off-page reference to a more detailed process may be generated as shown in Figure 9.13 whenever a design grows too large to fit comfortably on one page.

Using such a method, we may complete the detailed augmentation of this design. It is shown in two parts in Figure 9.14. Since the calculations shown are already at a code level for the language we have selected, they need not be further detailed.

```
================================================================================
Physical Augmentation
================================================================================
Purpose: to detail physical procedures and tests
--------------------------------------------------------------------------------
Steps:
1) Test Documentation:  On the LPS, write a footnote for the conditions
            which will terminate processing for each level of hierarchy
            and for each alternative set.
2) State Variable Initialization:  Set the initial values of State
            Variables at appropriate places on the Augmented LPS.
3) Physical Data Definition:  List all variables to be used for physical
            control in a Physical Data Dictionary.
4) Off-page referencing:  Fill in an off-page reference for each output
            statement on the Augmented LPS.
5) Physical Output Detailing:  Write the physical steps required to
            produce the intended output onto the Augmented LPS.
================================================================================
```

Figure 9.12: Starting to Build the Physical Program Design


```
                    ⎧ Print Invoice Information  {...See Page 2
      Invoice       ⎪ Add Sales Amount to Customer Sales Total
      (1)           ⎨ Add Profit Amount to Customer Profit Total
                    ⎩ Get Next Ideal Record
```

                                                             Page 2

```
                              ⎧ Move Invoice Number to Invoice Line
                              ⎪ Move Invoice Date to Invoice Line
    Print Invoice Information  ⎨ Move Sales Amount to Invoice Line
    (1)                        ⎪ Move Profit Amount to Invoice Line
                              ⎩ Write Invoice Line
```

Figure 9.13: Off-Page Referencing

```
                    ┌ Get First Ideal Record
                    │ Print Company Heading Information      {...See Page 2
          .Begin  <  Set Company Sales Total to Zero
                    │ Set Company Profit Total to Zero
                    └ Set No More Salesmen to False

                                    ┌ Print Salesman Heading Information     {...See Page 2
                                    │ Set Salesman Sales Total to Zero
                          .Begin  <  Set Salesman Profit Total to Zero
                                    │ Set Salesman Name(e) to Salesman Name
                                    └ Set Old Salesman Name to Salesman Name

                                                   ┌ Print Customer Heading Information      {...See Page 2
                                                   │ Set Customer Sales Total to Zero
                                          .Begin  <  Set Customer Profit Total to Zero
                                                   │ Set Customer Name(e) to Customer Name
                                                   └ Set Old Customer Name to Customer Name

                                                              ┌ Print Invoice Information      {...See Page 2
Company    Salesman    Customer     Invoice                   │ Add Sales Amount to Customer Sales Total
(1)    <   (1,S)?1 <   (1,C)?2  <   (1,I)?3  <                  │ Add Profit Amount to Customer Profit Total
                                                              └ Get Next Ideal Record

                                                              ┌ Print Customer Total Information      {...See Page 2
                                          .End  <               │ Add Customer Sales Total to Salesman Sales Total
                                                              └ Add Customer Profit Total to Salesman Profit Total

                                    ┌ Print Salesman Total Information     {...See Page 2
                          .End  <    │ Add Salesman Sales Total to Company Sales Total
                                    └ Add Salesman Profit Total to Company Profit Total

          .End  <  Print Company Total Information     {...See Page 2
```

Tests: ?1-No More Salesmen = True
       ?2-Old Salesman Name is not = Salesman Name or ?1
       ?3-Old Customer Name is not = Customer Name or ?2

Figure 9.14: Augmented Process Structure - Page 1
for Output #9

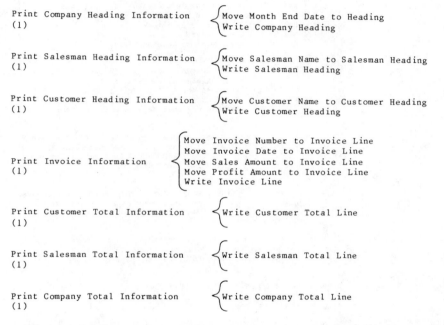

Figure 9.14: Augmented Process Structure – Page 2
for Output #9

Summary

The physical design begins with **augmentation** of the Logical Process Structure. We add state variable initialization and test footnotes for repeating and alternating universals. We also keep a Physical Data Dictionary. Then we begin to furnish the physical details of our specific output procedures, based on the particular language and hardware requirements. We now have the beginnings of the program design, itself.

This detailed design can easily be translated into COBOL with a great deal of speed and accuracy. The actual translation procedures will be discussed in Chapter 12. In the next two chapters we will take up the topic of some very important physical design that has yet to be addressed.

Physical
 Augmentation
 (1)
{
  Test Documentation
  State Variable Initialiation
  Physical Data Definition
  Off-page Referencing
  Physical Output Detailing
}

Figure 9.15: Chapter 9 Summary Diagram

Chapter 10 OUTPUT MAPPING DESIGN

Physical Mappings

Back in Chapter 3, a generalized overview of the Warnier/Orr
Structured Program Design technique was presented. In that
brief explanation of the SPD methodology, it was suggested
that program design was in reality an exercise in the application of a specialized branch of mathematics — set
theory — and that programs are transformations of an
input data set into an output data set. This set-to-set
transformation was called a mapping.

As explained in that chapter, the traditional single mapping
view of programming, "input-process-output," is insuffi-
ciently detailed to be a useful model for practical program
design. The usual program mapping of physical input into
physical output is not a simple one given to easy solution,
but a complex many-to-many mapping; many elements of the
input go into the production of many elements of the output.

The Structured Program Design method investigated in this
text instead breaks every program down into three mappings:
an **input mapping** which transforms physical input to
logical input, a **logical mapping** which transforms logical
input to logical output, and an **output mapping** which transforms logical output to physical output. (See Figure 10.1).

118

```
=================================
          Physical Input Data
=================================

            Input Mapping

=================================
          Logical Input Data
=================================

         Logical Process (Mapping)

=================================
          Logical Output Data
=================================

            Output Mapping

=================================
          Physical Output Data
=================================
```
Figure 10.1: SPD Mappings and Data Sets (Repeat)

So far in the book we have been analyzing the central or the "logical" transformation of logical input to logical output. Through the method explored in the last chapter, we can carry the examination of the "logical" mapping to a detailed level, a level that will represent a one-to-one mapping of design into program code. In this part of the book we will begin to look at techniques for designing the other two "physical" mappings shown. In this chapter we will be concerned with the last transformation pictured — the mapping of logical output to physical output.

Physical Output

Although we have been examining the structures of outputs all along in the design process, we have been making a

particular assumption about the operating environment the
output is to reside in. To avoid having to include physical
hierarchies on a Logical Output Structure, we have assumed
that the outputs we have worked with were being produced
under an operating system that could automatically detect
the end of a Page and print page headings when necessary.
In effect, the Logical Process Structure that we have created from this assumption produces a "one-page report", where
that Page is indefinitely long.

Unfortunately, most operating systems are not that intelligent yet. The program designer must eventually watch out
for and take care of the **physical packaging** of the output,
whether it is to tape, to disk, to screen, to paper, or
whatever. Let us now continue on with the examination of
the Monthly Sales Report whose LPS was augmented in the last
chapter. Only now we shall begin to worry about the physical output hierarchies that may be present.

If we cease to make the assumption that our program will run
under an intelligent operating system, then some new output
hierarchies start to become apparent. Look at the two views
of an output shown in Figure 10.2.

This is a side-by-side comparison of the difference between
the "logical" output we have been working with and a view of
the actual "physical" output required of the finished program. The logical output shown on the left is that which
would be produced by the Augmented Process Structure
developed in the last chapter. These lines printed on it
include not only the detail Invoice lines but also lines of
headings and footings for the other levels as well, such as
the Salesperson Heading line, Customer Total line, Company
Total line, etc. On the physical output there is other
information that must be output. For the sake of this example, let us assume that this output is for a generalized
Report with a Report Heading page to be printed out only at
the beginning of the output and a Report Footing page printed only at the very end; there is also a Page Heading and
Page Footing to be printed at the beginning and end of each
Page respectively; and each Page has room for a given number
of lines.

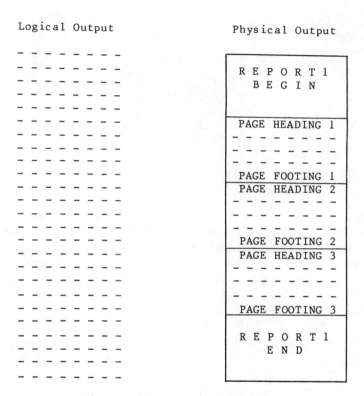

Figure 10.2: Output Views

Notice that the data to be physically output shows some distinct structure. In fact, this structure is a straightforward one that can be represented in the same manner as a Logical Output Structure, although it is not an LOS. It is a **Physical Output Structure,** and it appears in Figure 10.3.

The Physical Output Structure shows that there is a Report Heading and Footing at the Report level, a Page Heading and Footing for each Page within a Report, and Line Information for each Line within a Page.

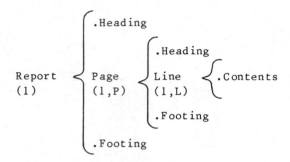

Figure 10.3: Physical Output Structure

The only problem with this structure is one that was originally mentioned in Chapter 2; **logical and physical hierarchies do not mix.** If the logical hierarchy of the output
data is Invoice within Customer within Salesperson for the
Company and the physical hierarchy is Line within Page for
the Report, we **cannot** create one processing hierarchy
which recognizes both structures. This inherent conflict
between logical and physical hierarchies is called a
structure clash, a term also coined by Jackson. We must
solve the problem of handling structure clashes before we
can build a program to produce the correct physical output
required.

Sequential Processing

There are fortunately two very good solutions to the problem
of structure clashes, both of which have been intuitively
invented by many programmers who have recognized the
problem. The first that will be presented is the simpler of
the two.

If we believe that the three mappings shown in Figure 10.1
provide a viable model for programming, then one solution to
the problem of the overlapping hierarchies seems obvious
— we could isolate the two clashing structures by time.
Under this solution we would, in effect, build two programs

that run one after the other. The first would be the one
based on the Augmented Process Structure we have already
designed. Instead of letting that program actually print
the report, though, we will have it dump its lines to a tape
file. That way it doesn't have to worry about physical
paging, and could actually build (as far as it is concerned)
a one-page report. After this program is finished, we would
rewind the tape created and run a second program whose job
it is to take the lines written on the tape and package them
into the physical format required. Such a program would
also be data-structured in accordance with the Physical Output Structure. Its general design is given in Figure 10.4.

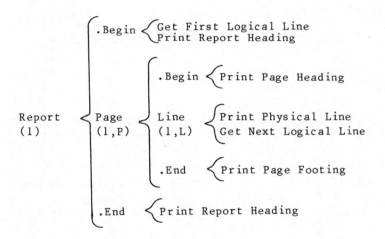

Figure 10.4: Physical Process Structure

This "two-program" solution has some very desirable
characteristics. It also has an undesirable side effect. To
begin with, let us consider its advantages.

● Advantage 1: It works. Sometimes the importance of this
advantage is overlooked.

● Advantage 2: It is simple. Instead of trying to design a single, complicated program that incorporates both hierarchies into one processing framework, we may create two relatively simple programs with simple, data-structured frameworks.

● Advantage 3: It is easy to enhance. If the structure of the physical output changes in some way (such as the page size being increased or decreased), both programs need not be affected, only the physical output process is affected. The so-called "ripple effect," where a change to part of a program causes unpredicted and undesired changes in some other part, is minimized, if not eliminated entirely.

● Advantage 4: It is a common solution. Since many programs will probably be output with the same physical format, the physical output process may be used again with other applications. Once a physical mapping program is built for an output device, it may be used by every program using that output format. This is quite analogous to the "interchangeable part" concept in the manufacturing world, and is equally powerful.

● Advantage 5: It allows device independence. Along with the ability to reuse output mapping programs for applications with the same output format, this method would allow us to interchange output mapping programs for a given logical output; the same logical output could be packaged as a report, a disk file, an on-line inquiry response, a telecommunicated message, or whatever, by simply interchanging physical output mapping programs.

Although it is clear that this solution to the problem of the output structure clash has many desirable advantages, it has one disadvantage that has caused many people to immediately reject it (and other solutions like it) in the past.

● Disadvantage: It is **slower** than necessary. Since the two-program solution must make two passes at essentially the same data, it takes roughly twice as long (as far as I/O processing is concerned) to run as a solution that makes just one pass at the data.

We will examine in a moment a solution that accomplishes the
same task with only one pass at the data, but first, a few
words about the above-mentioned evaluation.

Since it seems that the two-program solution will take
longer to execute than some other supposed solution, it is
often rejected out of hand as "inefficient" by many. This
is an improper and outdated attitude; it presupposes two
things which are not necessarily true. First, it presupposes that some other solution is possible; because efficiency is a relative measure, in order to compare, there
must exist at least two solutions to the same problem **that
both work.** If only one solution that works can be found,
efficiency is a moot point. Second, even when two solutions
to the same problem exist, it presupposes that machine
execution speed is always more important than all other
considerations combined. This is an impossible position to
defend. We have already pointed out at least five advantages to the "inefficient" solution, which may in total
outweigh the factor of execution speed. People time is a
more scarce resource and is also more expensive than
computer time. We might purposely choose to create software
that is slower than necessary (within acceptable limits) if
that software was easy to create and maintain.

Efficiency arguments among programmers are common, but
usually nonproductive. More often than not, the people time
expended in the argument delays the finished product by a
real-time factor many thousands of times greater than the
amount of the difference in machine time being discussed.

Efficiency is often confused with another concept that is
important: **program optimization.** Optimization, or mini-
mization, can occur in several areas in the machine environment: execution speed, resident program size, data storage
requirements, I/O access, response time, etc. The only
problem with optimization is that you usually can't optimize
every factor at once; there are trade offs. Optimizing
execution speed will often make a program physically larger,
while optimizing program size will make it quite slow. An
acceptable program solution may, in fact, not be optimal in
any of the above areas; it will probably be a **compromise**
of many factors, not the least of which will be the people
factors already mentioned.

Michael Jackson, in his book <u>Principles of Program Design</u>, states two rules for optimization that are applicable here. Rule one: Don't do it. Rule two: (For experts only.) Don't do it until last — until well after an "unoptimized" solution has been completed.

Inverted Hierarchies

Another solution to the problem of a structure clash lies with the use of a view of a data structured that is called an **inverted hierarchy**. However, do not be intimidated by the term. The meaning of the phrase will, with any luck at all, become clear as the use of the method is explained.

Let us assume for the moment that the two programs that we have mentioned, the Augmented Process Structure of Figures 9.13 and 9.14 and the physical output mapping of Figure 10.4 can run in parallel, i.e., side by side. (This is exactly the operating environment envisioned earlier —— the physical output mapping program is part of the "intelligent" operating system assumed at the beginning of logical design.) Although both programs would be started at the same time, the physical output mapping program would have to wait until the logical output mapping program had a line ready to print. Then it would take care of any necessary Report and Page Headings on the actual output before releasing the line given it. Then it would take care of any Page or Report Footings necessary. Every time the logical output mapping program had a logical line to print, the physical output mapping program would take care of the necessary physical output.

Under this scheme, we would have two parallel output data streams to watch: the one output by the logical mapping and the corresponding response by the physical mapping. The two data streams are shown in Figure 10.5. (For simplicity's sake, we have represented the physical page size as just three lines long.)

Notice that as the logical mapping readies logical lines to print, the physical mapping responds by printing an appropriate physical output. For the first line that the logical mapping transmits, the physical mapping must print the

Report Heading and the first Page Heading before printing
the line given it. For the second logical line transmitted,
the physical mapping simply prints the line. For the third
logical line transmitted, the physical mapping must print
the line and then the first Page Footing, since the first
page has now been completed. Notice that a heading on the
next page is not printed until another logical line is transmitted. With the last logical line transmitted, the physical mapping must print the line followed by the last Page
Footing followed by the Report Footing.

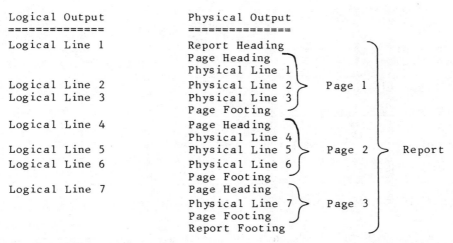

Figure 10.5: Output Data Streams for a 7-line Report

The Physical Output Structure presented earlier is obvious
in the physical output data stream. The only problem is
that the Physical Process Structure given back in Figure
10.4 is not allowed to operate all at once; it starts up
with the first logical line, waits until the next logical
line is sent before starting up again for a bit, then waits
for another logical line to be sent before starting up
again. This wait/start/wait cycle is depicted in Figure
10.6. The dashed lines show how much of the Physical Output
data stream is allowed to operate with each successive

startup. Every time it starts up it must print a physical
line, but sometimes before printing the line it must print a
Report Heading and a Page Heading, and sometimes just a Page
Heading.   After the line is printed, sometimes it has to
print a Page Footing and sometimes a Page Footing and a
Report Footing.

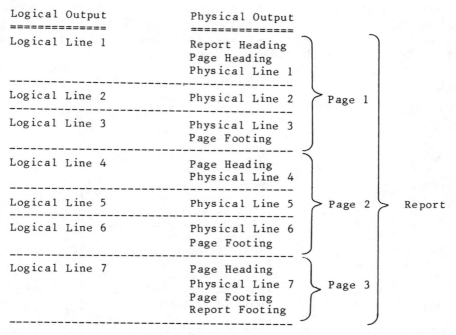

```
Logical Output                    Physical Output
==============                    ===============
Logical Line 1                    Report Heading
                                  Page Heading
                                  Physical Line 1
--------------------------------------------------
Logical Line 2                    Physical Line 2       > Page 1
--------------------------------------------------
Logical Line 3                    Physical Line 3
                                  Page Footing
--------------------------------------------------
Logical Line 4                    Page Heading
                                  Physical Line 4
--------------------------------------------------
Logical Line 5                    Physical Line 5       > Page 2   > Report
--------------------------------------------------
Logical Line 6                    Physical Line 6
                                  Page Footing
--------------------------------------------------
Logical Line 7                    Page Heading
                                  Physical Line 7       > Page 3
                                  Page Footing
                                  Report Footing
--------------------------------------------------
```

Figure 10.6: Wait/Start/Wait Processing for a 7-line Report

If we represent the data structure found when the data
stream is examined as a whole, we see the Report-Page-Line
hierarchy shown earlier in Figure 10.3; if we examine the
data stream seen only between one wait point and the next,
we see something else. The data structure seen between
waits is called an "inverted" data structure because the
hierarchy is "inside out" — Line-Page-Report.

Creating the inverted data structure for this Physical
Output Structure may be done in the same manner as all the
other data structures examined in the text; we may examine
the data elements output and the frequency with which they
appear physically. The output structure we are interested
in is the data structure between **any two wait/start/wait**

points. There are five physical data elements which may be present: a Report Heading, a Page Heading, a Physical Line, a Page Footing, and a Report Footing. The Physical Line appears for each Logical Line, but the other elements do not; this suggests some kind of alternative structure. The Report Heading only appears when the Logical Line to be printed is the Beginning of the Report. The Page Heading only appears when the Logical Line to be printed is the Beginning of a Page. Thus "Beginning of Report" and "Beginning of Page" are alternative universals necessary for the data structure we wish to create. Likewise are the universals "Ending of Page" and "Ending of Report" for the printing of the Page Footing and the Report Footing elements. The data structure suggested by this analysis appears in Figure 10.7.

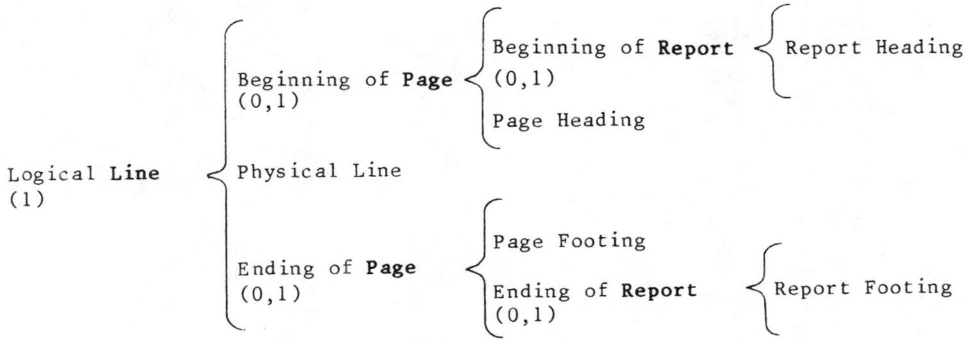

```
                         ┌                    ┌ Beginning of Report ┌ Report Heading
                         │ Beginning of Page <  (0,1)              <
                         │ (0,1)               │                    └
                         │                     └ Page Heading
                         │
Logical Line            <  Physical Line
(1)                      │
                         │                     ┌ Page Footing
                         │ Ending of Page     <                     ┌ Report Footing
                         │ (0,1)               │ Ending of Report  <
                         └                     └ (0,1)              └
```

Figure 10.7: Inverted Data Structure

This diagram suggests that for a Logical Line, we must first evaluate whether it is a line which will begin a Page, and if so, if it is the line which will begin the Report. If the line is both the beginning of a Page and the beginning of the Report (which the first line would be), then the Report Heading, the Page Heading, and the Physical Line are printed. If the line is the beginning of a Page but not the beginning of the Report, just the Page Heading and the Physical Line are printed. Similarly, the Page Footing and the Report Footing are to be printed when the Logical Line was the Ending of a Page and/or the Ending of the Report.

The reason this is called an "inverted" data structure should be apparent: instead of having Line within Page

within Report as a hierarchy, Line is highest, with a change
in the Page level checked for each Line, and a change in the
Report level checked each Page. **Remember, this hierarchy
appears to be inverted because we are only seeing a piece of
the total data structure at a time.**

With a little effort, the analogy of the Logical Process
Structure can be created from this inverted data structure.
It is shown in Figure 10.8.

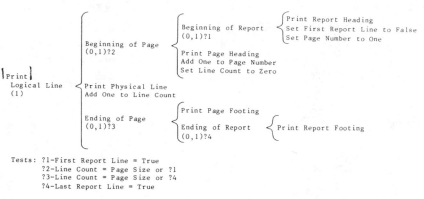

Tests: ?1-First Report Line = True
        ?2-Line Count = Page Size or ?1
        ?3-Line Count = Page Size or ?4
        ?4-Last Report Line = True

Figure 10.8: Physical Output Coroutine

The process structure shown here is a vitally interesting
one. This process structure is the mapping that must be
used if we wish to make only one pass at the data for this
output. It retains the separation of the logical mapping
from the physical mapping that the two-program solution
examined earlier does, without going through the data twice.
Each time the Augmented Process Structure portion of the
program has a Logical Line to print, it would invoke this
process (or one like it), which would handle the actual
printing of the line. Although it is most likely that this
routine will be coded as a subroutine in a COBOL program, it
is technically not a subroutine. Since the process could be
resident as a separate program operating concurrently with
the LPS program via interrupts (the wait/stop/wait
mechanism), this is a **coroutine.**

In actual practice, the physical output coroutine will reside in the same program with the logical process designed earlier. Some minor design modifications can be added to the Augmented Process Structure to reflect such a routine.

```
                          ⎧ Move Invoice Number to Invoice Line
                          ⎪ Move Invoice Date to Invoice Line
Print Invoice Information ⎨ Move Sales Amount to Invoice Line
(1)                       ⎪ Move Profit Amount to Invoice Line
                          ⎪ Move Invoice Line to Output Buffer
                          ⎩ Print Logical Line {...Figure 10.8
```

Figure 10.9: Logical Line Routine Usage for Output #9

In Figure 10.9, we have slightly modified the "Print Invoice Information" details examined in the last chapter. Instead of actually printing the Invoice Line once it has been built, the LPS part of the program would then move the line to a field called Output Buffer (perhaps an area defined in Working Storage) and then call the Logical Line routine, which is defined elsewhere. All Logical Lines printed by the Augmented Process Structure may be handled in this manner. By using this method, we have retained most of the advantages discussed earlier as far as interchangeability and enhanceability of the two-program solution, while making only a single pass at the data. The only thing sacrificed is perhaps a human factor; the inverted hierarchy is not as immediately understandable as the normal hierarchy. Fortunately, once an inverted hierarchy is developed for an output routine it is pretty much the same for every program which produces physical output with that format, so that not many different output coroutines will have to be designed or utilized. In many operating environments, they can be built right into the operating system (or even the output device).

Extensions

The Physical Output Coroutine just designed will serve only for simple reports; it assumes that the report is to be single-spaced, with page breaks only when a page is full. If

variable-length line spacing is desired, or if the requirements state that each new Salesperson is to begin on a new
page, or if no separate Report Heading or Footing is
required, then the output coroutine will have to be modified. New sections may have to be added; other sections may
have to be dropped or changed. Any level of intelligence
desired may be built into the physical output coroutine.
That, as the cliche' goes, is an exercise that will be left
to the reader.

Summary

One way to produce a report is to have one program output
the logical output data and a second program convert that
data set into the needed output format. The simplest way to
avoid running two separate programs is to write a coroutine
which is activated whenever there is logical output. This
coroutine is necessarily written with an inverted hierarchy
 — the "inside out" version of the hierarchy that would
be used if it were an independent program.

Chapter 11 INPUT MAPPING DESIGN

Input Routines

Of the three program mappings utilized in the Warnier/Orr Structured Program Design method, we have presented the development of two of them: the central, "logical" mapping from logical input to logical output, and the physical output mapping from logical output to physical output. The purpose of this physical output mapping routine, developed in the last chapter, was to isolate the "logical" part of the program from the real world; if the output format or device changes, then only the output mapping part of the program will need to be modified.

The last program structure that we need to design is the physical input mapping. It is exactly analogous to the output mapping we have already considered; it will act as a buffer between the "logical" part of the program and the real input. When the real input changes, only the input buffer part of the program will need to be enhanced.

In the last chapter, we discussed two primary solutions to the problem of physical buffering: The first was the "two-program" approach where the output data was passed twice, first output in an intermediate form and then repackaged in the physical form desired; the second was the coroutine

approach, where the "logical" section of the program transmitted one line at a time to the output coroutine, which
then packaged the line accordingly on the intended device.
In this chapter, we shall not consider the two-program solution to the input mapping routine; we shall consider only
the coroutine solution.

For the example presented in this chapter, we will return to
the Monthly Sales Report for which the logical solution has
already been developed (Chapters 7 and 9). To refresh your
memory, this was the output of Invoices within Customers
within Salespersons for the Company, with totals of the
Sales and Profits for each Customer, for each Salesperson,
and for the Company. In Chapter 7, we traced out the
development of the Logical Output Structure (LOS), the
Logical Data Structure (LDS), and the Logical Process
Structure (LPS) for this output. Since in this chapter we
will be concerned with input mapping routines, we shall be
primarily interested in the data structure of the required
input to support the output desired. The Logical Data
Structure derived for this output back in Chapter 7 is
repeated for your convenience in Figure 11.1.

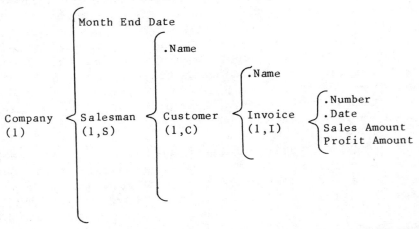

Figure 11.1: Logical Data Structure for Output #9 (Repeat)

Again, the LDS depicts the **minimal data requirements** to
support the output. It is produced solely from a knowledge
of the output requirements, and has no relationship to what
is actually available as input to the finished program.
(The data actually available as input to the program must,
however, have a relationship to the LDS.) The LDS presented

in Figure 11.1 says that the minimal data required as input to the output is in order by Invoice within Customer within Salesperson for the Company; further, the Month End Date must be provided at the beginning of the data set, the Salesperson Name at the beginning of each Salesperson, the Customer Name at the beginning of each Customer, and the Invoice Number, Date, Sales Amount, and Profit Amount for each Invoice.

In Chapter 7, we discussed one of the ways that the data shown on the LDS might be packaged. If we move all of the data appearing on the LDS down to the lowest level, we have a diagram of the **simplest** form that the input could take — a single sequential file with one record type. (This is also called a "flat" file.)

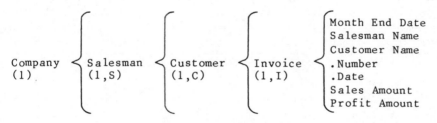

Figure 11.2: The Ideal Input File Structure
for Output #9 (Repeat)

Were we building a two-program solution to this problem, the first program would package the actual data coming in in the form shown in Figure 11.2. Then, the "logical" mapping, the LPS, could be used as a second program, taking the Ideal File generated in the first pass and creating the logical output.

To generate an input coroutine, we must take the same kind of approach that we did in the development of the output coroutine; we wish to fool the "logical" part of the program into believing it is reading an Ideal File, even if the Ideal File isn't actually present in that form. Where the Logical Process Structure portion of the program shows the

action "Get First Ideal Record" and "Get Next Ideal Record,"
we will install a routine that does that function.

So in a nutshell, the strategy we shall use is this: We
will examine the data structures of the data going into the
input coroutine (the actual input) and the data coming out
(the Ideal File) and develop a data-structured mapping to
accomplish the task. To begin with, let us consider the
output of the coroutine. We have already suggested that the
output of the input mapping is an ideal record, but it is
important to note the content of an ideal record. In Figure
11.3, you can see that each ideal record consists of four
parts.

```
 Company Data     Salesman Data    Customer Data     Invoice Data
+--------------+----------------+----------------+-----------------+
+--------------+----------------+----------------+-----------------+
+--------------+----------------+----------------+-----------------+
+--------------+----------------+----------------+-----------------+
+--------------+----------------+----------------+-----------------+
...etc...
```

Figure 11.3: Ideal Records for Output #9

Each ideal record must contain data for all the levels shown
on the LDS: the Company Data (the Month End Date), the
Salesperson Data (the Salesperson Name), the Customer Data
(the Customer Name), and the Invoice Data (the Invoice
Number, Date, Sales Amount, and Profit Amount). The input
coroutine that we are about to develop will have to gather
the data sufficient to fill each of these categories **just
once** each time it is called.

Let us consider now the real input data. A representation
of the actual input that this program is to use appears in
Figure 11.4. It consists of four files: (1) a Company File
with one record containing the Month End Date, (2) a
Salesman File with a record for each salesperson containing
the salesperson's name and number, (3) a Customer File with
a record for each customer containing the customer's name

and number, and (4) an Invoice File with a record for each
invoice containing the invoice's number, date, Sales Amount,
and Profit Amount, the Customer Number, and the Salesman
Number. Further, all files are **arranged sequentially;** The
Invoice File is a sequential file sorted in order by Invoice
Number within Customer Number within Salesman Number. The
Salesman File is a sequential file in order by Salesman
Number. The Customer File is a sequential file in order by
Customer Number. The Salesman File and Customer File
contain only the salespersons and customers that have
invoices for the period.

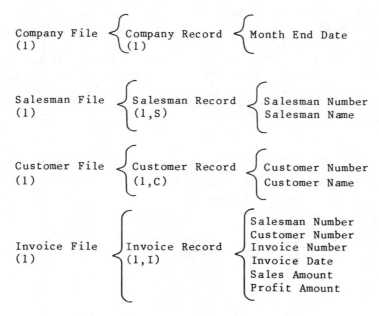

Figure 11.4: Actual Input Files

This set of files is very easy to use for the building of
the Ideal File. We will discuss shortly the process for
transforming other, more complex file organizations into the
ideal format. For now, the files that will be used are all
"flat" files, as represented in Figure 11.5.

Customer File: Salesman File: Customer File:

| Month End Date |

.Number	.Name

.Number	.Name

Invoice File:

Salesman Number	Customer Number	.Number	.Date	Sales Amount	Profit Amount

Figure 11.5: Physical File Organization

To begin our analysis, we must consider what the order of
the records to be processed must be. Assume for the moment
that the ideal record function is to be performed by a
clerk. The "logical" part of the program asks the clerk to
build the entire Ideal File. What actual input records
would have to be provided to the clerk, in what order, to
satisfy the request? The list of records to be provided
would look similar to that shown in Figure 11.6.

```
              Company Record
                Salesman Record
                  Customer Record
                    Invoice Record
                    Invoice Record
                    Invoice Record
                  Customer Record
                    Invoice Record
                    Invoice Record
                Salesman Record
                  Customer Record
                    Invoice Record
                    Invoice Record
```

Figure 11.6: Input Data Stream

This data stream is relatively easy to know; it is simply
the data stream represented by the Logical Data Structure
given earlier in Figure 11.1.

Since we now know the input and the output to this mapping routine, let us consider the relationship of the input to the output data sets. This is shown in Figure 11.7.


```
Company Record
    Salesman Record
        Customer Record
            Invoice Record - - - - - - > 1st Ideal Record
            Invoice Record - - - - - - > 2nd Ideal Record
            Invoice Record - - - - - - > 3rd Ideal Record
        Customer Record
            Invoice Record - - - - - - > 4th Ideal Record
            Invoice Record - - - - - - > 5th Ideal Record
    Salesman Record
        Customer Record
            Invoice Record - - - - - - > 6th Ideal Record
            Invoice Record - - - - - - > 7th Ideal Record
```

Figure 11.7: Ideal Records for Output #9 from the
Input Data Stream

An ideal record would be created at the points indicated by the arrows on the diagram. For the first record, we would have to consume the Company Record, the first Salesperson Record, the first Customer Record, and the first Invoice Record before we have read enough to build an ideal record. For the second record all the information except the Invoice Data is the same; so the second ideal record is created after consuming the second Invoice record; and so on, as indicated by the figure. As soon as all Invoices for a Customer have been consumed, we must be provided with another Customer record; as soon as all Invoices for a Salesperson have been consumed, another Salesperson record must be available.

From the discussion of mappings in the Chapter 3, we know this to be a **many-to-one mapping,** and as such it may be used as the basis for the input mapping routine. As with the output coroutine developed in the last chapter, this coroutine will also be based on an **inverted** data structure — the structure of the data present for each ideal

record present. The structure of the data present for each
of the ideal records generated appears in Figure 11.8.

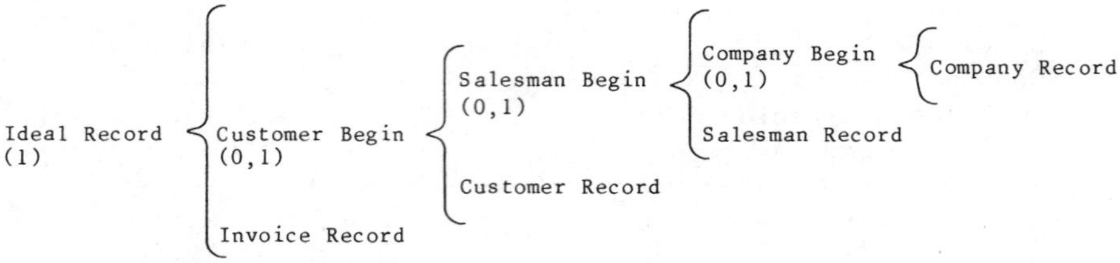

Figure 11.8: Ideal Record Data Structure for Output #9

This diagram indicates that for each ideal record, an
Invoice record is consumed. Prior to that, if the ideal
record is the first for a customer, a Customer Record is
consumed; when it is the first for a salesperson as well, a
Salesman Record is consumed; when it is the first for the
company, a Company Record is consumed. Notice that this is
just the top half of the inverted LDS; the Customer End,
Salesman End, and Company End universals do not appear since
there is no data to be input at the end of those levels.

From this structure, it is a simple matter to evolve a
mapping that will accomplish the generation of a single
ideal record each time it is performed. It appears in
Figure 11.9.

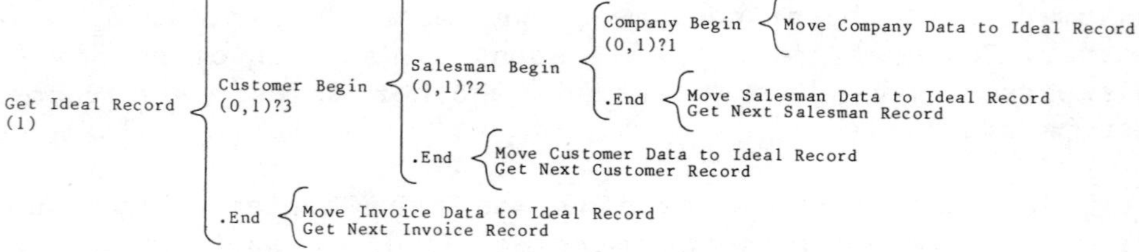

Tests: ?1-Ideal Record = Spaces
       ?2-Invoice Salesman Number is not = Salesman Number
          or ?1
       ?3-Invoice Customer Number is not = Customer Number
          or ?2

Figure 11.9: Get Ideal Record Coroutine

This coroutine assumes that an Invoice record, a Customer record, a Salesperson record, and the Company Record have all been read prior to its invocation. It also assumes that the ideal record area is initially filled with blanks. Notice that this routine tests to see where it is in the hierarchy, and then processes the data that is appropriate. It also replaces a record each time it consumes one (except for the Company Record, of course). After executing this routine, exactly one ideal record will have been built.

This routine can be used as the core of a process for buffering the Logical Process Structure central transformation from the real input. At the beginning of the Company level on the LPS is the instruction "Get First Ideal Record." This process may be detailed as is shown in Figure 11.10.

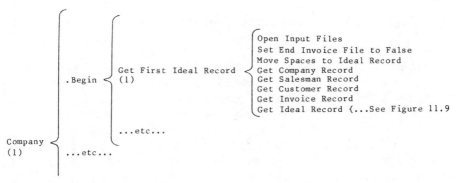

Figure 11.10: Get First Record Routine

This routine will open the input files, set up the "end invoice file" indicator, set the ideal record area to blanks, get the first record off of each of the four input files, and then invoke the Get Ideal Record routine just designed.

The "Get Next Ideal Record" routine found at the end of the Invoice level on the LPS is slightly different. (See Figure 11.11.) For one thing, it need not open the input files, nor set the initial state indicators, nor read the first records. It must, however, check the status of the "end invoice file" indicator to determine if there is another ideal record to build. If there is, it invokes the Get

Ideal Record routine, otherwise it sets the No More
Salespersons indicator true (so the LPS part of the program
knows it has exhausted all of the input data) and then
closes the input files.

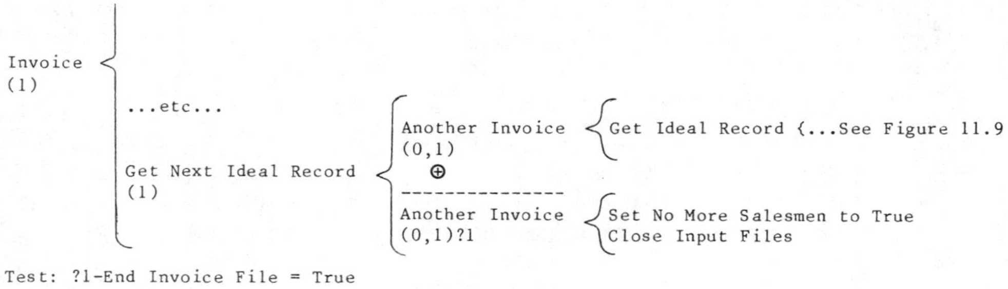

Test: ?1-End Invoice File = True

Figure 11.11: Get Next Ideal Record Coroutine

The technique of opening the input files, setting the
initial state variables, and doing the initial read's in the
Get First Ideal Record and checking the status of the detail
file in the Get Next Ideal Record is standard. These
"extra's" are required because of the way computer languages
tend to read input data; the "AT END" clause of the read
statement is executed **after the last record has been read**
instead of with the last record. Thus, the Get ideal record
routine must be called one more time than there are Ideal
Records to generate. Also, the "get record" statements
shown must be further detailed for COBOL. These "get's" are
shown in Figure 11.12.

Selecting Records

So far in this chapter, we have used a fairly simple input
file — one that had a record for each level of the
Logical Data Structure, where the records were all in the
proper order, were all edited, and had all been selected (no
extra records on any of the files). How would the design
change if, for instance, there were extra records on the

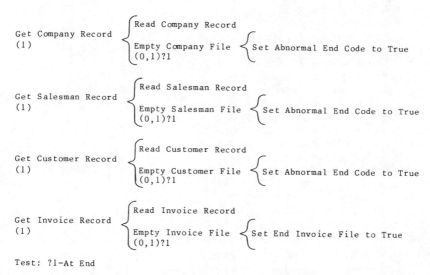

Get Company Record
(1)
    Read Company Record

    Empty Company File
    (0,1)?1   Set Abnormal End Code to True

Get Salesman Record
(1)
    Read Salesman Record

    Empty Salesman File
    (0,1)?1   Set Abnormal End Code to True

Get Customer Record
(1)
    Read Customer Record

    Empty Customer File
    (0,1)?1   Set Abnormal End Code to True

Get Invoice Record
(1)
    Read Invoice Record

    Empty Invoice File
    (0,1)?1   Set End Invoice File to True

Test: ?1-At End

Figure 11.12: Physical File Reads with "AT END" Alternatives

Invoice file? Not much. Let us examine a common occurrence; Let us suppose that the Invoice file, although
sorted, has not been edited. In other words, mixed in with
the invoice records that are useful are records that are
not; they contain bad values, unmatched fields, etc. Would
such a file ruin the design that we have so carefully built
so far? Not if we carry the idea of an "ideal record" one
more level. Consider the data streams shown in Figure
11.13. On the input data stream on the left, there are good
Invoice records mixed in with the bad ones, while on the
right we see, in effect, the "ideal" invoice records —
the good ones.

```
Bad  Invoice  Record
Good  Invoice  Record  - - - - - - >  "Ideal"  Invoice
Bad  Invoice  Record
Bad  Invoice  Record
Bad  Invoice  Record
Good  Invoice  Record  - - - - - - >  "Ideal"  Invoice
Bad  Invoice  Record
Bad  Invoice  Record
Good  Invoice  Record  - - - - - - >  "Ideal"  Invoice
Bad  Invoice  Record
Bad  Invoice  Record
Bad  Invoice  Record
Bad  Invoice  Record
Bad  Invoice  Record
Good  Invoice  Record  - - - - - - >  "Ideal"  Invoice
```

Figure 11.13: Editing the Invoice File

So far the design we have built assumes that only good
Invoice records will be provided. If bad records are
actually present on the "real" file, we can filter them off
by adding a new coroutine that fools the first one into
believing that it is reading only edited Invoices. Such a
coroutine would be as is shown in Figure 11.14. It would be
inserted at "Get Next Invoice Record" on Figure 11.9.

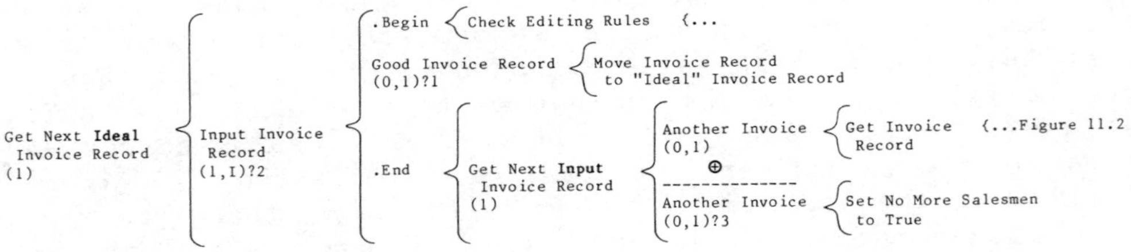

Tests: ?1-Invoice Record Passed Edit
       ?2-Invoice Record Passed Edit or No More Salesmen = True
       ?3-End Invoice File = True

Figure 11.14: Selection Coroutine

The routine shown above is also an inverted data structure, based upon the data relationships shown in Figure 11.13. This secondary coroutine allows the primary input coroutine to believe it is only processing edited Invoices. This secondary coroutine can also be considered a standard "model" for a coroutine; anytime an input file has more records on it than are needed, this kind of routine can be built. This is a model for a **selection coroutine**, because it selects off just the records that are needed. If there are extra Salesperson or Customer records present on the real input files, a similar coroutine can be built for them as well. We will examine some other useful model program structures in the last chapters of this book.

Decryption Rules

One other feature likely to be present in input mapping routines deals with the translation from data in its physical form into data needed logically. Such transformations are called **decryption rules**, since they take information that is physically coded in some manner and uncode it into useable information. For an example of a decryption rule, consider the Invoice File presented earlier in Figures 11.4 and 11.5. Each Invoice Record contained just the fields that were logically required as input. It is often the case that these fields will not be present in that form on the physical input files. For instance, instead of having a Profit Amount, each Invoice record might have contained a Profit Percentage. Thus, our input mapping coroutine would have to build the Profit Amount by multiplying out the Sales Amount and the Profit Percentage. This calculation is easily added to the design already created.

One note of caution with respect to decryption rules — they fall under the realm of **physical design** and not logical design. **The LDS does not contain the encrypted data elements present on the physical files.** Remember that the Logical Data Structure is independent of actual input, and the presence (or absence) of encrypted data on a physical file should be transparent to the logical design for the program.

However, the LDS is a useful tool for analyzing the existing data. Once it is created, we may go into the physical files present and determine if the data is there directly or will have to be decrypted from other data present. We can, if we wish, document the decryption algorithm for use in the design of the input coroutine, but again to emphasize — these rules are not "logical" calculations but "physical" ones.

"Abend" Processing

Notice that we have not as yet considered what to do if there is a failure of some kind —— a so-called "exception" to the program that we create. Under the Warnier/Orr philosophy, there **is no such thing**. There are two kinds of data present in any physical system: data that is recognizable and useable, and data that is not. Thus, there is only one way that a Warnier/Orr program should end: "normal end of job." If the possibility exists that the input files may be incomplete, we can plan for that eventuality and handle it. If, for instance, it is possible for the Customer File that we are processing to end prematurely (there are still Invoices left to process but there are no more Customer Records), we can (as was shown in Figure 11.12) set some state variable that indicates that the Customer File ended prematurely. A check of the status of this indicator would have to be included in the "Get Next Ideal Record" routine. The No More Salesman state variable, which is set to True when the Invoice File is exhausted, must also be set to True when the Abnormal End Code is set to True. This way the program will know that it must terminate its run because there is insufficient data to create an ideal record. A message stating why the program is quitting should also be included at the conclusion of processing.

There is only one criterion for knowing whether to include processing for such "exceptions": if the data provided to the program has been reliably screened for mistakes or flaws in the data, we will not have to include logic to screen for them again; if the data has not been reliably screened for mistakes or flaws, we must. Again, the processing necessary

is wholly and completely dependent upon the data being
operated on. If the data is unedited, we must edit; if the
data has been edited, we need not. It is as simple as that.

Summary

To allow the logical process part of the program to receive
only ideal records, we can produce a program to create the
ideal file from available files or we can create coroutines
to translate the actual files into the ideal format. Like
their output counterparts, physical input mappings require
inverting the physical data structures to suit the programs'
overall data structures.

Chapter 12 PROGRAM CONSTRUCTION: CODING AND TESTING

Programming Styles

Ever since there have been programs, there have been standards for programs. The problem with programming standards,
though, is that they are usually only good for telling you
if you have a poor program and will not generally tell you
if you have a good one. As someone once said, "You can't
make anything foolproof because fools are too ingenious."
Indeed, if you set programming standards based upon the
wrong things, you will consistently find that people will
write poor programs that conform to the standards. In turn,
new standards get set, and the cycle repeats. We know from
experience that this is a never-ending cycle that never
guarantees good results.

Standards that tell people what not to do are generally less
than completely useful, they usually say very little about
what **to do.**

In the seminars that we hold on Structured Program Design,
we often ask the attendants to make a list of the attributes
of a "good" program. This usually turns out to be an eye-
opening exercise. We usually get attributes like "no GO
TO's," "modular," "highly cohesive and loosely coupled," "no
negative logic" (a self-violating standard), "structured,"

148

etc. Unfortunately, programs that have no GO TO's, that are modular, that are highly cohesive and loosely coupled, that are structured, etc., may lack the obvious symptoms of bad programs but still be bad. In reality there are only two important attributes of a good program; **a good program must (1) work and (2) be maintainable.** The first attribute is usually easy to measure, the second, though, has a tendency to be subjective. The programs that are the easiest to enhance are those written in a style the enhancer is most comfortable with.

In this book, we will present only one standard for coding, and it is of the positive variety. Do not be misled by its simplicity, though. Its ramifications are profound.

Coding Standard:

● **Code the program so that it matches the data-structured design as closely as possible.**

This implies, naturally, that you must have a completed data-structured design to code from. When you have taken the time to detail a data structured design such as we have developed in the preceding chapters, the coding of the program becomes almost a trivial exercise. In fact, for coding in COBOL, only ten different statements are needed to be able to code any program.

Coding Conventions

In any program, there are only three things that must be codable: control logic, input and output, and arithmetic. For COBOL, the subsets are quite easy to define.

There are just four control structures possibly present on a Warnier/Orr diagram that must be translatable into code. They are the control structures presented originally in Chapter 2: **hierarchy, sequence, repetition, and alternation.** Translating each structure into code is simply a matter of setting up a correspondence rule. The correspondence rules presented in the next section are by no means the only ones

possible; they do represent the most convenient translations, though.

Customer   {.Begin {
(1)

        CUSTOMER.
              PERFORM CUSTOMER-BEGIN.
   Figure 12.1: Hierarchy Translation

Translating a level of hierarchy is quite simple. (See
Figure 12.1.) One can simply use the PERFORM statement to
invoke a lower level of hierarchy. The PERFORM ... THRU ...
option will not be needed in this coding style, as the GO TO
statement will not be used within PERFORMed paragraphs.

                              ⎧Open Input Files
Get First Record   ⎨Get Invoice Record {
(1)   ⎪Get Client Record {
                              ⎩Get Ideal Record   {

        GET-FIRST-RECORD.
              OPEN INPUT CLIENT-FILE, INVOICE-FILE.
              PERFORM GET-INVOICE-RECORD.
              PERFORM GET-CLIENT-RECORD.
              PERFORM GET-IDEAL-RECORD.
     Figure 12.2: Sequence Translation

The second control structure, sequence, is also easy to code. (See Figure 12.2.) Since COBOL executes statements in sequence within a paragraph, we shall simply place the statements within a level of hierarchy in the order that they are to be performed.

Company   Employee
(1)   (1,E)?1

Test: ?1-No More Employees = True

COMPANY.
        PERFORM EMPLOYEE.
        PERFORM EMPLOYEE
            UNTIL NO-MORE-EMPLOYEES = TRUE.

Figure 12.3: Repetition Translation (DOUNTIL)

Coding the third structure, repetition, requires two translations, depending on the form of the repetitive structure. As you can see in Figure 12.3, the DOUNTIL repetition, the "(1,n)" form, requires two statements. In COBOL the PERFORM ... UNTIL ... statement is functionally a DOWHILE, in that if the ending condition is true to begin with the PERFORMed paragraph is not executed. Since this automatically imposes a "(0,n)" repetition, we must first PERFORM the paragraph to ensure that it is done at least once. If the DOWHILE form of repetition is desired, the extra statement is not needed, as is indicated in the translation shown in Figure 12.4.

The last control structure, alternation, can also be coded in three different ways. The first form of alternation is a simple alternative wherein a condition is either true or not. This form of alternative and its translation are shown in Figure 12.5.

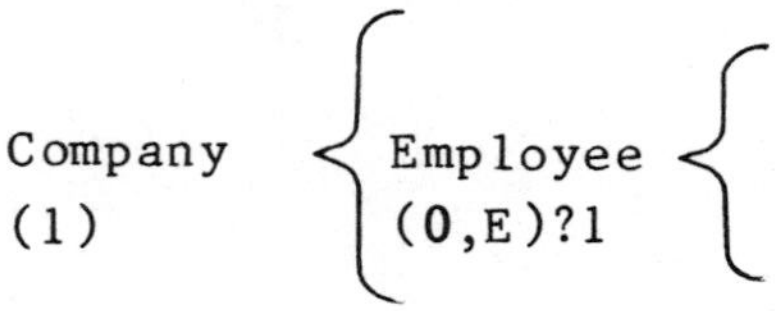

Company   Employee
(1)   (0,E)?1

Test: ?1-No More Employees = True

COMPANY.
        PERFORM EMPLOYEE
                UNTIL NO-MORE-EMPLOYEES = TRUE.

Figure 12.4: Repetition Translation (DOWHILE)

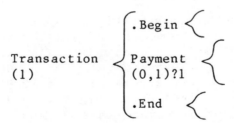

        Transaction   .Begin
        (1)   Payment
                         (0,1)?1

                         .End

Test: ?1-Trans Code = Payment Type

TRANSACTION.
        PERFORM TRANSACTION-BEGIN.
        IF TRANS-CODE = PAYMENT-TYPE
                PERFORM PAYMENT.
        PERFORM TRANSACTION-END.

Figure 12.5: Simple Alternative Translation

The second form of alternation is a complementary structure, where a condition and its negation are the only possible choices. This form of alternation and its translation are shown in Figure 12.6.

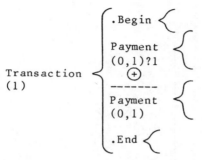

Transaction
(1)

.Begin

Payment
(0,1)?1
⊕

Payment
(0,1)

.End

Test: ?1-Trans Code = Payment Type


```
TRANSACTION.
        PERFORM TRANSACTION-BEGIN.
        IF TRANS-CODE = PAYMENT-TYPE
                PERFORM PAYMENT
        ELSE
                PERFORM NOT-PAYMENT.
        PERFORM TRANSACTION-END.
```

Figure 12.6: Complementary Alternative Translation

The third form that alternation may take is the "n-way" alternative — not simply a condition and its complement, but multiple mutually exclusive conditions. This is also called the CASE statement. (See Figure 12.7.)

Care should be taken to ensure that a noncomplementary alternative is not only mutually exclusive, but mutually exhaustive. Remember, also, if an alternative structure is present in the program simply to filter out unnecessary transactions, it belongs in an input coroutine and not in the "logical" processing part of the program.

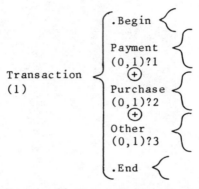

```
                         .Begin

                         Payment
                         (0,1)?1
Transaction                +
(1)                      Purchase
                         (0,1)?2
                           +
                         Other
                         (0,1)?3

                         .End
```

Tests: ?1-Trans Code = Payment Type
       ?2-Trans Code = Purchase Type
       ?3-Not ?1 and Not ?2


```
TRANSACTION.
      PERFORM TRANSACTION-BEGIN.
      IF TRANS-CODE = PAYMENT-TYPE
          PERFORM PAYMENT
      ELSE IF TRANS-CODE = PURCHASE-TYPE
          PERFORM PURCHASE
      ELSE
          PERFORM OTHER.
      PERFORM TRANSACTION-END.
```

Figure 12.7: Multiple Alternative Translation

In addition to the statements necessary for translating the
control structures into code, there are two other categories
of program statements needed. Four statements are needed to
get data into and out of the program: the READ, the WRITE,
the OPEN, and the CLOSE.   (See Figure 12.7.)   Also,
statements necessary to do arithmetic are required. (See
Figure 12.8.)

```
READ ....
WRITE ....
OPEN ....
CLOSE ....
```

Figure 12.8: Input/Output Statements

We need either the COMPUTE statement, or the ADD, SUBTRACT,
MULTIPLY, and DIVIDE, and also the statement for logical
substitution, the MOVE (Figure 12.9).

```
COMPUTE ....
-or-
ADD ....
SUBTRACT ....
MULTIPLY ....
DIVIDE ....

MOVE ....
```

Figure 12.9: Arithmetic Statements

To complete the program, only one other statement is
necessary — the STOP RUN or GOBACK.

Coding the Program

Using the translation rules provided, we may now proceed
with the coding of the program. The completed design for
the Monthly Sales Report that we have been detailing appears
in Figure 12.10.

```
                    ⎧ Get First Ideal Record ⟨...See Page 3
                    ⎪ Print Company Heading Information ⟨...See Page 2
           .Begin  ⎨ Set Company Sales Total to Zero
                    ⎪ Set Company Profit Total to Zero
                    ⎩ Set No More Salesmen to False

                                    ⎧ Print Salesman Heading Information   ⟨...See Page 2
                                    ⎪ Set Salesman Sales Total to Zero
                            .Begin  ⎨ Set Salesman Profit Total to Zero
                                    ⎪ Set Salesman Name(e) to Salesman Name
                                    ⎩ Set Old Salesman Name to Salesman Name

                                                    ⎧ Print Customer Heading Information   ⟨...See Page 2
                                                    ⎪ Set Customer Sales Total to Zero
                                            .Begin  ⎨ Set Customer Profit Total to Zero
                                                    ⎪ Set Customer Name(e) to Customer Name
                                                    ⎩ Set Old Customer Name to Customer Name

                                                            ⎧ Print Invoice Information   ⟨...See Page 2
  Company    Salesman    Customer    Invoice             ⎨ Add Sales Amount to Customer Sales Total
  (1)        (1,S)?1     (1,C)?2     (1,I)?3               ⎪ Add Profit Amount to Customer Profit Total
                                                            ⎩ Get Next Ideal Record ⟨...See Page 3

                                                    ⎧ Print Customer Total Information   ⟨...See Page 2
                                            .End    ⎨ Add Customer Sales Total to Salesman Sales Total
                                                    ⎩ Add Customer Profit Total to Salesman Profit Total

                                    ⎧ Print Salesman Total Information   ⟨...See Page 2
                            .End    ⎨ Add Salesman Sales Total to Company Sales Total
                                    ⎩ Add Salesman Profit Total to Company Profit Total

           .End    ⟨ Print Company Total Information   ⟨...See Page 2
```

Tests: ?1-No More Salesmen = True
       ?2-Old Salesman Name is not = Salesman Name or ?1
       ?3-Old Customer Name is not = Customer Name or ?2

Figure 12.10: Completed Program Design for Output #9
                         - Page 1

Print Company Heading Information
(1)
{ Move Month End Date to Heading
  Set First Logical Line to True

Print Salesman Heading Information
(1)
{ Move Salesman Name to Salesman Heading
  Move Salesman Heading to Print Line
  Write Logical Line {...See Page 5

Print Customer Heading Information
(1)
{ Move Customer Name to Customer Heading
  Move Customer Heading to Print Line
  Write Logical Line {...See Page 5

Print Invoice Information
(1)
{ Move Invoice Number to Invoice Line
  Move Invoice Date to Invoice Line
  Move Sales Amount to Invoice Line
  Move Profit Amount to Invoice Line
  Move Invoice Line to Print Line
  Write Logical Line {...See Page 5

Print Customer Total Information
(1)
{ Move Customer Total Line to Print Line
  Write Logical Line {...See Page 5

Print Salesman Total Information
(1)
{ Move Salesman Total Line to Print Line
  Write Logical Line {...See Page 5

Print Company Total Information
(1)
{ Move Company Total Line to Print Line
  Move True to Last Logical Line
  Write Logical Line {...See Page 5

Figure 12.10: Completed Program Design for Output #9
- Page 2

```
                          ⎧ Open Input Files
                          ⎪ Set End Invoice File to False
Get First Ideal Record    ⎨ Set Abnormal End to False
(1)                       ⎪ Move Spaces to Ideal Record
                          ⎪ Get Invoice Record ⟨...See Page 4
                          ⎩ Get Ideal Record ⟨...See Below

                          ⎧ Another Invoice   ⎧ Get Ideal Record ⟨...See Below
                          ⎪ (0,1)             ⎨
                          ⎪   ⊕               ⎩
Get Next Ideal Record     ⎨ ----------------
(1)                       ⎪ Another Invoice   ⎧ Set No More Salesmen to True
                          ⎩ (0,1)?1           ⎨ Close Input Files
                                              ⎩
```

```
                                                      ⎧ Company Begin  ⎧ Get Company Record ⟨...See Page 4
                                                      ⎪ (0,1)?2        ⎨ Move Company Data to Ideal Record
                                    ⎧ Salesman Begin  ⎨                ⎩
                                    ⎪ (0,1)?3         ⎪ .End           ⎧ Get Salesman Record ⟨...See Page 4
                  ⎧ Customer Begin  ⎨                 ⎩                ⎨ Move Salesman Data to Ideal Record
                  ⎪ (0,1)?4         ⎪                                  ⎩
Get Ideal Record  ⎨                 ⎪ .End            ⎧ Get Customer Record ⟨...See Page 4
(1)               ⎪                 ⎩                 ⎨ Move Customer Data to Ideal Record
                  ⎪                                   ⎩
                  ⎪ .End            ⎧ Move Invoice Data to Ideal Record
                  ⎩                 ⎨ Get Invoice Record ⟨...See Page 4
                                    ⎩
```

```
Tests: ?1-End Invoice File = True
          or Abnormal End = True
       ?2-Ideal Record = Spaces
       ?3-Invoice Salesman Number is not = Salesman Number
          or ?2
       ?4-Invoice Customer Number is not = Customer Number
          or ?3
```

Figure 12.10: Completed Program Design for Output #9 - Page 3

Get Company Record (1)
- Read Company Record
- Empty Company File (0,1)?1
  - Print Company Error Message
  - Set Abnormal End Code to True

Get Salesman Record (1)
- Move Invoice Salesman Number to Salesman Key
- Read Salesman Record
- Empty Salesman File (0,1)?2
  - Print Salesman Error Message
  - Set Abnormal End Code to True

Get Customer Record (1)
- Move Invoice Customer Number to Customer Key
- Read Customer Record
- Empty Customer File (0,1)?2
  - Print Customer Error Message
  - Set Abnormal End Code to True

Get Invoice Record (1)
- Read Invoice Record
- Empty Invoice File (0,1)?1
  - Set End Invoice File to True

Tests: ?1-At End
       ?2-Invalid Key

Figure 12.10: Completed Program Design for Output #9
- Page 4

Write Logical Line (1)
- Beginning of Page (0,1)?2
  - Beginning of Report (0,1)?1
    - Open Output Print File
    - Set First Logical Line to False
    - Set Last Logical Line to False
    - Set Page Number to One
  - .End
    - Print Page Heading (1)
      - Print Report Title Line
      - Print Report Period Line
      - Print Column Label Line
    - Add 1 to Page Number
    - Set Line Count to Zero
- .Middle
  - Print Physical Line
  - Add One to Line Count
- Ending of Report (0,1)?3
  - Close Print File

Tests: ?1-First Logical Line = True
       ?2-Line Count = Page Size or ?1
       ?3-Last Logical Line = True

Figure 12.10: Completed Program Design for Output #9
- Page 5

We may begin by coding the program level by level. The highest level, the Company level, may be coded as shown in Figure 12.11.

```
                        ⎧ .Begin {...
                        ⎪
            Company     ⎨ Salesman {...
            (1)         ⎪ (1,S)?1
                        ⎪
                        ⎩ .End    {...
```

Test: ?1-No More Salesmen = True

```
PROCEDURE DIVISION.
COMPANY.
        PERFORM COMPANY-BEGIN.
        PERFORM SALESMAN.
        PERFORM SALESMAN
            UNTIL NO-MORE-SALESMEN = TRUE.
        PERFORM COMPANY-END.
        STOP RUN.


DATA DIVISION.
WORKING-STORAGE SECTION.
01  TRUE              PIC X VALUE IS 1.
01  FALSE             PIC X VALUE IS 0.
01  NO-MORE-SALESMEN  PIC X.
```

Figure 12.11: Coding the Program

As the coding of the PROCEDURE DIVISION proceeds, one may also be defining the DATA DIVISION with the files, records, and fields that are used in the program. Rather than trace out the development of the program in detail, we shall present the finished product in Figure 12.11. Note the relationship of the design to the code; **each different bracket on the design becomes a module of code in the finished program.**

```
                    IDENTIFICATION DIVISION.
        PROGRAM-ID.  MONTHLY-SALES-REPORT.

        ENVIRONMENT DIVISION.
        SOURCE-COMPUTER.
        OBJECT-COMPUTER.
        INPUT-OUTPUT SECTION.
        FILE-CONTROL.
            SELECT INVOICE-FILE,
                ASSIGN TO INPUT, "INVOICE/FIL:2",
                ORGANIZATION IS SEQUENTIAL,
                ACCESS IS SEQUENTIAL.
            SELECT COMPANY-FILE,
                ASSIGN TO INPUT, "COMPANY/FIL:2",
                ORGANIZATION IS SEQUENTIAL,
                ACCESS IS SEQUENTIAL.
            SELECT SALESMAN-FILE,
                ASSIGN TO RANDOM, "SALESMAN/FIL:2",
                ORGANIZATION IS INDEXED,
                ACCESS IS RANDOM,
                RECORD KEY IS SALESMAN-KEY.
            SELECT CUSTOMER-FILE,
                ASSIGN TO RANDOM, "CUSTOMER/FIL:2",
                ORGANIZATION IS INDEXED,
                ACCESS IS RANDOM,
                RECORD KEY IS CUSTOMER-KEY.
            SELECT PRINT-FILE,
                ASSIGN TO PRINT, "PRINTER".

        DATA DIVISION.
        FILE SECTION.
        FD   INVOICE-FILE
             BLOCK CONTAINS 1 RECORDS
             RECORD CONTAINS 32 CHARACTERS
             LABEL RECORDS ARE STANDARD
             DATA RECORD IS INVOICE-RECORD.
        01   INVOICE-RECORD             PIC X(32).
        FD   COMPANY-FILE
             BLOCK CONTAINS 1 RECORDS
             RECORD CONTAINS 6 CHARACTERS
             LABEL RECORDS ARE STANDARD
             DATA RECORD IS COMPANY-RECORD.
        01   COMPANY-RECORD             PIC X(6).
        FD   SALESMAN-FILE
             BLOCK CONTAINS 1 RECORDS
             RECORD CONTAINS 34 CHARACTERS
             LABEL RECORDS ARE STANDARD
             DATA RECORD IS SALESMAN-RECORD.
        01   SALESMAN-RECORD.
             02  SALESMAN-KEY           PIC X(4).
```

Figure 12.12: Completed Program for Output #9
- Page 1

```
            02  FILLER                    PIC X(30).
    FD  CUSTOMER-FILE
        BLOCK CONTAINS 1 RECORDS
        RECORD CONTAINS 34 CHARACTERS
        LABEL RECORDS ARE STANDARD
        DATA RECORD IS CUSTOMER-RECORD.
    01  CUSTOMER-RECORD.
        02  CUSTOMER-KEY                  PIC X(4).
        02  FILLER                        PIC X(30).
    FD  PRINT-FILE
        LABEL RECORDS ARE OMITTED
        DATA RECORD IS PRINT-RECORD.
    01  PRINT-RECORD                      PIC X(132).
    WORKING-STORAGE SECTION.
    01  NO-MORE-SALESMEN                  PIC X.
    01  OLD-SALESMAN-NAME                 PIC X(30).
    01  OLD-CUSTOMER-NAME                 PIC X(30).
    01  FIRST-LOGICAL-LINE                PIC X.
    01  LAST-LOGICAL-LINE                 PIC X.
    01  END-INVOICE-FILE                  PIC X.
    01  ABNORMAL-END                      PIC X.
    01  LINE-COUNT                        PIC 9(3).
    01  PAGE-SIZE                         PIC 9(3) VALUE IS 55.
    01  ONE                               PIC 9 VALUE IS 1.
    01  TWO                               PIC 9 VALUE IS 2.
    01  TRUE                              PIC X VALUE IS 1.
    01  FALSE                             PIC X VALUE IS 0.
    01  PRINT-LINE                        PIC X(132).
    01  COMPANY-AREA.
        02  COMPANY-DATA.
            03  MONTH-END-DATE-IN  PIC X(6).
    01  SALESMAN-AREA.
        02  SALESMAN-NUMBER               PIC X(4).
        02  SALESMAN-DATA.
            03  SALESMAN-NAME-IN   PIC X(30).
    01  CUSTOMER-AREA.
        02  CUSTOMER-NUMBER               PIC X(4).
        02  CUSTOMER-DATA.
            03  CUSTOMER-NAME-IN   PIC X(30).
    01  INVOICE-AREA.
        02  INVOICE-DATA.
            03  INVOICE-NUMBER     PIC X(4).
            03  INVOICE-DATE       PIC X(6).
            03  SALES-AMOUNT       PIC X(7).
            03  PROFIT-AMOUNT      PIC X(7).
        02  INVOICE-CUSTOMER-NUMBER PIC X(4).
        02  INVOICE-SALESMAN-NUMBER PIC X(4).
    01  IDEAL-RECORD.
        02  IDEAL-RECORD-COMPANY-DATA.
            03  MONTH-END-DATE     PIC 9(6).
```

Figure 12.12: Completed Program for Output #9
- Page 2

```
        02   IDEAL-RECORD-SALESMAN-DATA.
             03   SALESMAN-NAME          PIC X(30).
        02   IDEAL-RECORD-CUSTOMER-DATA.
             03   CUSTOMER-NAME          PIC X(30).
        02   IDEAL-RECORD-INVOICE-DATA.
             03   INVOICE-NUMBER         PIC 9(4).
             03   INVOICE-DATE           PIC 9(6).
             03   SALES-AMOUNT           PIC 9(5)V99.
             03   PROFIT-AMOUNT          PIC 9(5)V99.
   01   REPORT-TITLE-HEADING.
        02   FILLER                      PIC X(31) VALUE IS SPACES.
        02   FILLER                      PIC X(20)
             VALUE IS "Monthly Sales Report".
        02   FILLER                      PIC X(27) VALUE IS SPACES.
        02   PAGE-NUMBER                 PIC ZZ9.
        02   FILLER                      PIC X(51) VALUE IS SPACES.
   01   REPORT-PERIOD-HEADING.
        02   FILLER                      PIC X(27) VALUE IS SPACES.
        02   FILLER                      PIC X(20)
             VALUE IS "For The Month Ended ".
        02   MONTH-END-DATE-HEADING      PIC 99/99/99.
        02   FILLER                      PIC X(76) VALUE IS SPACES.
   01   COLUMN-HEADING.
        02   FILLER                      PIC X(30)
             VALUE IS "Salesman    Customer          ".
        02   FILLER                      PIC X(30)
             VALUE IS "         Invoice       Date    ".
        02   FILLER                      PIC X(30)
             VALUE IS "  Sales Amount    Profit       ".
        02   FILLER                      PIC X(42) VALUE IS SPACES.
   01   SALESMAN-HEADING-INFO.
        02   SALESMAN-NAME-HEADING       PIC X(30).
        02   FILLER                      PIC X(102) VALUE IS SPACES.
   01   CUSTOMER-HEADING-INFO.
        02   FILLER                      PIC X(16) VALUE IS SPACES.
        02   CUSTOMER-NAME-HEADING       PIC X(30).
        02   FILLER                      PIC X(86) VALUE IS SPACES.
   01   INVOICE-INFO.
        02   FILLER                      PIC X(41) VALUE IS SPACES.
        02   INVOICE-NUMBER-OUT          PIC 9(4).
        02   FILLER                      PIC X(6) VALUE IS SPACES.
        02   INVOICE-DATE-OUT            PIC 99/99/99.
        02   FILLER                      PIC X(4) VALUE IS SPACES.
        02   SALES-AMOUNT-OUT            PIC ZZ,ZZ9.99.
        02   PROFIT-AMOUNT-OUT           PIC ZZ,ZZ9.99.
        02   FILLER                      PIC X(51) VALUE IS SPACES.
   01   CUSTOMER-TOTAL-INFO.
        02   FILLER                      PIC X(21) VALUE IS SPACES.
        02   FILLER                      PIC X(10)
             VALUE IS "Total For ".
```

Figure 12.12: Completed Program for Output #9
- Page 3

```
        02   CUSTOMER-NAME-E          PIC X(30).
        02   FILLER                   PIC X(2) VALUE IS SPACES.
        02   CUSTOMER-SALES-TOTAL     PIC ZZ,ZZ9.00.
        02   CUSTOMER-PROFIT-TOTAL    PIC ZZ,ZZ9.00.
        02   FILLER                   PIC X(51) VALUE IS SPACES.
    01  SALESMAN-TOTAL-INFO.
        02   FILLER                   PIC X(6) VALUE IS SPACES.
        02   FILLER                   PIC X(10)
             VALUE IS "Total For ".
        02   SALESMAN-NAME-E          PIC X(30).
        02   FILLER                   PIC X(17) VALUE IS SPACES.
        02   SALESMAN-SALES-TOTAL     PIC ZZ,ZZ9.00.
        02   SALESMAN-PROFIT-TOTAL    PIC ZZ,ZZ9.00.
        02   FILLER                   PIC X(51) VALUE IS SPACES.
    01  COMPANY-TOTAL-INFO.
        02   FILLER                   PIC X(19)
             VALUE IS "Total for the Month".
        02   FILLER                   PIC X(43) VALUE IS SPACES.
        02   COMPANY-SALES-TOTAL      PIC ZZ,ZZ9.00.
        02   COMPANY-PROFIT-TOTAL     PIC ZZ,ZZ9.00.
        02   FILLER                   PIC X(51) VALUE IS SPACES.
    01  COMPANY-ERROR-MESSAGE         PIC X(36)
        VALUE IS "**** ERROR ON COMPANY FILE READ ****"
    01  SALESMAN-ERROR-MESSAGE        PIC X(36)
        VALUE IS "**** ERROR ON SALESMAN FILE READ ***"
    01  CUSTOMER-ERROR-MESSAGE        PIC X(36)
        VALUE IS "**** ERROR ON CUSTOMER FILE READ ***"
    PROCEDURE DIVISION.
*** LPS SECTION OF PROGRAM *****************************************
    COMPANY.
        PERFORM COMPANY-BEGIN.
        PERFORM SALESMAN.
        PERFORM SALESMAN
            UNTIL NO-MORE-SALESMEN = TRUE.
        PERFORM COMPANY-END.
        STOP RUN.
    SALESMAN.
        PERFORM SALESMAN-BEGIN.
        PERFORM CUSTOMER.
        PERFORM CUSTOMER
            UNTIL OLD-SALESMAN-NAME IS NOT = SALESMAN-NAME
            OR     NO-MORE-SALESMEN = TRUE.
        PERFORM SALESMAN-END.
    CUSTOMER.
        PERFORM CUSTOMER-BEGIN.
        PERFORM INVOICE.
        PERFORM INVOICE
            UNTIL OLD-CUSTOMER-NAME IS NOT = CUSTOMER-NAME
            OR     OLD-SALESMAN-NAME IS NOT = SALESMAN-NAME
            OR     NO-MORE-SALESMEN = TRUE.
```

Figure 12.12: Completed Program for Output #9
- Page 4

```
                PERFORM CUSTOMER-END.
        COMPANY-BEGIN.
                PERFORM GET-FIRST-IDEAL-RECORD.
                PERFORM PRINT-COMPANY-HEADING-INFO.
                MOVE ZERO TO COMPANY-SALES-TOTAL.
                MOVE ZERO TO COMPANY-PROFIT-TOTAL.
                MOVE FALSE TO NO-MORE-SALESMEN.
        SALESMAN-BEGIN.
                PERFORM PRINT-SALESMAN-HEADING-INFO.
                MOVE ZERO TO SALESMAN-SALES-TOTAL.
                MOVE ZERO TO SALESMAN-PROFIT-TOTAL.
                MOVE SALESMAN-NAME TO SALESMAN-NAME-E.
                MOVE SALESMAN-NAME TO OLD-SALESMAN-NAME.
        CUSTOMER-BEGIN.
                PERFORM PRINT-CUSTOMER-HEADING-INFO.
                MOVE ZERO TO CUSTOMER-SALES-TOTAL.
                MOVE ZERO TO CUSTOMER-PROFIT-TOTAL.
                MOVE CUSTOMER-NAME TO CUSTOMER-NAME-E.
                MOVE CUSTOMER-NAME TO OLD-CUSTOMER-NAME.
        INVOICE.
                PERFORM PRINT-INVOICE-INFO.
                ADD SALES-AMOUNT TO CUSTOMER-SALES-TOTAL.
                ADD PROFIT-AMOUNT TO CUSTOMER-PROFIT-TOTAL.
                PERFORM GET-NEXT-IDEAL-RECORD.
        CUSTOMER-END.
                PERFORM PRINT-CUSTOMER-TOTAL-INFO.
                ADD CUSTOMER-SALES-TOTAL TO SALESMAN-SALES-TOTAL.
                ADD CUSTOMER-PROFIT-TOTAL TO SALESMAN-PROFIT-TOTAL.
        SALESMAN-END.
                PERFORM PRINT-SALESMAN-TOTAL-INFO.
                ADD SALESMAN-SALES-TOTAL TO CUSTOMER-SALES-TOTAL.
                ADD SALESMAN-PROFIT-TOTAL TO CUSTOMER-PROFIT-TOTAL.
        COMPANY-END.
                PERFORM PRINT-COMPANY-TOTAL-INFO.
        PRINT-COMPANY-HEADING-INFO.
                MOVE MONTH-END-DATE TO MONTH-END-DATE-HEADING.
                MOVE TRUE TO FIRST-REPORT-LINE.
        PRINT-SALESMAN-HEADING-INFO.
                MOVE SALESMAN-NAME TO SALESMAN-NAME-HEADING.
                MOVE SALESMAN-HEADING-INFO TO PRINT-LINE.
                PERFORM WRITE-LOGICAL-LINE.
        PRINT-CUSTOMER-HEADING-INFO.
                MOVE CUSTOMER-NAME TO CUSTOMER-NAME-HEADING.
                MOVE CUSTOMER-HEADING-INFO TO PRINT-LINE.
                PERFORM WRITE-LOGICAL-LINE.
        PRINT-INVOICE-INFO.
                MOVE INVOICE-NUMBER TO INVOICE-NUMBER-OUT.
                MOVE INVOICE-DATE TO INVOICE-DATE-OUT.
                MOVE SALES-AMOUNT TO SALES-AMOUNT-OUT.
                MOVE PROFIT-AMOUNT TO PROFIT-AMOUNT-OUT.
```

Figure 12.12: Completed Program for Output #9
- Page 5

```
        MOVE INVOICE-INFO TO PRINT-LINE.
        PERFORM WRITE-LOGICAL-LINE.
    PRINT-CUSTOMER-TOTAL-INFO.
        MOVE CUSTOMER-TOTAL-INFO TO PRINT-LINE.
        PERFORM WRITE-LOGICAL-LINE.
    PRINT-SALESMAN-TOTAL-INFO.
        MOVE SALESMAN-TOTAL-INFO TO PRINT-LINE.
        PERFORM WRITE-LOGICAL-LINE.
    PRINT-COMPANY-TOTAL-INFO.
        MOVE COMPANY-TOTAL-INFO TO PRINT-LINE.
        MOVE TRUE TO LAST-REPORT-LINE.
        PERFORM WRITE-LOGICAL-LINE.
*** PHYSICAL INPUT MAPPING SECTION OF PROGRAM ***********************
    GET-FIRST-IDEAL-RECORD.
        OPEN INPUT COMPANY-FILE, SALESMAN-FILE, CUSTOMER-FILE,
            INVOICE-FILE.
        MOVE FALSE TO END-INVOICE-FILE.
        MOVE FALSE TO ABNORMAL-END.
        MOVE SPACES TO IDEAL-RECORD.
        PERFORM GET-INVOICE-RECORD.
        PERFORM GET-IDEAL-RECORD.
    GET-NEXT-IDEAL-RECORD.
        IF END-INVOICE-FILE = TRUE
            OR ABNORMAL-END = TRUE
            PERFORM NOT-ANOTHER-INVOICE
        ELSE
            PERFORM ANOTHER-INVOICE.
    ANOTHER-INVOICE.
        PERFORM GET-IDEAL-RECORD.
    NOT-ANOTHER-INVOICE.
        MOVE TRUE TO NO-MORE-SALESMEN.
        CLOSE COMPANY-FILE, SALESMAN-FILE, CUSTOMER-FILE, INVOICE-FILE.
    GET-IDEAL-RECORD.
        IF INVOICE-CUSTOMER-NUMBER IS NOT = CUSTOMER-NUMBER
            OR INVOICE-SALESMAN-NUMBER IS NOT = SALESMAN-NUMBER
            OR IDEAL-RECORD = SPACES
            PERFORM CUSTOMER-BEGIN-PROCESS.
        PERFORM END-GET-IDEAL-RECORD.
    CUSTOMER-BEGIN-PROCESS.
        IF INVOICE-SALESMAN-NUMBER IS NOT = SALESMAN-NUMBER
            OR IDEAL-RECORD = SPACES
            PERFORM SALESMAN-BEGIN-PROCESS.
        PERFORM END-CUSTOMER-BEGIN-PROCESS.
    SALESMAN-BEGIN-PROCESS.
        IF IDEAL-RECORD = SPACES
            PERFORM COMPANY-BEGIN-PROCESS.
        PERFORM END-SALESMAN-BEGIN-PROCESS.
```

Figure 12.12: Completed Program for Output #9
- Page 6

```
COMPANY-BEGIN-PROCESS.
    PERFORM GET-COMPANY-RECORD.
    MOVE COMPANY-DATA TO IDEAL-RECORD-COMPANY-DATA.
END-GET-IDEAL-RECORD.
    MOVE INVOICE-DATA TO IDEAL-RECORD-INVOICE-DATA.
    PERFORM GET-INVOICE-RECORD.
END-CUSTOMER-BEGIN-PROCESS.
    PERFORM GET-CUSTOMER-RECORD.
    MOVE CUSTOMER-DATA TO IDEAL-RECORD-CUSTOMER-DATA.
END-SALESMAN-BEGIN-PROCESS.
    PERFORM GET-SALESMAN-RECORD.
    MOVE SALESMAN-DATA TO IDEAL-RECORD-SALESMAN-DATA.
GET-COMPANY-RECORD.
    READ COMPANY-FILE INTO COMPANY-AREA
        AT END PERFORM EMPTY-COMPANY-FILE.
GET-SALESMAN-RECORD.
    MOVE INVOICE-SALESMAN-NUMBER TO SALESMAN-KEY.
    READ SALESMAN-FILE INTO SALESMAN-AREA
        INVALID KEY PERFORM EMPTY-SALESMAN-FILE.
GET-CUSTOMER-RECORD.
    MOVE INVOICE-CUSTOMER-NUMBER TO CUSTOMER-KEY.
    READ CUSTOMER-FILE INTO CUSTOMER-AREA
        INVALID KEY PERFORM EMPTY-CUSTOMER-FILE.
GET-INVOICE-RECORD.
    READ INVOICE-FILE INTO INVOICE-AREA
        AT END PERFORM EMPTY-INVOICE-FILE.
EMPTY-COMPANY-FILE.
    DISPLAY COMPANY-ERROR-MESSAGE.
    MOVE TRUE TO ABNORMAL-END.
EMPTY-SALESMAN-FILE.
    DISPLAY SALESMAN-ERROR-MESSAGE.
    MOVE TRUE TO ABNORMAL-END.
EMPTY-CUSTOMER-FILE.
    DISPLAY CUSTOMER-ERROR-MESSAGE.
    MOVE TRUE TO ABNORMAL-END.
EMPTY-INVOICE-FILE.
    MOVE TRUE TO END-INVOICE-FILE.
*** PHYSICAL OUTPUT MAPPING SECTION OF PROGRAM *********************
WRITE-LOGICAL-LINE.
    IF LINE-COUNT = PAGE-SIZE
        OR FIRST-LOGICAL-LINE = TRUE
        PERFORM BEGINNING-OF-PAGE.
    PERFORM MIDDLE-WRITE-LOGICAL-LINE.
    IF LAST-LOGICAL-LINE = TRUE
        PERFORM ENDING-OF-REPORT.
BEGINNING-OF-PAGE.
    IF FIRST-LOGICAL-LINE = TRUE
        PERFORM BEGINNING-OF-REPORT.
    PERFORM END-BEGINNING-OF-PAGE.
BEGINNING-OF-REPORT.
    OPEN OUTPUT PRINT-FILE.
```

Figure 12.12: Completed Program for Output #9
        - Page 7

```
        MOVE FALSE TO FIRST-LOGICAL-LINE.
        MOVE FALSE TO LAST-LOGICAL-LINE.
        MOVE ONE TO PAGE-NUMBER.
    END-BEGINNING-OF-PAGE.
        PERFORM PRINT-PAGE-HEADING.
        ADD ONE TO PAGE-NUMBER.
        MOVE ZERO TO LINE-COUNT.
    PRINT-PAGE-HEADING.
        WRITE PRINT-RECORD FROM REPORT-TITLE-HEADING
            AFTER ADVANCING PAGE.
        WRITE PRINT-RECORD FROM REPORT-PERIOD-HEADING
            AFTER ADVANCING ONE LINE.
        WRITE PRINT-RECORD FROM COLUMN-HEADING
            AFTER ADVANCING TWO LINES.
    MIDDLE-WRITE-LOGICAL-LINE.
        WRITE PRINT-RECORD FROM PRINT-LINE
            AFTER ADVANCING ONE LINE.
        ADD ONE TO LINE-COUNT.
    ENDING-OF-REPORT.
        CLOSE PRINT-FILE.
```

Figure 12.12: Completed Program for Output #9
- Page 8

The finished program has a one-to-one relationship with the detailed design, thus the actual coding of the program takes very little time. This relationship extends to the separation of the three main sections of the program; the dominant section is the one resembling the detailed LPS, with subroutines for the physical input and output mappings.

Observe also that **the completed program has all of the obvious symptoms of a classic "structured" program:** it has no GO TO statements, it has no nested IF statements, it is highly modular, the modules are small, the modules all have one entry point and one exit point, the modules are highly cohesive and loosely coupled (statements that belong together are together and the program is easy to take apart

for enhancement), etc. These features did not appear
because they were a design goal; they are a naturally
occurring by-product of designing correctly.

An additional point bears an explanation. This program was
coded without regard to "efficiency" considerations; paragraphs with one statement are PERFORMed, tests are made that
need not be (the control test in Write Logical Line to
detect the last logical line and close the output file),
etc. Certainly this program may be "destructured" by
including code directly in-line and removing some of the
tests. However, the separation of the logical and physical
aspects of the program become blurred at that point, thus
eliminating some measure of enhanceability. From
experimentation we know that such **"destructuring" rarely
improves performance noticeably,** but does degrade
enhanceability measurably. Since this program is limited by
the speed of the peripherals as it is, "destructuring" will
not improve its throughput.

One last point about this program. The order that the paragraphs within the PROCEDURE DIVISION are presented is not
significant. The only paragraph that is fixed is the first
COMPANY paragraph; the remainder of the paragraphs may be
ordered in whatever fashion is convenient and/or desirable.

Testing

Having coded the program, we may move into the final phase
of the Structured Program Design method —— testing.
Contrary to popular belief, the purpose of testing is not to
find errors (although that certainly may happen). It is to
validate the operation of the program.

Testing will consist of three subphases: developing test
cases, developing expected results, and comparing expected
results with actual results.

In the first part of testing, we must examine the design and
determine the number of paths through the module we wish to
test. For instance, for the physical output mapping routine
shown in Page 5 of Figure 12.10, there are four test cases,
as shown in Figure 12.13.

```
Test Plan for Module: Write Logical Line
==================================================================
Test Case
==================================================================
1) Beginning of Page and
     Beginning of Report and
     Not Ending of Report
------------------------------------------------------------------
2) Beginning of Page and
     not Beginning of Report and
     not Ending of Report
------------------------------------------------------------------
3) Not Beginning of Page and
     not Ending of Report
------------------------------------------------------------------
4) Not Beginning of Page and
     Ending of Report
------------------------------------------------------------------
```

Figure 12.13: Test Cases

These four test cases exhaust all of the paths through the module, not only executing the alternatives, but bypassing them when appropriate. Setting out the data necessary to trigger each test case and the expected results is easy from the completed design. This is shown in Figure 12.14. From this table, it is a simple matter to arrange a test execution of the module to demonstrate the results.

The size of the program to be tested will determine the number of test plans to develop. For small programs, the entire program may be tested as a module; for larger programs it is desirable to test the programs in smaller chunks. Modules with more than about seven test cases may be considered good candidates for testing in sections.

Test Plan for Module: Write Logical Line
===
Test Case   Test Data   Expected Results
===
1) Beginning of Page and   First Report Line = True and   Output File Opened
   Beginning of Report and   Last Report Line = Undef   First Report Line Set to False
   Not Ending of Report   Last Report Line Set to False
                                                                  Page Number Set to 1
                                                                  First Page Heading Printed
                                                                  Page Number Set to 2
                                                                  Line Count Set to Zero
                                                                  Physical Line Printed
                                                                  Line Count Set to 1
----
2) Beginning of Page and   First Report Line = False and   Page Heading Printed
   not Beginning of Report and   Line Count = Page Size and   Page Number incremented by 1
   not Ending of Report   Last Report Line = False   Line Count Set to Zero
                                                                  Physical Line Printed
                                                                  Line Count Set to 1
----
3) Not Beginning of Page and   First Report Line = False and   Physical Line Printed
   not Ending of Report   Line Count < Page Size and   Line Count Incremented by 1
                                  Last Report Line = False
----
4) Not Beginning of Page and   First Report Line = False and   Physical Line Printed
   Ending of Report   Line Count < Page Size and   Line Count Incremented by 1
                                  Last Report Line = True   Output File Closed
----

Figure 12.14: Test Plan

Summary

Structured Program Design does not guarantee that you will
not make mistakes. Murphy's law prevents us from being consistently perfect. However, as Ken Orr often observes, "It
is better to be obviously wrong than obscurely correct."
With this technique it is easier to be obviously wrong, and
to correct errors when they are found. Many programmers
have found that with some care in the design and coding,
they can consistently get programs to run correctly on the
first or second try. Not only that, but the documentation
for the program is completed by the time the code is created. When enhancement comes, the design provides an excellent vehicle for maintenance. If the design is enhanced
before the code is, and if some care is taken to preserve
the one-to-one relationship between design and code, maintenance productivity can be improved many-fold. In fact,
maintenance can become seamless; an enhanced design and
program will look no different from a program that was
created with the same requirements. Thus as programs get
older they will not automatically degrade, but will maintain
their high degree of enhanceability throughout their
lifetimes.

Chapter 13 APPLICATIONS
PART 1
HIERARCHICAL REPORTS

Program Cannibalism

Most people in the data processing field are aware of the fact that there is a great deal of similarity between various software projects. A good portion of the programs that come up in application areas are quite similar in nature to things that have been developed previously. As a matter of fact, it is common practice in the industry for programmers to "cannibalize" sections of old code when creating new programs. This is a very intelligent approach to the creation of new software, since it tends to prevent the reinvention of the wheel, so to speak. It is an eminently practical one as well. In these days of rapidly increasing people costs, it becomes an important aid to programmer productivity.

Not surprisingly, this concept of building on existing knowledge can be carried on at a higher level as well, in particular, at a design level. In the next part of this book we will analyze the structures of some of the more common application problems. Each of the chapters in this part is self-contained and requires only a basic knowledge of COBOL and an understanding of the Warnier/Orr diagramming form. Although the model structures in these chapters are primarily oriented to COBOL, you will see that they could easily be adapted to any other programming language.

```
                          CUSTOMER PURCHASE REPORT
                          FOR THE MONTH OF MAY 1982
       CUSTOMER NAME
            PRODUCT #    DESCRIPTION    PURCH DATE    QUANTITY    PRICE    TOTAL

       ADAMSON REALTY
            000478     C-30 CASSETTE    05/01/82        100       1.59    159.00
                                        05/01/82        100       1.59    159.00
                                        05/25/82        250       1.59    359.50
                       PRODUCT TOTALS                   450                715.50*
            000599       NOTEBOOK       05/26/82         20       2.26     45.20
                       PRODUCT TOTALS                    20                 45.20*
            001022    TYPEWRITER RIB.   05/02/82         10       8.95     89.50
                       PRODUCT TOTALS                    10                 89.50*
          CUSTOMER TOTAL                                                  850.20**
       ANDERSON FINANCING
            000355       PENCILS        05/06/82        100        .05      5.00
       ...etc...
          CUSTOMER TOTAL                                                  158.45**
       REPORT TOTAL                                                     16482.11***
```

Figure 13.1: Output #11 Sample

Look at illustration Figure 13.1 to see an example of a
classic program problem — a sample of a report which
might be desired. This is a Customer Purchase report to be
generated for a medium sized supplier, showing, for a given
month, what Customers purchased what Products, with the date
and the amount of each Purchase given. Notice that this
report is broken down into three repetitive levels of
hierarchy; we show individual purchases, with subtotals by
Product and by Customer and with Company Totals at the end
of the report.

Any output having this general form is known as a hierarchical report, since it is broken down into various nested
repeating levels of hierarchy. Since outputs having this
general form are quite common, developing a model design for
this kind of program is apt to be quite valuable.

The first step that we will want to take in the analysis of
this output is to develop its Logical Output Structure.
Again, the reason for beginning with the output structure
goes back to Warnier's and Michael Jackson's data structure
theorem — the observation that the structure of the
program that we will want to create is going to be the same
as the structure of the output. Therefore, our first
objective will be to create a Warnier/Orr diagram which
graphically represents the structure of the device-
independent output requirements. This Logical Output
Structure is shown in Figure 13.2.

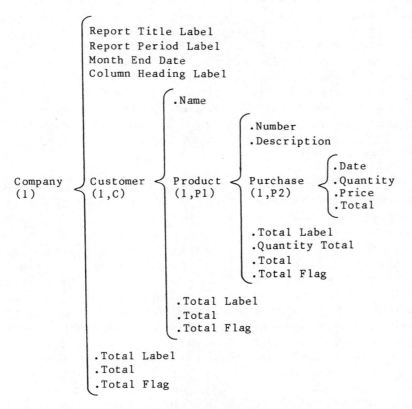

Figure 13.2: Logical Output Structure for Output #11

This LOS shows not only the hierarchical structure of the report, but also all of the data elements which must appear at various places on the output. It says at the lowest level, for instance, that for each purchase the output is to show the Purchase Date, the Purchase Quantity, the Purchase Price, and the Purchase Total. It also says that for each Product the output is to show the Product Number and the Product Description at the beginning of that product, and four elements of data at the end of each product: the Product Total Label (in this case, the words "Product Totals"), the Product Quantity Total, the Product Total itself, and the Product Total Flag (an asterisk).

For each Customer appearing on the output, the Customer's Name is to be shown at the beginning, and the Customer Total Label, the Customer Total, and the Customer Total Flag (the two asterisks) at the end. At the beginning of the Company level, the output will show the Report Title Label, the Report Period Label (in this case, the words "For the Month Of") the Month End Date, and the Column Heading Label. Note that these elements really do not just print once at the beginning of the report; they print at the beginning of each Page of the Report. However, for the purposes of creating this diagram, we treat the report as if it were only a one page report, to avoid having to deal with a physical hierarchy conflict and to maintain our objective of being device-independent.

At the end of the Company, the output is to show the Company Total Label, the Company Total, and the Company Total Flag (the three asterisks).

The next stage in the development of the program to produce this report is to examine the structure of the necessary and sufficient input to be able to produce this output. For the most part, this step simply involves the analysis and the elimination of unnecessary data elements from the LOS, such as the labels and the computable data elements. There is a bit more to it than that, however, as we have to be careful to incorporate any elements necessary for calculations that minimize data requirements and yet do not explicitly appear on the output, and also incorporate any hidden sort hierar-chies. In the case of this output we have no hidden ele-ments but do have a hidden sort hierarchy. In looking at

the output, you can see that Purchases are apparently being
listed in date sequence within each Product. Thus, we will
want to show that Purchases are to be input by Day within
Product, and we will thus add a level of hierarchy to the
Logical Data Structure to reflect this information.

You'll notice that although the Day level will appear on the
Logical Data Structure, it does not appear on the Logical
Output Structure, since there are no elements which appear
on the output with a frequency of once per Day.

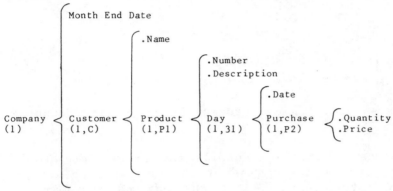

Figure 13.3: Logical Data Structure for Output #11

Thus in Figure 13.3, we show the data structure for the minimum data requirements to support this output —— the
Logical Data Structure. It shows that the required input
must be arranged by Customer within the Company, by Product
within Customer, by Day within Product, and by Purchase
within Day. The LDS also shows the data elements which are
required as input to produce this report. It says that we
have to be able to get the Month End Date at the beginning
of the Company, a Customer Name for each Customer on the
Report, a Product Number and Product Description for each
Product, a Purchase Date for each Day, and the Purchase
Price and Quantity for each Purchase.

At this time we can go ahead and produce a diagram of the
minimal processing that must be performed in order to
produce this output from a simple form of the required
input. Again, the structure of this process will be the
same as the structure of the output. This Logical Process
Structure is shown in Figure 13.4.

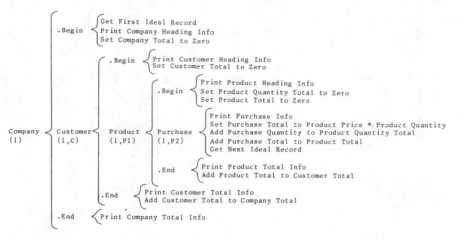

Figure 13.4: Logical Process Structure for Output #11

This process structure details the activities which must be done at the beginning and at the end of each level for the Company. For instance, at the end of the Company, we'll want to print the Company Total Information. At the end of each Customer for the Company, we'll want to print the Customer Total Information, and add the Customer Total into the Company Total so that it is correct by the time we finish the report. Similarly, at the end of the Product level, we want to print the Product Total Information and add the Product Total to the Customer Total, and so on. We initialize the totals at the beginning of the appropriate level, and we take care of the necessary logical input.

For the purposes of creating the LPS we **always** assume that the input will be the simplest possible input file — a single sequential file, with only one record type, with all records edited, with only the records necessary for the output, and with the records in the correct order. For this output this file would have to have a record for every Purchase, and on each record would be all of the elements shown on the Logical Data Structure. Furthermore, these records would be sorted by the hierarchy of the LDS — by Customer, by Product, by Day, and by Purchase.

This simplest of all possible files is again called the
Ideal File, since each record has all the information that
we need and the records are in the correct order. The Ideal
File will probably never reside in a computer, since it
wastes so much storage — it is simply a way of thinking
about input in it's simplest form. As long as we can make
any data that we do have look like the Ideal File to our program, we can produce code which has the structure shown.

Generalizing the Design

In order to globalize the process for designing hierarchical
reports we will have to speak in terms of a general output
instead of a specific one. In Figure 13.5, we have shown the
skeleton of an output which is primarily hierarchical in
nature. It says that, in general, the number of levels that
a hierarchical report might have is unbounded; that is,
there is no fixed maximum number of levels of hierarchy.
There might be two or three, or there might be ten or
twenty. As far as we are concerned, it makes no difference.

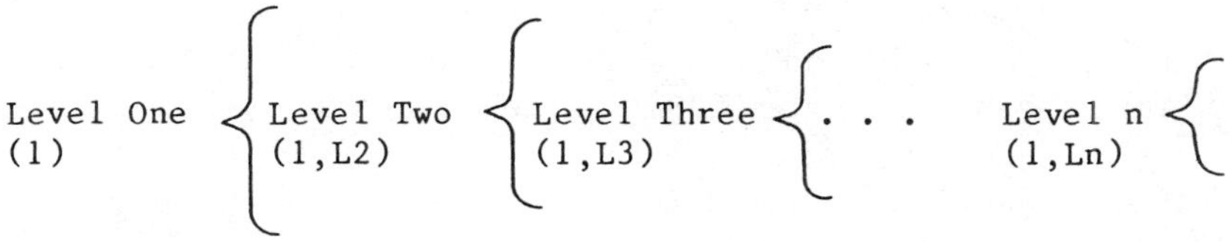

Level One   Level Two   Level Three   . . .   Level n
(1)   (1,L2)   (1,L3)   (1,Ln)

Figure 13.5: Model Hierarchy

Outputs which have this form generally have predictable
features about them. Any general level of a hierarchical
report, except for the lowest level, usually will have elements at the beginning of that level and elements at the
end. The heading elements shown at the beginning of a level
are typically identifiers of some kind which describe the
attributes of the level about to be reported. For instance,
on our sample output, the Customer Name appears at the beginning of the Customer level. It announces the name of the
Customer for whom Purchases are about to be listed. At the

beginning of the Product level, we find the Product Number
and Description, again, elements which announce or identify
which Product we are beginning to discuss. At the end of a
general level of hierarchy we typically find information sum-
marizing the information reported for that level, as we have
in our sample output. The lowest level on a hierarchical
report will have no distinction between beginning and end,
and will just have a group of detail elements which are
output.

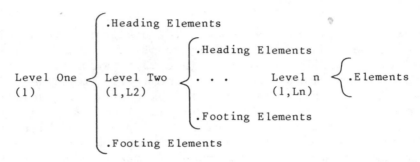

Figure 13.6: Model Logical Process Structure

Thus, the generalized Logical Output Structure for a simple
hierarchical report is shown in Figure 13.6. You'll note
that the LOS for the sample report given at the beginning of
this chapter has the same form as this model structure.

Not all hierarchical reports that you will run across will
automatically have elements at each of the places shown on
this diagram. There might be no subtotals at the end of a
particular level, for instance, or no identifying elements
printed at the beginning of a level. One thing might be
pointed out, however. If you happen to be designing an
output, putting a report like this together for a user, it
is always a good idea to create the output so that it follows this model. Reports that have this form are quite easy
for people to understand, not to mention the fact that they
are easy for us to work with.

The Logical Data Structures for such outputs are also pretty
predictable. Look at the model LDS shown in Figure 13.7.
for the most part, there will be elements which are required

at the beginning of each of the hierarchical levels and at
the lowest level. Since most of the elements at the end of
any given level are going to be totals of some kind, they
can be computed, and are not part of the necessary input.
Again, however, this is not always the case. There are
outputs which can indeed have required elements at the end
of a level of hierarchy.

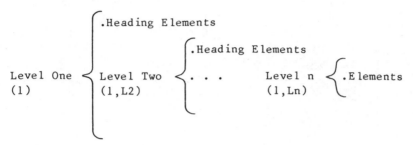

Figure 13.7: Model Logical Data Structure

At this point one more comment about designing outputs that
are easy to understand. You will recall that part of the
creation of the LDS involves incorporating data elements
which are required for calculations that minimize data
requirements but do not appear explicitly on the output, and
also incorporating levels of hierarchy not appearing on the
output structure to reflect the necessary sort sequence of
the data. These elements and hierarchies are called "hidden
elements" and "hidden hierarchies," since they do not show
up on the output structure. It is in general bad practice
to design outputs that have these kinds of features; outputs
which have no hidden elements or hierarchies are far easier
for people to use than those which have them. Again, if we
can help the user design these features away, we end up with
not only a more useful report for the user but fewer problems for ourselves when we go to design our program.

At this time, we are ready to present a generalized processing structure for a hierarchical report. One of the things
that we will have to settle first, though, is the concept of
the general Ideal File, which we mentioned earlier. For the
Customer Purchase Report that we started this module with,
we said that the simplest possible file that we could have
to produce this report from would be a single, sequential

file with one type of record on it. This simple file would
have a record for every Purchase made during the month; each
record would have to contain all of the data elements that
we had on the Logical Data Structure, and furthermore, the
records would have to sorted in the order of the hierarchy
of the Data Requirements chart. This Ideal File is shown
for your reference in Figure 13.8.

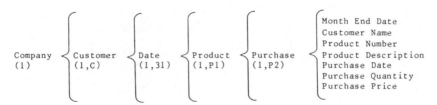

Company   Customer   Date   Product   Purchase   Month End Date
(1)   (1,C)   (1,31)   (1,P1)   (1,P2)   Customer Name
                                                              Product Number
                                                              Product Description
                                                              Purchase Date
                                                              Purchase Quantity
                                                              Purchase Price

Figure 13.8: The Ideal File Structure for Output #11

You'll notice that there is often no need to sort this file
on the highest and lowest levels of hierarchy. We do not
need to sort on the Company level because there is only one
Company on the report, and we may not sort on the Purchase
level because we can often depend on our sort to leave the
purchases within a day in the same order that they were in
before we sorted, in other words, we leave them in chronological order, the same order in which they were entered.
There are many cases, however, in which the lowest level
must also have some specific sort key, especially when the
sort utility does not preserve chronological order.

Again to emphasize, such a file will probably never actually
be created on the computer; it is simply a way of saying "If
I could get the data to look like that to my program, no matter what it really looks like, then I won't have any trouble
at all producing this report."

In general, we can say that the Ideal File for the model
output looks like that shown in Figure 13.9. We have a
record for each of the lowest level transactions, with all
of the required elements on each record, with the file
sorted in order by all of the levels of hierarchy of the

data requirements chart. This is the file that we will assume is available for the purposes of creating a model Logical Process Structure.

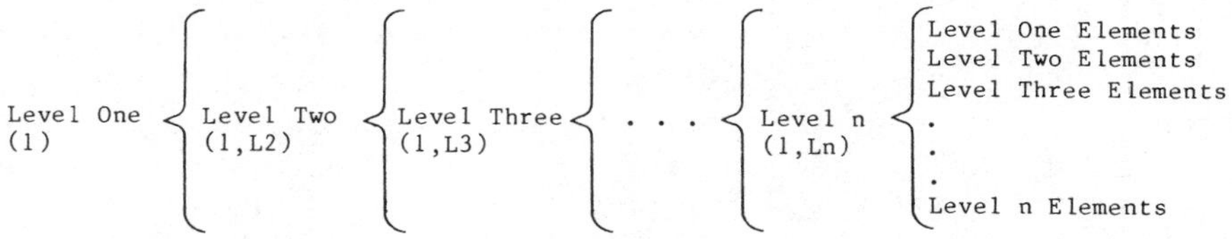

Figure 13.9: Generalized Ideal File Structure

As has been said earlier, our model LPS will have the same hierarchical framework as our LOS. The model LPS for a hierarchical report is shown in Figure 13.10.

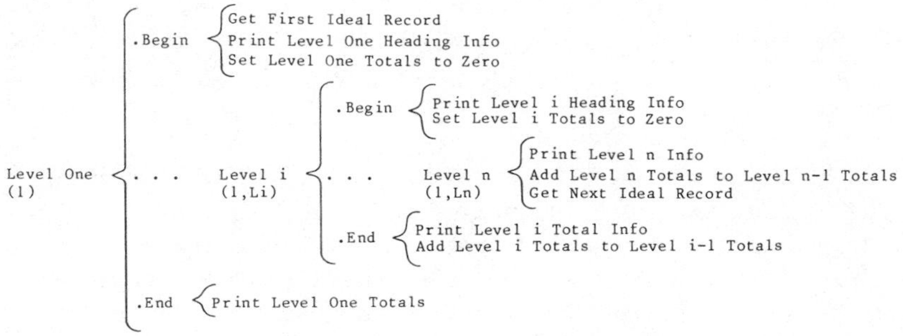

Figure 13.10: Generalized Logical Process Structure

At the beginning of the highest level we will want to Get the First Ideal Record. Then we must print the heading elements for that level and initialize any totals for that level. At the end of the highest level, we simply print the footing information, in other words, the totals.

At the beginning of each interior level, shown as Level i on the model LPS, we must print the heading information for that level and initialize all the totals for that level. At the end of such levels, we print that level's totals and add the totals to the next highest level.

At the lowest level, shown as Level n on the model, we must print the detail information for that level, add the detail amounts to the next highest level, and since we have now consumed all of the information that we got on our first Ideal Record, we have to get another Ideal Record. By reading one record ahead like this, we can always compare the record coming in to the one that we just finished, so that we know exactly what levels, if any, have changed.

As was mentioned earlier, this model is going to be quite useful to us. If we can learn to recognize outputs which have this form, and to apply the model correctly to them, we can increase our productivity on such jobs many-fold.

Please note that this model is for a very specific kind of output and cannot be used in exactly this form for outputs which differ from this model. The real danger in using model programs is that they tend to be viewed as a panacea; it is often the view that since they work so well for one type of output, they should work well for other kinds of reports as well. As you should be able to see, this is not the case.

Hierarchical report model programs abound in data processing. The programming language RPG is perhaps one of the oldest and best known of these types of models. Although RPG is based on a process-structured rather than a data-structured solution to this same problem, the model that it uses does indeed work, and consequently can be used to produce simple hierarchical reports faster than any other kind of language. However, this very useful trait is also RPG's greatest limitation. Because it is based on a specific model output format, outputs that do not fall into that category are nearly impossible to produce using RPG. This is why programming other kinds of problems is usually such a headache in that kind of language; for applications that fit their model, they work well, for applications that don't, they hardly work at all.

Since we now have a model processing structure for this type
of application, let's see if we can look at the model program code which we might produce. There is only one fundamental coding convention that we will adhere to: each bracket on our design will translate directly into one module of
code. In COBOL, that module will be a paragraph. Therefore, the code for the first few levels of this generalized
Logical Process Structure appears in Figure 13.11.

```
PROCEDURE DIVISION.

Level One.
    PERFORM Level One-BEGIN.
    PERFORM Level Two.
    PERFORM Level Two
        UNTIL END-OF-Level One = TRUE.
    PERFORM Level One-END.
    STOP RUN.

Level Two.
    PERFORM Level Two-BEGIN.
    PERFORM Level Three.
    PERFORM Level Three
        UNTIL END-OF-Level Two = TRUE
        OR    END-OF-Level One = TRUE.
    PERFORM Level One-END.

Level Three.
    PERFORM Level Three-BEGIN.
    PERFORM Level Four.
    PERFORM Level Four
        UNTIL END-OF-Level Three = TRUE
        OR    END-OF-Level Two = TRUE
        OR    END-OF-Level One = TRUE.
    PERFORM Level One-END.

Level Four.
    .
    .
    .
```

Figure 13.11: Generalized Program Control Structure

As we begin the PROCEDURE DIVISION, we must execute the module that will process our entire output. We perform the
functions found in the Begin Level 1 bracket, then Perform
the Level 2 process over and over again until we reach the
end of information for the output — in other words, the
end of the highest level, usually signified by the end of
the Ideal File that we are reading. After the file has run
out and we have finished processing the last of the Level
2's, we have to Perform the actions shown in the End Level 1
bracket. Then we can Stop Run (or Goback, as the case may
be).

```
PROCEDURE DIVISION.
    .
    .
    .

Level One-BEGIN.
     Instructions.
Level Two-BEGIN.
     Instructions.
Level Three-BEGIN.
     Instructions.
    .
    .
    .
Level n-1-BEGIN.
     Instructions.
Level n.
     Instructions.
Level n-1-END.
     Instructions.
    .
    .
    .
Level Three-END.
     Instructions.
Level Two-END.
     Instructions.
Level One-END.
     Instructions.
```

Figure 13.12: Generalized Detail Paragraphs

Next, we can define Level 2 processing, as is shown. Note that within Level 2 processing, we Perform Level 3 activities until we reach the end of that level, **or** the end of the highest level. This is to avoid missing a level break in our program. Then, we can define Level 3, and so on down to the next to lowest level.

These paragraphs can be called "control paragraphs" since, by themselves, they contain no actual processing, just invocation of paragraphs which do processing. All of the generalized paragraphs which actually perform some detail activities are shown in Figure 13.12. The Begin and End of each level, plus the lowest-level processing, can be called "detail paragraphs" since they contain for the most part only detail processing and no control except, perhaps, hierarchical invocation of utility routines.

To see how this model program can be applied to a specific problem, let us use it to create some code for the Customer Purchase Report that we have been examining. In Figure 13.13 we have simply plugged in the names of the levels into the model code. Please note, this is not necessarily the correct COBOL, since we have ignored reserved words. If the name of a level turns out to be a reserved word in COBOL, we can simply change it a little to make it an acceptable name. We will not do that for this example.

Again, note the fact that the tests in the Perform Until clauses check for a break in all levels above that one. This need not be done in this fashion, with explicit tests in the Until clause. It could just as easily be done by setting up a key for each level, which might be defined as in Figure 13.14. The lowest-level key, the Product key, would not only contain the number of the product, so we could tell when it changed from one record to the next, but it would also contain the Customer Key, so we could tell if that changed also. The Customer Key, in turn, would contain the Customer Name with which we could compare, and also the Company Key, which usually amounts to an end of file flag. If we set up two keys which have this structure, as we have in Figure 13.15, one for the record that we just finished processing and one which contains information from the newly gotten record, we can set up our control paragraphs as is shown.

```
PROCEDURE DIVISION.

COMPANY.
    PERFORM COMPANY-BEGIN.
    PERFORM CUSTOMER.
    PERFORM CUSTOMER
        UNTIL END-OF-COMPANY = TRUE.
    PERFORM COMPANY-END.
    STOP RUN.

CUSTOMER.
    PERFORM CUSTOMER-BEGIN.
    PERFORM PRODUCT.
    PERFORM PRODUCT
        UNTIL END-OF-CUSTOMER = TRUE
        OR     END-OF-COMPANY = TRUE.
    PERFORM CUSTOMER-END.

PRODUCT.
    PERFORM PRODUCT-BEGIN.
    PERFORM PURCHASE.
    PERFORM PURCHASE
        UNTIL END-OF-PRODUCT = TRUE
        OR     END-OF-CUSTOMER = TRUE
        OR     END-OF-COMPANY = TRUE.   .
    PERFORM PRODUCT-END.
```

Figure 13.13: Model Program for Output #11

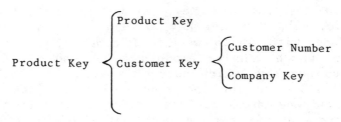

Figure 13.14: Staggered Key Structure for Output #11

```
01   PRODUCT-KEY.
     02   PRODUCT-NUMBER               PIC X(6).
     02   CUSTOMER-KEY.
          03   CUSTOMER-NAME           PIC X(20).
          03   COMPANY-KEY             PIC X.

01   OLD-PRODUCT-KEY.
     02   OLD-PRODUCT-NUMBER           PIC X(6).
     02   OLD-CUSTOMER-KEY.
          03   OLD-CUSTOMER-NAME       PIC X(20).
          03   OLD-COMPANY-KEY         PIC X.


PROCEDURE DIVISION.

COMPANY.
     PERFORM COMPANY-BEGIN.
     PERFORM CUSTOMER.
     PERFORM CUSTOMER
          UNTIL OLD-COMPANY-KEY NOT = COMPANY-KEY.
     PERFORM COMPANY-END.
     STOP RUN.

CUSTOMER.
     PERFORM CUSTOMER-BEGIN.
     PERFORM PRODUCT.
     PERFORM PRODUCT
          UNTIL OLD-CUSTOMER-KEY NOT = CUSTOMER-KEY.
     PERFORM CUSTOMER-END.

PRODUCT.
     PERFORM PRODUCT-BEGIN.
     PERFORM PURCHASE.
     PERFORM PURCHASE
          UNTIL OLD-PRODUCT-KEY NOT = PRODUCT-KEY.
     PERFORM PRODUCT-END.
```

Figure 13.15: Staggered Key Comparison Translation
for Output #11

Processing Empty Files

One other topic that may be addressed here is the model for
empty file processing. So far we have always assumed there
would be at least one record on the Ideal File, and have
written our programs accordingly. Is this a bad assumption?
Probably you have always been told that it is, that one
should always write programs that would work even if there
were no records to process. This is not really a better
assumption, just different. One can write a program that
will only work if there is at least one record to process on
a file, as long as one can make sure that the program is
never invoked when there are no records on the file. This
can be done with JCL or control language statements on some
computers. When it cannot be done, a simple change can be
added to the PROCEDURE DIVISION that will accomplish the
same thing. Look at the diagram in Figure 13.16.

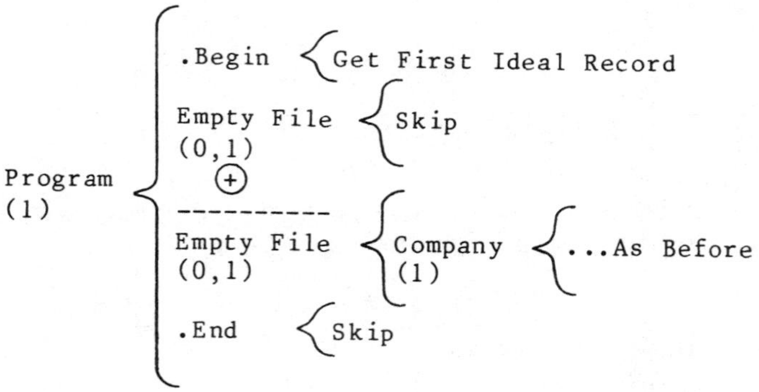

```
                          ┌
                          │  .Begin  < Get First Ideal Record
                          │
                          │  Empty File  < Skip
                          │  (0,1)
                          │     ⊕
            Program  <    │  ----------
            (1)           │  Empty File  < Company  < ...As Before
                          │  (0,1)          (1)
                          │
                          │  .End  < Skip
                          └
```

```
    PROCEDURE DIVISION.
        PERFORM PROGRAM-BEGIN.
        IF NO-MORE-RECORDS = TRUE
            PERFORM EMPTY-FILE
        ELSE
            PERFORM NOT-EMPTY-FILE.
        PERFORM PROGRAM-END.
        STOP RUN.
```

Figure 13.16: Empty File Model Structure and Translation
for Output #11

If we take the "Get First Ideal Record" out of the Begin
Company bracket in Figure 13.4, earlier, we can perform the
activities as shown. At the beginning of the program, we
can read the file. If there are no records, we can either
do nothing, as is indicated, or we might perhaps wish to
print a message that indicates that there is no data to
process. If there is at least one record, we will simply
perform the Company process as was detailed before, with the
exception that the initial read has already been done and
need not be done again in Company Begin. This "systems"
layer of insulation will work for any kind of program which
has the requirement and can be installed as the top of any
program.

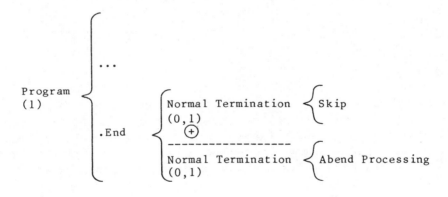

```
PROCEDURE DIVISION.
PROGRAM.
    ...
    PERFORM PROGRAM-END.
    STOP RUN.
PROGRAM-END.
    IF ABEND-INDICATOR = FALSE
        PERFORM NORMAL-TERMINATION
    ELSE
        PERFORM NOT-NORMAL-TERMINATION.
```

Figure 13.17: "Abend" Processing Model Structure and
               Translation for Output #11

"Abend" Processing

In a situation where the data input may be erroneous, we
need to include processing for an abnormal termination. The
same kind of structure that was used for an empty file
contingency may be used to do what has been classically
called "abend" processing —— processing to take place
when there was some problem with the data discovered during
the execution of the program. Outside the scope of the
normal "logical" processing for the output we may install a
level such as that given above in Figure 13.17.

In the "Get Ideal Record" coroutine, we may set an indicator
whenever an abend condition is detected. Recalling the
discussions of the input mapping routine in an earlier
chapter, this condition will also trigger the "No More Data"
indicator, so that logical processing is terminated in the
normal manner. At the end of the program, we may then check
the status of the "abend" indicator. If it has been turned
on, we many execute an "abend" reporting module as is shown.

Summary

Because hierarchical reports are so common in data
processing, it is useful to study the common aspects of this
kind of output. Familiarity with the generalized model
structures and code presented in this chapter will
facilitate faster analysis and design of similar software
problems.

Chapter 14 APPLICATIONS
PART 2
FILE MERGES

Utility Routines

In software systems there is a necessity for having standard-
ized routines to do common data manipulations. These
programs are often called **utility routines** — programs
for sorting, selecting, merging, etc. In this book we have
already examined a coroutine that can be used for a
selection utility (Figure 11.14). In this chapter we shall
examine the development of another useful utility routine,
one that will merge two or more files together into one.

Our approach to solving this problem will be the same as we
have used before; we begin with the desired results and work
backwards towards a program design. Also, we will be concentrating on different parts of the design at different stages. First, we will want to look at the language- and hard-
ware-independent processing structure (the LPS) in order to
give us a generalized idea of what must be done. Then, we
will add the specifics of our particular language and particular hardware environment to that high-level structure,
producing a workable program design.

The reasons that this File Merge application is worth investigating might escape some readers. After all, for most
installations, canned utility programs are already available

to accomplish file merges, and there is no real need for
developing new programs that perform the same task.   The
whole purpose of this technology is to get people to avoid
duplicating the design work of others, and it would seem
that this particular wheel has been invented for a long
time.

In the case of this model program it is not so much the
model which is valuable to us (although it is a useful one)
as it is the approach to solving a whole class of computer
applications — those programs which must produce a file
or a group of files as output.

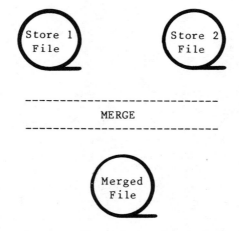

Figure 14.1: Two-file Merge

In Figure 14.1 is simply a pictorial description of what it
is that we are to design here. For this application we are
to take two sequential files from two retail stores, called
Store 1 and Store 2 appropriately enough, and merge them
into one output file, which is also sequential. The two
files coming in and the output file to be produced have
specific formats and arrangements, which are shown in Figure
14.2. Each of the two input files has a header record at
its beginning, which contains the File Date, the Store
Number that the file is for, and the Name of the file.

Following the header record, each input file contains a number of Customer Transactions. Every day each of the two stores has Customers buying goods and making payments. Each one of these purchases or payments which are made is called a Transaction, and a record is created for it. Each Transaction record contains the number of the Customer that the Transaction is for, and the appropriate information for that Transaction. Any one Customer may have many transactions at both stores, and would thus have records on both input files. **Both of the input files have already been sorted in Customer Number order.**

```
Input File Format (Both Input Files):

Header Record:        +--File Date--+--Store Number--+--File Name--+
Transactions:         +--Customer Number--+--Transaction Info------+
                      +-----------------+----------------------+
                      +-----------------+----------------------+
                      +-----------------+----------------------+
                      +-----------------+----------------------+
                      +-----------------+----------------------+
                      +-----------------+----------------------+
                      +-----------------+----------------------+


Output File Format (Merged File)

Header Record:        +--File Date--+--File Name-------------------+
                      +--Customer Number--+--Store Number--+--Transaction Info--+
                      +-----------------+----------------+-------------------+
                      +-----------------+----------------+-------------------+
                      +-----------------+----------------+-------------------+
                      +-----------------+----------------+-------------------+
                      +-----------------+----------------+-------------------+
                      +-----------------+----------------+-------------------+
                      +-----------------+----------------+-------------------+
```

Figure 14.2: Input and Output Specifications for a
Two-file Merge

The output file also has a header record containing the File Date and Name, followed by all of the Transaction records from both stores. You'll note that the format of each record has been altered slightly to indicate which Store a Transaction occurred at. Furthermore the output file must be produced in a particular order. **The Transactions on the output file are to remain in Customer Number order, but are also to be arranged by Store within Customer.** Thus, if a

particular Customer had Transactions at both Stores we would
want to show all of their records for Store 1 before their
records for Store 2.

There are two basic approaches that we could take, once we
have the information that has been given, toward the design
of a program to accomplish this task. The traditional
approach would be to take the two input files and begin to
figure out the process for transforming the input into the
output. This is done by a sort of empirical thought process, tracing out in one's mind how one might go about picking up records from one file and then the other file to preserve the order of Store within Customer. This is called a
"process oriented" design approach. It is also somewhat
input oriented, since the knowledge of the true format of
the input is also a guiding force in the design.

On the other hand, we could begin by analyzing the output
that we have been asked to produce without even considering
the actual input. We can investigate the structure of the
output, deduce what the structure must be of the necessary
and sufficient input, and then deduce the structure of the
process that would produce the output from the Ideal input
— the input that we would ask for if we had a choice.
This Ideal File would have all of the information that we
would need to be able to produce the output, and would be in
just the order that we would like it. If the actual input
that we are given is different from the input that we said
we would like to have, we can then design an input mapping
process to transform the actual input into the ideal input.

The first task in this design is to put away our knowledge
about the input files that we have been given to work with,
and begin our design as if we did not know what is actually
available for input. We'll come back to the input files
later in our design. For now, we would like to examine the
structure of the output that we are to produce. It is this
output structure that will eventually lead us to the basic
structure of our program.

The Logical Output Structure for this file is shown in Figure 14.3. This diagram indicates that the output consists
of a File Date and Name at the beginning of the file followed by a number of Transactions. For each transaction we

will output the Customer Number, the Store Number, and the
Transaction Information.

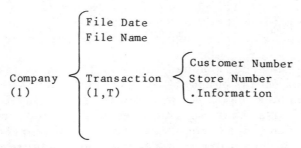

Figure 14.3: Logical Output Structure for a Two-file Merge

After producing the LOS we can analyze the data elements to
be output and produce a diagram of the necessary and sufficient input structure.   This is done by eliminating labels
and computable data elements, and by incorporating any necessary hierarchies to reflect the required sort sequence of
the output.   The resulting Logical Data Structure for this
output is shown in Figure 14.4.

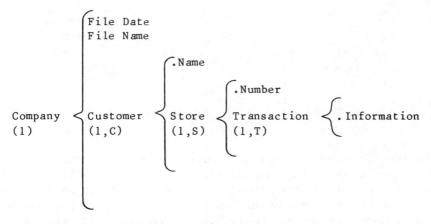

Figure 14.4: Logical Data Structure for a Two-file Merge

This chart says that in order to be able to produce this
output, we have to be able to get a File Date and Name at
the beginning of the output for the Company. Then for each
Customer on the output file we have to be able to get that
Customer's Number. For each Store within Customer, we'll
have to get the Store's Number. Finally for each Transaction we will need the Transaction Information. If we can
get the information shown at the places indicated on the diagram, we can produce the output file with no trouble.

Since we now have a graphic representation of the data requirements for this output, we can look at the arrangement
of this necessary data as an Ideal File. Obviously, there
are a lot of ways that we could actually keep this information so that the data requirements are preserved, but for
the purposes of creating a hardware- and language- independent process structure we will assume that our input is going
to be given to us in the simplest possible form — one
single sequential file with only one record type. Thus this
simple file will have to have all of the data elements left
on the LDS present on each and every record. We would need
to have a record for every Transaction and would need to
have those simple records sorted in the order of the
hierarchy of the LDS. This Ideal File is shown in the
illustration of Figure 14.5.

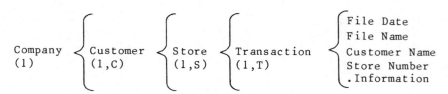

Figure 14.5: Ideal File for a Two-file Merge

We can now produce a Logical Process Structure for this output that will show the mapping from the Ideal File into the
output file. Since the Ideal File looks almost exactly like
the file that we have been asked to output, the Logical Process Structure is going to be quite simple. It is shown in
Figure 14.6. At the beginning of the Company, we will have

to Get the First Ideal Record and then Write out the Company
Header Information for the file. Then for each Transaction,
we Write out the new Transaction Information and Get the
Next Ideal Record. This LPS represents nearly a one-to-one
mapping from Ideal input to output.

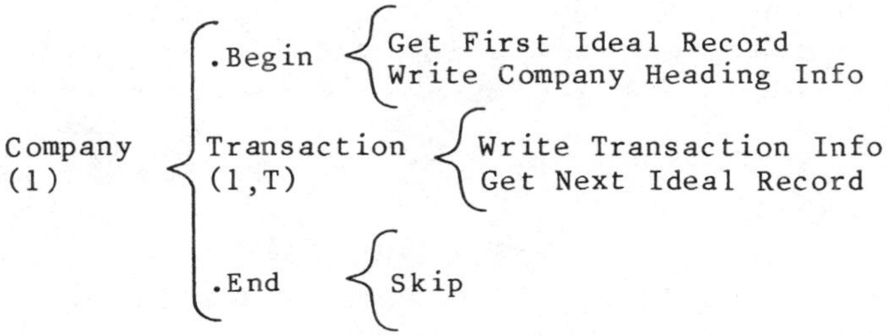

```
                    ⎧           ⎧ Get First Ideal Record
                    ⎪ .Begin    ⎨ Write Company Heading Info
                    ⎪           ⎩
                    ⎪
         Company    ⎪ Transaction ⎧ Write Transaction Info
         (1)        ⎨ (1,T)       ⎨ Get Next Ideal Record
                    ⎪             ⎩
                    ⎪
                    ⎪           ⎧
                    ⎩ .End      ⎨ Skip
                                ⎩
```

Figure 14.6: Logical Process Structure for a
Two-file Merge

Remember that this LPS is based on the Ideal Input File and
is not yet ready to be turned into a program. We must still
take care of the processing that is necessary because of the
way the input was actually given to us. The actual input is
not of the ideal form. We must make the observation that
nothing on this structure really has to change, we just have
to add to what is there. For instance, since there is no
Ideal File as such, the Get First Ideal Record and the Get
Next Ideal Record activities shown are not just simple read
statements of one single file. If we can make these two
activities into a procedure that would look at the available
input and then manufacture and ideal record from that input,
just as if the Ideal File had been available, then we can
use the structure as it is shown for the controlling
structure of our program. Thus we must design a process
that at the beginning will read all of the necessary files
and then build the first ideal record. Then at the end of
each Transaction we must design a process to again look at
the available input files and build the next ideal record.

Let us consider first the Get First Ideal Record routine and
see what it might look like. To build the first ideal
record we must get the header records off of each of the two

input files, save the File Date, Store Number, and File
Name, and then get the first transaction record from each
file. Since we would then have the first record off of each
file, and since we know that each of the input files have
already been sorted in Customer Number order, we know that
one of these two records contains the information for the
first ideal record. All that remains to be done is to
select the Transaction with the lowest Customer Number or
the Transaction from the Store 1 file if their Customer
Numbers are equal, and Build the Ideal Record. This much of
the Get First Ideal Record routine is shown in Figure 14.7.

Get First Ideal Record
(1)
$\left\{\begin{array}{l}\text{Open Input Files} \\ \text{Set No More Transactions to False} \\ \text{Get Store 1 Header Record} \\ \text{Get Store 2 Header Record} \\ \text{Get First Store 1 Transaction} \\ \text{Get First Store 2 Transaction} \\ \text{Build Ideal Record} \quad \{\text{...Figure 14.8}\end{array}\right.$

Figure 14.7: Get First First Record Routine for a
Two-file Merge

Since there are only two possible choices for which
Transaction record is to be selected, the Build Ideal Record
module is simplicity itself. It is shown in Figure 14.8.

Build Ideal Record
(1)
$\left\{\begin{array}{l}\text{Store 1 Is Low} \\ (0,1) \\ \oplus \\ \text{Store 2 is Low} \\ (0,1)\end{array}\right.$
$\left\{\begin{array}{l}\text{Move Store 1 Transaction Info to Ideal Record} \\ \text{Get Next Store 1 Record}\end{array}\right.$
$\left\{\begin{array}{l}\text{Move Store 2 Transaction Info to Ideal Record} \\ \text{Get Next Store 2 Record}\end{array}\right.$

Figure 14.8: Build Ideal Record Coroutine for a
Two-file Merge

When the Store 1 file has the low record, we will create the
Ideal Record from the Store 1 Transaction Information. When
the Store 2 file has the low record, we will create the
Ideal Record from the Store 2 Transaction Information. In
either case after the Ideal Record is built, we must Get the
Next Record from the file that was low. This is done so
that the next time we look at the two files, the records
seen are the current ones.

Notice that to begin with in this design, we simply show the
two conditions which may be present in the module, without
concern over how one knows which of the two conditions are
to be selected. The tests that are necessary to detect the
appropriate condition are added to the design as a second
step, and are shown in Figure 14.9.

```
                         ⎧ Store 1 Is Low  ⎧ Move Store 1 Transaction Info to Ideal Record
                         ⎪ (0,1)?1         ⎩ Get Next Store 1 Record  ⟨...Figure 14.10
Build Ideal Record       ⎨      ⊕
(1)                      ⎪ Store 2 is Low  ⎧ Move Store 2 Transaction Info to Ideal Record
                         ⎩ (0,1)?2         ⎩ Get Next Store 2 Record  ⟨...Figure 14.10
```

Tests: ?1-Store 1 Customer Number <= Store 2 Customer Number
       ?2-Not ?1

Figure 14.9: Tests Added to the Coroutine

To know that the Store 1 File is Low, we must determine that
the Store 1 Customer Number is less than or equal to the
Store 2 Customer Number. When the Store 2 Customer Number
is less than the Store 1 Customer Number (the negation of
the first test), the condition Store 2 is Low is to be
selected.

To complete this module, we need only consider what happens
when one of the input files is exhausted. The Get Next
Record routines for each of the two input files can be
detailed as is shown in Figure 14.10.

When the end of one of the files is reached, it may be
removed from consideration as the Low file by placing
arbitrarily high values into its Customer Number. This is
done so that for all subsequent invocations of the Build

Ideal Record routine the remaining file will have records
with a Customer Number lower than the file that has been
completed.

```
Get Next Store 1 Record  ⎰ Read Store 1 Record
(1)                      ⎱
                           Empty Store 1 File ⎰ Set Store 1 Customer Number
                           (0,1)?1            ⎱ to High Values


Get Next Store 2 Record  ⎰ Read Store 2 Record
(1)                      ⎱
                           Empty Store 2 File ⎰ Set Store 2 Customer Number
                           (0,1)?2            ⎱ to High Values


Tests: ?1-At End (Store 1 File)
       ?2-At End (Store 2 File)
```

Figure 14.10: Get Next Record Routines for a Two-file Merge

The same Build Ideal Record routine may also be used as a
part of the Get Next Ideal Record routine that must also be
detailed. As mentioned in Chapter 11, the Get Next Record
routine cannot simply invoke the Build Ideal Record routine;
there may be no records left to process. The Build Ideal
Record routine need only be invoked when there is at least
one more Transaction to read. If there are no more Transactions, the No More Transactions indicator may be set True
and the input files may be closed.

```
            ⎧ .Begin   ⎰ Get First Ideal Record ⟨...Figure 14.7
            ⎪          ⎱ Write Company Heading Info
            ⎪              ⎰ Write Transaction Info
            ⎪              ⎪
Company     ⎨ Transaction ⎪                              Another Transaction ⎰ Build Ideal Record ⟨...Figure 14.9
(1)         ⎪ (1,T)?2     ⎨ Get Next Ideal Record        (0,1)                ⎱
            ⎪             ⎪ (1)                            ⊕
            ⎪             ⎩                               -------------------
            ⎪                                            Another Transaction ⎰ Set No More Transactions to True
            ⎪                                            (0,1)?1              ⎱ Close Input Files
            ⎪ .End     ⎰ Skip
            ⎩          ⎱

Tests: ?1-Store 1 Customer Number = High Values and
          Store 2 Customer Number = High Values
       ?2-No More Transactions = True
```

Figure 14.11: Completed Program Design for a Two-file Merge

Generalizing the Design

This design works well for a simple two-file merge. Does it
extend upward to work equally well for merging more than two
files? Absolutely. As a matter of fact, since we were
careful to separate out the logical from the physical
aspects of this problem, only two sections of the program
design have to be modified to handle, say, three files. The
Get First Record routine must be modified to read the
headers and the first Transaction record off of each of the
input files. Then the Build Ideal Record routine must be
modified to select between three possible low records
instead of just two. The modified Build module is shown in
Figure 14.12.

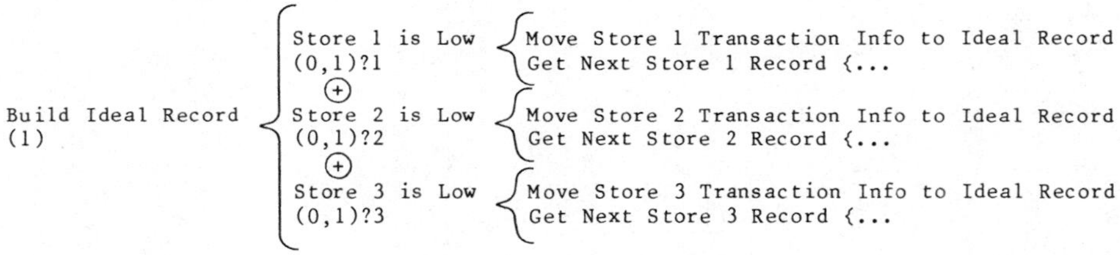

```
                          ┌ Store 1 is Low ┌ Move Store 1 Transaction Info to Ideal Record
                          │ (0,1)?1        └ Get Next Store 1 Record (...
                          │     ⊕
  Build Ideal Record  ────┤ Store 2 is Low ┌ Move Store 2 Transaction Info to Ideal Record
  (1)                     │ (0,1)?2        └ Get Next Store 2 Record (...
                          │     ⊕
                          │ Store 3 is Low ┌ Move Store 3 Transaction Info to Ideal Record
                          └ (0,1)?3        └ Get Next Store 3 Record (...
```

```
Tests: ?1-Store 1 Customer Number <= Store 2 Customer Number and
           Store 1 Customer Number <= Store 3 Customer Number
       ?2-Store 2 Customer Number < Store 1 Customer Number and
           Store 2 Customer Number <= Store 3 Customer Number
       ?3-Store 3 Customer Number < Store 1 Customer Number and
           Store 3 Customer Number < Store 2 Customer Number
```

Figure 14.12: Program Design for a **Three**-File Merge

You should again notice the ease with which the enhancement
for three files was made. Since the modification affected
the actual input and not the output, the only part of the
program that needs to be changed is the input mapping
coroutine and not the remainder of the design. For four,
five, ten, or a hundred input files the merge program would
be very much the same.

Summary

While file merges are often handled with the aid of software
utilities already available in a system, it is important to
have facility with this kind of problem. Having mastered
the techniques in this chapter, which are merely a direct
application of the methodology given previously, we can
easily create multiple file accessing modules for whatever
the need.

Chapter 15 APPLICATIONS
PART 3
MASTER FILE UPDATES

File Updating

The last model program design we shall examine in this book
is the Master File Update. The update model, as you might
well imagine, is going to be a particularly useful one if we
can manage to develop it (which we probably can or you would
not be reading this chapter right now). Master File Updates
are among the most common and most difficult of the normal
application programs which must be written, and thus a model
of the logic necessary to accomplish that function is going
to be of great value.

In Figure 15.1, you see a pictorial description of a
typical master file update function. The program design
that we will eventually develop will work for any kind of
master file, but for simplicity sake we are going to discuss
this problem as it pertains to a master file containing
customer information. This is to avoid getting bogged down
in generalities. We will have an already existing customer
file, here labeled "Old Customer Master File," to which we
will want to apply some transactions — transactions
which represent updates that we want to make to the file.
These update transactions will come in basically three
varieties: **additions** of new customers that aren't on the
old file, **changes** to be made to the data kept about a

customer who is already on the old file, and **deletions** of customers who are on the old file.

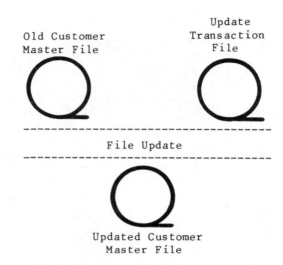

Figure 15.1: Master File Update

After applying all of these transactions, we will want to have a new customer file, here called the "Updated Customer Master File," which has the same format as the old file, but which now contains all of the updates. You'll note that there is only one file of transactions depicted in this figure; this need not be the case. The model program that we are going to investigate will handle **any number** of files in this **batch mode,** and we will even generalize the model so that it will function in an **on-line** environment.

Since the Warnier/Orr approach is an "output-oriented" technique, we are going to begin our analysis at the result and work backwards from that point. From the output we are going to be able to discern the necessary and sufficient input in the simplest possible form; we'll call that the Ideal File, since it will contain all and only the data that we would need in exactly the order that we would like to find it. Then, we can build a high-level generalized

processing structure to describe the transformation of the
simple input into the output. If the actual input that we
must work with is different in any way from the ideal input,
we can design an input mapping routine that transforms the
real input into the ideal form. At that point we should
have a workable design for a program.

Also in this chapter we are going to be taking advantage of
another of the features of the Warnier/Orr approach. The
process structures, the model logic for our programs, will
be the same as the structures of the data that we will be
operating on.

Let us begin with the output of the Master File Update and
see what turns up. The output file description is shown
below in Figure 15.2. On the Updated Customer Master File
we need to have a header record at the beginning containing
the Date and Name of the file. Then we have a series of customer master records — one record for each current
customer. On each record will be the Customer Number and
the Customer Information that we will keep about them —
name, address, credit history, whatever.


```
Customer Master File:

Header Record:        +--File Date--+--File Name--+
Customer Records:     +--Customer Number--+--Customer Information--+
                      +------------------+------------------------+
                      +------------------+------------------------+
                      +------------------+------------------------+
                      +------------------+------------------------+
                      +------------------+------------------------+
                      +------------------+------------------------+
                      +------------------+------------------------+
                      ...etc...
```
Figure 15.2: Master File Format for Master File Update

The Logical Output Structure for this file is quite simple
(Figure 15.3), and is in fact quite similar to the LOS for
the output file examined in the last chapter (Figure 14.3).

Again, the LOS shows us that the file for the Company consists of a File Date and File Name at the beginning followed
by from one-to-many Customer records, each one of which will
contain a Customer Number and Customer Information.

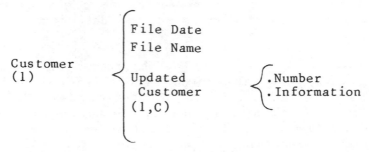

Figure 15.3: LOS for Master File Update

Having built a diagram of the structure of the output that
we want to produce, we shall now turn our attention to the
analysis of the data that will be needed as input to be able
to produce the output. As always, we will need to look at
each of the data elements on the output to see which ones
could be computed from other elements and which ones would
have to be required as input to be known. When we analyze
the four output elements identified, we find that each one
is a required data element — required in that none is
the result of a calculation. Furthermore, each element will
be required as input with the same frequency with which it
is to be output. Thus, **in this case the Logical Data
Structure and the Logical Output Structure turn out to be
the same.** (Compare Figure 15.4. to Figure 15.3)

As before, this diagram says that we will need to be given
the File Date and File Name at the beginning of the Updated
Company, and the Updated Customer Number and Updated
Customer Information for each customer on the file, in order
to be able to produce this output. If this data is not
available or cannot be derived from the input that we are
given, we cannot produce the output.

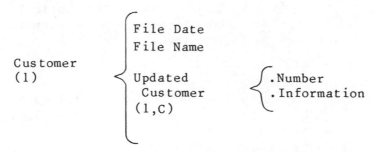

Figure 15.4: LDS for Master File Update

The Ideal File for this application is also quite simple; the simplest possible file format that we could use is that of a single sequential file with only one type of record on it, with each record on that simple file containing all of the data elements that are required (since we "ideally" would have only one record format). Also, there will have to be one of those simple records for each Updated Customer, so that we will have sufficient information to build the output file. Furthermore, these records will have to be in Customer Number order, since we also said that our Ideal File would be in the exact order that we would like. The Ideal File format is shown in Figure 15.5.

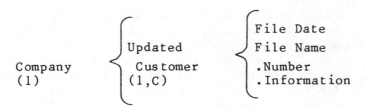

Figure 15.5: Ideal Input File for Master File Update

Again it should be stressed that such a file would probably never actually be built in a computer; it is just a way of

visualizing a very simple form of physical input arrangement
for the purposes of designing our programs.

Now we may develop the process which is necessary to turn
the Ideal File into the output file. **The Logical Process
Structure will have the same structure as the output file.**
It appears completed in Figure 15.6.

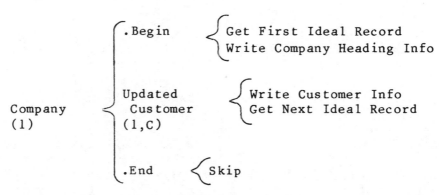

Figure 15.6 LPS for Master File Update

At the beginning of this process, we must Get the first
Ideal record, and then Write out the Company Heading
Information. Then for each updated Customer we must Write
out the updated Customer Information and then Get the Next
Ideal Record. We will keep doing this process until there
are no more records on the Ideal Input File to get.

You should notice that up until this point there has been no
analysis, indeed, not even a mention of the actual physical
input file or files that we were asked to work with. This
is a consideration that is always put off until after the
LPS is completed to avoid having to worry about too much at
one time. At this stage of the design we are halfway home;
we have a description of the process that turns the Ideal
File into the desired output. We will next turn our attention to the development of the mapping that will turn the
actual input that we were given into the ideal form.

Look at Figure 15.7. Let us for the moment say that we were
given an input stream that looks like the one shown here.

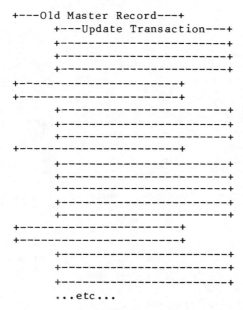

Figure 15.7: A Possible Input Data Stream

This input stream is sequential, and has two types of records on it: Old Customer Master records and Update Transaction Records all mixed in together. This stream thus contains all of the old customer information, plus a record for each change that is to be made to the old master file. Before we discuss the arrangement of the records on this stream, let's examine the information that is to be found on the two different types of records. Look at the illustration of Figure 15.8. The old Customer Master Records contain the Customer Number, a Master Code to indicate that this is an old master record, and then all of the old customer information. The Transaction records, of which there are three kinds, contain the Customer Number to which the transaction is to be applied to. If the transaction is an **addition** of a new customer, there will be an Add Code

followed by the new customer's information; if the
transaction is a **change** to an existing customer, there
will be a Change Code followed by the Change Information; if
the transaction is a **deletion** of an old Customer, there
will be just the Delete Code.

```
Old Customer Master Record:
      +--Customer Number--+--Master Code--+--Customer Info--+

Update Transaction Records:
   Add Record:
      +--Customer Number--+--Add Code--+--Add Info--+
   Change Record:
      +--Customer Number--+--Change Code--+--Change Info--+
   Delete Record:
      +--Customer Number--+--Delete Code--+
```

Figure 15.8: Input Record Formats on the Input Stream

This stream, with its two record types is in order by
Customer Number first, and also by Record Type within
Customer Number, i.e., Master Record before Transaction
Records for a Customer, if both are present. That gives us
some **predictable arrangements** of data for any given
Customer. Since the stream is in order by Customer Number,
we will find all of the records for a particular customer
all grouped together as shown in Figure 15.9, and not spread
out all over the place.

Also, since the records are in order by record type within a
customer, we will find the old master record for a customer
before any transactions for that customer. Not every customer may have an old master record and not every one will
have transactions, so basically we might find three kinds of
arrangements. We may have a customer with both an old
master record and some transactions, as Customer 1 has in
this figure. We also may have a customer who has an old
master record, but who has no transactions to apply to it,
as Customer 2 shown. We might also have the case where a
customer has no old master record, but has some transactions, as Customer 3 has.

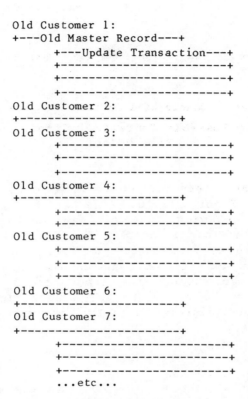

```
Old Customer 1:
+---Old Master Record---+
      +---Update Transaction---+
      +-----------------------+
      +-----------------------+
      +-----------------------+
Old Customer 2:
+-----------------------+
Old Customer 3:
      +-----------------------+
      +-----------------------+
      +-----------------------+
Old Customer 4:
+-----------------------+
      +-----------------------+
      +-----------------------+
Old Customer 5:
      +-----------------------+
      +-----------------------+
      +-----------------------+
Old Customer 6:
+-----------------------+
Old Customer 7:
+-----------------------+
      +-----------------------+
      +-----------------------+
      +-----------------------+
      ...etc...
```

Figure 15.9: Customer Information Arranged on the Input
Stream

All of these records have been reliably edited for **content**
prior to this point. Therefore, all of the fields on the
records contain the correct values, there are no duplicate
masters records, etc. However, there still might be some
problems that we can run across as we try to apply the
transactions. There may still be present in the input
stream errors in **context** — how the transactions are to
be applied.

Add Error: an Add for a Customer that already exists.

Change Error: a Change for a Customer that does not exist.

Delete Error: a Delete of a Customer that does not exist.

Figure 15.10: Possible Contextual Errors for a Master
File Update

There are three kinds of contextual errors that may be present. (See Figure 15.10.) If we find an "Add transaction" for a customer that already has a master record, then that transaction is invalid and cannot be applied. The same is true if we find either a "Change transaction" or a "Delete transaction" for a customer who has no old master record. As we go through the transactions for a customer, we will want to apply all of the transactions that we can but filter out and discard those that we cannot apply.

The Get Ideal Record Routine

The LPS designed to this point assumes the existence of an Ideal File. However, the Ideal File of already updated Customer records does not exist as such. To use the LPS for a program design, we must either make a complete pass of the input stream prior to this step and transform it into the Ideal form, or we could just take the two Get Ideal Record routines and build a mapping that looks at the available input and manufactures for us ideal records, one at a time. Then we can invoke that routine every time that we would like a record, and we can write our program just as if the Ideal File did exist. Thus, our immediate goal is to develop that ideal record manufacturing routine.

```
                                  ⎧ Open Files
                                  ⎪ Set No More Customers to False
    Get First                     ⎨ Set No More Records to False
     Ideal Record                 ⎪ Get File Header Record
     (1)                          ⎪ Get First Record from Input Stream
                                  ⎩ Build Ideal Record      {...
```

Figure 15.11: Partial Get First Ideal Record Routine for
              Master File Update


```
    Input Records:                          Updated Records:
    +---Old Master Record---+
          +---Update Transaction---+
            +-----------------------+
            +-----------------------+
            +-----------------------+
                                            +---Updated Master Record---+

    +-----------------------+               +---Updated Master Record---+

          +-----------------------+
          +-----------------------+
          +-----------------------+

    +-----------------------+
          +-----------------------+
          +-----------------------+               +---Updated Master Record---+

          +-----------------------+
          +-----------------------+
          +-----------------------+
                                            +---Updated Master Record---+
    +-----------------------+

          +-----------------------+
          +-----------------------+
                                            +---Updated Master Record---+

    +-----------------------+               +---Updated Master Record---+
    +-----------------------+
          +-----------------------+
          +-----------------------+

          +-----------------------+
                                            +---Updated Master Record---+
    ...etc...                               ...etc...
```

Figure 15.12: Physical Input and Output Data Streams

We shall begin with the Get First Ideal Record process,
which is partially shown in Figure 15.11. In this routine
we must open the input files, initialize two state variables
(one each for the end of the logical and physical files),
obtain the information for the file header record from
somewhere (you'll notice that it is not given to us
explicitly in the input that we are using), and then read
the first record from the input stream. Then, we will
invoke a routine that will go through as many of these input
records as is necessary to build one ideal record; an ideal
record, in this case, being an Updated Customer Master
Record.

As before, the structure necessary for the Build Ideal
Record mapping can be discerned by examining the data
structure of the input data stream and its relation to the
Ideal File. Examine the data streams shown in Figure 15.12.
Notice that not all customers present on the input file
necessarily survive the update function to become Updated
Customers; some of them may be deleted. So for one updated
Customer we must process from one-to-many Input Customers
(those present on the input stream). The data structure
present on the input stream for an Input Customer appears
in Figure 15.13. An Input Customer may or may not have an
Old Master record present. Following it may be from
zero-to-many Transactions, each of which is either an Add,
Change, or Delete.

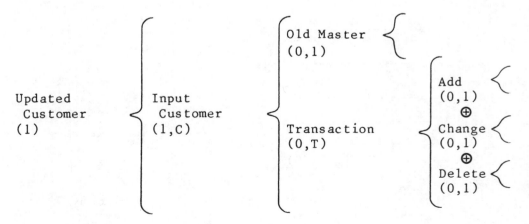

Figure 15.13: Physical Input Data Structure

Defining the Mapping

In order to begin to create Updated Customer records, we
will want to set up a save area to hold the Old Master
records that come in so that we can apply the Transactions
to them. That save area will be set up as in Figure 15.14.
The Master Save Area that we create will consist of a Master
Customer Number, and the Master Information.

Master Save   { Master Customer Number
     Area   { Master Information

Figure 15.14: Master Record Holding Area

In order to build a single Updated Customer record, we will
have to go through at least one, and possibly many, of the
customers present on the input stream, since the possibility
exists that we may want to delete some of the Old Master
Records. Therefore, we will want to be able to process
through as many of these Input Customers that we need in
order to find one that is to survive this update. The
diagram shown in Figure 15.15 indicates that in order to
Build (an) Ideal Record, we will have to go through at least
one and possibly many Input Customers. As soon as we have
an Input Customer that has an updated record to be written
out to the Updated Customer Master File, we will stop doing
this process, and move the record in the Master Save Area to
the Ideal Record area, just as if the Ideal File had been
read. Notice that the terminating test for the Input
Customer loop is when there is a record in the Master Save
Area or when the input stream has ended.

Within the Input Customer routine we will begin by setting
the Master Customer Number to the Number of the current
Customer that we have a record for and then blank out the
Master Information.

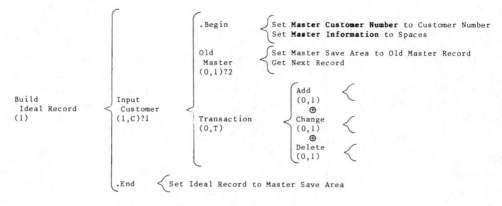

Tests: ?1-Master Information not = Spaces or No More Records = True
       ?2-Record Type = Master Code

Figure 15.15: Physical Input Mapping for the Input Stream

Having thus initialized the Master Save Area, we go on to
find that the Input Customer may or may not have an Old
Master Record, followed by from zero-to-many Transactions to
apply to that customer. We have not used the Exclusive OR
symbol on this diagram since in this case the possibilities
are not mutually exclusive. An Input Customer will **not**
just have **either** an Old Master **or** some Transactions; an
Input Customer could have (1) an Old Master and no
Transactions, or (2) an Old Master and some Transactions, or
(3) no Old Master and some Transactions. There is even a
case to be made that there are customers in these files that
have neither an Old Master nor any Transactions, but those
customers are quite hard to find.

Say that the first record that was on the input file was an
Old Master Record for a customer. We would begin this Input
Customer routine, initialize the Master Save Area, and then
make a test to see if the record type of the current record
is a Master Code, as is described in the ?2 footnote. It
would be, so we would want to Set the Master Save Area to
the Master Record that we had and, since we have now used a
record from the input stream, we'll have to go get another
record from the stream. This puts the Old Master Record for
an Input Customer into the Master Save Area so that we can
begin to apply any updates that we encounter for this
customer.

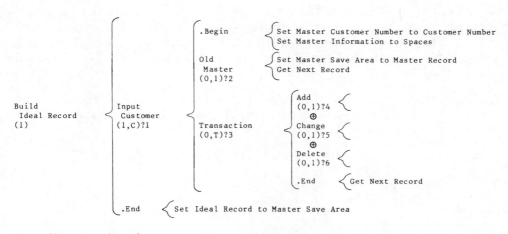

Tests: ?1-Master Information not = Spaces or No More Records = True
       ?2-Record Type = Master Code
       ?3-Input Customer Number not = Master Customer Number
              or No More Records = True
       ?4-Record Type = Add Code
       ?5-Record Type = Change Code
       ?6-Record Type = Delete Code

Figure 15.16: Transactions Mapping for Master File Update

After we found a master record, saved it, and then got the
next record from the stream, we are going to want to start
applying update transactions to that master record. Since
any given Input Customer is going to have from zero-to-many
transactions to apply, we will want to stay in this
Transaction loop, applying one Transaction at a time, until
we discover that we have run across either a different old
master record or a transaction for a different customer. In
either case, the customer number of the incoming record will
be different than the customer number in the Master Save
Area. So we'll keep processing transactions for this Input
Customer until we find, as referenced in footnote 3 in
Figure 15.16, that the Customer Number on the input record
just read is not equal to the Customer Number in the Master
Save Area, or we find that the physical input stream has
ended and there are no more records to process.

Let us focus for a moment on the process that we'll want to
perform when we find that we have a Transaction record on
the input stream. In Figure 15.17 we have shown that when
we find a Transaction record, it will be one of three types,
either an Add transaction, a Change transaction, or a Delete
transaction, and we will process it accordingly. As before,
the tests that we must make to know what kind of a Transaction it is can be found in the corresponding footnotes on
this diagram.

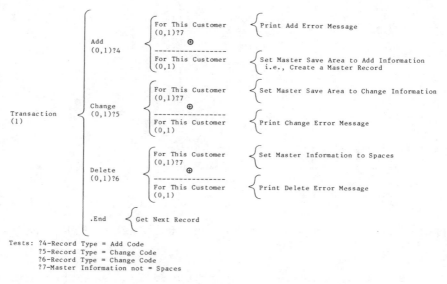

Tests: ?4—Record Type = Add Code
       ?5—Record Type = Change Code
       ?6—Record Type = Change Code
       ?7—Master Information not = Spaces

Figure 15.17: Transaction Routine

Regardless of what kind of transaction it is, after we have
processed the record we will Get (the) Next Record from the
input stream. Again, referencing Figure 15.16, we will keep
doing this process until we read a record from the input
stream that is not for this customer.

If we find that we have an Add transaction, we must make an
additional test. Any time we get an Add transaction it
could be an Add for a customer that already has a master
record, in which case the Add is incorrect and we will want
to skip it, or perhaps print an error message as is shown
here. On the other hand, the Add could be for a new
customer and we would want to go ahead and create a new

master record for that customer. So by testing to see if
the Master Information area contains blanks or not, we can
tell if the Add is for this customer or not, and take the
appropriate action shown.

Notice that the same kind of test must be made in order to
process a Change transaction. If we find the change is for
this customer, we should go ahead and apply the change. If
the change is not for this customer, then the change is
invalid, and we may print an error message. The same process also is required to correctly handle Delete transactions as well. Only when the Delete is for this customer can
we apply it correctly; otherwise, we will print an error message. Notice that in order to delete the record, all we are
going to have to do is reset the Master Information area
back to blanks. This reinitializes the Master Save Area
back to the same condition it starts in for each Input
Customer.

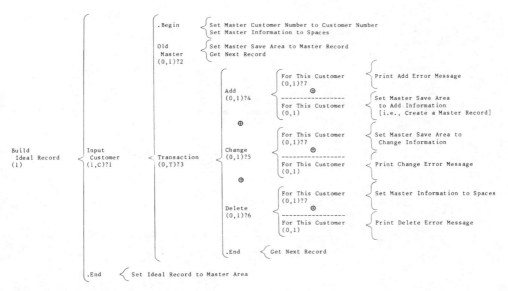

Tests: ?1-Master Information not = Spaces or No More Records = True
       ?2-Record Type = Master Code
       ?3-Customer Number not = Master Customer Number or No More Records = True
       ?4-Record Type = Add Code
       ?5-Record Type = Change Code
       ?6-Record Type = Delete Code
       ?7-Master Information not = Spaces

Figure 15.18: Build Ideal Record Routine for Master
File Update

The entire Build Ideal Record process appears completed in
Figure 15.18. This build routine may be used in the same
manner as the build routine examined for the File Merge in
the previous chapter; it is invoked at the end of the Get
First Ideal Record process and also within the Get Next
Ideal Record process, once it has been determined that there
is still perhaps another customer to process. We say
"perhaps" because the possibility exists that the last
customer on the input stream may be deleted and not become
another ideal record.

Since we cannot be certain that the last customer on the
input stream will generate an Ideal Record, we must test the
end of the Updated Customer loop here for either the end of
the logical file or to see if there is another Old Master to
process. (See Figure 15.19.)

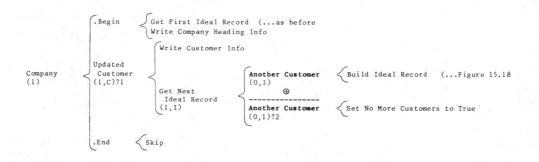

Tests: ?1—No More Customers = True or Master Save Area = Spaces
       ?2—No More Records = True

Figure 15.19: Augmented Process Structure for Master
File Update

With this final addition, the Master File Update model is
complete. There would still be some detail to add to this
design specific to the form of the Customer Information and
Transaction information actually being processed, but those
details will not be considered here.

Extensions of the Model

As with the File Merge model of the previous chapter, it is
not surprising to find that our file update model can be
used for many different kinds of update requirements without
much difficulty.   For   instance,   let   us   return   to   the
two-file problem posed at the beginning of the chapter
(Figure 15.1). The model so far works for an input stream
that has the master records and transaction records already
gathered together. What modifications must be made to the
design if we wish to process a separate sequential file of
transactions with a standard sequential master file to
create our Updated Customer Master File?

By extending the concept of the "ideal file", we can make
the modifications without any trouble.   The model so far
expects an already-merged input stream. If we simply detail
each of the Get Next Record routines with the appropriate
physical input actions, another level of input mapping is
added.   We need only design the specific physical input
processes to provide these parts of the program with the
records that they need. (See Figure 15.20.)

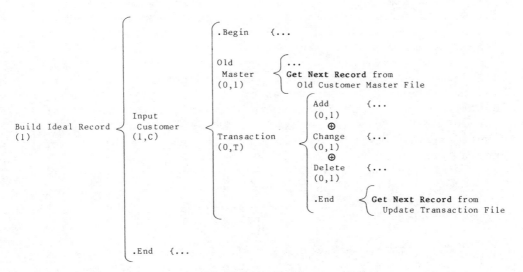

Figure 15.20: Enhancement Locations on Augmented
Process Structure

This is where we can begin to build on prior experience. The input mapping for the File Merge model presented in the last chapter can be used almost verbatim as the input mapping process for this program. The first record from both the master file and the transaction file will be read at the beginning of the program, and then a "build" routine will select the lower of the two records, or the master file record if they are equally low.

Using the extensions to this input mapping coroutine discussed in the last chapter, you can see that our model Master File Update program can be extended to work for as many master files as we want being updated by as many transaction files as we like. If the master file is fragmented into three files, and there are five files of transactions to apply to it, the model can be extended to handle such a circumstance with only a minimum of effort.

Direct Access Master Files

Another important subcategory of Master File Update programs is the update of a "direct access" master file, where the file containing the old masters may not be accessed sequentially but, rather, by a lookup on their key. (See Figure 15.21.) This extension of the model requires a slight modification to the original Build Ideal Record routine presented earlier in Figure 15.18.

The first change necessary, the dropping of the Input Customer loop, is done because of a change in the Delete function. While the update of a sequential master file requires that deleted records simply not to be output, for direct access master records it is customary to **flag** a record for deletion and still write it back out to the master file. The file is then **purged** at some later date. Thus, every customer on the transaction file will generate an ideal record, and the considerations mentioned earlier for the processing of the last record are not valid here.

For each customer present on the transaction file, we will begin as before by clearing the Master Save Area and initializing the Master Customer Number. The transaction file will **always** supply the next Input Customer Number for

the program to handle and for each new customer the master
file will be searched. If a record with the same customer
number is found, we will simply move it to our save area and
begin processing that customer's transactions.

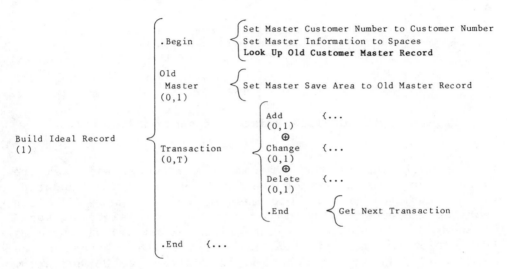

Figure 15.21: **Direct Access** Master File Update
Input Mapping

On-Line Updating

The final extension to be discussed is also one becoming
increasingly popular — the on-line master file update.
(See Figure 15.22.) In this situation, a file of input
transactions does not exist as such. The program is to get
the transactions one at a time from the operator of the
update "conversation". In this mode of operation, the
transaction processing becomes quite simple.

While back in Figure 15.17, each Transaction must be tested
for its contextual validity, in an on-line mode we can
filter out context errors at their source, and thus do not
need much of the logic provided.

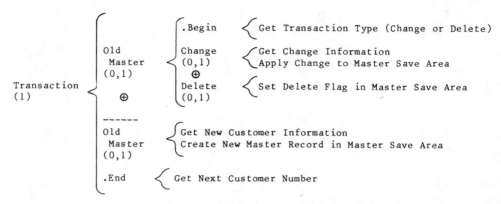

Figure 15.22: **On-line** Update Transaction Mapping

At the beginning of the program, the computer will ask the operator for the number of the first customer to be updated. If the customer has an old master, we will not allow the operator to enter information about an Add, since it would be invalid. As shown in Figure 15.22 we ask for the type of Transaction first, and then apply either the Change or the Delete. If the Customer has no old master, we do not allow the entry of a Change or Delete transaction, we only allow entry of an Add transaction.

Summary

File Handling typically entails complex consideration at the Input Mapping stage, the rest of the design being quite easy. Even the Input Mapping is becoming easier as direct access files and on-line processing are becoming ever more common. Remember, always, to handle the logical before the physical and the ideal before the real. That way, no matter how difficult the physical requirements are to satisfy, at least you don't have the rest of the problem to analyze at the same time.

Chapter 16 CONCLUSION

Getting Started

Having read this far into the book, presumably you will want to try the program design approach presented here. Before you do, though, there are a few important things that you should be aware of. Any time someone attempts to improve their productivity, there are certain dangers and pitfalls to be avoided.

The Warnier/Orr Structured Program Design methodology has been taught pretty much in the form presented in this text since around 1976. Before that, Warnier's LCP approach had been in existence since the mid-to-late 1960's, and has been taught regularly in Europe since the early 1970's. There are quite literally thousands of programmers world-wide who have been exposed to the Warnier/Orr method, and who apply it with varying degrees of success. Since my colleagues and I teach this method on a regular basis, we have had a chance to see some of the tremendous successes people have had with this method, and we have also seen a few failures. Fortunately, the failures have been few, and those that we have seen have almost always been due to political factors in changing to a new method, and not with the technical aspects of the approach. We have also found that failure with any new technology is fairly easy to predict and to prevent.

It has been our experience in teaching SPD that there are
two primary categories of people who are eager to learn it:
(1) those people who have just finished with a major
software disaster, and (2) those that are about to start on
a big project that they are afraid will turn into a major
disaster. The people who have already experienced the
disaster are probably a leg up; they know what kinds of
things can go wrong. Incredible as it may sound, the
introduction of a new productivity improvement technique
will not usually prevent a software disaster, and in fact,
may cause one.

For one thing, the Structured Program Design methodology is
quite likely to change the milestones used for measuring
progress in a programming project. If you look at the
percentage of time spent on the design of a program versus
the coding and testing of a program, traditionally you will
find that the ratio is about one to four; approximately 20%
of the time is spent in design, and about 80% in code and
test (this, of course, varies from one individual to
another). Under the SPD methodology, that ratio is likely
to reverse; we may find that 80% of our time is spent in
design, and only 20% in code and test. As the use of
automated code generators and test data generators becomes
more widespread, the code and test phase may entirely
disappear in the near future.

This shift of attention away from code and test towards
design has some important ramifications. Consider the first
project with a new methodology. Let us assume for the
moment that the project is one which would have taken us ten
weeks of dedicated effort using traditional methods. Of
this ten weeks, about two weeks would be spent in design and
eight weeks in code and test. Presumably, the Warnier/Orr
method will allow us to eventually design and build programs
quicker than before, so we shall assume an improvement of
100%; that is, instead of ten weeks, we now think we can do
the project in only five weeks. Here's the problem: if the
new ratio of design to code and test is followed, the five
week schedule will include four weeks of design and only one
week of code and test.

Traditional Programming Effort:

```
        Design                Code & Test
        !===+===!---+---+---+---+---+---+---+---+
Week 0    1    2    3    4    5    6    7    8    9   10
```

SPD Programming Effort:

```
            Design          C&T
        !===+===+===+===!---!
Week 0    1    2    3    4    5
```

Figure 16.1: Traditional vs. SPD

If we are using this methodology in a commercial environment, what is likely to happen to our manager's blood pressure between the two week mark where coding would have started under the old method, and the four week mark when coding starts under the new method? It probably will skyrocket. Since design has taken four weeks — twice as long as under the old method — management begins to be concerned that coding and testing will also stretch out twice as long to sixteen weeks!

Even if management is willing to gamble with the new technique, we have failed in this example to consider the effects of the learning curve on our first few projects.

The Learning Curve

When most people learn about a technique that is supposed to improve their productivity, their immediate temptation is to run out and use the method on the biggest and most critical project they have. This is not the best of ideas. Imagine the hunter that has just purchased a bow and arrow. That bow and arrow will obviously improve the hunter's productivity over bare hands and a knife. But would you, as the hunter, wish to go out into the woods to find the biggest, meanest, and most ferocious bear in the forest on which to try out this new gadget? Being essentially unskilled at the use of this new device, you would be quite

likely to miss with your first shot. Having missed with the
first shot, you may not survive to try a second.

The same kind of caution should come on the label of any
improved productivity aid. The kind of projects to work on
first are not the most critical and important ones that you
have; there will be plenty of time to work on those later.
If you attempt to tackle something too big, too soon, you
are apt to fail, and your failure will have nothing to do
with your abilities or with the improved method. It will be
because of the infamous learning curve.

If you look at someone's productivity over time, you will
find that most people produce work at a fairly constant
level. Whenever they go to a course or read a book about a
new method, something curious happens to that level of
productivity. It doesn't immediately rise to a new, higher
level; it doesn't even gradually rise to one. It first
drops below the current level before eventually rising to a
new level.

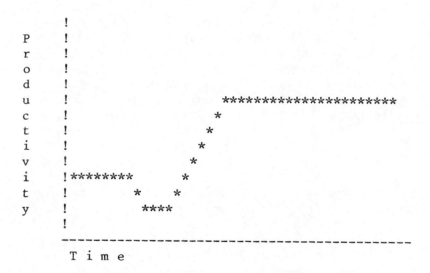

Figure 16.2: The Learning Curve

This curve is not unique to the Warnier/Orr method; it is
inherent in the learning process. It is simply indicative
of the fact that people do what they know how to do better

than they do what they don't know how to do, even if the new
technique is much better than the old one. As an example,
consider the productivity of my friend who now uses a word
processor instead of his old typewriter and is much more
productive with it. However, the first few times that he
used the word processor, his productivity wasn't higher. It
was lower — much lower. It improved, though, as he
became more comfortable with the new thing.

Notice the effect the learning curve will have on our
hypothetical first project. Now, instead of being a five or
ten week project, it is likely to take us twelve or fifteen
weeks — more time than it would have using the old
method. If the new ratio of design to code and test is
followed, that means we would be spending ten or more weeks
in the design phase alone. This is more time than the
entire project would have taken using traditional methods.
Even if management is not a problem, personal panic sets in
around week eight or so when we realize that the project is
due in two weeks, and we haven't started coding yet.

Overcoming the Learning Curve

There are a couple of things you can do to overcome the
effects of the learning curve. First of all, you should
start on a small project. It is suggested that the project
be no more than two weeks from beginning to end. It is also
important that this first project be something of a
non-critical nature.

If you pick a big, critical project to start with, the
learning curve will probably cause you to fail, as long as
failure is measured in terms of time and effort. No one,
least of all you, will be impressed with the new method.

If, however, you pick on a small, non-critical problem to
begin with, you have several things going for you. First,
the difficulty of the project is such that you are emotion-
ally comfortable with the prospect of trying something new.
When the project is truly small and simple, you have the
option of always falling back on the old method — the
one you know — if the new one doesn't work. Also, since
the project is simple and small, you are more likely to

recognize the correct solution when you see it. Building up
your confidence by doing a few simple projects in this
manner will convince you that the method really does work on
your problems, and it gives you the experience and the
background for developing solutions to bigger problems.
This methodology will increase your productivity. How much
depends on how much you use it, and to what level.
Warnier's statistics and the statistics that have been
reported in some areas of the United States suggest that a
100-200% improvement over traditional design is not out of
the question. Even if no improvement in productivity was
noted, though, the improvement in quality achieved with SPD
would be well worth the change.

GLOSSARY/FIRST REFERENCE INDEX

Abend: Acronym for Abnormal End. Used to describe any incomplete operation of a program. p. 146.

Algorithm: A set of actions which accomplish a particular mapping. Usually applied to mathematic transformations. p. 96.

Alternation: The grouping of elements into classes which may or may not always be present. One of the four fundamental constructs necessary for Warnier/Orr design. p. 8.

Augmented Process Structure: The Logical Process Structure with physical procedures and tests added. p. 29.

Batch: Traditional computer operational procedure where an input data set is transformed into an output set in its entirety. See On-Line. p. 206.

Calculation Rules: The actions by which the contents of a data element are derived. p. 63.

Central Transformation: The mapping of logical input to the logical output. Synonym for Logical Mapping and Logical Process Structure. p. 24.

Coding: Act   of   translating   a   program   design   into executable computer statements in a computer language.

Complementary Alternative: Two sets which are mutually exclusive and mutually exhaustive. Usually of the form "A or not A". p. 14.

Complex Alternation: Alternative construct with three or more mutually exclusive sets at the same level or hierarchy. p. 14.

Computable Element: A datum computed from other data. p. 63.

Concurrency: The grouping of elements into classes between which ordering is unimportant. Also, the grouping of elements into classes which may occur simultaneously. One of two advanced constructs used in Warnier/Orr design. p. 8.

Coroutine: A routine which may be run simultaneously with another. p. 130.

Data Dictionary: A list of data elements, definitions, and examples used for a project management strategy. Used to solve the problem of inconsistent naming in a program or system. p. 111.

Data Stream: A sequential list of data to be used by a program (input) or to be produced by a program (output). p. 33

Data Structured Design: Design method in which the structures of the mappings are based upon the structures of the data being transformed. p. 2.

Decryption: Translating data into a useful form from the form in which it exists. p. 145.

Direct Access File: A file whose records may be obtained or written at random. p. 224.

DOUNTIL: "Do Until" — a set of actions that repeats from one to many times. A traditional structured programming term. p. 11.

DOWHILE: "Do While" — a set of actions that repeats from zero to many times. A traditional structured programming term. p. 12.

DSSD: Data Structured Systems Development. p. 20

Element: An object, idea, or action found in the lowest level of a structure. p. 10.

Encryption: Translating data from a useful form into another form. p. 145.

Enhancement: A modification in a program to make it perform in a different manner.

Exclusive OR: Logical connective meaning "one or the other, but not both and not neither." The exclusive OR symbol, " $\oplus$ ", is called a circlesum. p. 13.

Exhaustive Alternative: Alternative structure which accounts for all possible choices. p. 14.

Flag: A piece of data used to test for the occurrence of an event. A flag is a state variable. p. 224.

Flat File: A data file having the form of a two-dimensional matrix. A sequential file of fixed length records each having the same format. p. 84

Function: A one-to-one or many-to-one mapping. p. 23.

Hidden Element: Data element necessary as input that is not present on an output. p. 70.

Hidden Hierarchy: A sorting hierarchy necessary as input that is not reflected on a Logical Output Structure. p. 70.

Hierarchy: The grouping of elements together into a larger class. One of the four fundamental constructs necessary for Warnier/Orr design. p. 8.

Ideal File: The simplest possible arrangement of data for input to a mapping. Usually a flat file. p. 83.

Ill-Behaved Output: An output whose Logical Data Structure is not a subset of its Logical Output Structure. p. 67.

Information System Life Cycle: The stages of development that a software system goes through. p. 26.

Input: Data which is provided to a program or system.

Inverted Hierarchy: An "inside out" mapping of a data set used to solve a structure clash. p. 126.

Label Element: A datum containing the name of another element or group of elements. p. 62.

LCP: Logical Construction of Programs.

LDS: Logical Data Structure.

Level of Hierarchy: The area within a bracket on a Warnier/Orr diagram. p. 8.

Logical: Independent of actual implementation devices and methods. p. 3.

Logical Construction of Programs (LCP): Warnier's program development method. p. 20.

Logical Data Structure (LDS): The graphic representation of the minimal data necessary to be able to produce an output. p. 60.

Logical Output Structure (LOS): The graphic representation of an output's requirements. p. 31.

Logical Process Structure (LPS): The graphic representation of the mapping to transform ideal input into logical output. p. 79.

Logical Group: One or more elements that are all output together. p. 85.

Logical Sequence: A group of data or actions which all occur the same number of times and under the same conditions. p.94.

Logical Substitution: A calculation having the general form "set A to B." p. 63.

LOS: Logical Output Structure.

LPS: Logical Process Structure.

Mapping: A transformation of one set of data into another. p. 21.

Nested Output: An output having multiple levels of repeating sets. p. 36.

On-Line: Mode of computer operation that is interactive with an operator, usually through a terminal. See Batch. p. 206.

Output: Data that is received from a program or a system.

Output Definition Worksheet: A form used to gather requirements information for an output. p. 37.

Output Oriented Design: Design method in which the outputs of a program or system are studied first. p. 3.

Physical: Dependent upon a specific implementation device or method. p. 3.

Physical Control Structure: The tests and branches that must be installed to physically implement repetition and alternation in the programming language to be used. p. 105.

Physical Input Structure: A Warnier/Orr diagram of the actual input available to the program.

Physical Output Structure: A Warnier/Orr diagram of the device-dependent format of the actual output. p. 121.

Physical Process Structure: A mapping detailed to the level where each elementary action is codable as one statement in the programming language to be used. p. 123.

Process: Synonym for mapping.

Purge: The act of removing deleted records from a file. p. 224.

Recursion: The relationship where a class contains an earlier or less ordered version of itself. One of two advanced constructs used in Warnier/Orr design. p. 8.

Relation: A one-to-many mapping. p. 22.

Repetition: The grouping of elements which occur many times with the same form or content. One of the four fundamental constructs necessary for Warnier/Orr design. p. 8.

Required Data Element: A datum required as input by a program in order to produce the desired output. p. 64.

Sequence: The relationship whereby one element is encountered before another in time or spacing. One of the four fundamental constructs necessary for Warnier/Orr design. p. 8.

Sequential File: A file whose records may be read and written only one after the other from start to finish. p. 137.

Set: A grouping of objects, ideas, or actions which all have a feature or features in common. p. 8.

Set Theory: Branch of mathematics which deals with the study of groups of objects, ideas, and actions. p. 10.

Skip: Elementary action used on mappings to denote an empty logical sequence. "Do nothing". p. 55.

Software: A computer program or family of computer programs that operate together.

SPD: Structured Program Design.

State Variables: Counters and switches necessary to inform one part of a program or a system about the condition or "state" or another. p. 108.

Structural Data: Data necessary to group or order other data. p. 77.

Structure Clash: Two or more hierarchies superimposed on the same set of data. Usually found between logical and physical data sets. p. 102

Structured Program Design (SPD): Name of Orr's program development method. p. 20.

Structured Programming: Second generation programming method stressing organized program coding methods. p. 1.

Subroutine: A set of actions invoked from many different places in a program. p. 130.

Subset: A set wholly contained within some other set. p. 67.

Universal: The name of a set of data or actions. p. 10.

Utility Routine: A subroutine or coroutine that may be used commonly by many programs or many parts of a program. p. 193.

Versions of Programs: The idea that programs and systems are modified into new programs and systems to reflect changing requirements. p. 26.

Warnier/Orr Diagrams: Pictorial form of representing data sets and mappings invented and used by Jean-Dominique Warnier and Kenneth T. Orr. p.2.

Well-Behaved Output: An output whose Logical Data Structure is a subset of its Logical Output Structure. p. 67.

BIBLIOGRAPHY

Higgins, David A., **Program Design and Construction.** Englewood Cliffs: Prentice-Hall, 1979.

Jackson, M. A., **Principles of Program Design.** New York: Academic Press, 1975.

Orr, Kenneth T., **Structured Systems Development.** New York: Yourdon Press, 1977.

_____, **Structured Requirements Definition.** Topeka: Ken Orr & Associates, Inc., 1980.

Warnier, Jean-Dominique, **Logical Construction of Programs.** New York: Van Nostrand Reinhold Co., 1976.

_____, **Logical Construction of Systems.** New York: Van Nostrand Reinhold Co., 1981.

_____, **Program Modification.** Boston: Martinus Nijhoff, 1978.

Library of Congress Cataloging in Publication Data

Higgins, David A.
    Designing structured programs.

    (Prentice-Hall software series)
    Includes index.
    1. Structured programming.   I. Title.   II. Series.
QA76.6.H525 1983   001.64'2   82-22976
ISBN 0-13-201418-1

Editorial/production supervision: Nancy Milnamow
Manufacturing buyer: Gordon Osbourne

© 1983 by EduCo. *Denver, Colorado*

Printed in the United States of America

10 9 8 7 6 5 4 3 2 1

ISBN 0-13-201418-1

Prentice-Hall International, Inc., *London*
Prentice-Hall of Australia Pty. Limited, *Sydney*
Editora Prentice-Hall do Brasil, Ltda., *Rio de Janeiro*
Prentice-Hall of Canada Inc., *Toronto*
Prentice-Hall of India Private Limited, *New Delhi*.
Prentice-Hall of Japan, Inc., *Tokyo*
Prentice-Hall of Southeast Asia Pte. Ltd., *Singapore*
Whitehall Books Limited, *Wellington, New Zealand*

DESIGNING STRUCTURED PROGRAMS

DAVID HIGGINS

EduCo. Corporation
Denver, Colorado

PRENTICE-HALL, INC.
Englewood Cliffs, New Jersey 07632

PRENTICE-HALL SOFTWARE SERIES
Brian W. Kernighan, advisor

DESIGNING
STRUCTURED
PROGRAMS